Screen Couple Chemistry

MARTHA P. NOCHIMSON

Screen Couple

Chemistry
The Power of 2

UNIVERSITY OF TEXAS PRESS
Austin

Copyright © 2002 by the University of Texas Press

All rights reserved

Printed in the United States of America

First edition, 2002

Requests for permission to reproduce material from this work should be sent to Permissions, University of Texas Press, Box 7819, Austin, TX 78713-7819.

♾ The paper used in this book meets the minimum requirements of ANSI/NISO Z39.48-1992 (R1997) (Permanence of Paper).

LIBRARY OF CONGRESS CATALOGING-IN-PUBLICATION DATA

Nochimson, Martha.
   Screen couple chemistry : the power of 2 / Martha P. Nochimson.—1st ed.
      p.   cm.
Includes bibliographical references and index.
ISBN 0-292-75579-1 (alk. paper)
   1. Man-woman relationships in motion pictures.   2. Love in motion pictures.
I. title: Power of 2.   II. title: Power of two.   III. title.
PN1995.9.M27 N63 2002
791.43'655—dc21   2002010533

Unreal, give back to us what once you gave:
The imagination that we spurned and crave.
                        Wallace Stevens, "To the One of Fictive Music"

People who talk about revolution and class struggle without referring explicitly to everyday life, without understanding what is subversive about love and what is positive in the refusal of constraint, have corpses in their mouths.
                      Raoul Vaneigem, *The Revolution of Everyday Life*

The fact that the features of the face can be seen side by side, i.e. in space—that the eyes are at the top, the ears at the sides and the mouth lower down—loses all reference to space when we see, not a figure of flesh and bone, but an expression, or in other words, when we see emotions, moods, intentions and thought, things which although our eyes can see them, are not in space. For feelings, emotions, moods, intentions, thoughts are not themselves things pertaining to space, even if they are rendered visible by means which are.   Bela Balazs,
      Theory of the Film: Character and Growth of a New Art

CONTENTS

      Acknowledgments xi

One **An Introduction to the Importance of Couple Chemistry under the Studio System** 1

Two **Johnny Weissmuller and Maureen O'Sullivan:** Tarzan and Jane 39

Three **Myrna Loy and William Powell:** The Thin Man Takes a Couple 85

Four **Fred Astaire and Ginger Rogers:** Music Makes Me 135

Five **Katharine Hepburn and Spencer Tracy:** Much Ado about "the Little Woman" 185

Six **The Post-Studio Synergistic Couple:** The Thin Aliens 235

Seven **The Thematic Couple:** A Post-Studio Innovation 285

APPENDIX
One **Fred, Ginger, and RKO** 313

APPENDIX
Two **Theorizing Chemistry in Entertainment via Neuroscience** 325

      Notes 329
      Bibliography 371
      Index 377

ILLUSTRATIONS

Tough but tender Gable and the uppity dame   15

Astaire and Rogers exploding gender cliches   17

Errol Flynn's macho response to Olivia de Havilland   29

Tarzan's savage masculinity is the partner not the master of the feminine   47

The eloquence of gesture in the Tarzan series   56

Tarzan (Johnny Weissmuller) baffled by an alien, civilized concept of femininity   58

Myrna Loy cuts a feminine figure at ease with sexuality   89

William Powell cuts a masculine figure at ease with female energy   93

Nick, Nora, alcohol, and the PCA   105

Fred Astaire deals with the problem of the reductiveness and confusion caused by social signs   145

Rogers and Astaire confront artificial and repressive boundaries and limits   151

Rogers proves that it's dangerous for men to take charge of female desire   175

The mutual gaze that created the onscreen Tracy/Hepburn legend *196*

Hepburn, Tracy, and constructed femininity *212*

Competing gender definitions in *Adam's Rib* *220*

The truth sought by Scully and Mulder was not "out there" but in them *251*

Keaton and Allen as aliens in a repressive society *266*

Luke (Tony Geary) and Laura (Genie Francis), the boy-man and the woman-girl *279*

Cosby and Rashad—shattering stereotypes *289*

A dream reconstruction of 1940s movies on *Moonlighting* *300*

Stereotypes of "ordinary life" in *Mr. and Mrs. Bridge* *306*

ACKNOWLEDGMENTS

To archivists, librarians, and collectors who give new meaning to the word *helpful*: Brigite Kueppers, Al Willis, Jeanne at the UCLA Fine Arts Special Collection; Ned Comstock at Special Collections at the Cinema-Television Library at USC; Richard Jewell, associate dean of the School of Cinema-Television at the University of Southern California; Caroline Sisneros at the American Film Institute; Scott Curtis, former research archivist at the Margaret Herrick Library; Barbara Hall, research archivist of Special Collections at the Margaret Herrick Library; Ronald Grele, director of the Oral History Project at Columbia University; Paul Becker; Charles Niles, Boston University Special Collections; Rudy Behlmer, the great studio historian; Steve Wilson, Special Collections at the University of Texas, Austin.

To academic and personal friends who openhandedly went out of their way to support me: Karen Backstein, Krin Gabbard, Arthur and Phyllis Skoy, Joan Richardson, Daniel Traister, my colleagues at Mercy College—especially Louise Feroe, Nina Lee, Heather Blenkinsopp, Paul Caputo, and Don Phillips—Linda Laufer, and Cynthia King. To my openhanded and openhearted colleague John J. Pierce. To Stephen Negron, my heroic computer consultant, always there with the right stuff when I need him, and to Gilberto Perez for his generous, collegial reading of parts of the manuscript. To Aaron Warner, director of Columbia University Seminars, and to the Columbia Film Seminar.

The author expresses appreciation to the University Seminars at Columbia University for assistance in the preparation of the manuscript for publication. The ideas presented have benefited from discussions in the University Seminar on Cinema and Interdisciplinary Interpretation.

To my colleagues at the University of Texas Press, especially my perceptive editor, Jim Burr, whose humor, good sense, support, and knowledge about wine has seen me through. Thanks to Sue Carter for her patient, thorough, insightful copyediting.

To my friends and compatriots in the industry, including Robyn Astaire, widow of Fred Astaire, and Thomas White, lawyer for the estate of Fred Astaire; Betty Comden; Catherine Coulson; Nancy Grahn; Terry Lester; Patrick Mulcahey; Susan Newman; Stephen Nichols; Johnny Sheffield, who played "Boy" in the original MGM Tarzan films.

With love: To my children, David and Holly, those thin aliens. To Richard, my own true Mr. Synergy.

Screen Couple Chemistry

CHAPTER One

AN INTRODUCTION TO THE IMPORTANCE OF COUPLE CHEMISTRY UNDER THE STUDIO SYSTEM

What do the four following lines of dialogue have in common?

"(Scream) Don't let me go: hold on to me."
　　　　　　Tarzan the Ape Man (1932, Dir. W. S. Van Dyke)
"Boys, boys and girls, and you too Honey."
　　　　　　Flying Down to Rio (1933, Dir. Thorton Freeland)
"Pardon me if I seem to intrude."
　　　　　　Manhattan Melodrama (1934, Dir. W. S. Van Dyke)
"Yes, yes, in a belligerent sort of way."
　　　　　　Woman of the Year (1942, Dir. George Stevens)

Quite a lot. Each is the first line of dialogue exchanged between an onscreen couple that proceeded to knit itself into the public imagination as a fundamental part of the cultural capacity to imagine both erotic intimacy and human connection. Each of the above quoted lines of dialogue resonated far beyond its filmic moment, or even the film in which it appeared. In each case, a partnership was generated that took on a life of its own, beyond the plans of the individual actors, the creative teams that made the movie, and even the studios that theoretically controlled all the materials and personnel concerned. The disparate tones, contents, and resonances of the lines are indicative of the divergent destinies that governed the making of the series of films that ensued. However, in each case, screen chemistry was the catalyst, and in each case screen chemistry resulted in a partnership that was much more than the sum of its parts.

The first line of dialogue, spoken by Maureen O'Sullivan as Jane to Johnny Weissmuller as Tarzan, is little more than a cliche of the exotic action picture genre, a stereotypical female call to a strong male for protection, but it masked the gender-bending, generally unconventional, and purely serendipitous Tarzan series that would ensue. Somewhat more predictive, the second line, spoken by Fred Astaire as Fred Ayres to Ginger Rogers as Honey Hale—separating Honey out from the "boys and girls," playfully leaves her in gender limbo. This line suggests the ludic strangeness that would make RKO all but bludgeon the reluctant pair into their nine-picture partnership under its auspices, not counting the last picture they made together ten years later, once again because studio pressure, this time from MGM, made it a reality.

The third line is spoken by Myrna Loy as Eleanor Packer to William Powell as Jim Wade, as she, a perfect stranger, flings herself into the backseat of a taxicab with him. This line is still more prefigurative, tinged with the arch couple humor invented for the screen by these two highly harmonious actors, who contentedly collaborated with MGM's plans for their repeated pairing, after they recovered from the surprise of their amazing compatibility, a surprise quite similar to Eleanor's sudden eruption into Jim's life. Finally, the last line is spoken by Spencer Tracy as Sam Craig while looking at Katharine Hepburn as Tess Harding, responding to a question by a third party inquiring whether the two had met. This line prefigures quite vividly the combative attraction that Hepburn and Tracy would themselves consciously cultivate in nine films, while a bemused MGM hierarchy gave them their lead. However belligerent or intrusive, willing or unwilling, the merged energies of these acting pairs inspired the creative teams around them toward onscreen ironies and even luminous challenges to conventional filmic representations of love, courtship, and marriage that elevated often pedestrian scripts to unconventional eloquence. These four couples combined the unexpected with the immense popularity usually reserved for predictable cliches in the mass media as the hallmark of their special kind of Hollywood pairing, widely acclaimed both in its own time and now, here called the Synergistic Couple.

The Synergistic Couple, with its vortex of wild forces, is a natural outcome of the American mass media insofar as it has made its enigmatic, major creative contributions by what might seem to be its greatest limitation, the triumph of energy over craft, a situation that deserves a closer look. The *craft* of the popular has always been dazzlingly effective at distraction, or escapism as it is generally called, but limited in its capacity for expression about the human condition. By contrast, the raging *energy* released by Hollywood has, under certain conditions, become a distinctive vehicle of expression. The chemistry of the onscreen media couple is one important aspect of commercial filmmaking that can create those special conditions through which the torrents of popular culture energy are channeled as a form of intelligent communication. The energy circulating between certain acting pairs, their chemistry, can become a singular mode of contemplating intimacy, its mysterious fusion of two into a manifold one, that terrible and wonderful sliding of individual boundaries. How to deal with this kind of connection that often grabs us without permission and leaves us confused about where self ends and the beloved begins? How to deal with its vertiginous pleasures that, as the song says, make us forget the "ordinary things that everyone ought to do" and thereby may make us run up against established cultural values and priorities? The wordless chemistry of onscreen couples, widely recognized as a source of pleasure and even seduction, is also surprisingly effective at enabling Hollywood to say much on the subject. This is particularly true of the Synergistic Couple, the kind of movie couple that this study will distinguish as the most dangerous, fascinatingly powerful type of couple in commercial, mass media film.

The energy of the onscreen couple, which becomes at its most intense a form of synergy between two actors, has been relatively easy to recognize, but difficult to discuss, if only because of the abundance of acting pairs to consider. The Hollywood studio era of the 1930s and 1940s produced a fairly large number of screen couples, and audiences immediately reacted. The post-studio media have produced a much smaller group, but still substantial in number, and these too have commanded powerful audience response. Audiences have room for spontaneous engagement with a virtually infinite number of such experiences, but critical exploration into the fascination of the screen couple requires selection and some sorely needed distinctions, to be made in these pages. Among the best and worst cases of what Hollywood screen couples have told us about our need for intimacy will be represented of necessity by a chosen group of captivating acting pairs.

The most focused attention will be given to the quartet of onscreen acting teams evoked above in their introductory exclamations: Johnny Weissmuller and Maureen O'Sullivan as Tarzan and Jane; William Powell and Myrna Loy as Nick and Nora Charles; Fred Astaire and Ginger Rogers; and Spencer Tracy and Katharine Hepburn. Our travels will begin and linger with them, and their contrasts with other onscreen acting teams of their day that were neither as enduring nor as complex in their depiction of love and emotional closeness. Ultimately, we will also hazard the terrain of the contemporary media. To speculate about what screen couples have inherited from the great screen couple traditions, we will look at the work of Woody Allen and Diane Keaton; Joanne Woodward and Paul Newman; and the character pairings of Mulder (David Duchovny) and Scully (Gillian Anderson) on *The X-Files,* Luke (Tony Geary) and Laura (Genie Francis) on *General Hospital,* Maddie (Cybill Shepherd) and David (Bruce Willis) on *Moonlighting,* and Cliff (Bill Cosby) and Claire (Phylicia Rashad) Huxtable on *The Cosby Show.* The beauty and danger of the four screen couples from Classic Hollywood on which this study will initially—and primarily—focus spans the spectrum of the kinds of films produced in Old Hollywood: comedy, musical, melodrama, mystery, and exotic action adventure. It also spans the length of the heyday of the studio system. Weissmuller and O'Sullivan worked together from 1932 to 1942. Powell and Loy worked together from 1934 to 1947. Astaire and Rogers worked together from 1934 to 1939 and then again in 1949. Finally, Tracy and Hepburn worked together from 1942 to 1967. These discussions will provide a basis for exploring today's media screen couples.

Each of these couples was bigger than the films they made together, the beauty of their several rapports seeming to break free from the constraints of any particular story, the relationship itself becoming a freestanding energy vortex. Their too great impact on moviegoer sensibilities imperiled the public's social grounding in reality, often blurring the boundaries between actuality and illusion, as in some part of the audience's mind the real personhood of the actors slipped into the identities of the onscreen lovers, and chemistry slipped into history. The public imagined the screen couples as offscreen intimates, without actually marking the place where slippage had taken place. Today, removed from the white-hot glare of momentary celebrity into abiding cultural significance, their transcendence no longer disorients our historical sense of the real. All the purely sociological motives offered by critics that explain audience interest in their charisma as escapism—relief from particular political and economic conditions, the influence of marketing pressures—exhausted themselves as the films left their immediate circumstances. In the long run, we know them to be seminal imaginative experiences. If moviegoers long ago used these couple fantasies primarily as trivial distractions, that is not the full extent of their import. They are a cultural legacy of how we thought (and think?) about desire and love. Their enduring strength is a phenomenon that is ripe for contemplation in terms of meaning.

THE GREAT COUPLE TRADITION

Studying these four couples affords many opportunities for renewed appreciation of their achievements, and it affords clarity about the nature of their difference from the large number of insignificant screen couples produced in Old Hollywood. Close scrutiny also promotes understanding of how they built a foundation for those impressive and expressive screen couples of today that similarly generate audience loyalty, exhilaration, and sometimes outright frenzy. This appreciation and clarity, however, will depend on the evolution of a precise definition of the screen couple—an amorphous category that is due and overdue for rigorous articulation—and on the articulation of a historical perspective on the way the great couple tradition developed in commercial entertainment. For the purposes of this articulation, a significant distinction will be made between screen couples that bear narrative and psychological weight and those that are trivialized. Movies and television shows dominated by action relegate the couple relationship to a few strategically placed scenes, and cannot be said to contain a screen couple in any important sense, but rather to feature a shorthand for romance that adds color or sizzle. The screen couple of the weighty type, by contrast, is the kind that is of interest to this study. The first crucial characteristic to be discerned about this kind of significant popcult, onscreen pair is that it is not a perfunctory narrative element but rather depicts an intimate relationship that is the central dynamic of the movie or television show. Its nuances are as crucial to the storytelling as the outcome of any action in which the characters may be involved.

Weight and importance in screen couples will also be distinguished in terms of the heft of repeated collaborations of specific actors who together spark chemistry. The media have for a long time featured co-stars who work together numerous times as the narrative and psychological core of a series of movies or a television series. Ostensibly, there is little more to this couple phenomenon than its commercial value as a box office attraction. However, the importance of this kind of repetition is not only economic; in fact their commercial success is, from a long-range perspective, the least interesting feature of such a professional association. This study will distinguish the capacity of some acting pairs to create a body of work for the media that, because of their synergy, establishes in its totality a comprehensive, dimensional portrait of intimacy for mass audiences. The result of these ensemble images of connection is a widely accessible, extended, and sometimes surprisingly cogent meditation on the relationship between the couple bond and social pressures.

The chosen quartet of "golden age" screen pairs have this weight and heft, and although they might not include everyone's favorite choices, they will be universally recognized as prime examples of those screen couples from Old Hollywood whose repeated work together articulated a multifaceted fantasy universe in which the various couples they played reflect off each other to create a nuanced portrait of passionate connection as one single movie could never do. That is, there is an intertextual Fred Astaire and Ginger Rogers universe made up of their many performances together that forms a multi-perspective portal for mass audiences into a complex understanding of love, courtship, and the human capacity for bonding. The same is true of the movies made by Weissmuller/O'Sullivan, Loy/Powell, and Tracy/Hepburn. As exemplars of the most intense portrayal of the couple in the mass media, they are useful and revealing about the great tradition of the screen couple as an ongoing and widespread industry phenomenon.

The present examination of their films and the production conditions that brought them together will show how the significant screen couple—including its descendant the television couple—differs from more trivialized couple representations, even though both types emerged from the same economic and cultural roots. Historically, both significant and trivial onscreen pairs evolved as an efficient and cost-effective business practice. In an industry organized into studios, the deployment of contract actors as couples to attract audiences was economically feasible and rewarding. At the same time, the historical development of all onscreen romantic pairs was also a matter of storytelling practice: audiences were generally unsatisfied unless the joinings and separations of couples punctuated the plot conflict in some respect. In fact, as David Bordwell, Janet Staiger, and Kristin Thompson have estimated in *The Classical Hollywood Cinema*, between 85 and 95 percent of mass culture movies before 1960 contained a significant romance element.[1] Most of these were perfunctory screen pairs, which I will classify as the Functional Couple, the most trivial kind of screen couple, which fulfills only the minimum economic and narrative functions. This kind of screen pair will hover in the background of this study, forming the mass of duo presences whose contrast to the chosen quartet of couples from the studio era, and a selection of couples from the post-studio era that will be discussed at the end of the study, establishes the richly nuanced qualities of the latter. The screen couple, in its most significant form, has a significance beyond business and basic narrative issues. It is about the way we process information about eroticism and intimacy. That process is not divorced from business and narrative issues, but is in its fundamental identity a matter of the energy by which the intertextual world of the significant popular culture couple is created, star chemistry. Star chemistry is crucial to our understanding of the major issues surrounding the weighty onscreen couple: the star system, the slippage between art and life, and the conflict between image and story text in cinema.

Star couple chemistry is the primary element that separates the trivial from the weighty screen couple and that determines the potential for films about couples to establish meaning. It is a troublesome fascination that in the short run beguiles us. But certain manifestations of couple chemistry also have an interesting, often happy, astringent quality. Star chemistry can be manipulative, burying the audience in escapist illusions about love. Yet it can also work in the reverse way. It can liberate the film from the illusions otherwise fostered by the kind of simplistic plot favored by the commercial film industry under the studio system.

A very early development of mass movie culture in Hollywood was its emphasis on plot over image as the primary structure of the movie, despite the visual nature of cinema. This emphasis on plot remains with us today. Critics and audiences overwhelmingly talk about the meaning of a film in terms of its story. Easy absorption of simple plots was and is more consumer-friendly than a complex modernist formation of narrative out of the juxtaposition of images. Any attempt to establish meaning for mass audiences through visually based narrative, typical of avant-garde and artistic cinema, appeared (and still appears) to threaten them with confusion. However, another early commercial film interest, the star image, reasserted and still reasserts the power of the visual for mass audiences. Mass audiences are not threatened by star images, which reduce story to second place behind the attractions of the star, as attention shifts to the glance of an eye, the turn of a head, an expression, and away from the logic of the plot, which can go to hell in the process. For this reason, the pleasure of the star image is generally assumed to work against meaning in a film. However, the power of the visual reasserted by star chemistry can sometimes work not against meaning but against the reductiveness of the typical mass culture story, particularly when the core of the film deals with intimacy.

When an onscreen couple generates powerful energy and boosts the image to prominence as a structural element in the film, chemistry becomes an important part of storytelling, a phenomenon about which serious study of popular culture has been silent, primarily because chemistry is a part of Hollywood history that film studies has rarely dealt with.[2] Chemistry, though a central feature of the mass media concept of entertainment, lurks vaguely on the periphery of informed discussion. For good reasons. It is unquantifiable, a given rather than a constructed phenomenon, difficult to study—much like the challenge for physics of dealing with smoke and clouds. To the mind trying to pin down its smoke-like elusiveness, it is a disturbing phenomenon. But it is that very disturbance that has proven to be the key to its importance. And one of the most disturbing aspects is the sense of it as an almost invincible enemy of truth. Yet, as we shall see, a more precise understanding of this phenomenon involves making distinctions between its existence as escapist distraction and its existence as the antidote to escapism. Making that distinction requires a clear mental separation of the three types of couples produced by Old Hollywood: those that had star chemistry—Synergistic Couples and Iconic Couples—and those that didn't—Functional Couples. These distinctions will, by the end of this study, help us to understand a new type of couple that evolved in the post-studio era, the Thematic Couple.

The most basic, largest, and least inspired category of screen couples was the Functional Couple, a simple cog in the wheel of the churning plot, adding little if any screen chemistry to the experience of the movie, and therefore interesting to this study only as a matter of contrast. Nothing could be clearer than the distinction between a sparkling star pair and a plodding Functional Couple. The Iconic Couple lies in between the magical Synergistic Couple and the plodding Functional Couple: such pairs, though they may have some degree of star power, tend to reiterate empty cliche. The Thematic Couple, a post-studio descendant of the Iconic Couple, differs from the latter in its tendency to be yoked to more dynamic and more socially realistic scripts than the old Iconic Couple. Another feature of the Thematic Couple is its tendency for image to be subordinated to rational purposes as opposed to tapping into the subconscious level. With the Functional Couple as a contrast or background, we will examine the subtle, interesting, and important distinctions among Synergistic, Iconic, and Thematic Couples, three types of screen pairs built around stars that furnish varying amounts of chemistry. These three types each have significantly different relationships to the typical Hollywood plot, and use the star image differently in connection with the values carried in the formulaic stories common to Old Hollywood, and to some extent the post-studio mass media.

Of the star pairings under the studio system, the most important and influential category of star couples for this study and for the implications of popular culture's contribution to human understanding is the provocative Synergistic Couple. The stars that formed Synergistic Couples empowered popular culture to make genuine expressions about intimacy by breaking up conventional narrative recipes for storytelling. A simple way of speaking about the difference between the Synergistic Couple and other star pairings is through a partially negative definition: Synergistic Couples were never closely connected with a narrative recipe by means of which a variety of partners might produce similar effects. Their effect was uniquely possible only with each other. The narratives of the films of Synergistic Couples might easily be analyzed for formulaic elements, but none of the routine story elements was particularly instrumental in the success of the film. In fact, what was characteristic of Synergistic Couples was that their energy tended to disrupt the formulas in interesting ways so as to create highly distinctive perspectives on the social practices embedded in the usual narrative pattern. The Synergistic Couple brought a healing energy to a world of cliches. The Astaire/Rogers characters, for example, would typically stumble around a mazelike world of superficial distractions that stood as barriers to their desire for intimacy with each other, though *their* wholeness as a couple was always manifest in dance. Typically, the energy finally released in dance brought them to the moment of clarity that released them from a still dysfunctional culture. Weissmuller and O'Sullivan's Tarzan and Jane combined into a potent couple energy that enabled them to cope with a world shattered into hostile camps because of greed, redeeming the situation by their enduring completeness, while the world remained as rapacious as ever. Powell and Loy's Nick and Nora, similarly, redeemed the family by their integrity as a couple, while dysfunction (generally also related to greed) ravaged families around them. Finally, the Tracy and Hepburn characters, in their best work, transcended through the organic bond between them a world lying in political, economic, and ethical ruins. As the exception to the rule, the Synergistic Couple gave the audience a way to stand at a distance from the more repressive aspects of society and to think about themselves and their desires in a new way.

Synergistic Couples showed Old Hollywood at its most creative and stood apart from the largest category of star couples, the Iconic Couple, which was really a showy and charismatic version of the Functional Couple. The Iconic Couple succeeded in making cliches glamourous and established dramatic and comic recipes that could work for comparatively large numbers of interchangeable star partners: glamour, replaceability, and cliche were the hallmarks of the Iconic Couple. If the Functional Couple worked as a mundane cog in a plot that in Hollywood fashion chugged along well-defined tracks, the Iconic Couple, no less a part of the obligatory formulaic movie plot of the studio era, made cliches seem more exciting and truer, more entertaining because of the technology of the glamourized star images involved. The difference between Synergistic and Iconic Couples is the difference between star power that rocks old ways of thinking and star power that gilds tired old cliches. This distinction requires a complex comparison between the almost fully manipulated image of stereotype and the substantially raw image powered by wild energy.

The Iconic Couple is a powerful form of Hollywood illusion, lending to stereotypes a seductive charm. Energizing the cliched plot of the typical Hollywood movie, the Iconic Couple gives enchanting bodies and faces to the gender stereotypes that the mass media catered to. The unofficial king of Iconic Couples was Clark Gable. And so I will call the usual pattern of casting Iconic Couples the Gable Plus One phenomenon. Then, as now, the men tended to be the primary consideration in the formation of the couple, though occasionally there were female actors who might be in the dominant position: it would be possible to speak of a Dietrich Plus One formula and much later, in the fifties, of a Crawford Plus One casting decision. During the studio era, it would also be possible to rename the Gable Plus One phenomenon for John Wayne, Cary Grant, Humphrey Bogart, Gary Cooper, Melvyn Douglas, Maurice Chevalier, or the less enduring but once quite popular Joel McCrea, Randolph Scott, John Payne, and Dennis Morgan.

But Gable makes a convenient focus, both for his abiding popularity and for his distillation of the Iconic Couple male. He played the male partner in a number of couple series with several actresses who had powerhouse images themselves: Joan Crawford (eight films), Lana Turner (four films), Myrna Loy (six films), and Jean Harlow (six films).[3] Perfectly adaptable to a large number of acting partners, Gable required only that they be sexually attractive, possessing a headstrong femininity that could serve as a foil for his stereotypical but thrilling patriarchal lessons in love—lessons that were inherent in the less colorful Functional Couples, but not nearly as much fun. Gable brought a special energy to his three-part taming process, lending a charm to the first step, in which he established that women need a firm hand; the second step, by which they learned that he was right; and the third step, whereby they learned the joys of internalization of lessons one and two, indicated by the smile on their formerly wayward faces. Many of the Gable formula films are now all but forgotten—*Dance, Fools, Dance* (1931, Dir. Harry Beaumont), *Susan Lenox: Her Fall and Rise* (1931, Dir. Robert Z. Leonard), *Dancing Lady* (1933, Dir. Robert Z. Leonard), *Test Pilot* (1938, Dir. Victor Fleming); others have made it into film history and maintain a modest reputation—*Red Dust* (1931, Dir. Victor Fleming), *Cain and Mabel* (1936, Dir. Lloyd Bacon), *Honky Tonk* (1941, Dir. Jack Conway). One or two classics used Gable's image to enduring advantage: *It Happened One Night* (1936, Dir. Frank Capra) and *Gone with the Wind* (1939, Dir. Victor Fleming). However, more powerful than any of the films themselves, the pattern lingers on. The Iconic Couple in classical Hollywood energized a formulaic script and makes submission to cultural stereotypes seem like a party.

As cultural stereotypes increasingly lost favor as a mode of characterization in the post-studio era, the Iconic Couple became an iffy proposition, though it did not disappear. In the last chapter of this study, we shall see how it became both duller than it had been under the studio system and less important, though it still continued to feature stars. At the same time, a new category of onscreen star pair, which I will call the Thematic Couple, partially filled the vacuum it left, emerging in the post-studio era. I will discuss this type in depth in Chapter Seven. As more freedom became available to moviemakers, scripts stopped unequivocally enforcing traditional stereotypes and began to tentatively question them. Actors energizing this kind of script often disrupted traditional stereotypes without disrupting the script. This type is most meaningfully represented by Paul Newman and Joanne Woodward, in their numerous screen collaborations; Bruce Willis and Cybill Shepherd, in the television series *Moonlighting;* and Bill Cosby and Phylicia Rashad, in the television series *The Cosby Show.* But thoughts about the Thematic Couple in the post-studio era take us ahead of our story. To critically appreciate that kind of star coupling, and the fin de siècle version of the Synergistic Couple, it is necessary to first consider in depth and detail the foundation for the couple tradition in mass media entertainment built during the studio era.

The chemistry of the Gable Plus One package is as undeniable as the chemistry of the Astaire/Rogers series. Yet the differences between these two categories of chemistry go to the heart of my attempts to understand the possibilities and limitations of the Hollywood that existed between 1930 and 1950. Primarily, attending to these two kinds of couple chemistry helps us to see with fresh eyes not only the figure of the couple in Classical Hollywood, but also the expressive consequences of the relationship between filmic sound and visual elements and the literary/formulaic/ideological elements in the popular culture movie.

RAW AND COOKED IMAGE IN HOLLYWOOD

There has been a dearth of thinking about couples in Hollywood movies. Astoundingly, there is no serious, extended criticism of the work of any of the four classical Synergistic Couples identified here, a situation that has left this study almost completely dependent on primary sources. Moreover, in what criticism exists about the couple phenomenon, the tendency has been to address the content of the script, the concept of the love story, and their cultural and ideological implications. This kind of study, though important, leaves out the most telling aspect of the screen couple: image. In this investigation I will consider the stories too, but the main emphasis will be on the relationship between the story and the image imprinted by charismatic screen couples. Screen couple chemistry is an *energy* issue, by itself a conceptually neutral element of moving pictures, the release of high-impact images into Hollywood movies. Screen couple chemistry is not inherently attached to any particular social values; rather it becomes attached to values depending on the way it is narratively used. It is necessary to discriminate among the possible ways of invoking values through screen chemistry. That discussion must be based on an understanding of the way chemistry is processed industrially through the filmic image, its vehicle, and how the processing affects absorption of the image by the spectator.

Most discussions of Hollywood assume that the processing of images is always thorough and that in all cases spectators read these images through social codes that subtly glamourize the conventional values promulgated by scripts supervised by the conservative/reactionary Production Code Administration. But in the case of screen chemistry, when its force turns into screen couple synergy, there are raw documentary elements in the image as well as elements fabricated by studio manipulation of technologies. That uncontrollable aspect of the Synergistic Couple contains not only fascination but also the potential for spectators to receive impressions that go beyond socially devised languages and systems. When this potential is realized, meanings that challenge formulaic cultural understanding are forged. In the specific case of the screen couple, an understanding of chemistry goes to the heart of why stereotypical representations of intimacy are connected with the more processed Iconic Couple, while unorthodox representations of intimacy follow from a more intense raw presence in images generated by Synergistic Couple chemistry.

In the case of the Iconic Couple formed by the Gable Plus One package, Gable's macho manhood chemistry is itself subordinated by an aggressive structure of stereotype and formula that objectifies the sensuality of Gable and his partners through a narrative of a domination/submission pattern of love. By contrast, in the case of the films made by the focal synergistic quartet, chemistry plays a more primary role. In, for example, the Astaire/Rogers series, Astaire's offbeat indeterminate masculinity, Rogers's equally ambiguous femininity, and the odd mutuality of their battle of the sexes forced their vehicles to adopt less aggressive narrative structures that took oddly indeterminate forms to accommodate their deluge of screen chemistry. Such synergy as theirs both disrupts a formulaic script and evolves a counterpointed visual continuity that forms the basis of a new perspective on old stereotypes.

The same can be said for the association between offbeat gender definition and the raw aspect of image in the other three couples in the focal quartet. Weissmuller/Tarzan's strange combination of male physicality with a whimsical, even receptive, nature usually associated with women fuses in a dynamic pairing with O'Sullivan/Jane's oddly unthreatening combination of receptive, fragile English Rose beauty and aggressive openness to difference and adventure typically associated with men, all of which erupted in a synergy requiring an unusually pliant narrative. Powell and Loy, both of whom had been cast as evil characters in earlier films, brought this edgy legacy to bear in the Thin Man mystery series, making for a darkly shaded, somewhat unsettling portrait of their intimacy. Finally, Hepburn's androgynous energy paired with Tracy's stolid bourgeois patriarchal energy charges with visual expressiveness and unique psychological complexity their often simplistically overwritten films.

Documentary image as a raw element of photography doesn't exist as a pure entity in any form of photography as, even in the most naked of photographic glances at the external world, there is always the issue of framing, which is inevitably connected with the values, ideas, and background history of the photographer. The studio-created Hollywood image is in general far more managed than it is documentary in character. However, the term "documentary" can, and should, also be applied to Hollywood movies, albeit as a highly qualified concept, particularly in relation to the Iconic Couple.[4] There is a documentary element even in Gable's highly manipulated image. He *was* in front of the camera and there *was* a specific magnitude and tone to the energy that his body projected, but it was consistently subordinated to the purposes of molding and maintaining Gable's stardom, encased, unshifting, a thinglike, dependably consistent icon, one that never revealed the ineluctability of the body. Gable's energy was the foundation of his image, which proposed a false, glamourized idea of body, as an armor that his inner force illuminated but never animated.

The patent-leather hair, with one or two wayward strands; the dark, hostile eyes sometimes shot through with a gleam of warmth that registered the minimal recognition that the narcissist can have of the presence of another who pleases him for a moment; the dimples in the tightly sculpted face; the thin moustache above the cherubic lips; the one oddity that perhaps energized his charm, his protruding ears: the composition was never stirred by any emotion that rearranged the sculptural effect. The preservation of that image superseded his delivery of lines and emotions in a scene, which, subordinated to the static image, was always mechanical; never a surprising improvisational gesture that could not be imagined by the spectator before it was performed. Much the same could be said for the stars he worked with. Joan Crawford, for example, exuded a raw chemistry that had a documentary origin in her, but it too was packaged to fit a static iconic image: her sultry, enormous eyes and full, sulky mouth, all molded into a characteristic expression of cruelty and pathos: the

Classic Gable Plus One: Gable, tough but tender, and Myrna Loy as the "uppity dame" ripe for subduing.

victim/adventuress. Crawford's large-boned body swaggered through the film frames as well defined as a statue, calling attention to itself, offering itself to be dominated. She clicked into place with Gable, but she clicked into place within any story formula tailored to her goddess/sacrifice image.

But if Hollywood fame often depended on the ability of an actor to find such a reproducible image to contain and delimit the necessary star energy, and the Hollywood couple might often mean a matched pair of icons, there were star couples that altered the logistics of the artificial star package. Fred Astaire, for example, when he worked with Ginger Rogers, to take perhaps the most cliche-shattering and abiding of the four pairs to be studied here, entered the frame with more raw energy than fixed image. "Being debonair" became a rigid pose for Astaire with other partners. But with Rogers, his image armor was in the immaculate, but ultimately removable tuxedo, which the audience knew was only a covering. In the Astaire/Rogers series, the Astaire tuxedo brings into conjunction both the external constraints of social order and an almost indescribable inner energy of resistance to all the formality to which his character is subjected. Moving along a spectrum of changing shapes, the inner protean Astaire is sometimes light enough to escape into the air through his white-tied collar, sometimes as physically obdurate as a balking mule. In his synergy with Rogers, he sometimes meets her with a puckish, elfin pliancy, maneuvering to soften her hard-edged self-protectiveness through play; other times he prods her and coaches her physically as an animal speaks to another (intractable) animal, drawing from within her rhythms she is rejecting. There are still other times when he meets her with an Oberon-like force, surprising her like a lightning strike. If Astaire's formal clothes satisfy the Hollywood mandate for reproducible images, when he worked with Rogers, there was that within the uniform that amplifies the documentary, mysterious energy of the human body.

On her part, Rogers, too, had a synergy with Astaire that complicated the standard glamour of her obligatory Hollywood feminine allure accessories. Rogers's cloud of blond hair, her clingy gowns, her feathers, satins, lamés, sparkles, and high heels may be the uniform of Hollywood seduction, but with Astaire, she exuded an energy from within the glamour drag, unreproducible by any starlet or female impersonator; the energy was inimitable, even by her. Her shifts in body and emotional tone matched, provoked, and answered Astaire's

This composite of Astaire and Rogers is not a frame-by-frame sequence from "Cheek to Cheek" in Top Hat. The selections made by the compositor, however, highlight the way this pair exploded gender cliches. Despite the obligatory subordination/submission masculine and feminine gear, Rogers begins and ends as a match for Astaire's power.

in a documentary surge of life force. Rogers ran the gamut from ice queen implacability to irrepressible effervescent playfulness. But she could also exude a searching energy of earnest intention to pursue her own agenda that excluded him completely, as well as a kind of openness to him that verged on ecstasy. Her permutations existed in immediate, spontaneous response to his; in the case of raw synergy, there can be no standard blueprint.

The differences between the Iconic Couple, represented by the Gable Plus One phenomenon, and the Synergistic Couple, represented by the work of Astaire and Rogers, were not the result of a studio decision, but rather of the opportunities created by the collaborative conditions of the studio system. As far as explicit studio policy was concerned, from the earliest days of the studio system, screen chemistry was a commodity. But if the studios had to see chemistry in that way, its reality evaded them. It was not a commodity, even in Hollywood, but an energy that sometimes was generated by the spontaneity that marked the collaborative commercial film process. In an effort to understand the Synergistic Couple phenomenon, which was permitted because *it was thought of* as a marketable commodity in Hollywood, this study will explore the emergence of screen chemistry as the result not of the decisions of the studio hierarchy but rather of the vortex of multiple perspectives that was an everyday part of the fragmented studio structure. The inability of any one point of view to dominate the collaborative process built into the studio system, combined with its fostering of situations in which stable acting partnerships could be formed that involved highly conflicted energy, is at the basis of screen chemistry. Studios permitted, and even forced, performers to explore the interesting, if on occasion exasperating, results of working through the dynamics of difference.

The fact of onscreen chemistry in movies must be closely read in terms of the production conditions from which those films evolved, in terms of both studio policies and the particular creative teams that made them, for it is no small point of interest that couple chemistry is an inherent and spontaneous quality that flourished in spite of and in some ways because of a manipulative industry formed by highly specific historical conditions. The historical conditions are almost as important as the innate energy in considering couple chemistry, as there was a symbiotic relationship between screen chemistry and the studio-generated star system. If the star system became a feature of the American culture industry by virtue of screen chemistry, screen chemistry moved from a notable phenomenon to force majeure because of the star system. During the studio system years in Hollywood, the star system and screen chemistry fed each other. Painted with the broadest brush, the situation was this: The political and economic power accorded to a star created a dynamic whereby that actor became increasingly at liberty to release the inner force more freely, which etched the performer more deeply into the public imagination and promoted stardom more indelibly, which led to more emphasis on the power of the screen energy in the actor's instrument, and so forth. This was true for all stars and all star pairs; the distinction of the Synergistic Couple was that its energy was more resistant to the control of studio technology over its release.

Nonetheless, the significance of the Synergistic Couple depends on the energy with which the studio sought to process it. Ironically, the energy of the star couple image became a significant element of meaning *because of* the presence of the artificial features of movies so cultivated by the studio system: the formulaic narrative and idealizing costumes, makeup, and lighting. In non-Hollywood films that use loose, personally imagined narrative elements, improvisation, and a desire to reach for the purity of unlabeled documentary image, actor chemistry is just another form of raw image.[5] In contrast, studio products heighten the impact of star chemistry by the extreme tension created between that raw energy and the multitude of artificial technologies used by Hollywood.[6] The effect of the synergistic actor's raw energy is magnified on the screen when it is virtually the sole raw element of the composition of mise-en-scène and story that are formed by the highly artificial Hollywood formulaic plot, as well as by manipulated lighting, costume, and makeup. The star's raw energy, and especially the combined energies of a star couple, appears even more powerfully because of its inevitable resistance to the artificiality, as elemental life forces in ordinary situations will appear even more intense if there is an attempt to cultivate them. So let us say it is the imposition of the formal, quasi-military, somewhat repressive, and certainly ideologically resonant lines of the tuxedo on Fred Astaire, combined with the artificial glamour of Rogers's wardrobe, that ratchets up the power and the visibility of the non-ideological force of the energy of their chemistry. And the synergy of Astaire and Rogers is ratcheted up by the artificiality of the script and setting. Detractors of the studio system and of Hollywood in general give the men in charge of the mass media high marks for effective manipulation of the movies in terms of the ideologies they transmit and economic successes they create. And often these evaluations are correct. Yet studio politics and their attendant cultural ideologies have never been successful at fabricating the real magic of Hollywood, such as that given to them by the accident of Rogers and Astaire.

Serious consideration of the clash between the manipulated technologies of Hollywood and the raw energy of couple chemistry that the studios tapped into but never could create forces us to rethink how the spectator receives the image and the potential for Old Hollywood to make meaning in ways that confounded studio control. Much of current film studies has approached the making of meaning in the movies as a function of ideology. That is, film has been widely explored in terms of how it re-inscribes the value systems of Western society in general and capitalism in particular through its visual modes of storytelling. Ideology is understood to be a powerful set of assumptions built into the structure of our institutions, which set the boundaries to our beliefs and behavior. Much of American ideology embedded in the structure of government, education, business, religion, and the armed forces has been identified as an inevitable limitation on our thought and actions. The dominant ideology is said to coerce beliefs in hierarchy, patriarchal entitlement, a preference for competition over cooperation, dominance/submission over mutuality, and the rational over the emotional. While it is accurate to say that ideology *often* functions in this way, however, ideology is too frequently seen as a total form of tyranny, and this is not correct. There are many fissures and ruptures, of which film studies must take heed. The tendency in film studies toward an anxious certainty that the rational supersedes the emotional, preventing us from thinking beyond the parameters established by ideology, has created unnecessary blind spots, particularly with regard to screen chemistry. The overemphasis on the power of ideology has made it impossible, heretofore, to discuss screen chemistry as anything other than a socially manipulated weapon in ideology's arsenal. However, all evidence in the films themselves points toward a form of chemistry quite independent of ideology, and cutting-edge experiments in neuroscience support this observation. Reason and the ideology it creates, this work suggests, are but one of a number of modes of making meaning. The implication of these experiments for film studies is that they establish theoretical support for a raw, non-ideological image, which, along with learned ideology, plays a role in the way we make meaning as we view and make meaning of films—including our engagement with screen couples.

As neuroscience has been making clear, the rational constructs of ideology are not necessarily the final determinants when it comes to making meaning; nor are the non-rational areas in the mind that are more linked to inherent body and emotional processes totally in control.[7] Rather, these different brain functions are mutually important in the process of making meaning, possibly differing to the greatest degree in terms of their positions in different parts of the cycle of making meaning. The raw image may be understood as that part of the screen image that speaks to the subcortical, preconscious mind, which seems to initiate the process of making meaning. In this initial engagement with the screen image, the spectator is responding below the level of rational awareness. (For a more detailed discussion, please see Appendix Two: "Theorizing Chemistry in Entertainment via Neuroscience.") By contrast, those aspects of the screen image associated with Hollywood technologies that are part of the social coding may be understood to be read by the reasoning centers of the mind, which have a second-cycle involvement in thinking. In this light, the raw energy of screen chemistry may be theorized as part of the way movies make meaning. In its ability to replicate the first stage of thinking through body image, screen couple chemistry is plausibly one aspect of the entertainment industry that produces a cycle of relationship between image and concept so rapid that it comes as close as we can ever come to infusing an uncoded experience into the meaning of the Hollywood movie. Paradoxically, then, chemistry, despite its reputation as the mark of the repressiveness of the Hollywood system, may also be the sign of potential resistance to the constraints of escapist storytelling. The juxtaposition of the raw image with the artificiality of Hollywood technologies will be explored in the films of the Synergistic Couples in Chapters Two to Five, as a way of creating a new perspective on the way the mass public reads, enjoys, and is stimulated by the clash between chemistry and formula in Hollywood movies. A larger goal of these discussions is to explain why the culture forms enduring attachments to the screen couples that embody the irritant juxtaposition of convention and unbound energy, while it forms only temporary interest in screen couples that are purely conventional/ideological.

SYNERGISTIC AND ICONIC STAR COUPLES

The two categories of couple chemistry that I have labeled the Iconic Couple and the Synergistic Couple can be best distinguished by examining the degree to which they create a dynamic between coded information and raw energy in a Hollywood film. The more numerous kind of star couple, the Iconic Couple, was, of the two types, less rich and exciting in its dynamic. It was composed of two icons, one star image linked to another star image in a way that left each a discrete separable module that could be plugged into a reasonable facsimile of the partnership with another actor. By contrast, the energy interchange of the Synergistic Couple, which could not be reproduced at will, exerted a disruptive influence on the formulaic elements in the film and emerged from an unpredictable process of combination, a multiplication process in which a third entity was created, a hyphenated identity, from which neither could be extricated as a discrete portion of the couple. There was no comparable recombination possible. Synergistically linked actors became third-entity pairs by virtue of their psychological balances or imbalances, by virtue of accident, or by virtue of luck, which resulted in the reduction of blockage of energy flow between the two partners and also between partners and spectator.

A comparatively rare phenomenon, but one strikingly important to the American culture industry, the Synergistic Couple distills the paradox of mass culture. Neither a mechanical reproduction nor a subversive attack on industrial culture, synergistic chemistry was at the same time an economic foundation of the Hollywood studio, and a live, unpredictable energy that made Hollywood capable of authentic expression about human existence. This form of couple chemistry occurred unpredictably between actors, as we shall see in chapters to come, in a number of different forms, generated by a variety of different historical circumstances, but consistently as a function of the fate of that sort of spontaneous kinship within the parameters of the studio system. The images created by Synergistic Couple chemistry generate a system of relations on the screen that, in a substantial way, proposes a narrative of its own, the chemistry no longer a matter of a single element in the screen frame, but of a small energy ecosystem that collides with the verbal narrative as well as the composition of the mise-en-scène. This creates an unusual (for mass entertainment) powerful subconscious engagement of the spectator with the narrative as well as with the image, the primary significance of which is its demonstration that popular culture can produce profoundly meaningful rather than only trivial escapist pleasures for a mass audience. Although it has been supposed that the greater the subconscious involvement of the spectator, the greater the chance for the traducing of the spectator with the simplistic and repressive formulations of the narrative, the films made by Synergistic Couples show the opposite to be true. Because of its disruption of the rational elements of the narrative, Synergistic Couple chemistry lessened the ideological stranglehold of entertainment on the audience.

By this light, the pleasures of Synergistic Couple chemistry show up as the opposite of the escapist fascination they have been presumed to be because they have been confused with the escapist pleasures generated by the Iconic Couple. Their films have been mistakenly lumped in with the usual Hollywood film, managed by studio executives in collaboration with the Production Code Administration to ensure a product that would appeal to the lowest common denominator and that would include no ideas that would disturb or turn away potential ticket buyers. The usual Hollywood narratives tended to be stories that, in the despairing words of screenwriter Ben Hecht, "have slapped into the American mind more human misinformation in one evening than the Dark Ages could muster in a decade. One basic plot only has appeared daily in their fifteen thousand theaters—the triumph of virtue and the overthrow of wickedness."[8] Worse still, the naive, simplistic Hollywood concept of conquering virtue and defeating vice was generally imagined through a particularly narrow and exclusive ideology that regarded virtue as the exclusive property of moneyed white Christians and vice as the likely option of all others. However, if Hecht gives a reasonably accurate description of the customary Hollywood plot, he does not describe Hollywood movies, to which there was, in the more important films, abundantly more than the plot. This is a truth that escaped an entire industry that, in its production and creative communities, and especially in the adjunct to the Hollywood studio system known as the Production Code Administration, never seemed to understand how much information is carried by image and how complicated the relationship was between simplistic plot and highly indeterminate image.

What we think of as Hollywood—so often exclusively associated with assembly-line production of standard items—actually often involves elements of disturbance, as well as formula. What is more, the history of Hollywood has been affected more powerfully by what has jarred its formulas than by what reinforced them. While Iconic and Synergistic Couples were both comparatively successful in their day, Synergistic Couples have proven to be enduring, while by and large Iconic Couples have proven to be limited in appeal to the times in which they were produced. Moreover, the kind of Iconic Couple movie that does endure as a powerful popular culture force, like *Bringing Up Baby* (1938, Dir. Howard Hawks), *Gone with the Wind* (1939, Dir. Victor Fleming), and *Casablanca* (1942, Dir. Michael Curtiz), notably involves one-time star pairings that either demonstrate how potent the anti-recipe factor is in creating powerful mass media fiction or suggest that the pair might have become synergistic had they been appropriately cultivated by the industry. What makes *Gone with the Wind* an enduring power, despite the standard Gable Plus One dynamic between Gable and Leigh, is the atypical, disturbing indeterminacy at the end of the film, which drew from the actors an energy that went beyond the formulaic macho man/uppity woman recipe that informs the bulk of the film. Gable's Butler reaches an unusual place for the actor in the last scene, in which there is a flicker of something more raw and documentary as he grapples with a battle that can be neither lost nor won. Leigh, an actor infinitely greater in scope than Gable, is given a chance to break formula, to some extent, as Scarlett reaches a moment that takes her beyond the obligatory formula for Hollywood's all too headstrong, sexy heroine/villain. Had Gable's Butler killed or tamed Leigh's O'Hara in the prescribed Hollywood manner, despite the film's big-budget production, *GWTW* would probably have, like most of the Gable hits, been popular in its day but then would have faded into history. Somewhat different in composition, *Casablanca*, despite the inordinate number of cliches in its script, opens up an indeterminacy in the relationship between Humphrey Bogart's Rick and Ingrid Bergman's Ilsa, with his anti-hero refusal to act and her steel fist in a velvet glove assertiveness that in the movie dwarfs the heroism of the reputed resistance hero to whom she is married. The atypical gender configurations bring out something not quite formulaic in the actors' relationship with each other that raises questions about what might have been accomplished between them had they been rematched several times. Similarly, the pairing of Katharine Hepburn and Cary Grant in *Bringing Up Baby*, in most ways a formulaic comedy, demonstrated their capacity in this film for creating a synergy that drew brilliantly both on Grant's unusual combination of iconic star image and the physical freedom to render it pliable and bending as wax and on Hepburn's similarly unusual freedom to unleash powers that disrupt the iconic star female image. Though highly regarded now, it was decisively rejected by the public in its time. Perhaps it threatened so much gender bending that unfortunately the nascent Hepburn/Grant synergy exhibited in *Baby* (they worked together four times, but never as excitingly) alienated the mass audience (unlike the case of Astaire and Rogers) and so was not nurtured by the film industry.

The industry failure to support the destabilizations of gender revealed in *Baby* is indicative of the irony (and maybe tragedy) of popular culture. In the short run, except when luck intervenes, institutionally, it favors its least dynamic aspects. The popular culture production hierarchy has always been more comfortable with the typical Iconic Couple, which Hollywoodizes the raw energy of chemistry by shunting it back into stereotype, as a mechanical blueprint for sexual tension between a dominant male and an uppity female. The misplaced confidence in manipulatively defined couples is encouraged by their commercial success in the short run. When the energy of actor chemistry is contained in this way, it continues to exert its own kind of attractions but favors the formulaic plot and is used by the Hollywood creative team for predictable results in a predictable, if momentarily exciting, story. Iconized chemistry is embryonic platitude, culturally captivating in its appeal as long as historical conditions embed the relevant cultural ideologies, but lacking the strangeness and shifts that bleed formulaic stories into more culturally enduring representations of the clash between the ideal and the ungovernable in human life.

We have already considered how the Gable Plus One phenomenon is acutely expressive of the pleasures of actor chemistry reduced to formula. A closer look at Gable's films is instructive in terms of the bound and free elements of his charisma. Gable's consistent cliched presence in apologist narrative for male violence, insensitivity, and pigheadedness now can be examined for its obnoxious and even boring qualities; yet the undeniable appeal of Gable's energy remains. In *Dancing Lady*, his cheerful force disguised the phallic sadism of the protagonist, cynical choreographer Patch Gallagher, who slaps dancer Janie Barlow (Joan Crawford) on the buttocks after hiring her for a job in the chorus, in what became a typical Gablesque act of gratuitous mastery and possession. She, with fawning, spaniel-like devotion, thanks him, ostensibly for the job, but in a way that helps the audience understand it as a grateful reaction to his abusive touch. Later in the film, Gallagher works out with Janie in a gym—in the film he is identified by his last name, she by her first—and repeatedly alternates between injuring and massaging her, to which she also responds in a spaniel-like fashion.

In *Test Pilot,* as test pilot Jim Lane, Gable raises his image to a godlike level as he makes the analogy between the sky, which draws him toward the possibility of death, and a seductive woman in a blue dress, whom he survives by slapping her into place. Myrna Loy, as his wife, Ann, is represented as longing to be slapped by him, so that she can do better in the importance category than sitting beside him as he gets drunk after returning from his missions or watching anxiously from the ground. In *Gone with the Wind* (1939), as Rhett Butler, he expresses the conviction, when Scarlett (Vivien Leigh) says she will faint if he continues to kiss her, that that's just what she needs, to be kissed until she faints. He rapes her when she withholds sex after the birth of her daughter. And when Scarlett tries to tell him how deluded she has been about her love for him, he leaves her without listening to the words he has purportedly longed to hear. At the time of the production of these films, Gable's energy disguised, through its charm, the abuse in all these scenes, not to mention the formulaic conclusions of the films, in which male domination is firmly established over a defeated, once uppity woman. In his time, Gable could pull off his signature gender routine with a remarkably large number of female colleagues.

Other kinds of cliched domination/submission patterns could be provided by Iconic Couples who, though more effective with each other than with any other partner, still lacked the unsettling energy of the Synergistic Couple and existed to glamourize Hollywood cliches. For example, Olivia de Havilland and Errol Flynn were not as appealing to audiences with other acting partners as they were with each other, but were strikingly formulaic in their repeated relationships with each other in the seven films in which they co-starred. The group of Iconic Couples that showed a particular affinity for each other within the almost machine-tooled repetitiveness of their formulaic pattern is equally represented by the numerous collaborations of Jeanette MacDonald and Nelson Eddy (eight films).[9] This category of Iconic Couple created a form of static repetition, which unlike the repeated partnerships of the Synergistic Couple, did not grow but rather gave the public an industrial replication of the pattern that abundantly offered the short-term satisfactions of predictability and familiarity.

The recipe for the Errol Flynn/Olivia de Havilland film will serve nicely as an example. Within a space of six years, this Iconic Couple became encrusted in a familiar combination: Flynn's insouciant derring-do, scorning the injustices of the powerful who would oppress him and all God-fearing men, and de Havilland's ladylike playfulness, challenging Flynn's masculine prerogative until he humbles her to his will and simultaneously raises her to the level of his acquired power. They constructed this relationship as the gender pattern of choice in the medieval period (*The Adventures of Robin Hood*, 1938, Dir. Michael Curtiz), seventeenth-century England (*Captain Blood*, 1935, Dir. Michael Curtiz); the nineteenth-century American West (*Dodge City*, 1939, Dir. Michael Curtiz, *Santa Fe Trail*, 1940, Dir. Michael Curtiz, and *They Died with Their Boots On*, 1941, Dir. Raoul Walsh); Victorian England (*The Charge of the Light Brigade*, 1936, Dir. Michael Curtiz); and twentieth-century America (*Four's a Crowd*, 1938, Dir. Michael Curtiz). Their repeated teaming as a movie couple created an image of historical inevitability in the stereotypical dynamics of their relationship, while reducing the historical events through which they courted and loved to a pile of nonsense.

Their first film, *Captain Blood*, set the pattern. Despite the grittiness of the film's violence, atypical for the studio system period but permitted by Warner Brothers, the studio that produced the Flynn/de Havilland films, *Blood* is a cliched production. Flynn steadily entombed his charisma behind the constructed Flynn image; his charmingly engineered gestures threaded their way through English and American history, bringing to heel the ever pert yet refined de Havilland. A conventionally phallic Hollywood hero, Flynn managed his energy to produce more subtlety and a more nuanced European quality about aggression than there was about Gable's bluster. Flynn masked his bravado with a thin veneer of civility, which was proudly flaunted in his films as the difference between him and the crudely phallic boors who opposed him. He had a charming lyrical smile that belied a quiet, iron will that he imposed on bullies who made unreasonable demands. His small, chiseled facial features were not particularly distinguished except for their clean modeling, and he eventually articulated the drama of his face with a pencil-thin moustache à la Gable. Flynn cultivated the gestures of heroic nonchalance in his body, which was more distinctive than his face. His feline grace gave him the air of a tomcat; his voice, even more distinctive, had a calculated, purrlike, soft lyrical lilt. Probably his most deliberate strategy was his smile, with its brilliant white flash of teeth that intimated the bite and sneer of defiance ready beneath his soft manners. The Flynn situation required (and got) an adversary on whom that irony was never lost; Flynn's acting armor would have cracked had he been forced to deal with an imperceptive or too overtly brutal antagonist. The smile also served him well in the context of command. When he was surrounded his loyal crew—men who would follow him anywhere—the flashing smile expressed a "good old boy" exuberance as he dashingly issued orders.

He formed a matched pair with de Havilland, with her catlike daintiness, her softness always ready to make way for righteous indignation, and her kittenish enthusiasm. She joined him in a coupling of civil ferocity and grace, though his scenes with her tended to be subordinated to his action plot, aggressively suggesting the stereotypically subordinate role of women in the typical, man-centered Flynn movie. For example, *Captain Blood* purports to take place in the seventeenth century in England, a time of religious and political tyranny when Englishmen were scooped up on the flimsiest of pretexts and either executed or transported as slaves to Jamaica for the economic gain of the Crown. Among these is Dr. Peter Blood (Flynn), transported for ministering to the wounds of a rebel against the Crown. Most of the movie is spent on action scenes in which Peter mobilizes *his men* and intimate scenes with heroine Arabella (de Havilland), thrown in sparingly to suggest Blood's ultimate destiny once he wins the day. Even the intimate scenes, however, tend to take place as a sidebar on the manly field of action rather than in private, secluded, *intimate* spaces. The scene in which Flynn is auctioned off as a slave before de Havilland's eyes is what passes for personal contact in a de Havilland/Flynn film. In this very public scene, the irrepressible Blood offends Colonel Bishop (Lionel Atwill), the better of the two slave owners in Jamaica, by being too independent about the routine physical inspection of newly arrived slaves. When Colonel Bishop pounds on Blood's chest and smacks him across the face for not opening his mouth for a tooth inspection, Blood smiles and then imitates Bishop's inspection posture, looking Bishop up and

Arabella's (Olivia de Havilland) feminine pleasure at her power to rescue Captain Blood (Errol Flynn) from Colonel Bishop elicits not a responsive pleasure but stereotypical macho disdain of womanly initiative.

down. For his arrogance, Blood is almost sold to the mines, the worst fate for a slave. Bishop's niece Arabella (de Havilland), who, appropriately for a heroine, takes a dim view of buying and selling people, takes pity on Blood and buys him herself. This saves his life but violates the domination/submission pattern for heroes and heroines. He resents her interference, bowing to her before joining the other Bishop slaves and saying, with lyrical irony, "Your very humble slave, Miss Bishop." In order to maintain the necessary gender recipe, which is played out with relish between them, all subtlety in the situation is sacrificed.

The definitive and public nature of each of their gestures ignores the complexity of Arabella's position as a woman in seventeenth-century society, and the complexity of any erotic interplay between men and women of any time. It also trivializes the terrible bondage into which Blood and the other men have been sold as a charming excuse for flirtation. The simplemindedness of the couple construction also dominates the outcome of the film, when Blood becomes the governor of the island and makes all well, suggesting that class injustice can be eliminated by the right couple, rather than acknowledging how complexly it is built into the fabric of society. The escapism and anachronisms are compounded by Arabella's behavior with her abusive and extremely powerful uncle, toward whom she acts as if she were a spoiled teenager in Marin County today.

The stage is set for not only a trivialized and eroticized battle of wills but also a trivialized and eroticized picture of class warfare. The sporadic meetings between Arabella and Blood are recipe encounters that use a slave society as the background for ritual courtship. If de Havilland has somewhat more spontaneity than Flynn, there is no chance for it to engage any free energy on Flynn's part, possibly the reason why Curtiz edited the slave auction scene so precisely, cutting back and forth between the two instead of using two-shots, which would have made painfully obvious the modicum of energy between his hero and heroine. The sexual "chemistry" between the two is predominantly fabricated by the juxtaposition of shots of Flynn's shamrock-scented posturing with shots of de Havilland's flashing-eyed, perky defiance of social customs. Smooth and polished, the rapport has nothing of the improvisational or wild energy about it. As such, the couple pairing does nothing that touches the profound non-reasoning centers in the mind, in a way that might have disturbed the spectator about the unexamined racism of Arabella's family and friends or complicated the simplistic portrayal of this highly stratified and brutal society. On the contrary, because it lulls the spectator's senses, the canned if attractive nature of the Flynn/de Havilland byplay lures the audience into accepting the escapist, conventional Hollywood logic of the satin-clad, ringlet-tossing maiden who dares and the rebel and pirate who becomes governor of Jamaica. This pattern of charming and intense endorsement of plot stereotypes is reproduced in all the films of this couple series.

By contrast, because of the unpredictable and uncontrollable energies of the synergistic acting pairs, repeated castings proved to be anything but a pure Hollywood version of mass production. Unorthodoxly countering heavy pressures to mechanize and formulate the movies in each series, the reengagement of energies in the Synergistic Couple series represents a very different form of repetition. At various points in their cycles, these acting pairs fell into the trap of consumer commodity, but more often they brought us repetition as exploration, renewal, and regeneration. The repetition became, at its best, an exploration of the attraction/repulsion of Otherness, and its implications for social institutions. The crucial factor was whether the charisma in the acting team could reverse the typical industry imbalances that emphasized the logic of the screenplay over the image. The more closely the film was tied to a powerfully articulated story, the more likely that the mysteries of human connection would be circumscribed by cultural ideologies inevitably promoted by the storyline. The more energy behind the couple image, the more likely that a film could complicate its vision of human relations.

In the chapters to come, as we examine the synergistic partnerships in films like *Tarzan and His Mate* (Johnny Weissmuller and Maureen O'Sullivan), *Top Hat* (Fred Astaire and Ginger Rogers), *The Thin Man* (William Powell and Myrna Loy), and *Adam's Rib* (Spencer Tracy and Katharine Hepburn), we will find less editing and less harmony among the filmic elements and more dissonance analogous to the disruptive energies between the couple partners. There will be more than a few slippages in the images that record the characterization of the male and female protagonists. The fluid transformational energies of the Synergistic Couples challenged the cliched romantic images and the ritualized sexual power games mandated in Hollywood scripts, which yielded time and again to their dynamic improvisational interactions, which were transmitted almost wholly by the non-narrative aspects of film image, sound, light, darkness.

Hollywood's zero degree aesthetic, which strives to erase the inherent conflicts among filmic elements, also tries to close the door on facets of representation that might trouble conventional ideas, like unsynchronized or wild sound, shadows, evocative lighting, disruptions-of-continuity editing. Shot patterns were supposed to bring a sense of clarity to the spectator about the details of the story. A close-up was intended to emphasize a story point, just as the lighting was supposed to indicate realistic images of times of day and year, and make visible what needed to be seen so that the story could be followed with the least amount of difficulty. Any attention to sound or image as a thing in itself disrupted the reassuring dependability of narrative (arguably a metaphor for the assumed dependability of masculinity) with the shifting, mysterious materiality of sound and image (arguably a metaphor for the assumed anxiety associated with the attractions of the feminine). On this basis I will argue for the significance of the presence of all these destabilizing visual and aural elements in the films of Synergistic Couples, and for the connection between this "wild" presence and the unconventional parity between the synergistic partners.

It is necessary to emphasize at this point that the categories I have constructed for the purposes of this study are primarily heuristic in nature, and not at all tidy. Purity is not a pronounced characteristic of the collaborative, commercial film industry. All couples in the mass media are somewhat formulaic in nature, and many have moments when they disrupt and dazzle with untrammeled energy. The categories used here denote the significant differences in proportion in these elements. Iconic Couples generally domesticate their star energy through formula; Synergistic Couples generally release it. While significantly more tensions operate within the films of the Synergistic Couple, such tensions may also crop up occasionally in the films made by the Iconic Couple, because the energy domesticated by the screen icon can never be completely checked. Visual and sound images can never be completely synchronized through editing and manipulation, nor can they be completely reduced to the film's pure story purpose, because there will always be an image that pops out of the film by virtue of a beauty or ugliness that goes beyond what is needed for narrative comprehension. In the same way, actor chemistry cannot be completely suppressed to suit escapist needs. There can always be a line of dialogue delivered in a tone that is arresting in itself, in a way that briefly disturbs the mass media control over its elements. In the otherwise formulaic *Test Pilot*, there is a stunning moment during which Myrna Loy, as Ann, jolts the viewer with the raw energy of a line delivery. Ann and Jim (Gable) engage in some otherwise cliched banter about his stereotypical fantasy about the sky as a treacherous woman in a blue dress who one moment "sits in his lap and purrs" and the next tries to kill him. Ann, jealously, tells him she wants a blue dress, that she looks good in blue. "What do I get for it?" asks Jim, in a smooth setup for Ann's next line, which Loy delivers in a way reminiscent of the raw chemistry she continually displayed in the Thin Man Series: "I'll purr in your lap." The line suddenly crackles with a primordial power and the film jumps off track, but just for a second. Immediately, Gable and Loy return to their customary, polished line delivery. When Loy worked with Powell in the Thin Man series, such moments were the pattern on which the film was built. However, Loy's momentary rupture in a film in which she was being used as an icon exemplifies how this kind of tension among the materials of filmic representation is one of the main conditions of film production, and thus is never totally absent from the filmic medium, whether it is worked by experimental and independent directors of the collaborative teams of the commercial film industry. Experimental and independent filmmakers producing films for an elite audience may more often play with and emphasize this tension. Commercial studio practice may more customarily suppress it. But there are elements in the commercial film industry, like the Synergistic Couple, that bring the tension forward, ripping the seamless illusion with which Hollywood films are associated.

Space limitations unfortunately prevent me from embracing the full range of couple irritants in commercial entertainment. For example, I regret that I will not be able to discuss camp couples in movies—the pairing of Dick Powell with Ruby Keeler (seven films), Mae West and W. C. Fields (one film), Rock Hudson and Doris Day (three films), and Jon Hall and Maria Montez (six films)—which throw an interesting light on the tension between the energy of image and narrative formulas in commercial entertainment. So do the repeat pairings of some very popular and somewhat indeterminate screen pairs—neither quite iconic nor quite synergistic—that were not able for various reasons to work together enough to give them the kind of heft demonstrated by the chosen quartet, like Cary Grant and Mae West (two films), Jeanette MacDonald and Maurice Chevalier (four films), and Gene Kelly and Judy Garland (three films).[10] Among the other interesting screen couples who do have abundant heft and the potential for providing valuable nuances for our understanding of how mass media define intimacy that could not be discussed here because of the demands of space, some of the more interesting include Groucho Marx and Margaret Dumont (seven films) and Judy Garland and Mickey Rooney (ten films).[11] Then there are the few movie couples that might have been included here even though they are marginal as Hollywood products because they exemplify missed opportunities in mass culture. One such example is the teaming of James Gleason with Edna May Oliver in a delightful but virtually forgotten series about a pair of "sixty plus" aficionados of mystery—Hildegard Withers and Oscar Piper—which was continued by the teaming of Gleason with Zazu Pitts and with Helen Broderick after Oliver left the series.[12] Simply because of the spectacle of two utterly unglamourized senior citizens cavorting with style, relish, and pizzazz, it is unfortunate that these have been virtually erased from cultural consciousness. The more couples studied, the more complete becomes the picture of not only the spectrum of commercial images of intimacy, but also the relationship between the mass media and ideology.

ONSCREEN COUPLES AND IDEOLOGY

My approach to couple chemistry, only a step toward exploration of the range of onscreen couples, seeks to expand on the range of screen couple issues explored in Virginia Wright Wexman's *Creating the Couple: Love, Marriage, and Hollywood Performance*, the only other serious book-length study of the phenomenon of the couple in Hollywood films. *Creating the Couple* focuses on the ideological effects of the star system on Hollywood's representation of sexuality and marriage, and on specific, distinctive stars rather than on actors who were coupled onscreen.[13] Wexman's conclusion that the couple is yet another way Hollywood has of reinforcing conservative social values and stereotypes is based on her very narrow focus on Hollywood movies. While I am inclined to agree with Wexman's conclusions about *her material*, her discussion is partial in nature. Wexman speaks not at all about those pairs that I identify as Synergistic Couples and their capacity to disturb, nor does she imagine the possibility of thinking beyond ideology. Focusing on the capacity of the Hollywood couple for formula and cliche, Wexman is mistrustful of the pleasure they create as the bait for swallowing ideological assumptions that are repressive and demeaning to many of the constituencies in the audience, notably women and people of color. I too am mistrustful of a particular kind of Hollywood couple. But I am also mistrustful of Wexman's emphasis on the link between the great interest in the couple in the American mass media and capitalism. The films themselves, as well as studio documents, show that the economic system was not as decisive an influence on the creation of Hollywood couples as she indicates, nor is intense interest in fantasies about couples limited to any one economic system.

The movie pair is a central feature in films produced by countries organized by a wide variety of economic systems. Observation of films made in Communist countries in their earliest and most idealistic stages—historical periods in which the prevailing idealization of group camaraderie could not have been more different than the individualism of the United States—suggests that there is no simple and unassailable connection between capitalism and the couple. In fact, such films may even suggest that the prevalence of couples in movies is more related to pan-cultural response to dramatic storytelling than to the ideologies of the producing countries. Film directors like Alexander Dovzhenko, writing within the context of the Communist ideology, also use the union of the romantic couple as a powerful narrative element onto which the triumph of Communism and the structural element of narrative closure are displaced. The rupture of a romantic couple in *Earth* (1930, Dir. Alexander Dovzhenko) is every bit as much of a metaphor for the wounding of the community and collective farming as John Wayne's betrayal of Marlene Dietrich in *Pittsburgh* (1942, Dir. Lewis Seiler) is a metaphor for the wounding of individualism and capitalism. And just as Wayne's recognition of his sins toward Dietrich is a healing that facilitates the capitalist war effort during World War II, so the triumphant rebirth of the romantic couple in *Earth* brings hope for collective farming (and humanity's relationship with nature) at the end of that film. In even more extreme ideological circumstances, Viktor Ullman, in the chamber opera *The Kaiser of Atlantis*, set in the concentration camp at Theresienstadt, also displaced onto the romantic couple his passion for the assertion of the potential for life in the face of the threat of annihilation. Ullman was not constructing screen drama, of course, but his inclination toward the figure of the couple in drama in circumstances of such extreme suffering must make us think again about the role of the romantic pair in dramatic structure.

This study, however, is not just about the role of the couple in drama, but about our misunderstanding of screen chemistry and our oversimplification of the pleasures involved with screen couples. A clear look at screen chemistry and screen couples is not only beautiful but also dangerous—to the more conservative notions about the mass media. Synergistic chemistry represents danger to the script, which it disrupts with its seminal power, not to the audience, which it is erroneously believed to have misled about the nature of love. This danger has not been recognized principally because Synergistic Couples have not been properly distinguished from less interesting and more manipulative pairs created by mass culture.

In much of Hollywood's output, both old and new, the couple image *is* manipulated into a form of idealization that short-circuits analysis. In the formulaic script couple and in the Iconic Couple, the chemistry of the acting pairs is harmonized or even homogenized to form one seamless, captivating image. By contrast, in the Synergistic Couple, two forms of idealization are brought into collision in a way that disrupts each ideal and stimulates vision and thought. Yet such disruptions ensure that the film will be propelled rather than arrested by the seamlessness of the couple. The Synergistic Couple represents energy in a dialogue between two powerfully matched male and female partners whose images depict interchange rather than sudden, heart-stopping paralysis. The disruptive energy dialogue of the Synergistic Couple also enters into a secondary dialogue with the constraints and defining articulations offered by a script. It pours a regenerative and hopeful energy into one of the most static parts of Hollywood fantasy, the domestic formula, which, particularly in the studio era, tended to present the home as a distinct area cut off from the larger society and the universe. The Synergistic Couple reconnected the domestic realm to the larger reality, suggesting that beauty (in both men and women) was a metaphor for the rich bounty of the pleasures of intimacy, with its capacity to confound the constricting incursions of social structures upon the human spirit. In the hands of the creative teams that built movies around these couples, metaphors for the intimacy of the couple became a form of resistance to threats against humanity involved in the urban mysteries (the Thin Man series), the mysteries of the organic world (the Tarzan series), the mysteries of temporal and spatial forms (Astaire and Rogers), and the enigmas of cinema itself (Tracy and Hepburn).

As we confront, encounter, engage the films of the Synergistic Couples in abundant detail, we will discover that there is a kind of filmic physics in the forces that are put into play through narrative, the movement of bodies, words, and gazes, when Astaire and Rogers, Powell and Loy, Weissmuller and O'Sullivan, and Tracy and Hepburn enter the filmic field. While, in a literal and simple way, all movie couples represent the relationships between the two sexes and can be construed as models for our behavior, the ones that can go no further may indeed be considered problematic, provoking no more than direct imitation that often leads to disillusionment, since life cannot and should not be like a movie. By contrast, these Synergistic Couples that became part of popular culture between 1930 and 1950 exist beyond such limited uses as those of mechanical imitation; they exist as a form of poetry that offers hope. They embody in poetic form the possibility for balance among opposite and contrasting forces as they work through their stories toward closure in a way that satisfies our longing for understanding of the conflicting elements in our lives. Such longings also drive neuroscientists to experiment with left and right brain impulses and chemists and physicists to experiment with the combinatory drama of matter and energy. Synergistic Couples thus are misunderstood as models for behavior. They are more accurately comprehended as meditations on the larger picture of human existence when questions of intimacy, connection, and love are given priority.

Studying the mass media couple tests our seriousness about exploring popular culture because the pleasure connected with the screen couple presses all the hot buttons of the film scholar: The wariness of the onscreen couple's seductive powers. The connections the onscreen couple has with old, discredited social, sexual, and class ideas. The belief that we know that the managers of the culture industry are simply manipulating the audience for profit. The desire to cut through harmful illusions. While the study of beauty may be dangerous, it is worth the risk. Exploring what excites our desire as spectators promises many rewards in teaching us how we read mass entertainment when we are most enthralled, and in freeing us to discriminate among various kinds of enchantments so that we may conceive of a healthy kind of pleasure and celebrate its contributions to cultural survival. Exploring what excites our desire as spectators also gives us the opportunity to probe the uncomfortable and even frightening situation of our manipulation by the media, for the managers may not be as powerful in this respect as they seem, nor the pleasure that they seem to make possible as much under their control as they would wish. The major value of the exploration that follows is its attention to these issues.

CHAPTER Two
JOHNNY WEISSMULLER AND MAUREEN O'SULLIVAN
Tarzan and Jane

The most inexplicable of the Synergistic Couple phenomena to be discussed in this study is the onscreen partnership of Johnny Weissmuller as Tarzan and Maureen O'Sullivan as Jane. Whereas Loy/Powell, Astaire/Rogers, and Tracy/Hepburn each had the kind of proven talent and expertise that reassuringly generates rationalizations for their dazzling synergies, O'Sullivan and Weissmuller leave the observer defenseless against the bald fact of chemistry at its purest. In looking at this pair, we are forced to immediately confront chemistry as a pure synergy of forces that defies theory as a fully explanatory method yet leaves room for theory to trace its existence through the glaring presence of a negative space in Hollywood's manipulative production system. This is a fitting place to begin the discussion of synergistic couple chemistry, as starting with O'Sullivan and Weissmuller can remind us that the skills that will be referred to in discussing the other three couples may be important in determining the direction of their specific synergies but that there can never be purely cultural reasons why that synergy existed in the first place.

The casting of Tarzan and Jane was a last-minute decision, arguably a bad business practice. Yet what can be judged a mindless state of panic can also be apprehended as an openness to the spontaneous insight into opportunities that logic, dependent on previous example, would inevitably miss. Reason could not validate either Weissmuller or O'Sullivan as casting choices. Both were unknowns, and neither had acting training. Of the two, only O'Sullivan, who had been making movies for about two years when she was signed as Jane, had significant experience in front of the camera. Before being signed as Tarzan, Weissmuller had been in one film, *Glorifying the American Girl* (1929, Dirs. Millard Webb and John Harkrider), as an Adonis figure in a musical spectacle number and had spoken no lines. Clearly, Weissmuller was hired for his body and his reputation as an Olympic swimming champion, while O'Sullivan seems to have been taken on because she brought to life the look and feel of the sweet, sophisticated, feisty girl conjured in the imagination of the writer, director, and producer during the story conferences.[1] But those decisions were made after the two had been brought to the attention of the right people at the right time by the merest chance. Weissmuller was noticed serendipitously at a pool. And O'Sullivan's demonstration of the right qualities in her screen test was accidental. O'Sullivan has said that had not screen test director Felix Feist been assigned to direct her, as he well might not have been, she wouldn't have gotten the part: "I'd been playing nothing but these wispy, forlorn little things; so that's the way I thought I'd play the test. It was all I knew how to do. But Felix Feist told me to drop all that and be more direct, the way I really was."[2]

The impurity of the process was compounded by the catch-as-catch-can sequence of directors on the set. Although W. S. Van Dyke is the director of record for the first Tarzan film, and although he certainly was involved in developing *Tarzan the Ape Man* (1932), the actual hands-on directing seems to have been done by whoever was available. In her last interview, O'Sullivan said that Van Dyke picked up "a shot or two" on *Tarzan the Ape Man* and that most of the directing was done by the second unit director, Jimmy McKay, with William Wellman directing one or two days.[3] Until the later films in the series, the lack of a single directorial focus was part of the daily production reality. Interestingly, the two best pictures of the series were made under these conditions. Arguably, as the production circumstances became more orderly and controlled, the films in the series decreased in quality.

The endurance of the Weissmuller/O'Sullivan collaboration could never have been predicted, as the initial film was a low-priority venture for MGM. Not only was the gathering of the cast and crew haphazard, but the genre was not taken seriously—the transcript of the story conferences reveals that the director of record, W. S. Van Dyke, had doubts about whether the movie would appeal to anyone but children—and the studio was stunned by its success. Staff producer Bernard Hyman was so surprised and so anxious to build on the unexpected success that he made a number of trips to theaters early in its release to observe the audiences in hope that spectator responses would alert him to the specific source of its appeal.[4] Moreover, the thrilling onscreen magic of Weissmuller's boyish charm and O'Sullivan's radiant, loving abandonment as Jane with Weissmuller's Tarzan, certainly not a reflection of an offscreen connection, was not even rooted in a fully acceptable acting partnership.

O'Sullivan was responsible and dependable, but Weissmuller was a quirky, unpredictable actor who shared with Tarzan some of the character's reckless, moment-to-moment gusto and enthusiasm. Weissmuller's spontaneity could certainly yield an infectious frisson of delight, as when, in 1924 he and a fellow swimmer named Stubby Kruger disrupted the Olympic swimming contests with an unscheduled comedy swimming act, after which a screaming crowd demanded two encores.[5] But his exuberance was sometimes out of control. O'Sullivan obligingly emphasizes the charm of his "wild child" personality in her public statements about him, describing him as a "big kid. He was fun. He was just what he looked like. He loved to laugh. He had no pretensions whatever about being a champion swimmer.... He was just like anybody else ... like a prop man or like one of the electricians. He was just a real nice guy. And, a good friend. I was very fond of Johnny. He never would have occurred to me a romance [sic] or anything, it was just, we had fun together."[6] Moreover, because of his freewheeling energy, according to O'Sullivan, the animals really did love him, particularly Cheetah, "which is probably the reason he hated me, because he was jealous."[7] Johnny Sheffield, who as a young boy was picked by Weissmuller to play his screen son, has adoring memories of Weissmuller, suggesting the kind of warmth and uncalculated energy that draws children, remembering him to this day as a good father who "was always kind and attentive." Going further, Sheffield remembers Weissmuller as "a Star (with a capital S) and he gave off a special light and some of that light got into me. Knowing and being with Johnny Weissmuller during my formative years had a lasting influence on my life. I didn't know it then, but as time passed I see very clearly how Big John was different from most and how being around him started a clock ticking in my head a lot like the one in his. He was NEVER defeated during his swimming career. The most important thing was that Johnny Weissmuller had time for me."[8]

But Esther Williams, who swam with Weissmuller at the Billy Rose Aquacade in 1940, remembers him as an outrageous exhibitionist who sexually harassed her continually and whom she found devastatingly attractive but alarming. "Johnny Weissmuller didn't just play Tarzan. He thought he was Tarzan.... Heaven knows, he was handsome.... He thought he was God's gift to women.... He had remarkable genitalia that he loved to exhibit and was constantly stripping his clothes to his swimsuit and beyond so that everyone could appreciate his extraordinary male attributes."[9] Many years later, when she met Maureen O'Sullivan at a fund-raising event, she asked O'Sullivan if Weissmuller exposed himself to her, which O'Sullivan confirmed, saying she coped with it by not making a fuss.[10] This was a part of Weissmuller's spontaneity and "friendship" on which O'Sullivan never commented publicly, not even in her last interviews, when Weissmuller was long dead. As Williams does not attribute Weissmuller's behavior to any viciousness on his part, but rather to a pure lack of moral limits, a lack that he displayed unthinkingly and in all circumstances, there is reason to credit her speculation that Weissmuller sexually harassed O'Sullivan as well. So while it seems quite clear that O'Sullivan never thought of him romantically offscreen, she was forced to contend with him sexually in a way that played out onscreen, where she was both more (there were limits to how carried away he could be) and less (she had to enter into the spirit of his play enthusiastically) protected from him personally.

Moreover, aside from the likelihood of Weissmuller's unwanted attentions, she was certainly physically beset by the working conditions. In a 1934 interview in *Photoplay*, O'Sullivan bemoans the "miseries of nudity." She has no problems about voluntary nudity. "It worked perfectly in the Garden of Eden, until the snake came along and said, 'Yah! Yah! You're naked!'" However, her "enforced nudity" as Jane was another story. Freezing in cold water, she was told by the sound man, "I can hear your teeth chattering, Miss O'Sullivan. You'll have to control them." She remembers always being sick while working as Jane, always aching somewhere, and always being bitten by the adult monkeys. "It took us a year to make the picture, you know. And I just chalk it up as three hundred and sixty-five days of unexcelled discomfort."[11]

Documentation suggests that what emerged from all this seemingly careless unprofessionalism should have conformed to the contemptuous model of mass culture established by influential cultural critics Max Horkheimer and Theodor Adorno, who defined the "culture industry" as a totalitarian leveling of aesthetic experiences for mass consumption, a diminution of unique poetic expression into infinitely reproducible images of indistinguishable performers and interchangeably disposable stories slotted for immediate consumption and recycling.[12] Certainly, the Tarzan series was regarded as a product by MGM, which produced it, having recycled the Tarzan books by Edgar Rice Burroughs. Arguably O'Sullivan and Weissmuller were undistinguished actors by themselves. Plausibly neither of them had any particular acting talent, and factually neither had the film business expertise to bring to bear any original perspective on their characters. By all accounts they did what they were told. Yet the movies themselves have the final word. Against all odds, Weissmuller and O'Sullivan brought to the films what turned out to be a decisively important freshness. Weissmuller brought a highly unusual physical beauty that was charged onscreen by an almost uncanny ease with physicality, and O'Sullivan brought her ingenue charm, petite elegance, and a splendid emotional openness and readiness. Once together, they were not interchangeable with other actors of their type, nor were their films disposable or dull, mechanical imitations of each other. In concert, Weissmuller and O'Sullivan amassed a riveting energy dynamic that paradoxically frustrated, decentered, and even inverted the studio plans for a controllable product at the same time that it eminently fulfilled studio plans for garnering substantial profits. Their chemistry and its effect on mass culture partook of the pristine fortuitousness that is so much an element, though certainly not the entire picture, of the history of screen chemistry in Hollywood.

The first of the four industry paradoxes of this type to be explored in this study, Weissmuller and O'Sullivan created a mass media portrait of lovers that cannot be fully deconstructed as a machine-made article for immediate consumption and recycling. Strip away the contrivances of the publicist, the fabricated glamour of makeup and costumes, the molding of appearance through lighting, and the editing—significantly, as we shall see, editing plays a far smaller role in the films of Synergistic Couples than in the filming of more formulaic iconic pairs—and there is something left to talk about that is not of industrial manufacture. The combined O'Sullivan/Weissmuller images radiated something not created by, but brilliantly expressive of, the human dilemma with culture. Their paired images left energy traces on the film frame—such "wild" energy traces in such unusual abundance, in the unforeseen power of their onscreen interaction with each other, that they cannot be explained away in the terms of current critical discourse as manufactured illusion or reduced to stereotypes and cliches.

In fact, far from recycling platitudes, *Tarzan, the Ape Man*, the first of the six MGM Weissmuller/O'Sullivan Tarzan movies, lays down an uncommon premise for the series with its wholly inadvertent experimental approach to gender and to ethnicity. The film is relatively indeterminate in nature, as compared with the usual boilerplate Hollywood genre film. Ambiguously, it has both a conventional and an unconventional narrative focus. At the core of all the films in this series is the theme that the destiny of both African- and European-based culture was changed after a white, European man was discovered living in harmony with nature, and to some extent in harmony with the neighboring indigenous African peoples on the Mutia Escarpment, a sacred area in Africa.[13] The wild-child motif was not a new one, either for the history of Western literature in general or for the movies themselves. Only one year before, W. S. Van Dyke had directed a film called *Trader Horn* (1931) in which a woman, kidnapped as a child, was discovered living a "savage" existence with an African tribe. However, although Van Dyke and MGM assumed that they were duplicating in *Tarzan the Ape Man* their successful production of *Trader Horn*, the assumptions underlying the two films turned out to be very different in the finished cuts. The fact that we now know that Jimmy McKay may actually have done most of the shooting of the first film would not seem to account for the difference between the two supposedly similar films, as we have abundant documentation that Van Dyke was crucial in the *development* of both even if he did not participate in the first Tarzan film as the primary director.[14]

Horn told a tale of unmitigated white supremacy that followed in the tradition of the old colonial narratives of women settlers triumphantly repatriated from their "captivity" by Indian tribes to their original, European, "appropriate" way of life. *Horn* featured a narrative that explained the circumstances of its heroine in a clear and unambiguous fashion, detailing the outrage of her abduction and the felicitousness of her rescue. In contrast, *Tarzan the Ape Man* leaves Tarzan's strange appearance in the jungle a mystery—one that would never be explained in the series, although it is fully explained in the Burroughs novels. How did he come to be where he is? The Weissmuller/ O'Sullivan series indicates no terrible rupture with a happy European past in the film (the explanation in the novels). The lack of such an original scene of trauma and discontinuity, in combination with the powerful sense of Tarzan's harmony with the jungle, leaves the situation interestingly committed to the appropriateness of a life lived by a European man outside of the constraints of European civilization, and without commitment to the primary desire in the *Horn* narrative for a return to European roots. In fact, given what the film does show, there are clear suggestions that repatriation would be a tragedy for Tarzan, and clear praise for his extrication of Jane Parker from her European heritage. The violence of Jane's conversion from European society is presented not as an outrage but rather as an apocalyptic redemption. The love relationship that erupts between Tarzan and Jane Parker conventionally should have been, but was not, the scandal of her refusal to repatriate. It was instead the source of Jane's freedom.

The story of the first Tarzan film follows the lines of most Hollywood movies in that it proposes the stereotypical European girl-as-narrative-prize, esteemed and desired by all but reserved for the singular hero. However, it and the succeeding Tarzan movies complicate the familiarity of the stereotype in two ways. First, there is the narrative's unusual focus on what Jane wants, decentering the customary clash of the men over the female trophy by animating the trophy as a female person, possibly more in touch with her desires than the men. Second, there is the identity of the hero, who is not Hollywood's customary cream of European society but rather a man who is defined by the dominant men in Jane's family and acquaintanceship as little more than an animal.

In moving through six narratives that redefine the importance of female desire as central to the story, rather than peripheral to the desire of the men who want her, and in redefining the masculine ideal, the MGM series used both a simple narrative structure and the obligatory Hollywood emphasis on happy endings in an unusual way. In asserting itself as a story in which the couple makes for a double protagonist structure, the film also departed radically from the books written by Edgar Rice Burroughs, in which Tarzan is a lone hero, Jane being not only a side dish but also disposable. He gives her up at the end of the first novel, for her own good, thereby proving himself a true Christian gentleman. In the Burroughs series, Tarzan assumes the identity he is born to have once he encounters his "true" cohort. In the films, Tarzan defines himself increasingly in opposition to a highly problematic white Christianity. Where the Burroughs books integrate Tarzan back into competitive, capitalist society, sometimes imagined as a jungle and sometimes imagined as the European class system, the MGM Tarzan series is about freedom from the competition and commercialism that feature women as trophies through Tarzan's fortunate if inexplicable adoption of an alternative set of values based on the organic interconnection between humanity and nature—and between man and woman. The crucial interconnection between Tarzan and Jane, fostered by the natural world of the jungle, challenges generally accepted American individualistic values and behavior of competitive, class-structured society, a challenge that endures and ripens throughout the series.

OTHERNESS

The powerful bond between Tarzan and Jane remains strong throughout the six films of the MGM series, but their relationship evolves as it is weathered and textured by the competing value systems that their union brings into collision. In all cases, the interior experiences of both Tarzan and Jane are balanced; never is the learning process one that accommodates Jane to the dominance of Tarzan, as in the Gable/uppity female films and the Flynn/de Havilland series described in Chapter One. Rather, the confrontation of Otherness is deepened with each film.

In the first film, *Tarzan the Ape Man*, each learns to follow an awakened desire that lay dormant while each was bound by his or her own context. When they meet, they begin a process of the recognition of the Other as a living entity and energy outside his or her desire and identity within a new context formed by their union. The symbol of the possibility of their seemingly impossible union is the death of Jane's father, James Parker (C. Aubrey Smith), the price of his greedy and unsuccessful pursuit of ivory; his death signals the demise of any easy assumptions about Jane's obligations to European heritage.

In the second film, *Tarzan and His Mate* (1934, Dirs. Cedric Gibbons and Jack Conway [uncredited]), despite the masculine predominance implied by the title, Tarzan and Jane both further explore the differences that have brought them together and still threaten to separate them. The difference between the patriarchal title and the

In the synergistic MGM Tarzan series, savage masculinity is the partner, not the master, of the feminine.

mutuality in the actual events of the movie demonstrates the lack of awareness on the part of MGM about what they were creating. Nevertheless, as in the first film, a highly unusual tale is told. A safari of European men led by Harry Holt (Neil Hamilton), James Parker's apprentice from the first film, again enters the sacred Mutia Escarpment to get the ivory that James Parker found but did not live to acquire, and to reclaim Jane. Although this plot might seem to be a simple recycling of the first, it is not. In the 1932 film, Jane did not confront the values with which she entered the film, principal among them a kindred assumption with her father that the quest for ivory was a perfectly acceptable business. In the 1934 film, Jane begins to understand that to stay with Tarzan she will have to change more than her geographical location and external lifestyle. Revisiting her father's quest through Harry's reappearance—when it suddenly strikes her that Tarzan had never understood the commercial reasons her father had for visiting the elephant's graveyard—she begins to see it as an unwarranted invasion and to move further toward a conscious choice of values different from those with which she was educated. When Tarzan, for his part, suddenly apprehends that Parker's death had disguised the Europeans' intentions of looting the sacred burial ground, he begins his long struggle against the European attitude toward life and nature—which because of audience identification is made alien for the normally Eurocentric audience—and Tarzan himself takes on a greater understanding of the depth of the differences between himself and Jane. The second film generates Tarzan's series-long lesson that, unlike a battle with an animal, the struggle with a civilization is not over when the body dies, but lives on in the intractability of ideas. The symbol of Jane's further commitment to Tarzan and her increasing estrangement from her heritage is the death of Harry Holt, her would-be European suitor, which represents the demise of any chance that she will generate a typical European family of her own.

The relative intractability of the opposition between Jane's heritage and her choice is further explored in the next two films, *Tarzan Escapes* (1936, Dir. Richard Thorpe) and *Tarzan Finds a Son* (1939, Dir. Richard Thorpe). Both movies explore the ways in which Jane's deep conditioning by her education and feelings of loyalty to her European forebears lead her to separate from Tarzan in what she believes to be a temporary rupture, but which the audience understands could mean the end of their life together. In each film, she abets plans of newly invading Europeans that initially seem benign to her. In the 1936 film, Jane believes she is helping her family, and in the 1939 film, she thinks she is helping her son, but in both cases, she has been deceived by two different kinds of emotional allegiances into facilitating strategies for satisfying European greed. Tarzan comes close to rejecting her in *Tarzan Finds a Son*, when Jane actually lies to him in her blind fidelity to her "people," but once she achieves clarity about her confused values and Tarzan forgives her, they are united against the Eurocentric civilization of her past. The next two films, *Tarzan's Secret Treasure* (1941, Dir. Richard Thorpe) and *Tarzan's New York Adventure* (1942, Dir. Richard Thorpe), find them fully united against European violation of their family, once on the Escarpment, and then on the turf of the invading culture itself, in New York. In both of the final films of the series, greed and the fascination exerted by Western technology threaten their son, Boy (Johnny Sheffield). In *Secret Treasure*, Boy is endangered when his fascination with the Western technology shown to him by a scientific expedition (including a movie projector) makes him vulnerable to the rapacity stirred up in the scientists when they discover the abundance of gold on the

Escarpment. In *New York Adventure,* technology again makes Boy vulnerable to the danger and corruption of Western culture when a plane carrying hunters crashes on the Escarpment. Boy's desire to fly in the plane creates a situation in which Tarzan and Jane appear to be dead, leaving him no real alternative but to accompany the hunters to New York, where they intend to exploit him as a freak attraction for a circus. After Tarzan and Jane are extricated by the efforts of Cheetah, their chimpanzee family companion, from what seemed to be a fatal situation, they confront not only the greed of European culture but the law that may protect it when they travel to New York to save Boy.

The first Tarzan film initiated the series of six films through a succession of accidents, false starts, and anything but a coherent vision on anyone's part. The films that emerged do have a coherence, however, one that cannot be attributed to auteur-like control but that clusters around the extraordinary chemistry of Weissmuller and O'Sullivan. The evocation of Tarzan and Jane's story as an ongoing, sophisticated, and complex exploration of the Other is not achieved by the scripts, which are ordinary mass-culture narratives. It is achieved by the counterpoint between the spontaneous filmic images of Weissmuller and O'Sullivan as Tarzan and Jane and the stories, giving depth and power to simple themes. It is quite one thing to say that the hunters, ivory traders, and scientists are greedy, and quite another to embody an alternative within the Synergistic Couple that makes the audience profoundly experience the difference between individualistic conquest—ironically so similar to the system that produced the film—and a loving human connection that that same system was inadvertently able to portray. The unorthodox vision of the Tarzan series could not have been realized except through the serendipity of the O'Sullivan/Weissmuller synergy.

Weissmuller's Tarzan is a truly unorthodox male figure who stops the film with his physical beauty and his difference as much as does O'Sullivan's Jane. First glimpsed in *Tarzan the Ape Man* as a figure in motion in the dense jungle foliage, Weissmuller is a mobile body, free of the male uniform of constricting garments worn by the males among Jane's European friends and family. Tarzan enters the film as an ambiguous sound—the distinctive Tarzan yell that hovered between formula and uncanny visceral experience throughout the series—that may or may not be human. When Tarzan comes to rest in a tree for his initial full frontal appearance, he crouches forward in a simian posture that is complicated by his contrastingly human glance, alert with intelligent curiosity about the European invasion of his pristine land. A figure of flesh and innocent strength, he stands in contrast—to his advantage—with Jane's stately, mannered, but ivory-obsessed and gun-crazy father and with the pragmatic, self-controlled Harry Holt, who wants to be a decent man but who is driven to cruelty and violation by his part in James Parker's scheme to plunder the wild of its treasures. Conviction is conveyed about this opposition not primarily through the script, but rather through the physical energy of the juxtaposed images. Neil Hamilton and C. Aubrey Smith, with their stiff, conventional acting bodies, incarnate the antithesis of Weissmuller's relaxed, spontaneous physicality.

O'Sullivan's Jane immediately understands Tarzan's Otherness, and she is drawn toward it and away from Hamilton and Smith, contrasting images that translate more profoundly into the experience of the film than the conventional dialogue and storyline, which only gives verbal acknowledgment to what is already powerfully on the screen. When the Parker safari first encounters Tarzan in the trees above them and Jane restrains her father from shooting him because Tarzan doesn't comply with old Parker's demand that he descend from the tree, the image of the guns clusters with the image of European body-as-armor and in counterpoint with the naked, innocent, yet more inherently powerful flesh of Weissmuller's Tarzan. After Tarzan abducts Jane—the minute her father's attention is distracted by the sudden attack of a hostile African tribe—the stunning image of Weissmuller's energy casts a guilelessness over his violation of Jane's personal space as he investigates her clothing and then tries to initiate physical contact that is unquestionably sexual in character. His action is a very different kind of incursion into personal space than the already abundantly documented readiness of Harry and her father with whip and gun, wordlessly casting European culture in a dubious light.

However, the immediacy of Weissmuller's filmic image is not employed in the film as an apology for Tarzan's seizure of Jane against her will. On the contrary, that very immediacy confounds the seemingly imminent romanticized rape scenario after Tarzan bears Jane into the trees. During the first confrontation between Tarzan and Jane, the openness and spontaneity that Weissmuller and O'Sullivan possess as individuals authenticate Tarzan's sudden inability to press his will on Jane, even though there is nothing and no one to stop him. With no "story explanation" of the scene, the innocence embedded in the chemistry of the actors' bodies conveys a recognition of the other's humanity such that it limits the progress of the violation begun by the abduction. The preliminary exploration of Jane's clothes by Tarzan, once he has removed her to a branch high above the jungle floor and the European safari, is thus transformed into the prologue to not possession but the understanding that he can never possess her by force. At the same time, O'Sullivan's spontaneous image conveys Jane's encounter with male energy released spontaneously as a force with natural limits, not as the typical Hollywood mythological limitless naturally mastering force to which she must submit. No words could have conveyed the Tarzan/Jane shock of recognition.

The Weissmuller/O'Sullivan synergy of raw power is released on the screen to communicate the couple issues of bonding from the moment when Tarzan sets the newly-carried-off Jane down on a large branch between himself and a small chimpanzee. Tarzan and the chimp fight like children over Jane's "mysterious" handkerchief, a manufactured rather than organic object that Tarzan tears into strips in an action that speaks of both his curiosity about the nature of this fine web of threads and an impatience with the artifice of the dainty thing, so inimical in every way to a life lived through the bounty of nature. At the same time, O'Sullivan's Jane, finding herself at last in the "savage" situation she has been craving—the motive for her sudden appearance in Africa on a surprise visit to her father— embodies the moment with extraordinary nuance and articulation of the tension between her open sensibility and her breeding. Nature and nurture collide in her as she watches a grown man whose body speaks a language of connection and engagement that defies all her experience with the Western version of manliness, a form of male maturity achieved through detachment and distance. Protecting Jane from the curiosity of his fellow apes and chimps is a matter of ritual shoving and loud, proprietary shrieks in a language that is anything but Indo-European in origin. Jane begins to speak body language when she holds on to the inside of Tarzan's thigh for balance and out of fear of the other animals. The intimacy and the nuance of this gesture is typical of the articulation of this extraordinary film. O'Sullivan's Jane exists not within the grid of language once she meets Tarzan but in the realm of almost pure physicality, generating from the actress such a gesture as steadying herself with her fingers on the inside of Weissmuller's thigh, a gesture that would have all kinds of other implications in her own society, and certainly would have been unthinkable in any other Hollywood film of the time, but *was not remarked on by the PCA*, as was the nude swimming in the next film, *Tarzan and His Mate* (1934). Perhaps the PCA was silenced because of the way the film altered ordinary terms of Hollywood representation, or perhaps because they had no way to think about, let alone prohibit, the silence and delicacy of the gesture, embedded within an almost purely visual scene, filled with wild imagery and sound.

Jane's first encounter with Tarzan utilizes few utterances, and those are restricted mainly to ad-lib screams of fear when Jane finds herself in the treetops, and then when Tarzan's exploration of Jane moves past her clothing to her body. The relation of Weissmuller's Tarzan to O'Sullivan's Jane as a male physical creature to a female physical creature stands as the most intensely material representation of eroticism in the films made by Classical Hollywood. At the same time it initiates what was to become a pattern in the Tarzan series of minutely detailing the difficulties of intimacy. The wild energy traces from the acting pair in the screen images mark it as an incomparable, authentic visualization of intimacy as an awakening of the spirit in the body that is prohibited by the ordinary rules of culture, but that is also alien to the practices of jungle life.

When Tarzan drags Jane into his "nest," he pushes and pulls at her body as we have just seen him push and pull unhesitatingly at the simians around him to let them know how he expects them to behave. Here too there is no hesitation until the quite literally blinding moment when it occurs to Tarzan that he cannot continue in this manner. Extraordinarily for the time, there is no eroticizing of Tarzan's manhandling of Jane, unlike in previous Hollywood silent scenes of a similar nature, for example those between Rudolph Valentino, as an exotic primitive, and his co-stars. There is pure invasive energy depicted on the screen on Tarzan's part and pure defense on Jane's part. However, the sudden wild gaze in Weissmuller's eyes—unlike the mesmerizing glance of Valentino (that standard of the image of primitive man at the time), which rendered his female partner a helpless victim—does not mesmerize Jane, but rather triggers her understanding that this is a very different man as it initiates Tarzan's realization that something new is happening. With spectacular purity, Weissmuller's Tarzan reaches a physical as well as an emotional realization that within the woman's otherness exists a self as individual as his own. It is a stunning visualization of the birth of an idea growing up from the roots of material experience. At the same time, as O'Sullivan's Jane sees Tarzan's cataclysmic realization, she, who has previously been accustomed to thinking of herself as the object of desire but never of men as figures who could make her feel desire too, awakens to a new sense of maleness as a force as organic and attractive as her own female power, and to a potential if frightening possibility of negotiation between the two.

The synergistic energy traces on the film made this encounter viable in a way that had not been possible in *Trader Horn*. In that film, Horn (Harry Carey) and Peru (Duncan Reynaldo), his stereotypical young protégé in African adventure, rescue Nina (Edwina Booth), a European woman abducted by Africans as a baby, raised to be a "savage" and worshiped as a blond goddess by the tribe. The film is a hodgepodge of moldy cliches: the superiority of the Nordic patriarchs over "black savages"; the seductive womanhood of the Nordic heroine that must be saved from the desires of lesser men; the danger of women (white, of course)—here made even more dangerous by Nina's life among black Africans; and the necessity of return to authentic civilization. There is no evidence in the *Tarzan* script conferences or script notes now available to us that the creative team was conscious of doing anything very different in the first Tarzan movie from what had been done in *Trader Horn*. Yet different it was, and it would seem that many of the continuing differences emerged because of opportunities offered by the chemistry of the two co-stars, which moved the team rather spontaneously toward something new and expressive in the mass media.

Once Weissmuller and O'Sullivan gave body to that impulse, their energy took over the creation of the series. Before Weissmuller and O'Sullivan were on board, as the conference notes testify, the team had conceived of a feisty Jane, which moved the team toward its seminal casting decisions, but they then took on lives of their own in the making of the movie, as the elements of a process will do. The teleology of the making of the movie is echoed by the teleology of the plot of the movie, as the life Jane sought by moving out of her niche in England and into Tarzan's realm arrived in a form she could never have foreseen, and at the same time awakening Tarzan, by her entrance into his territory, into a new form of his human potential to fit into the natural ecosystem almost as animals do.

The singularity of the combined Weissmuller/O'Sullivan image became a filmic language in itself. It spoke of something different from the ideas communicated by the dialogue and the plot structure, creating a film image very different from the typical manipulated image in Hollywood entertainment (then as now). Manipulated image inevitably joins the dialogue and plot structure in reiterating conventional ideologies, as was the case with *Horn*, which used the exotic location of the jungle to restate the Hollywood cliche of romance in which the female is the submissive object of male desire and in which desirability is a function of the cultural worship of Nordic beauty. Nina, the abducted European woman, clearly stuns the African tribe into submission and inspires love in Peru as a pale blond "fetish," literally the word used for her by the tribe. Even today, in the most recent Tarzan movie, Disney's 1999 feature-length cartoon based on Burroughs's Tarzan story, Jane and Tarzan cannot in any way project the raw image potential in the charismatic human body and, following in the mold of Disney heroes, are clearly modeled on Nordic ideal images. There is no opposition at all between the figures and the cliched romance between Tarzan and Jane, in which Jane is at all points subject to Tarzan's authority—even when he has less command of English than she has. Certainly manipulated image also fits right in with stereotypical story in the deservedly forgotten Buster Crabbe Tarzan film, *Tarzan the Fearless* (1933), made immediately after MGM's *Tarzan the Ape Man* by a small company called Principal Productions, which was trying to ride on MGM's coattails. Eschewing Jane Parker, Principal Productions gave Crabbe's Tarzan Mary Brooks (Julie Bishop), a young woman who comes into the story as an idealized photographic image on the desk of Tarzan's European mentor—she does not even exist originally as a living creature. Thus Crabbe's Tarzan is emphatically not involved in a mutual awakening, but rather in the customary lust of male for female object, following a tradition of creating the couple by virtue of their idealized Nordic features.

Trader Horn, *Tarzan the Fearless*, and the Disney Tarzan all conform to the analysis of the couple in the Hollywood movie made by Virginia Wright Wexman in *Creating the Couple*. In her formulation, the Hollywood couple as a constructed illusion of romance (which I have labeled as the Iconic Couple) addresses the audience so as to make culturally specific (Nordic) ideals of beauty seem natural and universal and so as to universalize culturally specific patterns of gender relationship. The partnership of Weissmuller and O'Sullivan shows, however, that the mass media couple does not *inevitably* glamourize the Nordic look as the essence of beauty—basically a racist statement without words—just as this Synergistic Couple shows that the domination/submission gender pattern so typical of Hollywood is not inevitable.[15] It is true that Weissmuller and O'Sullivan are both ravishingly beautiful. However, looks were not the reason that they proved to be far more successful, compelling, and enduring than Crabbe and Bishop in the copycat Tarzan film that followed the next year. Crabbe and Bishop were also beautiful, and far more Nordic looking, particularly Crabbe. Weissmuller is, in fact, Slavic in origin and rather suggestive of a hybrid of the Oriental and the Western, though O'Sullivan certainly qualifies as a Nordic beauty. But even O'Sullivan's British appearance is highly qualified by a maverick spirit that creates an important and fascinating tension with her conventional beauty. The distinction between the two pairs is the raw energy of the images of O'Sullivan and Weissmuller as contrasted with the rote, cliched technique of Crabbe and Bishop. O'Sullivan and Weissmuller mark the film with images that are viscerally *incompatible* with the stiff body tone of the characters conditioned by a greedy civilization, while Crabbe and Bishop are in filmic image every bit as starched by Western body conventions as are the villains.

Tarzan the Ape Man is full of seminal moments between Tarzan and Jane that charge the screen with images that oppose the regimented Western body and propel the audience into not just thinking about but also experiencing, through the conviction of filmic raw image, the kind of authentic body existence that the European characters can neither understand nor inhabit because of the distancing effects of their ideology of greed and conquest. One of the most delightful as well as significant of these moments is the sequence in which a frustrated and anxious Jane tries to bridge the chasm between herself and Tarzan by teaching him basic English, and she runs up against a linguistic conundrum. The reference pronouns "you" and "me" are at odds with the physical reality of two bodies, as Jane discovers when she says, "Thank you for saving me," and can't explain to him that she is "only me to myself." They do better with the nouns "Tarzan" and "Jane," which are easier to attach unequivocally to their bodies. When Tarzan hits her shoulder and says "Jane," hits his chest and says "Tarzan," they are on firmer ground, if communication becomes painfully repetitive as Tarzan continues to study his lesson, hitting their bodies while reciting their names alternately. Taking it one step further, the two of them explore the way in which bodies are language. Tarzan determines that Jane is hungry through physical

The comparative eloquence of gesture in the Tarzan series, a language beyond the limits of verbal structure.

vibration of her belly with his hand, a gesture that is patently non-erotic but that momentarily disturbs Jane's European definition of personal space. She quickly understands that Tarzan's gesture conforms to the much less distant concepts of personal space that are in play among Tarzan and his animal companions. The extraordinary concentration of the two actors during this scene conveys a palpable sense of comparative linguistics that makes all the stereotypical dialogue meaningful primarily as a demonstration of the limits of civilized language. Similarly, when Tarzan and Jane later play in the water and Jane tells him how attractive he is, wondering aloud what he would look like in clothes ("pretty good") and imagining the women in London spoiling him, the magnitude of their non-linguistic communication is apparent, despite Tarzan's loving obliviousness to Jane's words and Jane's humorous feeling that she loves saying things to a man who can't understand a word she is saying.

In *Tarzan and His Mate,* the scene in which Jane models some European finery that Harry Holt has imported to the Escarpment in hopes of luring Jane back to England is seminal in its establishment of the Weissmuller/O'Sullivan chemistry. (The underwater swimming scene in which "Jane" appears nude with Tarzan is more notorious but less important in terms of their chemistry, since O'Sullivan did not do her own nude swimming.) The clothes scene takes place as Holt and his partner in the ivory trade, the womanizing Martin Arlington (Paul Cavanagh), set up camp before making their trek to the elephant graveyard. In an extremely prurient scene, Holt and Arlington "tempt" Jane with silk stockings, hats, and perfume, which they encourage her to don over her nearly naked, animal-skin-clad body, like two perspective johns outfitting a whore. Once again, the series places European values, particularly male courting practices, in a worse than dubious light. However, Jane is oblivious to the lurid subtext and to Arlington's lascivious voyeuristic pleasure as he watches her shadowy silhouette in the tent, lighted from within, changing her clothes. O'Sullivan's unself-conscious ease with her virtually nude body, and her equally innocent joy in playing with the glamourous clothes as a child might explore his or her body (not as an arsenal for seduction) is again a physically charged image, radically different in its spontaneous body tone from the forced physical carriage of the manipulative Englishman. Tarzan's arrival seems to suggest that clingy gowns, perfume, and stockings are natural aphrodisiacs, as, in a hilarious scene, Tarzan ignores all propriety and clearly will not be denied sex as he whisks Jane up to their tree nest while Jane tries to engineer a socially correct exit for them before the eyes of the devastated Holt and the amazed Arlington. But the next morning, it is clear that at the very most Tarzan was intrigued by the curiosity of the clothes, which he actually finds funny.

Tarzan wakes up next to Jane, who awakens with a smile on her face, the import of which is quite clear and utterly convincing, though the PCA uttered not a word of protest about a clear violation that sexuality must not be implied even between spouses—and certainly not between the unmarried, as Tarzan and Jane were. Tarzan's utter lack of concern with the skimpy satin evening gown is apparent when he pulls off her dress in one smooth gesture as he propels her into the water, as if he were removing irrelevant plastic from a fruit basket.

The nude swim (for Jane, at least) is not performed by O'Sullivan and so does not depend on their chemistry; further comment on the slippage of their chemistry onto this juxtaposed "special effect" is warranted. That slippage of their chemistry onto all aspects of the films is the crucial issue for watching/reading the MGM Tarzan films. The slippage determines the relationship of ideology to the films. Because of its location and subject matter, the MGM Tarzan series resonates with ideological issues that it rarely overtly acknowledges, plowing through events that vibrate vividly with references to race, gender, class, and power. Divided between Europeans and Africans, the casts of characters are outspokenly racist on these issues, often expressing beliefs that are repugnant by today's standards. Those expressions, however, are constantly juxtaposed with the emergence of the sympathetic raw filmic image of body in the films, by which the disregard of the Western Europeans when they brutalize the African

Tarzan (Johnny Weissmuller) baffled, not charmed, by Jane's (Maureen O'Sullivan) garments, importing into their paradise an alien, civilized concept of femininity.

bearers they coerce into serving them is tacitly contextualized. Slowly the series developed some overt contradiction of the racist, sexist, and generally exploitative attitudes of the villains. But by the same token, more dialogue attention to values weakened the series, as the dialogue was inevitably shallow and cliched. Toward the end of the series, the more Tarzan and Jane spoke with each other and the more articulate they became about their values and the values of Western culture, the more they were constricted by the limitations of the culture that produced the films. Thus Jane tells Tarzan in the last of the Weissmuller/O'Sullivan films that she is in every way his inferior in strength and goodness, while he assures her that she doesn't need to be strong since she is beautiful and that she is good. This superfluous, wrongheaded dialogue clashes with previous films, in which Jane was not only courageous and strong but clearly self-sacrificing, as both she and Tarzan knew. Similarly, before they take off for New York, Jane makes overt her hard-won understanding of the deficiencies of her culture: "We're going into places where men's minds are more tangled than the worst underbrush in the jungle. . . . Everywhere we'll be met with lies and deceit. Your honesty and directness will only be handicaps. It'll break my heart to see your strength and courage caught up in the quicksands of civilization." Of course, this is the film in which Tarzan proves that even on its own turf, civilization is no deadlier than mud for him, but the point here is that although Jane's is an accurate summation of the lessons of the previous five films, it diminishes the tone of the last film by moving too far into the realm of the word and away from the realm of the image and chemistry. As long as the powerful contradictions remain tacit, filmic, the couple is strongly represented as a convincing and meaningful alternative to the civilized villains who were never as powerful in the authority of their filmic existence as Tarzan and Jane. The power of Tarzan and Jane radiated fully as long as they were primarily filmic in nature and as long as the civilized villains and their attitudes were construed as invaders of the sacred space of the Escarpment, a location that does not appear in Tarzan films outside of the MGM series.

SACRED SPACE

In the Tarzan films outside of the Weissmuller/O'Sullivan series, there is nothing like the Escarpment—other Tarzans roam an undefined jungle space. Within the Weissmuller/O'Sullivan series, however, the purity and mystery of the Escarpment is given a great deal of screen time. What the Europeans call "savage" is redefined by the Escarpment into sacred, pure, and/or authentic. There is a great deal of manipulation involved in the creation of the Escarpment landscape, even in the early films. There are mechanical rhinos and crocodiles, acrobats wearing monkey suits, and matte paintings for special effects.[16] But alongside these technologically induced artificialities are a multitude of documentary nature images and imaginative use of set materials so strange that they provoke some of the energy charge of the documentary image. In a scene from *Tarzan the Ape Man*, a fight between the safari crossing a river on a raft and a colony of water hippos on the Escarpment uses an energizing spectrum of wild nature photography and edited sequences with mechanical animals, bleeding the pristine beauty of the terrain into the carefully sculpted action scenes. A similar intercutting occurs between Tarzan and Jane's backlot scenes and authentic shots of the sky over untouched forest growth. Tarzan's nest, an animal lair, is so strangely constructed that it too becomes a part of the purity of the sacred territory.

The lack of sacred space in the multitude of Tarzan films outside of the O'Sullivan/Weissmuller series corresponds to the diminution or disappearance of Jane's role. In most of these films Jane doesn't exist; where she does exist, she is subordinate to Tarzan, who singlehandedly (if under her anxiously admiring gaze) effects a conventional, one-dimensional, and finalizing heroic solution. In the MGM series, Tarzan is a very different and unconventional kind of hero. Despite the persistent labeling of the group of films as the "Tarzan series," as if it were a homogeneous, monolithic entity, the MGM movies construct unusually parallel positions for Tarzan and Jane, which arguably functioned as an embryonic foundation within the mass-culture industry for today's concerns about gender. Much has been achieved in the way of challenging representations of men and women since 1932; I do not claim that O'Sullivan and Weissmuller represented the full spectrum of gender issues that are now in the minds of the teams responsible for even the most formulaic of entertainment. Most glaringly missing, and this will be true for all of the couples discussed in this study, is the representation of the confusion and fear involved in the evolution of a sexual identity in the context of confusing and threatening social signals to the growing child. Each partner in each Synergistic Couple arrives in the film with a secure sense of his or her masculinity/femininity. What is helpful for us to recover, however, is those film images that are precursors of modern attitudes toward erotic connection and that helped to generate today's questioning because they are not stampeded into a stereotypical male fantasy—presented as if it were the one and only cultural reality—in which the danger of female energy is braved and disposed of by a male figure who is judged by whether or not he has the capacity to dominate her.

In the synergistic Tarzan series, Jane is a dangerous female, but the danger she poses is to a set of Western values focused on domination and possession that are presented as highly dubious. Tarzan represents an alternative option for Jane, an interesting departure in itself, since it focuses on her desire. He embodies another form of the strength valued in men by Western culture. Unquestionably brave, he is not judged in these films by his capacity to bring Jane under his control, but rather for his commendable difference from the men formed by Western culture who want to bring her under control. This is why Jane is not dangerous to him but remains a potential danger to her British compatriots. O'Sullivan's Jane is perilous, as only a British ingenue can be. Radiant, bell-voiced, and delicate as porcelain, poised and cultivated in her physical carriage, she radiates an inner fire that marks her as both attractive and uncannily effective in getting her way: she is braced by a well-bred, steely self-possession that is the civilized equivalent of savagery. Walking off the boat that has brought her to her father's trading post, to a reunion with him after many years, O'Sullivan's Jane brings a whiff of England that sets her apart not only from the African milieu and culture but also from other Englishwomen in the area. They pull into themselves, holding fast to European convention and identity. O'Sullivan's Jane projects an outgoing vigor opening onto new experience; she holds her cultivation out to be tested and to test. She is primed to initiate audience expectations that she will be put in her place, with style and erotic force, by the hero. But this is not what happens.

Transcripts of the story conferences for the first Tarzan film reveal that the creators were conscious of creating a "different" heroine in Jane. The discussions about Jane's relationship to her father are, however, the most telling of the transcripts. The men are bemused by the idea of a wonderfully adventurous girl who is self-possessed, independent, sexual yet capable, and able to set limits. She is, as they invent her, a stunning departure from all stereotypical female roles in contemporary jungle flicks of the period (and many women depicted routinely by other film genres), which tended to feature maidens born to be saved—Tarzan's European love interest in the films made by MGM's competitors at the time—and wild, exotic women born to be tamed—Nina in *Trader Horn,* Tondalayo in *White Cargo.* Most of the characterizing details for Jane discussed in the story conference transcripts show up in the finished film: her refusal of a cup of tea when she arrives in Africa in favor of an alcoholic drink called a Sundowner (October 24, 1931, pp. 2–3); her unashamed removal of her travel clothes in front of her father, much to his embarrassment (Bernard Hyman says of this scene in the script, "I liked the embarrassment of the old man. . . . he feels a little self-conscious. It's sophisticated and it gives her a nice character" [October 23, 1931]). The conference notes also indicate that Hyman wanted a girl for Jane who was "very sophisticated. We don't want her doing anything ingenuish. I think if you don't, you'll get a swell contrast later when the spirit of Tarzan gets her" (October 23, 1931, pp. 2–3). Novello's contribution here was that such a role called for a genuine Englishwoman: "There's nothing so silly as an American girl saying conventional English things. It makes her sound affected, where an English girl is perfectly natural saying them . . ." This was apparently in response to a test by an unidentified American actress (perhaps the now forgotten Leila Hyams) whom Hyman thought suitable, except for her diction, which he assumed could be improved by tutoring. Leila Hyams has claimed that she turned down the role before it was offered to O'Sullivan, so perhaps Novello won his point by default. Van Dyke seems to have been initially less on target with his take on Jane, thinking in terms of portraying her as a kind of child-woman and imagining her jumping on her father's back and saying giddy-up. Happily this was discouraged by Hyman, who didn't think "that's the kind of humor you want" (October 23, 1931, pp. 2–3).

Of major interest is how liberating the team's departure from the Burroughs series is. Since Burroughs would not give permission for MGM to use anything but the names of his characters, freedom had been written into their contractual obligations. From a literary perspective, this is a bizarre situation. As it turned out, however, the logic of literary integrity would have meant the death of a liberated perspective for the series. For the odd contract guaranteed that even the books that were the source of inspiration for the film would not control the creation process that generated it. As one more element of the composing process, the novels complement the team synergy; as the blueprint for the film, they would have stymied the sympathetic energy of the team. The result is rich and strange, a transformation of the value structure of the Burroughs novels along with the transformation of the narrative structure. Whereas the film bears within itself a multitude of unorthodox gender roles and definitions, as well as a strangely deviant view of race relations, Burroughs's novel of twenty-eight chapters is straightforwardly and thoroughly sexist and racist. Jane does not appear until chapter 13, and then only as an apparition before Tarzan's dazzled eyes (a white woman at last!). They do not meet until chapter 19, and then they enjoy only a brief idyll before Tarzan, the real Lord Greystoke, sacrifices his love for Jane to what he conceives of as her need for the civilization that he cannot give her. Tarzan refuses to reveal his paternity as the son of Lord and Lady Greystoke, who perished in the jungle, and forfeits Jane to his cousin, along with his rightful inheritance. Movies based on novels are typically thought to be dumbed down; here we have the opposite. At least in the beginning, the films in the Tarzan series—the product of a creative, collaborative media process—grew far beyond the conservative Burroughs novels, which articulate the notion that a sojourn in the jungle is stimulating, but that the rightful place of the couple, and certainly of women, is European civilization, under the control and protection of white men.

Inviting vague audience apprehensions that she needs discipline, minutes after her reunion with her father, Jane sheds her travel clothes in front of her father, without shedding that steely English core, daring her father to be embarrassed by her freedom. Yet the combination in O'Sullivan's Jane of entitlement—bequeathed by a strong social identity—and a questing spirit drives audience desires in a new direction even before she meets Tarzan. Never particularly known as a charismatic actress outside of the series, she was scripted in all other films in which she worked to stereotypically represent respectability because of the conventions surrounding the cliche of the Englishwoman. Here, however, O'Sullivan shines with a luster that no other "Jane" could touch—certainly not the pedestrian Brenda Joyce, who succeeded her after she left the series. O'Sullivan's screen chemistry emerged in tension with the script and with Weissmuller's particular charisma, charging every frame with a sense of longing and dissatisfaction with European civilization that brought conviction and authenticity to Jane's scripted arrival in Africa.

Jane's initial longing is for a whole family, or as much of it as is possible for her, her long-absent father. But the film illustrates that the wholeness of family is impossible within the terms of European culture. James Parker is a man who, despite his great love for his daughter, ultimately will prove a dysfunctional parent when he gives up his life, and thus his time with her, in a futile and greedy quest for fortune as an ivory trader. Jane has been separated from her father since girlhood because he has established his business in Africa as a trader. Their first meeting is an explosion of tears and physical affection with which he can hardly cope. A blustering profiteer, he clearly falls short of Jane's expectations, though she never seems to notice that he is a disappointment to her hope and desire to be "a savage, like you"—a characterization that hardly describes this transported Englishman. Nor does O'Sullivan's energy find its match in the offer to her, almost as soon as her boat docks, of what generally passes for romance; handsome Harry Holt, her father's assistant, immediately loses his heart to her, but she listens to professions of affection from this stiff-upper-lip man with something more like charity and wistful bemusement than passion. O'Sullivan's infusion of the energy of a fiery adventuress into Jane is engagingly mysterious, whereas the other actors around her are prosaic. Clearly a decent woman by virtue of her upbringing, Jane pulsates with longings that are entirely innocent. In a departure from Hollywood screen practice, Jane's power is not one that leads her to connive or even to jeopardize men inadvertently. The script tells a story of Jane's innocent, even pure quest for something she cannot identify; O'Sullivan's charisma makes that untainted push beyond ordinary limits a screen fact. European men embody ideals too fragmented to satisfy Jane's longing for wholeness.

Hollywood women with more than their share of glamour, charisma, and radiance typically either buckle under to the authority of culture or die in the typical Hollywood production. Jane quietly breaks all those rules. She will neither die nor be domesticated to the conventional female role, nor will she break a man or be broken by him. She will, rather, find a kind of female freedom almost unheard of in mass media films of the time, and certainly atypical of all other jungle epics. Jane finds her freedom when Tarzan appears, not as the man to tame her but as her masculine equivalent, like her a European who poses a danger to European constraints, limits, and the fragmentation of an economics of selfishness.

The mutual deviance of the synergistic Tarzan and Jane finds its validation in nature as a mode of cooperation and connection that authorizes their existence as connection while the other European relationships, even those that supposedly involve love, are defined in terms of separation, isolation, objectification, and alienation. This counterpoint between separation and connection illuminates all aspects of the series. For Tarzan, once he has seen her, separation from Jane is a kind of death, his Kryptonite, the only thing that can really defeat him. This dramatically distinguishes him from all the other men in the series, from Weissmuller's diminished definition of Tarzan once O'Sullivan left the series, and from all other Tarzans. James Parker, her adoring father, voluntarily accepted separation from Jane to pursue his career, and the other European men who desire Jane covet her as a prized possession, luring her with promises of wealth and glamour; they also try to take her by force and lie to her "for her own good." Weissmuller's synergistic Tarzan neither wants to nor is really able to do any of these things.

Tarzan's first impulse is to take Jane by force, yet he rejects this impulse in a violent shock of recognition. Arguably this is the moment at which the series, as a synergistic entity, comes into being, since his restraint differentiates him from the conventional European men in the series (and other Tarzans), for whom romance is violence and conquest. Jane's ability to inspire passion and tenderness in many men is abundantly demonstrated in the first two films of the series, but what the European men have to offer is always characterized as overly aggressive in contrast with the lingering resonance of Jane's initial contact with Tarzan in his nest. The responses of the European men to Jane characteristically begin to approach the generosity and warmth of Tarzan's as they are about to die. In *Mate*, Martin Arlington, though he appears to the Western men in the film as a perfectly respectable person, is defined for the audience as a grasping, unscrupulous man inordinately motivated by a lust for possession. He grabs Jane against her will to kiss her, and apologizes only as a strategic ploy in a continual pursuit of her. Soon after that, he shoots Tarzan when no one is there to see and then, believing that he has killed Tarzan, lies about proof of Tarzan's death in order to encourage Jane to leave Africa with him. Only at the point of his death does Arlington realize that he has valued all the wrong things and that he would give his life for her. In the earlier film, Harry Holt, a less devious man than Arlington, more openly "manages" Jane when he agrees to restrain his desire to kill the "Ape Man" if Jane will call Tarzan to account for himself about the death of one of the people on the ivory trader safari. Jane calls Tarzan, who despite the brevity of their first encounter immediately comes to her, and Harry shoots repeatedly, despite Jane's screaming protests, until Tarzan is wounded. By the time of the second movie, Harry has learned not to behave that way, but he continues to lower himself in Jane's estimation by trying to bribe her, with fashionable clothes, to return to England with him. He dies in this film because he has allied himself with the double-dealing Arlington. Exposure to Jane culminates in a noble death, however, as he sacrifices himself in a vain attempt to save the lead "boy" on the safari from an attacking tribe.

Tarzan offers a way for Jane's life to be based on respectful connection rather than exploitation. But the series does not merely repeat this rather unusual couple pattern. Both Tarzan and Jane evolve as mates. Tarzan's repeated confrontations with the values of civilization are significant only when they involve Jane's atavistic return to patterns that guarantee separation between the two, her failure to understand the incompatibility of the motives of people of "her kind" with her chosen life with Tarzan. In the first film, she begins to understand when she sees that Harry's casual killing of an ape who he mistakenly thinks is a danger to Jane is to Tarzan what the death of a friend is to any human. But it is only by the fifth of the films, *Tarzan's Secret Treasure*, that Jane separates in a significant way from "her people" and begins to protect Tarzan and the now present Boy (Johnny Sheffield), the son that she and Tarzan are raising, lying to the new European invaders about the gold that exists in abundance on the Escarpment. Dramatically this becomes possible because the growing Boy is now the vulnerable point through which the villains can cause trouble; he is fascinated by the technology, revealed to him in dribs and drabs, of the culture that Jane has left. The advent of Boy thus leaves the way open for Jane's decisive evolution away from European values, which reaches its apex in the last film O'Sullivan made with Weissmuller. In *Tarzan's New York Adventure*, the kidnapping of Boy requires Tarzan to go to New York City with her, as she eloquently pays direct tribute to all that she has learned about him since the first film.

Tarzan also evolves through the synergistic series. He is tested repeatedly as to whether his value system is really equal to that of the powerful civilization from which he has won Jane. Tarzan represents a vision of possessions, and particularly land, that is in direct contrast with capitalist assumptions that land that is not being used to bring in money is land that is empty and waiting to be occupied. Tarzan's commitment to the land is to its organic integrity; it is represented as being full to bursting with both plant and animal and indigenous African cultures, which only the Europeans think of as so many obstacles to be overcome and erased.[17] Tarzan mobilizes audience perspective in understanding the Europeans and their guns and cages as an intrusion, and there is never any resolution in the synergistic series that doesn't erase the invasive Europeans in favor of the organic systems represented by plants and animals, and even to some extent by the African cultures. The African cultures represented when their territory has not been invaded are familial, shown in acts of nurturing. This is also true of the dangerous animals, who conjoin with the Africans to provide violent scenes in which Tarzan can prove his valor. There is a running motif throughout the series in which several adorable lion cubs attract the attention of a European, who foolishly wishes to play with them as if they were domestic cats. The protective behavior of the lion mother is presented as an appropriate part of her culture. Even more strikingly, just before a swarm of hippopotamuses attack the ivory traders who are rafting toward the Escarpment in search of the elephant burial ground, there is quite a lot of emphasis on the affectionate grouping of a mother hippo and her baby.

The cartoonlike villains in the non-synergistic Tarzan films are generally bad *individuals,* deviants from good European society who alienate the audience by exhibiting disrespect for a particular sentimentalized, natural region. In the synergistic Tarzan series, the invading Europeans are portrayed as symptomatic of the way Western civilization does not recognize that it is trampling on a multitude of other civilizations as viable and fully articulated as, and more animated by life force than, its own. The foundational Tarzan film establishes the assumptions about culture that inform the entire series. European civilization—represented in almost all cases by the British and only sporadically by the French, Germans, and Americans—is rotted by greed. Lust for wealth and economic gain manifests itself in what Tarzan identifies, once his language skills are more developed, as the "white man's" betrayal of all organic life: family, nature, fellow human being, and self. Tarzan is, from the beginning, unalterably opposed to this European mode of behavior; Jane evolves toward his perspective and away from that of the culture of her birth, and ultimately expresses this, in the last two films of the series, with the verbal eloquence of which Tarzan, who profoundly and almost literally em*bodies* alternative values, is never capable.

In contrast to the many other action movies and cartoons that have been made based on either the characters or the situations in the Edgar Rice Burroughs novels about Tarzan, the MGM Tarzan series with Johnny Weissmuller and Maureen O'Sullivan represents a highly articulated world full of competing cultures, those of animals, Europeans, and indigenous African peoples within an attentively drawn ecosystem. Unlike the non-synergistic plot-driven Tarzan features, in the MGM series questions about whether the villains will get the ivory from the elephant graveyard or take Boy away from Tarzan and Jane are subordinated to a panoply of questions about what it means to be human. From *Tarzan, the Ape Man* (1932), the film of origin, to *Tarzan's New York Adventure* (1942), the films probe whether living as a human being is primarily a matter of the ability to manipulate cultural technologies, whether European or indigenous African, in the largest sense—clothing, language, power hierarchies, as well as guns, airplanes, cameras, and the media—as most of the people for whom the films were intended as entertainment ultimately believed/ believe. As part of this thematic substructure, the films either brush or emphatically consider questions of comparative cultural technologies—animal and human languages; animal and human hierarchies; animal and human grooming and bonding. Much of the role of Johnny Weissmuller's Tarzan as the imaginable vision of what a European male might be in a framework alternative to the Eurocentric value system highlights issues of separation/connection, touch/distance, the direct/the mediated in terms of how people interact politically, linguistically, and emotionally/sensually. Jane's importance to Tarzan, and his to her, is that they and they alone have the potential to test the utopian desires for satisfaction and completion that go begging in European-based civilization.

Because of Tarzan's alternative relationship to touch, distance, and directness, he also offers another lens on cross-racial transactions distinct from that offered by the Europeans in the series. Although Tarzan's engagement is not completely sympathetic by today's standards, it does undermine the racism of Jane's relatives and friends. For Tarzan, the African cultures occupy the same place that the Europeans and hostile animal cultures occupy, as competing groups. This leveling of the European hierarchy, which places men above animals and white men above other races, is symptomatic of a pronounced slippage between human and animal in the synergistic Tarzan series, which resonates with the importance of the raw image of the body in the series. In the synergistic Tarzan films, there is never the pure sense of lions, rhinos, and crocodiles from the human perspective, dressing the set for verisimilitude and as plot obstacles that create the excitement of adventure. There are certainly many "exciting" action scenes in which Tarzan fights animals, but there is always, at the same time, the sense of the animals from their own perspective, as belonging to a large interconnected group that has group intelligence, and organized modes of behavior that become dangerous only when their territory is invaded. The Europeans behave as if they are entitled to slaughter, which is one of the reasons Tarzan, who hates guns, often loathes the people of his root culture. Tarzan fights situationally, justified in his behavior by the need to defend and protect. His attitude toward the black Africans is somewhat different. He does not hate Africans; they are a fact of life as a competing culture. He certainly is willing to kill them in great numbers to save Jane, but he usually blames the European's propensity for upsetting the balance of nature and of the order of the African cultures for this necessity. Ordinarily, he does not involve himself in the business of the African tribes, and there is no need for him to kill. When in *Tarzan's Secret Treasure* Boy brings home Tumbo (Cordell Hickman), an orphaned child of one of the neighboring black African tribes, Tarzan and Jane include him as they would any child. Racist comments and actions by the Europeans (and Jane, too, in the earlier episodes) are quite common, but there is some tension created between their attitudes and Tarzan's.[18]

This is not to claim that racist social assumptions were not in the minds of the creative team that made the series. Discussing the climactic scene in which Tarzan and his friends are almost killed by an enormous gorilla held in captivity by a tribe of Pygmies, Van Dyke and Hume want more violence and display a clear racism in their narrative strategies for getting it. Hume, a particularly bloodthirsty writer, appears to want to see one of the extras pulled apart by a gorilla, the actual knifing of a lion that fights with Tarzan, and the murder of "all the black ones" (extras) by the gorilla. Hyman responds negatively to Hume on the first two points. Van Dyke prefers to show one representative death of a black extra. Van Dyke pushes for, and the finished film suggests that he got, more extreme visuals for this scene. "If the execution is at night, we can get away with a lot of stuff we couldn't otherwise, because we can make it shadowy and vague. We wouldn't have to do it at night. We can shoot it in the daytime for night" (October 21, 1931, p. 5). At one point, Hyman expresses some concern about the level of audience understanding, which Van Dyke thinks isn't an issue:

Hyman: We ought to cash in on the futility of their position.
Van Dyke: But that's evident.
Hyman: But we should cash in on it.

The racism here is casual; no thought is given to it, and the conversation quickly drifts to other narrative issues. Only the Production Code Administration made an issue of it, mandating a radical reduction of images of violence perpetrated on black bodies for the final cut.

Certainly, also, racist social assumptions that already existed in the audience were not strengthened by the synergistic Tarzan films when they were first shown—and even today in audiences predisposed to racist beliefs. On the one hand, once the black tribes in the films are aroused, they behave in terrifying ways that tap into deep-seated fears about dismemberment and the volcanic violence of the body that are typically associated with racist-inspired xenophobia. On the other hand, the tribes are represented as organized cultures, particularly as they fit into the larger poetic vision of Tarzan's world. Absolutely abstaining from the presentation of complex political answers to the questions they raise about what it is to be human, the films take Tarzan's apolitical position. From his perspective, all cultures, African or European, are dismal failures, the Europeans more so because of their guns, and because it is they who cause the trouble by disturbing both the natural order and the boundaries established by the tribes, which Tarzan considers valid. By the time of *Tarzan's Secret Treasure*, Jane concurs and voices this belief to the European invaders. In fact, Tarzan's distrust of white people as Other to him, given the fact that by any biological account of race he should identify with them, turns this category into a constructed form of behavior rather than a natural fact.

Tarzan's understanding of the animal and human cultures around him, however, does not mitigate the problem of the human condition. His solution is not politically credible. It works for him as a totally unique being; thus the synergistic Tarzan and Jane work as a poetic vision of connection. This is good news poetically, but no news of significance if one wishes to approach the films from a sociological vantage point. Tarzan and Jane cannot serve as direct role models. The purity of their connection is organically linked to their dismissal of culture as irrelevant to their lives, a solution that has never worked, and indeed ultimately does not work for them. In their final film together, the synergistic poetry shatters on the confrontation between Tarzan and the capitalist on his own turf. In this film there is an abundance of deconstruction of social behavior by Cheetah, the chimpanzee companion of the family. She cavorts in civilized feminine apparel, climaxing her display by reclining on a bed in a negligee in a way that utterly discredits the erotic construction of clothing. She plays with getting water from a cooler, befuddled at first by being able to see the water, but not to lick it, but then imitating a human user of the machine in a devastating satire of our estrangements from our senses. But Cheetah can only suggest civilized illusions. She cannot change European power relations with Tarzan. The Escarpment can overwhelm the European invaders, but Tarzan is not credible when summoning his elephants to save his son from the exploitative entrepreneur of the circus on Long Island to which Boy has been abducted. It is, of course, gratifying to audience desire to see Tarzan successfully mobilize the chained circus elephants, who know his language and respond by breaking their chains and blocking at every turn the car in which Boy is being transported against his will. But elephants cannot break the chains their trainers have learned to bind them with. And villains who are willing to kill and kidnap do not care about elephants who get in the way. Even though the happy family is last seen swimming on the Escarpment—the familiar act of affirmation in this series—this was Tarzan's last stand in a significant way. The subsequent Weissmuller Tarzan films were negligible, even as light entertainment, devoid of conviction and poetry, devoid of O'Sullivan's Jane, and not coincidentally, devoid of the presence of a jungle replete with myriad viable communities. The post–O'Sullivan/ Weissmuller Tarzan fought with science fiction communities of bizarre high priests and sadomasochistic exotic ritual sacrifices. The Tarzans after Weissmuller—with the exception of Christopher Lambert in *Greystoke: The Legend of Tarzan, Lord of the Apes* (1984)—were even less interesting. They degenerated into almost naked, inarticulate muscle men, caricatures of men somehow placed in a jungle, now become empty space because they are devoid of constructed artifacts. Having no Jane to negotiate with and no family, they had perfunctory, cliched adventures dealing with problems that tended to involve protecting Europeans and European values from a fearsome nature.

In other words, after the Weissmuller/O'Sullivan partnership dissolved, Tarzan became a nearly naked Lone Ranger.

POETICS

The later degeneration of the series notwithstanding, however, the poetry of the synergistic Tarzan films endures and deserves a great deal more critical attention and appreciation than it has received. In keeping with the centrality of the opposition between connection and fragmentation in the series, one way in which it is profitably understood is as a poetry of touch centering on the Synergistic Couple. While Jane comes from a culture structured by appropriate distances, Tarzan's is the regime of touch. Ordinarily, the Europeans in the Tarzan films do not touch their environment. Touch is reserved for erotic encounters, and thus, for Jane's European cohort, touch is wholly sexualized. Ordinary contact with the world tends to be made through their African servants, or "boys," as bearers are called, a racist appellation that strikes a nerve today but that faithfully preserves the racist language of the time. In the first film, African servants carry Jane's trunks into her father's living quarters, and they subsequently bear all the safari materials. The closer to touching the world one is in the view of Europeans in these films, the lower one is in the hierarchy. Lower-class Europeans may do menial work, which marks them as lower on the scale of humanity. It is the Europeans who use the guns the "boys" bear, and the act of shooting is an act of violence at a distance, devoid of physical touch. One of the strangest elements of this motif in the series is captured in a line spoken by Jane when she first arrives in Africa. Asked by Harry Holt if she can shoot, she replies, "Like an angel." This slippage between the European idea of transcendence and the propensity of the Europeans to destroy at a distance seems to establish her as a kind of sacred warrior virgin, but since it is a position from which Jane evolves, it cannot be said to represent the point of view of the series. In fact, although the films seem to rather neutrally record the European priority on distance, even before Tarzan appears to intrude the body most emphatically into the European scheme of things, there is, in all the synergistic films, a sly mockery of European denial of the body through the comic slippage of touch into sexual innuendo, and Cheetah's imitation of European negations of the flesh:

clothes, makeup, consumption of alcohol, drinking, smoking. One particularly interesting joke about the problem of the European and touch occurs in *Mate*, with the arrival of Martin Arlington. Harry Holt orders Beamish (Forrester Harvey), his white Cockney subordinate, to draw a bath for Arlington, whom he is sure will need one, having traveled the long way from England to Africa. After Arlington gets into the tub, a prospect that made the PCA very nervous, Beamish's attempt to hand him the soap results in his falling repeatedly into the tub with the "naked" Arlington, to which the PCA amazingly made no objection, but which certainly humorously, even carnivalesquely, commented on European sexual mores and Western issues about physical contact, here portrayed as too much closeness.

That the Africans do not participate in Western-style denial certainly does not neutralize the problem of racism in the film, but it does place the Africans rather in a less ridiculous position as regards the central issue of touch. However, the dangers of both the European cultures and the African cultures are defined with respect to touch—the one too distant from touch, the other surfeited by too much touch, in contrast with the balance that Tarzan and Jane develop with respect to the nuances and subtleties of touch, which is always in danger of repression by the Europeans and devouring excess from the African cultures and the cultures of dangerous animals. Such balance as Tarzan and Jane reach ultimately becomes tied to the Escarpment as a mysterious and magical place not visible on any map but reachable from places that are recorded officially. Accident is the preferred mode of coming upon the Escarpment, for all intent is tinged with the corruption of civilized greed or the corruption of African belief in the sacred nature of the place. Much like Shangri-La in Frank Capra's *Lost Horizon* (1937), the Escarpment is depicted not as a temporary escape from civilization, like a spa or a movie, but as an alternative system in which a permanently structured way of life offers the possibility of a balance between the delirium of flesh and its spirituality in a way that demotes verbal language from its position of centrality. Another way in which the films position touch and organic immediacy is that all six films use a sound design of natural sounds—water, animals, air, fire, foliage, drums, and chanting of indigenous cultures—unimpeded by any nondiegetic European music, which only appears diegetically as the transmission of a radio or a phonograph.

Tarzan first appears in the series as a savage in the eyes of the Europeans and as a magical, quasi-sacred figure to the Africans.

Certainly the European point of view is the one immediately available to the audience, since we first hear him as a mysterious cry, without intelligible English meaning, and when we first see him, he is swinging through the trees with the apes, very much as one of them, not as a higher form. Coming to rest, he peers down at Jane and her cohorts in a position that is not quite upright, both bestial and yet somehow attractive. We are seeing with Jane's unevolved eyes. The prefiguration of how our vision of the "Ape Man" will change is that Tarzan is above the Europeans, looking down on them, flying above them easily while they hack and trudge on the ground. By the end of the series, the sound of the Tarzan cry in times of trouble has achieved a status far more reassuring than the sight of a European man with a gun, and the sight of Tarzan in the trees has become an apparition not of bestiality but of the fusion of freedom and connection in a world made richer for his unabashed engagement with organic life.

The series, thus, has a direction; out of the studio intention to simply reproduce a formulaic success emerged something more. The crux of that evolution is Tarzan's meeting and mating with Jane, and hers with him, for, on their own, each is only potential. Invasion and penetration are explicitly rejected after Tarzan abducts Jane. Instead there is a slow and delicate exploration of the other through her gift of language and his materiality within the physical elements of the environment. Possession is attempted by him and abandoned in the face of her refusal to be thus possessed, giving way to their mutual exploration of how to say what they must and what is on their mind. This process moves into its first moment of illumination in the water, the destination of Tarzan and Jane, and then with Boy and the animals—because of the serendipity of a casting decision to employ an Olympic swimming champion with no acting training. This utterly commercial decision, to capitalize on Weissmuller's fame and magnificent physique, nevertheless enabled the creative team to dramatize the conjunction of Tarzan and Jane using the element of water, beginning with their initial playful scene in which all that separates them is momentarily dissolved in the materiality of this physical element that is revealed by them in all its magical potential for both individuation and connection, a magic repeated over and over with increasingly varied and resonant implications.[19]

Because of Jane's passionate partnership with Tarzan, she becomes a kind of crucible within which civilization alters. Her allegiances to a gamut of cultural values like progress, law, conquest, economic profit, and hierarchy are challenged and tempered with each successive film by the cyclical, sensual, interconnected values inherent in nature and materiality. With each successive sequel, the picture of Jane's function is more clearly articulated, as we watch her move toward her final position in the series, where she fully commits to a paradoxical position. She aspires to bring the inheritance of abstract language and other technologies of our culture to the defense of immanence.

Jane's turning point comes in the fourth of the six-film series, *Tarzan Finds a Son!* In the first three films Jane maintains a rather distant position from Tarzan's values, letting herself be drawn into the materiality of his existence erotically, emotionally, and through their water rituals of connectedness. But she eventually finds herself intellectually seduced by arguments about progress as a fundamentally enabling cultivated asset or by appeals to family loyalty and cultural identification. She thus becomes the point of entry into Tarzan's abundantly organic world for get-rich-quick schemes that will involve the pillaging of natural resources (*Tarzan the Ape Man* and *Tarzan and His Mate*) or the abduction of Tarzan by entrepreneurs who want to exploit him in a circus as a spectacle for voyeurism (*Tarzan Escapes*). In the fourth film, Boy becomes a mutual point of vulnerability of both Tarzan and Jane. Rescued by the couple from a plane crash, Boy is sought by the rich and prominently social Greystoke family five years after. Some of the Greystokes want to take Boy from Tarzan and Jane to become his guardians and so control his wealth; one more honorable Greystoke simply wants Boy to take his "rightful" place in the family and in England. Interestingly, both of these projects involving privilege and power are equally rejected by the film in favor of a much more valuable inheritance and rightful place, the world of mutuality and balance created by Tarzan and Jane. The mechanism is the transformation of Jane, a profoundly altering process, after which she is never again tempted by conventional values. It is noteworthy that at no point in this film does Jane wish to return to England, though she is at first swayed by guilt for keeping Boy from all the wonders of civilization. After betraying Tarzan in a scene unique in the series in which she exploits her sexuality to hide her plans from him, she quickly realizes she has put Boy into the hands of villains. When the safari is captured by the obligatory African tribe attack, Jane is given her chance to redeem herself by embodying, for the first time, the values of immanence and the intelligence of materiality on her own initiative—instead of observing it, tourist-like, in Tarzan.

Noting that there is a break in the village stockade fence when a monkey comes through a loose set of bamboo stalks, she instructs Boy to run at her cue, to go find Tarzan as fast as he can, and to make sure that he does not look back, no matter what he hears. Boy obeys her, and as she has expected, her body forms a human shield for her escaping son. She takes the spear in her back as Boy escapes. In placing her body in this way, Jane irrevocably moves into the regime of touch, here depicted as essentially ethical and intelligent as well as loving and connected, and, most explicitly, placed as a better alternative to the values of conventional culture. There are two fascinating points in this connection that show how unconsciously and accidentally meaning gets constructed in the Hollywood-influenced media. First, this evolution was scheduled to be Jane's last, as she was originally scripted to die of the wounds sustained by her rescue of Boy. Only at the last moment was the script rewritten to save Jane for two more films. Had Jane died, the series would have collapsed into a heap of conventional gender depictions that mandate death for mothers—a metaphor for their lack of importance—and Freudian transfer of the children to the authority of the fathers. The series would also have collapsed into a cliche among other cultural cliches that mandate death for women who transgress patriarchal culture—here, Jane's punishment for leaving Western patriarchy and England for the jungle and Tarzan.[20]

Cliche was prevented by the unpredictable negotiation of competing opinions and desires that is inevitably part of the collaborative process in the mass media. Maureen O'Sullivan did not want to play Jane after *Tarzan and His Mate*, but had hung on through *Tarzan's Escape* and *Tarzan's Revenge*, and agreed to do *Tarzan Finds a Son!*, at the end of which Jane was supposed to die. Three days before the film was scheduled to begin shooting, using a script in which Jane was killed off at the end, a sudden objection changed everything. On January 6, 1939, Edgar Rice Burroughs wrote a letter to Al Lichtman, an MGM vice president, strongly suggesting that they review the ending. "I believe that you will find that it will react badly at the box office, for during twenty-five years' experience with Tarzan fans I have found that Jane is extremely popular and that when I leave her out of the Tarzan books . . . we receive many letters of complaint. No matter how inartistic a happy ending may be, you are going to discover that the Tarzan fans prefer it."[21] There are no available documents showing Lichtman's response, but the ending was changed to keep Jane alive, and somehow

O'Sullivan was pressured into working in two more Tarzan films. However, by this time Cyril Hume, who had been a writer for the first Tarzan film, was desperately trying to be released from any continued association with the series, for an interesting reason. He could not conceive of a future for the series unless Jane and Cheetah were dead. He had already begun writing the next film, in which, as he saw it, Tarzan and Boy burn down the tree house, and a new woman, Sylvia Starke, an "international glamour girl," comes into Tarzan's life and wins the heart of both Tarzan and Boy. Bernard Hyman decisively rejected Hume's approach; Hume left the series; Tarzan, Jane, and Boy continued in *Tarzan's Secret Treasure*.[22]

This interplay of forces kept in motion the Weissmuller/O'Sullivan evolution of the passionate partnership of Tarzan and Jane, and the evolution, thereby, of Tarzan as a spiritualized body, the destiny of his capacity to operate as a physical force imbued with the intelligence of the flesh that responds to its material environment with profound sensitivity and a kind of deep judgment of the autonomic system. Tarzan's allegiance to Jane creates in him a fuller incarnation of ethics through language and civil modes of interaction, moving him from an initial limitation within the regime of touch to a wider sense of strategy and respect for the separate otherness of first Jane and then other beings, all this without losing his organic sense of the wholeness of living creation. It is in forgiving Jane at the end of their fourth film that Tarzan, as the materiality of connection, irretrievably admits separation and thus abstraction into his world as a necessary tension. Always a foe of guns (an interesting departure from Hollywood's usual image of phallic power and authority) and exploitation of the land, and always a critic of progress who cannot see why time has to be "saved" instead of entered into, Tarzan, at the moment in which he forgives Jane's quite horrible betrayal, moves irrevocably out of the shadow of the simple cliche of the noble savage (a previously ever-lurking trap for the character) into a complex hero who knows his enemy.[23]

Jane's seduction and betrayal of Tarzan in this film involves the European style of exploitation of their sexual connection, which grates on the audience not only because of its ethical connotations but also because of its betrayal on a nonverbal level of the chemistry of the raw image. It is a filmic moment of evil, in which Jane takes on an almost nightmarish image that fuels the pain of the narrative, when by this betrayal Jane imposes on Tarzan separation, the one situation that is anathema to his life. Preparing to hand Boy over to the Greystoke family, Jane tricks Tarzan into a deep gorge and removes the vine by means of which he can climb out, thus isolating him and leaving him isolated for an indeterminate period of time. Thus Jane has perpetuated on Tarzan all the most heinous evils of European society associated with the villains of the series. Her mistake is drastic and one that Tarzan is not prepared to forgive despite his continued love for her. It is only when he sees the blood on her back from the spear wound that he reconnects with her. Because the conclusion of the film was the product of a hasty, last-minute rewrite, the scene is not played out as fully or as satisfyingly as it should have been. But the continuity of the series is clear. Tarzan has recognized Jane's reentry into the regime of touch, this time not borne by pleasure but with the awareness that it may cost her her life; that recognition enables him to accept the fragmentation, discontinuity, and breaks in the wholeness of his culture that her presence in his life entails. As a result, in the last two films, Weissmuller's Tarzan plays out the continuity of this event with an increased authority on behalf of his way of life that involves, among other things, a new visualization of the inception of the narrative from his point of view; in the last two films the Europeans are seen moving into the Escarpment, where previously, as audience, we came upon Tarzan from the perspective of the invading safaris. That Tarzan gains a vocal point of view, instead of inhering as a pure immanence that makes him always the spectacle, opens up further the complex fascination of the European as other rather than as locus of natural authority and reality.

The Synergistic Couple of Tarzan and Jane thus endures and continues to fascinate and appeal because of its unorthodox use of mass culture to depict and to some degree even to explore complexly gendered relationships. This couple does not go as far as subversion; ultimately Tarzan and Jane become a sanctuary outside of history, reassuring us that we are not locked into what is shown as the impossibility of culture and therefore downplaying the seriousness of the impasses it portrays and alleviating the need to make profound cultural changes. Nevertheless, if the consolations offered by the Synergistic Couple of Tarzan and Jane leave these films teetering on the edge of escapism, it is important that we distinguish this pleasure as an enigmatic kind of escapism that in part irritates and challenges by following the emotional and visceral logic of its material the way "high" art does, while at the same time existing as a studio product, at points blocked by cliche, stalled into fighting its own energies.

Three telling examples of how complicated the tension between the logic of the material and the logic of the system can be are the depictions in the series of the roles of the following three elements in the depiction of Tarzan and Jane as a couple: the African tribes, procreation, and law.

In five of the six series films set in Africa, all people designated as African are black; the whites are Europeans passing through. Fulfilling the stereotypes of the thirties and forties, the Africans fall into two categories: subservient and savage. Now it is also true that the Europeans fall into unflattering stereotypical categories: the violators, the buffoons, and the fatally mistaken. But the Europeans are given identities, whereas the Africans, with minimal exceptions, are a mass of undistinguishable bodies either being whipped or sadistically calling for blood. Europeans may be lacking, but they are distinctly identified with the audience for which the films were made; the Africans in their masses are distinctly Other, a jumble of sounds and gestures that leaves the audience across a familiar divide from what are clearly people but not like "us." This is the logic of the studio. Its worst manifestations are in the sadistic portrayals of the deaths of the safari "boys" that occur in every one of the African-located films. Its most enlightened manifestations are in the first two films, which highlight the domestic arrangements of the Africans in real footage taken in Africa, of the *National Geographic* type, which is the closest the studio logic of the time ever comes to multiculturalism.

However, the tribes also function as part of the logic of the material in these films, which defines Tarzan and Jane in terms of touch. The central couple in this series represents the epitome of spiritualized flesh, the perfection of touch, the capacity to know an Other as well as the environment, to connect with living organisms, and to act within the limits prescribed by respect for other creatures and living ecosystems. All around them are cultural groups for which touch has become destabilized toward one extreme or another. In this sense, the African tribes function as the extreme of too much touch as counterweight to the extreme of too little touch represented by European civilization. The Europeans represent spirit divided from flesh such that it becomes capable of cannibalizing its own through sins of distance—murder by gun, theft of social inheritance and position, lies and duplicitous negotiations. The tribes represent the spirit engulfed by flesh such that it becomes capable of cannibalizing its own through sins of closeness—murder by physical torture and the employment of savage beasts; the actual corporeal consumption of human beings (as opposed to the abstract consumption of one's place in society); mercurial, non-negotiable shifts in intent. The logic of the material identifies neither of these extremes as better than the other; Tarzan and Jane represent the ideal resolution of both extremes. Narratively, however, the Europeans always operate as the force most threatening to Tarzan and Jane, while the Africans always operate as the impediment, if a rather frightening one, to the Europeans, a block to European greed or treachery that gives Tarzan and Jane a chance to reestablish themselves in a situation destabilized by white people and their guns. The tribes always attack just when the avaricious Europeans are about to either kill Tarzan or Jane or separate them (which amounts to the same thing in the stories). Narratively, this dynamic suggests the extreme of bodily closeness rising up to compensate for the abstracted separation from the body of the Europeans. The appearance of the tribes always means enough impediment to the European greed to give Tarzan a chance to reestablish the ideal balance of body and spirit between himself and Jane and between them and the world ecosystems. Arguably, there is here a grudging tribute to the physical world in the face of economic and cultural exploitation, as well as a grudging tribute to otherness. Ultimately, unimpeded by the prejudices of the studio hierarchy and the Hays office, the tribes would have become an explicit ally of Tarzan's, but this was not possible in Old Hollywood. It is interesting, maybe even essential, to note that even in these days of greater latitude and multiculturalism, this rapprochement has not happened yet. Instead, as racial issues became more explicit in this country, the tribes disappeared altogether from later Tarzans, first from the Weissmuller and O'Sullivan films, then from the films made by Weissmuller without O'Sullivan, and then from the post-Weissmuller movies. Is it a coincidence that the tribes (cultural other) disappeared as Jane (the sexual other) was fading from the picture? The simultaneous decline of the series and the disappearance of the tribes and of Jane suggest that a crucial balance was upset because the previously submerged issues of touch, gender balance, cultural otherness to Western society, and anticapitalist thought were coming too close to the surface. Popular culture was not ready to deal with the weighty, challenging undercurrents in the Tarzan mythologies it had created, as distinct from the reactionary worldview of the Burroughs source texts.

Similar interesting terminal moments occur in the series with respect to procreation and the law. With the fifth film, in which Tarzan and Jane get a child, the PCA insisted that it not be their own and that this be clear. The logic of this demand was that the child would be the proof of their sexual activity, and the film series had been careful not to actually show any of it graphically. Thus Tarzan *finds* rather than conceives a son. Studio compliance with the PCA demand, as was quite common, brought about a far more unconventional situation than would have resulted had the PCA let things alone.[24] In today's language, it depicted parenthood as a constructed rather than a natural behavior. That is, Tarzan and Jane's passionate commitment to the child becomes one of choice rather than instinct. Similarly, Tarzan and Jane's sexuality, which is abundantly communicated without graphic depiction, is separated from procreation, permitting a portrayal of not only the freedom of sex from the generation of children but also sexual pleasure and freedom, particularly for women. In the last film, where this issue becomes an explicit narrative point, when Jane is challenged in court for custody of Boy, it is rather clearly suggested that only a villain would insist on parenthood as a natural rather than a behavioral position. The synergistic series was brought right to the brink of confronting procreation, sexuality, and parenthood, but, as with the issue of the tribes, studio logic foreclosed the potential in the logic of the material, and this too was erased from the later Tarzans.

Finally, there is the issue of the law as the abstract form of European cultural organization. In the sixth film, Tarzan makes the encounter he has been heading for since the first film. He comes up directly against the law of European culture. After Boy has been taken by some circus people to be exploited as a spectacle for American audiences, Tarzan and Jane leave the jungle and, in New York, on Jane's advice, they get into the civilized game of the legal system to extricate Boy from the clutches of the villains. This encounter brings to the surface almost all the questions that have been lurking in the previous five films, all of which can be summarized in one question: What is the role of Jane's civilization in the life of this couple? The answers that emerge from this film make it the most conventional film in the series. Once the questions are verbalized, the logic of the studio dominates the film. Tarzan and Jane are dissatisfied with the law, but they ultimately reconcile with it when, after Tarzan has turned the city upside down to get Boy, he receives a suspended sentence from a noble, white-haired judge who is invited to fish in the waters of the Escarpment. None of the deep-seated paradoxes of Tarzan as an embodied law are dealt with except in the shallowest terms, and certainly his irrevocable opposition to abstract law is barely touched. At the same time, this film could have offered some interesting reflexive possibilities, since Tarzan, Jane, and Boy are being exploited for American audiences. None of that was implied except in the most remote terms, in regard to Cheetah's impersonations of civilized behavior, on whose small and hairy shoulders also fell the impossible task of taking up the slack of the missing tribes to provide the extreme of too much touch to balance the extreme of European distancing. It is also noteworthy that with the tribes being missing in New York, there is an important absence that, when recognized, begins to account for a sense that something is wrong with the rhythms and tone of the picture and that there is an increasing flatness in the depiction of the connection between Tarzan and Jane.

CONCLUSION

While the early films in the series stand as brilliant examples of what the system could produce, in some important ways, the synergistic Tarzan series lost its battle with the kind of cliche that the studio system produced when it asserted itself. The simple change that occurred was a "normalization" of the balance between image and story convention. By the end of the series, image had taken a backseat to narrative action. The directors of the last of the Tarzan films gave less play to the images that could be generated by the O'Sullivan/Weissmuller chemistry and more to the formulas that had grown out of the early films. Whereas most of the action in the early films took place wordlessly between Tarzan and Jane, in the later pictures, they spoke more with each other and Boy, bringing the level of the film down to what was permitted by the PCA and what was routine for the scriptwriters. As their abiding synergy became less of a force in the films, all the other synergies that had resonated with it also faded. While the stories continued to feature Tarzan and Jane's defense of the purity of the Escarpment from invading European safaris, the creative teams violated it with increasingly clever technology for Tarzan and Jane. Their home was no longer the evocative nest built by Tarzan but the jungle home as imagined by the European mind, filled with jungle equivalents of Western technology, like elevators pulled by elephants. The Escarpment became more of a mirror image of the West and less an alternative system. The relationship between Tarzan and Jane and nature became, at the end, more a notion of the script than an embodied fact of filmic image. The later emphasis on trained animals rather than on the spontaneous relationship between the two and animal immediacy anthropomorphized the creatures and eroded the filmic fact of the difference between Tarzan/Jane and the Europeans. Similarly, the swimming scenes, which originally had been represented as wild interludes, became synchronized family routines. Oddly, the decreasing emphasis on the African peoples also was a symptom of the fading energy of the series. The absence of their energetic fury against the European invaders, particularly in the last film, which took place almost entirely in New York, worked toward a homogenization of Tarzan and Jane with European, and therefore Hollywood, norms.

Nevertheless, the early films abide, reminders of an important legacy left by a creative team that understood how to use the synergistic chemistry of Weissmuller and O'Sullivan. The films express sophisticated insights about the difficulty of intimacy, affirm the powerful desire for it that endures despite dehumanizing economic motives and the fearful energy of the animal world, and assert the possibility of crossing cultural boundaries that only seem irrevocable. They also challenge simplistic assumptions about Hollywood, suggesting the impact of slippage between raw images and Hollywood formulas. This slippage ensures that more than one meaning can be taken from each adventure. From one perspective, the poetics of touch in the series devalues larger social issues and places a priority on purely personal satisfactions. From another perspective, the series acknowledges the enduring complexity of human greed, the capitalist system of exploitation, and selfishness in Western culture, a tangle of obstacles to the good life that can only be opposed from the organic perspective that integrates spirit and body. Emphasis on the separation of Tarzan and Jane's special Escarpment from the world favors the first interpretation, while emphasis on the inevitable frustration of the fortune hunter by the Escarpment favors the second. As the Escarpment is both separate and inevitably intruded upon, an even more satisfying perspective would find complex impulses both toward and away from larger social issues marbled with each other as Tarzan and Jane's adventures oxymoronically link nature and culture. In doing so, they set the stage for the exotic setting to become a rich part of the great couple tradition in the American media.

CHAPTER Three

MYRNA LOY AND WILLIAM POWELL
The Thin Man Takes a Couple

The chemistry of the Synergistic Couple, as we have seen, is a force that altered escapist movie formulas in the Tarzan and Jane series, disrupting and feeding the studio system at the same time, paradoxically using cliche as a springboard to authentic expression. Yet there are nuances to the significance of Hollywood's Synergistic Couple that cannot be probed through the collaboration of Johnny Weissmuller and Maureen O'Sullivan as Tarzan and Jane, for example, the relationship between acting proficiency and couple chemistry. Both Weissmuller and O'Sullivan were limited in their skill as actors, which may in their case have been a crucial part of their chemistry; there was little learned device to block their mutually flowing energy. Weissmuller and O'Sullivan, however, are but one paradigm of the Synergistic Couple. The partnership of Loy and Powell, more nuanced, is another paradigm, demonstrating not only that cultivation is no necessary barrier to Couple Chemistry, but that it can produce an intense form of expression by virtue of the interplay between elemental energy and strong culturally learned performance modes. The onscreen partnership of Loy and Powell also emphasizes the importance of the collaborative process at the core of the studio system in bringing the Synergistic Couple to the screen. Only partly dependent on the potential rapport between the acting partners, the Synergistic Couple is also a function of the response of the collaborative team to the possibilities the acting pair presents. Loy and Powell always enjoyed working with each other, but only the Thin

Man series, six of the fourteen films they made together, permitted them significant onscreen release of the synergy between them.

The rich collaboration of Myrna Loy and William Powell includes both a synergistic series of six Thin Man mysteries and eight other films in which the potential in their chemistry for disrupting and vivifying formulas only shines through in starts and gleams. The well-honed performance styles of the two actors meant that they could be used to advantage in formulaic comedies and melodramas as a star Iconic Couple. Powell and Loy were practiced enough to add flash and panache, in the manner of the Iconic Couple, to both recipe comedies, like the story of a Bohemian man who unstarches an uptight female executive in *Double Wedding* (1937, Dir. Richard Thorpe), and recipe melodramas, like *Evelyn Prentice* (1934, Dir. William K. Howard), a story about a high-powered lawyer who opts to defend his wife from a murder charge after he discovers that the victim of the crime might have been her lover. It was only when the creative teams were sensitive and bold enough to let the production sail into unpredictable seas, as in the six Thin Man films starring Loy and Powell as Nick and Nora Charles, that their witty performance styles and inimitable rapport were free to find an organic center and a counterpointed relationship to the mystery/melodrama scripts. Although the Thin Man series is far from constituting a coherent vision formed by an auteur, it remains a vibrant example of the polyglot, collaborative best of Old Hollywood. The Synergistic Couple performance of Myrna Loy and William Powell as Nora and Nick Charles represents a more aware use of couple chemistry than do the films of Johnny Weissmuller and Maureen O'Sullivan as Tarzan and Jane.

Deservedly, the Thin Man series is still widely admired for its charm and offbeat storytelling. In the series, Loy and Powell created a couple unusual for Hollywood films, a married pair who continued to enjoy each other and whose interest didn't lie in the usual couple scenarios that inform their non–Thin Man films: how two become a couple—which is never explored in the stories involving Nick and Nora; or how two break up and reunite—which never happens to Nick and Nora. Rather, Nick and Nora, as a couple, model a successful negotiation of the conflicts that tear at families and couples around them. The drama of Nick and Nora is how they stand together to disarm the social conflicts that could destroy their marital microcosm, conflicts that do explode through the general culture macrocosm. Shot through with self-destructive impulses run rampant, the social milieu in which Nick and Nora live always threatens to fragment even the closest human relationships. The mysteries plumbed wittily by Nick and Nora are the secret social depths of antagonism, hierarchy, and exploitation, revealed in the corrupt transactions unearthed by the Charleses as they, and not the hopelessly incompetent police force, solve one murder after another throughout the six films of the series. The police force is stymied because, as another form of antagonism, hierarchy, and exploitation, it is part of the system that produced the foul play in the first place. Unlike Tarzan and Jane, Nick and Nora do not stand apart in a sacred refuge from social upheaval. Rather, they are unique because although fully members of a community built on artificial and destructive values, they share a spontaneous synergy, embodied vibrantly by the synergy between Powell and Loy, that permits them to be direct and open about seemingly irresistible social pressures and thus to play with them rather than to be controlled by them. In contrast, all around them, the tormented denizens of each new murder scenario in each of the six films are driven to catastrophic and fatal extremes by the secrecy in which they shroud their dreadful socialization. Even more interesting, by virtue of a marriage that is a reflexive comment on the culture, Nick and Nora are also a reflexive comment on the films they generate. If their inspired, serious horseplay moves the formulaic mystery plot vigorously toward conclusion, it also disrupts the storytelling sufficiently to reveal plot as well as cultural cliches for what they are.

A Thin Man formula structures the plotting of all the films; however, as a formula it is somewhat unusual for Hollywood, as it draws attention to one issue that Hollywood is generally at great pains to ignore or deny: class structure. The six films offer mysteries that are crucially concerned with how class contrasts between the lower working and criminal classes associated with Nick and the professional and upper classes associated with Nora fragment families. The class issues bleed into gender issues when Nora's money and position open the door to questions about who controls whom in the Charles marriage. The running gags about their class and gender difference produce a proliferation of private jokes between Nick and Nora that let them chew over social cliches about marriage, money, and desire. What are private jokes between them are the stuff of crime in others. While Nick and Nora tease each other self-mockingly about Nora's money and how Nick's marriage to her has made it possible for him to wallow in lazy luxury, the other characters are betraying and killing each other as they jockey for social position and money through marital arrangements. The stories complicate the Charles's edgily merry, cynically self-lacerating attitudes toward their marriage, a deeply felt connection but also, as Nick keeps admitting, to some extent a financial arrangement. Nick and Nora are of their culture. Tangled up with Nick's self-proclaimed mercenary motives for marriage to the wealthy Nora is the acid-etched picture of the disconnection, loneliness, and isolation of the people in the culture around them who marry miserably for money, and maim and/or kill each other, and their children and parents, as well as competitors, for mercenary reasons. At the same time, the singular chemistry of Loy/Powell is embodied in Nick and Nora's eccentric, electrifyingly erotic and spiritual rapport, plainly missing in the couples floundering about them.

The seriousness of what society does to intimacy comes through in Nick and Nora's hard-edged compatibility. Time has veiled Nick and Nora in sentimental nostalgia, as two lovable cutups with a terrier, but with a closer look at the films, their abrasive qualities burst off the screen. The performance styles of Loy and Powell facilitate highly stylized characterizations; their synergy, enabled by the maverick ideas of the creative team that made the Thin Man movies, moves through the stereotypes and formulas with raw energy. Loy's Nora radiates all the haughty grandeur of her class. Tall, slim, condescending, and always appareled in stunning, regal, intricately designed, and infuriating (for those in the audience who will never be able to afford such things) "outfits," Nora tends to regard the foolishness of the world through a basilisk stare, one of the staples of her acting style in the days when she played evil femme fatales. Loy's Nora holds her nose quite literally in the air. When she speaks, it is in that irritating, paradoxical combination of clipped and drawled pronunciation that characterizes Hollywood's version of upper-class tones, but that is ordinarily reserved for the most unpleasant of silver screen debutantes. Nora sports a number of the annoying qualities characteristic of the other women of her social group, and none of the endearing softness of the stock figure of the upper-class ingenue, who is routinely victimized by a very cruel world and against whom Loy's Nora would typically be positioned as the villainess in a conventional Hollywood film. But in the synergistic Thin Man series, Nora's class

Nora's (Myrna Loy) blend of hauteur and playfulness permits her to negotiate, with style and freedom, her discovery of Nick (William Powell) comforting a pretty young girl.

armor is rendered virtuous and even sexy while the other upper-class characters are rendered as pathetic cliches. She wears well in the world as it is, according to the series, where other women are casualties of the culture wars, because her pose bends, gaps, and moves with living energy, while other poses break under the pressure of life.

THIN IMAGES

As with all Synergistic Couples, it is the raw, documentary energy in the images produced by Powell and Loy that embeds that characteristic, uncanny sense of vitality into the Thin Man series. These are not movies that ask us to believe rationally that Nick and Nora are a wholesome force of nature in a culture sickened by its own artifices. The synergy between Powell and Loy engages the spectator on another, more profound level than is possible for the other more mechanical actors and their more mechanical means of relating.

Unlike Weissmuller and O'Sullivan, who in their series really depended on each other scene by scene for their energy vortex, Powell and Loy, in the Thin Man series, irradiated the screen both separately and together, like two wild forms of visual power moving apart and together to form their synergy as a third kinetic manifestation, formed by the mysterious melding of the two. Nora's entrance into the first film of the series, *The Thin Man* (1934, Dir. W. S. Van Dyke), brilliantly establishes the power of Loy's screen image to convey Nora's ability to slip between bedrock propriety and all the wild forces that expose the limits of correct social behavior and even its elements of masquerade. While the plot (the story of the disappearance of Clyde Wynant, the Thin Man of the title) is entering its expository stage in a fashionable nightclub, suddenly Nora bursts into the scene in a point-of-view shot unusual for the period, her well-dressed arm being pulled energetically by the Charleses' pet dog, the small but relentless terrier Asta. A cut to a frontal shot of Nora's careening body thrown to the floor in the melee, Christmas presents flying pell-mell, displays her staggering wealth as well as her staggering torso. She is expensively shod, a tiny stylish hat perched atop her stylishly coifed hair, the fur collar of her magisterially cut walking suit standing up around her neck like the cape collar that later showed up around the neck of the evil Queen in Walt Disney's *Snow White* (1937). This is the stuff of classical Chaplinesque movie comedy, the chance for the "little fella" in the audience to laugh at the haughty and mighty. Yet Nora's recovery from her spill breaks the mold, as she gamely fights her way up from the floor, unconcerned about the ridiculous figure she has cut, shrugging off the eager help of the restaurant staff, who come to her aid in the spirit of those who wait upon the affluent. There is a spirit moving incongruously behind the regal clothing, the regal posturing, something that could be called vulgar or just spontaneous, caught as raw image by the camera.

Indeed, the image was raw in fact. Loy was preparing to stroll into the bar, with Asta on the leash, to find Nick, as directed in the script, when Van Dyke sprang a surprise on her. "'Can you fall?' Woody asked. 'Do you know how to fall?' I said, 'I've never worked for Mack Sennett, but I'm a dancer. I think I can do it.' I would have done anything for Woody, because I was devoted to him."[1] The scene was shot without rehearsal. Van Dyke just put the camera, normally used at a height of four or five feet, right on the floor where Loy was supposed to touch down, defying the very real possibility that she might hurt herself quite seriously. "As I say, he had put a camera on the floor and he put a mark where I was supposed to land you know, with my chin or something—I was supposed to—that was it—and we never rehearsed it. And, but, being—having the control I had—I had to have the confidence to do it. . . . I tripped myself and I slip across the floor—I went down and slipped across the floor and almost hit the marker—it was absolutely incredible."[2] Exhilaration of this kind carried them through to future improvisations. Collaborations on such idiosyncratic and unpremeditated inventions are far more significant to enduring *Thin Man* pleasures than the script, which while passably written shows the constraints placed on movies by the PCA and the studio heads. The script itself borrows a significant number of witty, sophisticated lines from the novel, but, in typical Hollywood fashion, uses reductive ethnic stereotyping whereas the novel, while dealing in ethnicities, is less conventional.

On his part, Powell's Nick, already present in the nightclub, is irritatingly comic in his role of spectator, incongruously patronizing as he watches Nora topple, especially since he is the one of the pair that would be more likely to collapse onto a barroom floor. Nick is most often a leering, drunken (seeming) buffoon, an unusual hero in Classical Hollywood. Where Loy/Nora stands with that ramrod carriage that summons images of young girls schooled relentlessly in balancing books on their heads, Powell/Nick has the loose-jointed bearing of a man just about to fall into a heap. Radiating the cliche of the unfettered and even unruly body of the lower-class man, Powell/ Nick violates personal space readily and just as readily descends into physical vulgarity reminiscent of Groucho Marx's wild body postures and stoop-shouldered walk. The audience's first glimpse of Nick in the first film of the series, *The Thin Man*, is of his jiggling buttocks as he, with back to the camera, demonstrates to a group of rapt bartenders how to make a martini. Like the mask that Julius Marx made of his face in order to become Groucho, Nick's face is stamped by the indelible mark of Classical Hollywood's movie villain/interloper, the moustache, but unlike Marx, who, as interloping upstart, turned cliched heroes into so much mush, Powell turned disreputability into the mark of genuine suavity. Unlike Marx, Powell was not a true representative of the immigrant lower class; born in Pittsburgh, he was acknowledged by the film audience as "one of us," not—like Marx—an odd (if strangely amusing) Jew from that highly suspect hideout of Others, New York City. In the novel, Nick is described as looking Greek, whereas Powell brought to the screen—with his large, slightly protruding, heavily browed eyes and his sensual gap-toothed smile—the danger not of the foreigner but of the American underclass that would not keep its place. A social threat, Powell as Nick utilizes those physical attributes that made Powell a screen villain during his early, extremely successful years in silent films. In addition, he represents a threat to gender conventions because Nick hardly maintains the prescribed rigid "masculine" control over his body. Powell's Nick is saved from absolute transgressiveness only by a deep, rich voice (albeit one that he sometimes permits the manic freedom to screech into falsetto) and a comfortable sense of conventional masculine entitlement. By virtue of the peculiarly wild energy that Powell released into Nick, he is exasperating. But the collision between that energy and the conventional control Nick has over the plot causes the character to exude authority not only among members of the class from which he comes—acted using pretty standard comic acting technique—but also among flatly depicted members of the upper class, who attempt to patronize him. Nick's exciting combination of Hollywood cliche and Powell's wild energy also creates an interesting thematic issue. Just as Loy's energy has implications for her portrayal of Nora's free relationship to the artifacts of luxury that are the signs of her class, the vibrancy of that combination between formula and force in Nick makes the emotionally felt experiences of his conventional male authority disquieting for the audience when we are reminded that he is, by some lights, a kept man: his freewheeling ease is grounded in the money he throws around thanks to the estate appended to his wife.

The rapport between these two extremely atypical romantic leads is immediately obvious in their first scene together in the series, at the beginning of *The Thin Man*. They set the tone for their ebullient defiance of Hollywood casting patterns in a scene that is built of two seemingly irreconcilable opposites; it is both archly witty and genuinely earthy, a paradox that could not be recreated with the numerous other attractive and talented acting partners with whom each worked. In all other filmic partnerships, they could be one or the other but never both at the same time. The scene that introduces the attractive ambiguity of their marriage takes place right after their wild entente in the bar, packages flying and Nora tumbling, after which they encounter Dorothy Wynant (Maureen O'Sullivan, here cast for her superficial qualities in a formulaic upper-class-girl role), who brings

Powell cuts a masculine figure at ease with female energy.

the Charleses into the plot by asking for Nick's help in finding her father, Clyde Wynant. When she leaves, Nick and Nora sit down for a drink, bantering not about the Wynant disappearance, which will form the spine of the story, but about Nick's flirtation with young, pretty Dorothy. In a scene in which they both play with the characters that society has assigned them, Nick and Nora move easily and fluidly in and out of personas. Speaking in her society and wifely voice, Nora crisply comments on Dorothy's attractiveness, without lowering herself to an openly jealous remark. Speaking as an erstwhile streetwise hustler and currently bourgeois husband, Nick evades her implication, describing Dorothy impersonally, "Yes, she's a very nice type." Moving on to more playful options, Nora sheds her socialite crispness, hitting Nick with a slang expression: "You got types?" At this, Nick reverses the situation and speaks as a smooth upper-class flatterer, telling her that she constitutes a type of which she is the only example—his only type. Each continues playacting a role opposite to the one cast by society, improvising an on-the-spot Abbott and

Costello–like scenario that allows them to work off the energy generated by Nick's flirtatious moment with Dorothy. Nick "admits" that Dorothy is his daughter, and in the tone of the melodramatic confession sighs, "You see it was spring in Venice, and I was so young I didn't know what I was doing. We're all like that on my father's side." Nora, staring with rapt attention at him, as if each word were an important legal pronouncement, replies, "By the way, how is your father's side?" Breaking abruptly and with a playful comic timing from his heavy-breathing purple style, he moves smoothly into an alternate emotional register, regular-guy matter-of-fact pose, and counters, "Oh, it's much better, thanks. And yours?"

The charm of this apparently lighthearted repartee masks its serious creation of a multilayered reflexivity of the fiction being offered to the mass media audience. First, these are actors portraying characters who admit they are acting. More important is the palpable synergy behind their gestures, which creates a level of reality beyond what they do and say. This more profound level makes the audience experience, not just rationally acknowledge, a vision of all typical social interchanges as forms of acting using preset cultural codes. Part of Nick and Nora's synergy is that they are so playful, so aware, and they have access to a deeper level of existence than conventional characters. Other characters get stuck in one pattern, one tonality, and find it hard to negotiate the complexity of emotional dynamics like jealousy and possessiveness. Nick and Nora's ability to move through a variety of tones by means of fantasy immediately casts ordinary logical social structures as narrow and dishonestly artificial, roles that bind people into feeling disconnected. This quality of dialogue introduces the audience to what is really primary in the film, not the murder plot, with its heinous betrayals and fragmentation of human life, but the connectedness of this couple in all its uncanny ability to pull wholeness from the dynamics of disconnection.[3]

The on-the-set tone during the filming of the Thin Man series, at least the early films, was improvisatory and open. Loy and Powell, although they were two very different kinds of people in their private lives, were nurtured by a spontaneous, unpredictable, and eccentric director. Van Dyke played jokes on and with the actors he directed. The documentation paints a picture of a somewhat loose cannon, a little cruel, but a fiery proponent of immediacy. He would, on occasion, "do terrible things like having chairs wired . . . and you'd sit down and get an awful shock."[4] He did not introduce Powell and Loy in a formal way when they worked together on *Manhattan Melodrama*, which immediately preceded their partnership in *The Thin Man*. Instead he let them run into each other in character, Loy's character, Eleanor, flinging herself into the back of a taxi in which Powell's character, Jim Wade, was already sitting. Loy assumes that Van Dyke was too busy to introduce them in the usual way, which is possible. But a man who shocks his actors for the hell of it might also introduce his actors in this manner for creative reasons. Loy's connection with Powell was immediate: "From that very first scene, a curious thing passed between us, a feeling of rhythm, complete understanding, an instinct for how one could bring out the best in the other."[5] It may well be that the lack of a formal introduction released a rapport that etiquette might have altered or even precluded, as it was Loy's belief that the combination of her ability to be detached and Powell's outrageousness was the key to their partnership. Their first moment exploded into that combined balance and imbalance for them to explore before they were distanced by a more socially conventional set of responses.

The immediacy of that contact played into Loy's work mode as an actor. She was a thoughtful actor, but not because she prepared carefully for a role; she thought about herself in the wake of her experience with a partner. She never theorized in advance, but worked out choices in the context of her instinctual response to the dynamic her partner presented to her.

> I instinctively keyed my women to the personalities of the men. Male-female relationships were much more clearly defined in those days. My job was to vivify the abilities of the men. Clark [Gable], for instance, suffered so much from the macho thing that love scenes were difficult. He kept very reserved, afraid to be sensitive for fear it would counteract his masculine image. I always played it a little bit tough with him, giving him what-for to bring him out, because he liked girls like that. . . . I played differently with Bill. He was so naturally witty and outrageous that I stayed somewhat detached. Always a little incredulous . . .[6]

When she speaks of her choices in *Mr. Blandings Builds His Dream House*, working with Cary Grant, however, we do see that "vivifying" her co-star can mean kicking him in the pants too. In the notes made in preparation for her autobiography, Loy contrasts her acting choices working with Powell with those made with Grant: "I thought, Oh, he's so funny when he's, [sic] when he is irritated so then I decided that instead of playing the sort of vis a vis that I played with Bill, I was going to play this woman the other way."⁷ The other way meant irritating Grant with a female who gets waited on hand and foot. Loy's attentiveness to her acting partners was not lost on them. Both Powell and Grant remembered her work being what actors now call "in the moment." Grant has said, "Even when she fed me lines off camera, I'd look over and she'd be pulling down her hem or straightening her stocking in subconscious wifely gesture.... When you get someone who catches it and throws it back that's what acting is all about. Myrna kept that spontaneity in her acting, a supreme naturalness that had the effect of distilled dynamite."[8] Powell has said, "When we did a scene together, we forgot about technique, camera angles, and microphones. We weren't acting, we were just two people in perfect harmony. Many times I've played with an actress who seemed to be separated from me by a plate-glass window; there was no contact at all. But Myrna... has the happy faculty of being able to listen while the other fellow says his lines. She has the give and take of acting that brings out the best."[9]

Clearly, although Loy was conscious of gender implications as she worked, it is only in hindsight that she expresses the kind of consciousness that would have permitted her to challenge formulaic roles. Yet her "vis a vis" with Powell was a challenge to stereotypical representations of women, wives, and lovers pushed the limits of her own definition of herself as a woman and an actor. The vis-à-vis, which came from within both of them as they both saw and lived it, had an interesting connection with their offscreen feelings for each other. There was never any romance between them, but whatever worked for them as acting partners took the occasional slip into real life.

> We became very close friends, but, contrary to popular belief, we were never *really* [sic] married or even close to it. Oh, there were times when Bill had a crush on me, and times when I had a crush on Bill, but we never made anything of it. We worked around it and stayed pals. In this world today, nobody seems to understand how you can just be terribly close and love somebody a whole lot and not sleep with him. If Bill and I had been lovers, then we would have had fights. And if we'd been married, it would have been even worse.[10]

The negotiations that brought Powell and Loy together in *The Thin Man* depended on Van Dyke's working methods, which involved an acute political sense of how to build momentum within the studio for his goals and his lightning speed as a director. Van Dyke had only three weeks for *The Thin Man*. Usually a film took six to eight weeks to film, but Van Dyke shot *Thin Man* in sixteen days, counting two retake days.

Van Dyke's speed was in large part what made him so valuable to MGM; he was efficient and cost-effective. However, if the studio thought of his speed in terms of profit margin, Van Dyke and Loy had another idea about its value. Van Dyke told her, "Actors are bound to lose their fire if they do a scene over and over. . . . It's that fire that brings life to the screen." According to Loy, "He wanted spontaneity, and speed ensured it. Of course, he had us going like crazy, but by that time I could come in, look at new lines, and do them. You had to in those days, because they changed scripts overnight. . . . Woody demanded extraordinary deeds and you needed the discipline to go along with it or you couldn't work with him. He ultimately became too fast; it became an obsession. But his pacing and spontaneity made *The Thin Man*."[11]

All of Nick and Nora's repartee activates the Powell/Loy synergy, creating counterpoint with the plot, but there are also dozens of very special moments when the actors clearly were on a roll and director W. S. Van Dyke let the production slide with them, releasing even more of their unique power to evoke a reality beyond the reality of the plot and the shallow characters that take it all so seriously. The most impressive of these moments is in the first film. A character has arrived at Nick and Nora's apartment to push the plot along by making a phone call that will yield some new information. As he is speaking to an invisible person at the other end of the phone line, Nick and Nora wordlessly play exuberant games with each other, in a physical battle of the sexes that he initiates by poking his finger vulgarly into the button of her very elegant blouse. As she defends herself playfully and they get into a rhythm of physical thrust and parry, the plot dialogue briefly scatters as they give the audience a sudden apprehension of that other, less obvious level of action, which effectively subordinates the plot. Perhaps the most enigmatic and briefest moment of this kind takes place in *Another Thin Man*, in a completely throwaway moment as Nick and Nora prepare to go to sleep in one of the bedrooms of a vast Long Island estate threatened by mysterious doings. It is the end of a scene, and Nora hands Nick his pajamas, but the scene does not end with the gesture. It lingers on the two of them as they stare at each other for no scripted reason and Nick suddenly grins and makes a clicking noise with his mouth that relates to nothing in the story. The effect is uncanny, suddenly infusing into the flow of events their personal dynamic and all the erotic and intimate possibilities under the surface of their daily actions.

Although they worked together and separately on many formulaic pictures that called on them to create a seamless illusion of the reality in their dialogue and situations for the film, in the Thin Man series Loy and Powell move freely among formulas, letting the seams and the contractions of the characters and of their screen personas emerge. As they do so, they deconstruct the society in which these characters move, which locks its denizens into one-dimensional roles that twist and mutilate them. The "lighthearted" Thin Man series is another example of what happens when inner conflicts are exposed energetically as a form of spectatorial pleasure in a Synergistic Couple. Such a representation, rare for Hollywood, but crucially important to its history where it does occur, offers a way to make an end run around the pressures in the culture industry to avoid disruption and troubling thoughts about social institutions. Here the shifts Nick and Nora negotiate together, permitting a unity in difference between male and female, upper and lower class, the limits of decorum and a less limited openness to spontaneity, offer a means for making a searing condemnation of a repressive culture by the contrast between an ideal of freedom they embody and how society works.

BREAKING THE MOLD

The six films in the Nick and Nora series vary significantly in their quality and in their capacity to open the mass media to indirection and ambiguity that can penetrate the surface of a deeply troubled society. *The Thin Man* is generally (and accurately) accepted as the most successful of the group. It defines the type of rigid, conventional, formulaic pattern that characterizes the plot structure of this synergistic series as well as its counterpoint with Nick and Nora's capacity to shift position and tone. The typical Thin Man plot involves crime in high places, and generally unsuspected rotten places in the heart of a greedy and uncaring society. In this first film Nick and Nora are drawn into the lives of the Wynants, a wealthy, prestigious, though graceless and dysfunctional, family that Nick has worked for in the past. Nick and Nora investigate the disappearance and murder of Clyde Wynant, the patriarch, about whom we find out in the obligatory revelations scene at the end that he was dispatched by the Wynants' easily corruptible lawyer, MacCauley, a greedy middle-class professional who preys on a family too busy preying on each other to notice. Wynant has betrayed his wife with his secretary, and in return she has divorced him and married a gigolo-like younger man who is around only for the money. The morbid Wynant son is overly attached to his father, and the Wynant daughter, Dorothy, suffers from a fear that she bears such corrupt genes that no decent future is possible. While the family is plunged into confusion by adultery and frantic grasping for the family fortune, Nick and Nora bring clarity to the situation as they playfully overturn one rock after another and make the serpents under them visible. *After the Thin Man* (1936, Dir. W. S. Van Dyke), also quite a good movie, is again about the sexually confused, greedy, and moribund upper class; this time Nora's family. Nora's distraught cousin is hopelessly in love with a husband who has married her for her money. When he is murdered, she is blamed for the crime, which Nick and Nora discover was committed by the man she rejected for her depraved husband, a man who seemed to be the best and brightest among them and the young wife's one true friend. Again Nick and Nora bring light to the situation because they are not similarly afflicted by sexual and materialistic frenzies of possession. The quality of the series stays high in *Another Thin Man* (1939, Dir. W. S. Van Dyke), again about greed and mayhem in the upper class, this time involving the betrayal of an obnoxiously overbearing and self-involved father by a self-involved, adopted child devoid of conscience or the capacity to love. The parent-child plot, not coincidentally, is the center of the first narrative in which Nick and Nora are parents, and contrasts with the Charleses' parental situation. *Shadow of the Thin Man* (1941, Dir. W. S. Van Dyke), a racetrack mystery, begins the downhill slide of the series, but maintains its cynical view of moneyed, pedigreed people. It is full of minor and major crime figures, but the murders turn out to have been committed by the silver-haired, patrician patriarch engaged by the state congress to investigate corruption at the track. The problems of hierarchy and patriarchy plague Nick and Nora in this film, and they do negotiate them with grace and charm, but the trajectory of the film begins here to move Nick and Nora toward the more formulaic wife and husband that both Loy and Powell went on later to play with other acting partners in postwar Hollywood, making the film less captivating than its earlier series mates.

The slight move toward cliche in *Shadow of the Thin Man* becomes disastrously pronounced in the next film, *The Thin Man Goes Home* (1944, Dir. Richard Thorpe). The fifth film in the series is a wartime film that clearly fell victim to the industry move to erase what ambiguity there was in its films to create the needed climate of moral certainty on the American home front. It almost drowns in conventional cliches about marriage and family, a problem that can be traced to the assignment to the creative team of Frank Capra's favorite writer, Robert Riskin. Riskin devised a script in which he confuses Nick with the Gary Cooper hero and Nora with the Jean Arthur heroine in Frank Capra's *Mr. Deeds Goes to Town* (1936) and gives the quintessentially urbane, nonconformist Nick a small-town background complete with a cliched, conventional, salt-of-the-earth country doctor father and a silver-haired, women's auxiliary mother who speaks with a British cadence. This corruption of the Nick and Nora series even goes so far as to demonize the corrupt city in contrast with virtuous small-town life, a tone utterly out of keeping with a series that was, when in its right mind, one of the primary Hollywood valentines to the diversity and energy of the American city. The murder involves a dysfunctional, greedy husband and wife, a couple that could have served as an interesting contrast with Nick and Nora. Instead, the small-town focus skews the story into a classical Oedipal tale in which reprobate Nick finally gains the approval of his mainstream father by solving a hometown mystery. Nora, formerly a polished woman who casts a suitably cold eye on the pieties of good society, is reduced to a dizzy "little woman" who sentimentally immolates herself in the cause of Nick's bonding with dear old dad.

Song of the Thin Man (1947, Dir. Edward Buzzell), the final film in the series and the last film Loy and Powell made together, returns the series (minus Robert Riskin) to the Charleses' urban stomping ground. In keeping with the postwar emergence of jazz into Hollywood films, the Charleses investigate a murder in the promising milieu of jazz musicians, but unfortunately as a pale imitation of the film noir of the period, a strange and disquieting irony, since the initial 1934 *Thin Man* was a pioneer in the aesthetics that later created the postwar film noir. Here the murders are also involved with a dysfunctional couple torn apart by the kind of greed and sexual rage that the series finds endemic to the human condition, but which Nick and Nora have accommodated by their ludic approach to issues of property and sexuality in marriage. However, the members of the creative team working on the last gasp of the series were unable to mobilize the synergistic chemistry of Powell and Loy to advantage, and *The Song of the Thin Man*, while more accomplished than *The Thin Man Goes Home*, ends the series with only a small thump of social satire, showing just a bit too much whimper, in this last portrayal of Nick and Nora, of the lingering effects of the wartime erasure of ambiguity.

At their best, Nick and Nora had the flash and manic subversiveness associated with the brief, unforgettable pairing of Mae West and W. C. Fields, who created an indelible impression as a couple in only one film: *My Little Chickadee* (1940, Dir. Edward F. Cline). More long-lived, and closer to the bone in their depictions of the way we live now, Loy and Powell sashayed through shadowy crime scenes that were synecdoches of the contemporary culture as one large crime scene, permitting the audience to laugh at an image of itself impaled on the fixed bayonets of respectable society, Nora rolling her eyes and sending up woman as visual spectacle and precious object of male possession (while constituting a dazzling spectacle herself) and Nick soaked to his eyeballs in liquor and mocking male authority (while wielding it). Except in the execrable *The Thin Man Goes Home*, Nick and Nora have physical, intellectual, sexual, and linguistic equality while at the same time paradoxically inhabiting the social inequities of the male and female roles. Defying classical categories, they are each depicted as equally rational and emotional in dealing with the mysteries of murder, despite the need for both of them to struggle with their internalization of cultural expectations that she will be the subordinate emotional partner under the control of his rational supervision.

The Thin Man series is not structured by Hollywood's familiar gender formula: woman/body—man/mind. If Nora is on spectacular physical display, so is Nick. Each is introduced in the first film from behind, foregrounding the body and delaying the psychological identification with face and expression. When we first meet Nick, shaking a container of martinis with his entire body, and Nora, as her body is being dragged into the bar by Asta, we can say that Nick is, in typical masculine fashion, in control while Nora is out of control, in typical female fashion, dragged by an animal and thus associated with the purported feminine closeness to animality and nature. But there is nothing typical about the full definition of either position. Nick's concoction of the perfect martini requires an atypical male absorption in his body, his surrender to the rhythms of the world: there are different rhythms for each drink. Nora's entrance uses the cliche of female closeness to animality and body to make a joke of Hollywood's traditional images of female glamour, as she is splayed on the floor in her expensive, sophisticated outfit, her impressively wrapped Christmas purchases flying out of her grasp like so much chaff in the wind. (This deconstruction of glamour has already been introduced in a previous scene in which a gangster looks at a picture in a fashion magazine and the audience sees a point-of-view shot in which he imagines the girdle beneath the slender silhouette of the model, causing him to say, "You women sure take a lot of punishment.") Indeed, the body that is out of control is that of the masculine Asta, and he is frantically searching for his human alter ego, Nick. So, implicated in this image of seemingly typical female bodily instability is an untypical subtext of Nick's male bodily instability, since he is associated with body and animal through Asta. There is also yet a further implication that it is not Nora's undependable femaleness being depicted here but a loving association with maleness that dishevels and buffets her. Nick and Nora, when they are most true to their original definition, are gender doubles of each other, all masculinity and femininity intricately interconnected since each contains its opposite within itself. This contrasts dramatically with the bipolar gender definitions of all the supporting characters in the Thin Man series, each of whom is neatly and conventionally gendered along the lines of male/dominant/control/mind and feminine/submissive/chaos/body.

The synergistic pairing of Loy and Powell in the Thin Man series depicts a love dependent on tensions between the stereotypical social categories and their carnivalization by Nick and Nora. The films gain their power by playing with the tension between the flow of Nick and Nora's gender doubling and the rigid boundaries of cultural categories. For this, in hindsight, we can say that Loy and Powell were superb for the roles in part because the need for some transgressive element in both Nick and Nora was answered by the slippage of the public images of Loy and Powell from their early careers playing villains onto the law-abiding, but never socially defined, Charleses.

Powell had moved from playing villains to playing detectives, so there was a transition from his earlier public image, but Louis B. Mayer opposed the casting of Myrna Loy because of her existence in the public imagination as the sadistic Fah Lo See in *The Mask of Fu Manchu* (1933), and indeed her frequent appearance on screen as an oriental vamp. L. B. Mayer was more than somewhat uneasy about director W. S. Van Dyke's choice of Myrna Loy for Nora Charles, because she had already been typecast as a villainess, generally nonwhite. Van Dyke, who was rather low in the MGM pecking order, was responsible for casting Loy, and also for swaying Mayer. But, much of the power of Nick and Nora comes from the double public image that this series created; indeed, Irving Thalberg, the head of production at MGM, is said to have thought, in general, that all effective film actors had a slight sense of villainy in their eyes.[12] Thoughtful examination of Loy's facial expressions in the role of Nora reveals how important to her effectiveness is that suggestion of feline cruelty and willfulness that lurks under her wifely smile. Similarly, a thoughtful examination of Powell's expression reveals how much his authority comes from his association with the ruthlessness and sensuality of the gap-toothed Snidely Whiplash leer. This double sense of domesticity and kinkiness gives an electric charge to the comic panache of Nick and Nora juggling the categories of respectability. Who but the former sadistic daughter of Fu Manchu could stand up to Nick's jokes at her expense, as in a brief scuffle between the two after Nora's entrance with Asta, in which Nora's social position as the "little woman" is played off against her actual ability to stand toe to toe with her "lord and master." When the maitre d' politely asks Nora to leave with the dog, Nick halts him, saying these are *his* dog and wife, in that order, and adding that the *dog* is well trained. Who but a former deviant, such as Powell had played, would make such a statement in public? Nora calls Nick on this, chiding him for not giving her first billing, but it is her bearing toward him at this point that drives home her parity with him, the words only supporting her haughty stare. Nick's pompous posturing vis-à-vis the maitre d' is also punctured by the film. The dog is *not* well behaved. He will obey none of Nick's commands as Nick tries to demonstrate his obedience. Again, the film throws a curve. Nick has a sense of humor about his male entitlements, and comically behaves as if the recalcitrant Asta is going through his paces with dispatch as Nora smirks. Social conditioning exists only in the mind.

In this filmic world, Nick and Nora alone know that social values are powerful only because people have been conditioned to believe "it is so" if society says "it is so." In their fictional world, they alone are able to laughingly give lip service to artificially imposed cultural mores, while living another kind of interrelationship. Being willing to see society as performance carries Nick and Nora through at least the first four films; the complexities of going along and making a private joke of cultural norms surfaces in the last two films, in which it becomes painfully clear, as we shall see below, that Nick and Nora can take things only so far in attending to the issues of a dysfunctional society.

The protection of the image of American society was the prime directive of the Production Code Administration, but it had almost nothing to say about the subversions of the Nick and Nora series. The PCA files on the Loy/Powell Thin Man series deal in cliches and illustrate that in the thirties the PCA was often more mild nuisance than anything else. In a seemingly endless deluge of memos, the PCA objected to the display of liquor consumption in the Thin Man films. However, although there are no memos in the files of the individual pictures in the series in which either Van Dyke or his production team disputes the PCA nor any memos in which the PCA relents about any of its objections, the films are oozing with cocktails and dialogue about drinking. Indeed the exposition of their characters takes place in a bar, as we have seen above. It is unlikely that the PCA ever retreated from its anti-drinking stance, yet it approved all the films in the Thin Man series. What is most likely is that the principals at the PCA were charmed by the series and simply ignored their own (numerous) memos. After all, Breen wrote MGM to congratulate them on the "most interesting screen entertainment which we have witnessed in a long time" (May 12, 1934). His memo makes not one single reference to the prodigious consumption of alcohol by the central couple.

This reflects the kind of capriciousness typical of PCA decisions. The local review boards didn't object either. All the Thin Man films passed local review boards in New York and Massachusetts routinely without exclusions, and most of them too in Pennsylvania, as well as in the very curmudgeonly states of Ohio and Kansas. They were rejected only in Latvia, Esthonia, Nanking, and Hungary, but not in relationship to any display of alcohol. There they were rejected for too much violence and criminal content.

As Nick and Nora never depicted explicit sexuality or revealed

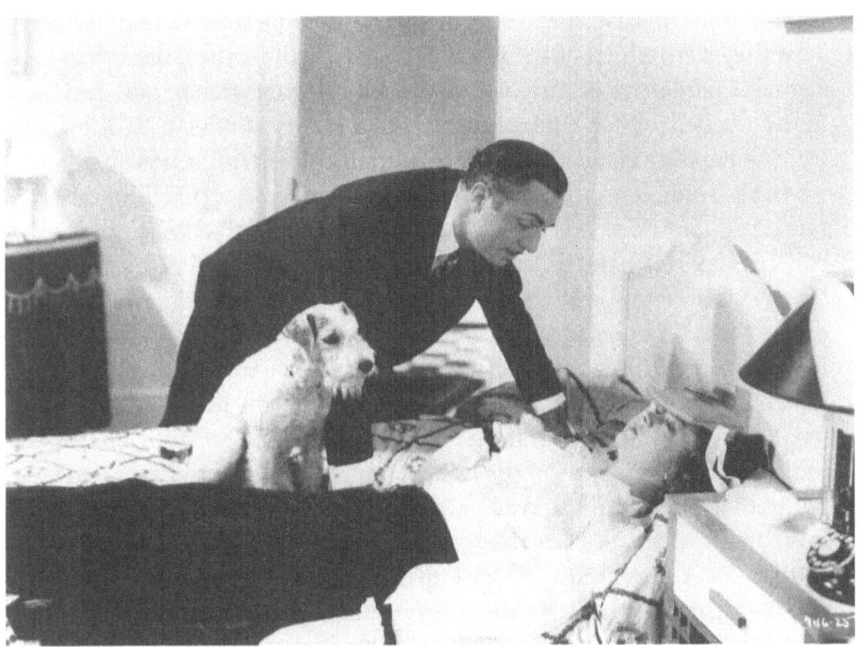

Nora's (Loy) comic hangover, one of the many jokes about drinking to excess to which the PCA closed its eyes in the Thin Man series.

themselves to the cameras in any state of undress, the specific comments of warning about eroticism were directed toward the Charleses' double entendres and rather mild sexual references. One exchange that came in for scrutiny occurs when Nora and Nick are bantering about the newspapers' exaggerations of some violence; Nora says that Nick was shot six times in the tabloids, and Nick responds, "He didn't get anywhere near my tabloids." Other contested lines bear only the slightest traces of innuendo, as for example "after what I have been to you"; "I was just a gleam in my father's eye." Still other lines that came in for censure have an innocent, merry middle-school silliness about them, as when the police are searching Nick and Nora's bedroom (pointedly without a warrant) and one policeman looks into Nora's bureau, causing her to exclaim, "What's that man doing in my drawers?" (Interestingly, the PCA file shows no objection to the critique of our law enforcement system in this interchange.) Each of these lines and many other equally playful innuendoes remain in circulating prints today. However, some of them were edited out of prints shown in Australia, Pennsylvania, Ohio, Alberta, and Ontario. That they were edited out at all reflects that, by the forties, there was a notable hardening of the position of the PCA from what it had been in the thirties. By the time of *Shadow of the Thin Man* (1941), they were demanding and getting a more puritanical repression of sexuality. In that film, a mystery about a corrupt syndicate controlling the racetrack, the PCA warned MGM about two minor characters, a corrupt reporter named Barrow and Claire Porter (Stella Adler), a blonde working girl with the airs and graces of a lady; the film was not to give the audience any suggestions that the two were living together. In the finished film, they are not even a couple. However, as was typical, when one situation was censored another sprung up to take its place without comment from the PCA. In the finished film Claire is obviously the mistress of the boss of the syndicate, and there is no doubt that Claire and the syndicate boss are living together. It's hard to imagine what the PCA thought it accomplished by forcing this shift. A PCA memo also objects to the display of lingerie in the Charles apartment, a suggestion not heeded, as the scene in which Nick holds up one of Nora's nightgowns admiringly remained in all prints in circulation. Interestingly, although the PCA explicitly disapproved of references to the dog, Asta, urinating, images of Asta and urination are shoved in the audience's face in the main title, which displays a cartoon image of Asta staring at a fire hydrant on which a possibly threatening cat sits. And references to liquor are equally prominent as Nick terminates his day in the park with his son; sitting on a park bench two blocks from home, he hears Nora shaking a martini. In addition, the film breaks some of the series' ethnic stereotypes by featuring a Jewish police lieutenant. (On its own initiative, however, it also features a "mammy" caricature of a black maid.) In 1941, the Hays office watchdog was trying harder to bite, but with only limited success.

Relative to *Song of the Thin Man* (1947), the last film in the Thin Man series, the PCA did police the erotic rapport between Nick and Nora in a way that diminishes their representation in the film. The series was partially moribund by this time, bereft of most of its original creative team. Having lost its original writers a few films back, it had also lost its original producer, Hunt Stromberg, and its original director, W. S. Van Dyke. All that was left from the original core team were Loy and Powell. The film involves the Charleses in the death of a bandleader, and so there are many scenes of women in formal gowns. In its usual ineffectual way, the PCA registered unprecedented complaints about the series costumes, asking that "the greatest possible care must be taken" that the women's dresses not reveal their breasts. We can see the effect of this dictum as the film opens and Gloria Graham as a big band singer is wearing a dress with a high neck, a low hem, and a surprisingly unrevealing slit up the side. However, the creative team, although in many ways much weaker than the original team, still managed to defy the PCA, following the letter but not the spirit of the law. Graham's dress is made of a material so clingy that, because of a very clever lighting design, her nipples appear to be outlined under the fabric. The same can also be said of Jayne Meadows's gown in the opening scene, as she plays Janet Thayer, the rebellious daughter of a super-rich family. The PCA also warned that Nicky Jr. (Dean Stockwell) was not to be shown getting lessons in safecracking, so the film didn't show it. Nora merely talks about the lessons instead—not actually much of a difference in the kind of role model for children built into the film. Continuing its record of inconsistency, the Hays office said nothing about Nicky talking about the pinups he had been peeking at in Nick's *Esquire*. The Hays office succeeded in a small way by having unimportant lines cut out of the film, such as "but his mother barked" and a remark about "inside a cool martini glass," while leaving intact Nora's line "I'm practically under the table now, but not the way I want to be." But the PCA did make an impact with its stern disapproval of the ending of the film in the Charleses' bedroom, which was judged "unduly sex-suggestive and could not be approved." The film did not end in the Charleses' bedroom, but on a shot of Nicky Jr. sleeping with Asta. The joke on the PCA is that this too is a transgressive scene. Asta has been forbidden to sleep in Nicky Jr.'s bed. However, nobody wins. The joke isn't a good one, and the PCA victory is a completely pyrrhic one, forcing a rather cloying ending on the film and doing very little to avert suggestion in a film that focuses continually on Loy's body, beginning with a couple of gangsters ogling her behind, continuing with an odd feathered hat that steals each scene in which she appears, and keeping our eyes on Loy's sleeping body as she dozes off in the locations in which she and Nick search for clues.

The slippage of villain/villainess image onto husband and wife in the Thin Man series is significant too because it challenges cliches about Hollywood's propagandistic naturalization of culturally created, ethnically specific values in portraying the couple. Loy and

Powell are good-looking people of Anglo-Irish backgrounds, but in the Thin Man series they cannot be said to work onscreen in terms of idealized Nordic looks as they do in the more forgettable non-series comedies and melodramas. The enduring fascination of Loy and Powell as Nick and Nora is the way they make strange (defamiliarize) ethnic domination of conventional American standards of beauty by Nordic features. The attraction of their pratfalls, mugging, and especially the intimations of something dark under the actors' features suggests that it is not the stereotype that charms the audience but the subversion of its idealization. The power of Loy and Powell, in some way, then, is that being the supposed acme of Nordic excellence, they are in the best position to portray the artificiality of that illusion and to represent the merely human under the mask of social desire.

In *The Thin Man*, as social type is fictionalized, so are the social taboos of sexual exclusivity, social class, and materialism. Sexual exclusivity goes first. Dorothy Wynant's mild flirtation with Nick becomes and stays a private joke between Nick and Nora. Later, Dorothy runs to Nick for protection during a Christmas party at the Charleses'. She is upset because of her difficult and even violent mother, who is looking for the missing Clyde Wynant to get more money from him. Sobbing, Dorothy goes into the bedroom with Nick for a private moment of comfort. Nora breezes in as Nick puts his arms about Dorothy to reassure her that she is overly excited about her troubles. Dorothy is prepared to "explain" the situation to Nora, as if this were a serious infraction, but an exchange of shot-reverse shot nose wrinkles between Nora and Nick makes a joke of that capriciously drawn line that establishes the socially contracted exclusive couple relationship. While other couples are fragilely compounded of social roles and definitions, and therefore are threatened by any deviation from the role, for Nick and Nora being a couple is too profoundly organic a union to be threatened by a hug from a "cute chick."

Social class and materialism dwindle into a set of abstract constructions too. All Nick's friends are "mugs," with their cheap clothes, loud behavior, and New York accents. But during the course of the film, everyone, except Nick and Nora, becomes visible as mugs. Nora's class of people are mugs in better clothes who speak in clipped accents. Material possessions, so coveted by the greedy villains in the Thin Man series, are depicted in terms of the presents flying out of

Nora's hands, objects in the wind of human passion and compulsion. Their instability renders the demarcation of economic classes fictional. Indeed the classes are anything but pure categories in the series. Coupling routinely takes place across the limits of class division, Nick and Nora being the prime example and the sign of the cultural reality of flow that reduces to puppet-like pretensions the operating principles of the supporting characters, who violently contort their energies to appear to conform with rigidly codified behavior while they give in to their chaotic urges. They are rendered absurd at every turn, since in the Nick/Nora milieu family composition betrays the reality of flesh and nerve beneath artificially devised class labels. And anyone can play any social role. In *Another Thin Man*, Lois (Virginia Grey), the adopted daughter of upper-class Colonel McFay (C. Aubrey Smith), is of lower-class origin but resembles him utterly in presenting a mannered veneer that hides a crude, self-absorbed shadow self, perhaps the consequence of the exploitations and repressions of the social machine.[13]

The tension between the imposition of standardized social roles and institutions and spontaneous human desires and passions charts the evolution of Nick and Nora throughout the series in a way that stands as a significant exception to one of the patterns of Hollywood coupledom traced by a succession of feminist film critics following in the tracks of Laura Mulvey. Mulvey observed that in mass media entertainment, male heroism requires the sacrifice of female autonomy, a kind of obsessive, automatic, Hollywood Taming-of-the-Shrew reflex, in which shrewishness is replaced by a multitude of forms of female uppity behavior: flirtatiousness, seductive power, ditzy recklessness, unorthodox eccentricity. The hero is attracted to the autonomy of the heroine, but this sparks a desire to put an end to it by establishing his authority over her, domesticating her, and denuding her of the power of the glamour that first attracted him to her: the Gable Plus One phenomenon, discussed in Chapter One. In the Thin Man series, the couple is already formed when the series begins; Nora never loses her glamour, and if Nick's authority comes from his affiliation with Nora, it is not because he possesses and subjugates her, but rather because of the opposite, that he is willing to enter into the never-ending struggle with her that pits his desire for control against her formidable ability to wield power through her glamour. That neither of them is fooled either by his will to control or by her capacity for assuming the shape of female allure, that neither of them is willing to relinquish his or her power, highlights their difference from the characters caught in the maelstrom of murder and mayhem and the central truth of their endurance as a Synergistic Couple. As Nick and Nora, Powell and Loy offer a striking contrast to those couples who fit the Mulvey pattern, those who won contemporary popularity but have since disappeared—and also a contrast to Loy and Powell's eight other co-starring roles in non-series films, as we shall soon see.

Indeed, the energized and energizing collision between them in the first four Thin Man films turns on who will use Nora's glamour and how that affects the crime investigations. In these films, Nora, always in full makeup, professionally coifed, and dressed like a fashion model, is continually mistaken for Nick's mistress and thus propositioned by hoodlums Nick has previously sent to jail, who comprise Nick's main group of friends. She moves through hordes of thugs downing liquor in their bi-coastal habitats, coping with illiteracy and crudeness, or through mansions inhabited by the social elite, who either sleepwalk through their lives or throw their considerable weight around. Her glamour shows up against these backgrounds as purely artificial yet potent as a symbol of power. In the first film, when Nick is getting ready to reveal the killer, his first requirement is that she have a "nice evening gown" to preside over the mock dinner party for the suspects. Their forthright understanding of glamour as armor and costume that the two of them manipulate sets them apart in this film from the Wynants, particularly Clyde's wife, Mimi, who clearly believe that a woman is what she wears. There is no confusion between Nick and Nora about that kind of role-playing with identity—he'd as soon wrap a martini shaker in one of her designer originals as look at it on her, and he does so at the beginning of the second film, *After the Thin Man*. They do not naturalize glamour, nor is it a secret the way it is in films in which women simply appear in their finery as if it were an effortless feminine reality. Virginia Wexman critiques the representation of romantic couples in Hollywood where women's "work as participants in the manufacture of glamour is denied by depicting the results as . . . produced by nature and by associating this beauty with the unworldly transcendance [sic] of romantic love."[14] By contrast, in this film, the artificiality is all too plain, and the foolishness of forgetting how it was produced is even plainer. Nora's glamour is portrayed as technologically created and economically dependent on her large inheritance; glamour is one part of the financial structure that entangles men and women in webs of self-destruction from which they cannot extricate themselves.

Clyde Wynant has understandably left his grasping wife, Mimi, but incomprehensibly, has left her for an equally grasping mistress, Julia Wolfe. Both Mimi and Julia, like most studio-era protagonists, confuse being a woman with having the best that money can buy. But the beauty disguise is not restricted to women in this series. Among the slippages of convention in the series, in *After the Thin Man,* manufactured male glamour is the ruin of a woman. Selma Landis (Elissa Landi), Nora's high-society cousin, has chosen to marry the glamourous Robert Landis (Alan Marshall) over the loyal and steadfast David Grahame (Jimmy Stewart). Robert in turn has confused the glamour of cafe chanteuse Polly Burns (Penny Singleton, before she became Blondie) with her reality; she is actually a pathetic, manipulative woman. Landis manipulates Selma, and Polly, in cahoots with her boyfriend, Dancer, manipulates him, in both cases for money. Ultimately Robert is murdered by David, who frames Selma for the murder, obsessed as he is by the need for revenge because the foolish Selma has injured the once loyal David's sense of self-value in passing him over for smooth, pretty Robert, a sham lover. These are mistakes to which Nick and Nora are immune, the reason why they can solve murders that baffle others who are stuck in mainstream values, their sight narrowed by mainstream blinders to alternate possibilities. Nick and Nora demonstrate this in a truly delightful scene in the Li-Chee club where Polly sings. Surrounded by a table of thugs, Nora is once again mistaken by the thug next to her for Nick's mistress, whom the thug compares favorably to all the previous mistresses. "She's hot ain't she?" he drools, adding that when Nick "gives her the sack" she should look him up. "I soitenly will," replies Nora, reminding us how artificial the social mask is, as she uses his New York inflection, and curling her lip as she says it. Nick and Nora look at each other in superior amusement at the thug's confusion about glamour, wives, and relationships, as the audience is given a place to perch safe from the precise kind of confusion Robert Landis has only minutes before demonstrated about Polly. Almost immediately the superiority gives way to something more complex and interesting, as Nick and Nora demonstrate an advanced form of tension surrounding female glamour. As Nora tries to talk seriously with Nick about Robert's obvious infatuation with Polly, Nick tries to shove her into the position of trophy wife by throwing her glamour in her face as a kind of mollifying compliment. Instead of answering her, he tells her she is the most fascinating woman "on this side [western] of the Rockies." Wise to his ploy, and absolutely confident that he knows she is, she parries his thrust in resistance to his attempt to turn her charm into his power to control her, saying, "Wait 'til you see me on the other side." This graceful yet profoundly serious struggle is, paradoxically, fatal and yet not hopeless. Nick will never get over trying to dominate her, she will never let him, and neither will ever write off coupledom with the other for the threat each poses to their most powerful individual interests. Most mysterious of all, it will be the outcome of these eternal struggles that some good, truth, and justice will prevail in their world.

The two create coupledom as an irresolvable balance of tensions, not a harmony based on male ability to dominate female, by keeping her "in her place." The balance is an ongoing struggle in which the usual social dominance/submission pattern keeps threatening and the Charleses keep playing with it. Nick variously sends Nora against her will to Grant's Tomb in a taxi, has her locked up in jail, and locks her in a closet in his arrogant male belief that she will only get in the way of serious male business. He is never right, and she never stays put. Nick is obnoxious in his humorously toned manifestations of power, but she is quite equal to the task of giving as good as she gets. In the first two films, her power takes an almost purely defensive form: her strong and witty verbal rejoinders, and her equally strong silences, in which she cuts the ground out from under his posturing with a look, not often presented as a woman's weapon in early Hollywood.

As the series develops, in *Another Thin Man* and *Shadow of the Thin Man,* in which the Charleses become parents, Nora meets a very different fate than the typical Hollywood mother, a position that guaranteed for most onscreen moms death, the loss of the babies, anonymity (i.e., the eponymous heroine of *Stella Dallas,* 1937, Dir. King Vidor). Nora remains front and center, very much alive, and, though possessed of fluctuating degrees of influence, she remains a focus of desire. *Another Thin Man* concerns the murder of tyrannical, parsimonious Colonel McFay by his adopted daughter, Lois (Virginia Grey), who wants the colonel's money and the freedom to use it her way and not the colonel's. In this adventure, Nora, matron and mother, has probably her finest hour as a force majeure.

The class issues in this film become ever more edgy when McFay, an unpleasant old despot, lures Nick out to his Long Island estate under false pretenses to investigate threats against his life by Phil Church (Sheldon Leonard), a gangster recently released from prison who lives on a neighboring estate. In seeking protection, McFay is forced to reveal that Church's enmity is founded on some past business dealings that "might" have involved him in shady transaction, and that also might implicate Nora's father, his former partner. Although McFay goes out of his way to clear Nora's father of any wrongdoing, he is such a patently slippery operator that a taint clings to Nora's upper-class background that has never before been implied. Furthermore, the invention of McFay reveals the fantasy in Nick's claim that he has given up detective work because he is managing Nora's father's business affairs. In this adventure, we see that Nick understands nothing of the workings of the estate, details that have been handled by McFay all along. Nick breaks the stereotype of the American father by being unconcerned with being the breadwinner and provider; he quite happily coasts along on Nora's money as it is doled out to him. His humor about this part of male identity emerges clearly when McFay's revelations lay open to question whether Nora's inheritance is indeed safe; Church "took the fall" for business irregularities and now may want to claim a significant share of what Nora thought was all hers. Nick, unfazed, quips that without Nora's fortune he can always make a good living as a detective—though he isn't sure what Nora and Nicky Jr. will live on. Against this background of dubious patriarchs, Nora emerges as a more assertive person.

Indeed, all the women in this landscape have to take care of themselves and their men. However, Nora's difference from the rest points to some interesting new layers of the Charles filmic universe. In this film, aside from Nora, the independent women are all linked to Church. After the colonel is murdered, Church becomes the primary suspect. He has made vocal threats and has disappeared. While Nora is assisting Nick in solving the crime, a moll named Mrs. H. Culverton Smith, called "Smitty" (Muriel Hutchison), is the steadying support person in Church's plans to regain the fortune he believes he is entitled to. Smitty is interesting. With a husband in prison, and her husband's friend trying, on his pal's behalf, to extricate her from her relationship with Church, Smitty looks like the blonde moll who serves the coffee and is ever available for sexual favors, but she turns out to be a self-possessed businesswoman whose business is crime. In a surprising scene between Smitty and Church, Church negotiates with her to escalate their business partnership into a romantic one as well. In this scene, Smitty emerges as anything but the conventional, golden-haired bimbo. She is not the crime lord's possession, but an individual vendor. This relationship, like all couple configurations in the synergistic Nick and Nora films, becomes a foil to the continuing revelation of the layers of the Charleses' intimacy. Smitty and Church are far more conscious of the need for respect and parity in partnering than most of the confused denizens of the series, regardless of class, but they are still locked within a social system that shatters all intimacy with self-interest and greed.

Lois McFay and Phil Church also have an understanding and a partnership, which Smitty does not know about, just as Lois knows nothing about Smitty's role in Church's life. Lois wants a wild life, and high times, not the quiet existence of a Long Island debutante. When Church got out of prison and began making his demands, Lois liked what she saw and joined forces with him. Church has developed one of those methods for murder—actually ludicrously impossible but slick sounding in a final revelation scene—that were so common in mystery movies of the classical period, involving a pseudo-scientific plan that makes it possible to make a gun go off (and hit its target) while the murderer is observed to be somewhere else. Church, planning to be very visible at a gambling club while the colonel is murdered, arranges with Lois to put his handy-dandy murder machine into operation, giving her five minutes to be sitting with Nick and Nora while the fatal shot rings out.

Smitty and Lois take their destinies into their hands, working the system to undermine conventional male entitlement, even to be partners with male initiative, only to get involved in the pattern of users being used. Thus Smitty compares as unfavorably with Nora as have the submissive women who are parasites on male authority. Nora's synergistic alliance with Nick allows her to move ever more bumptiously onto the larger stage of life with her customary playful honesty. One of her most delightful sorties as a partner in detecting shows her gaining important information because the police try to manipulate her as the "little woman." The investigating officers try to get Nora to break Nick's alibi—that he was with her at the time McFay was shot—by playing on the insecurity that is so much a part of the liaisons typical of this society. They try to make Nora "tell the truth" about where Nick was by making her feel that Nick doesn't deserve her loyalty, that he has betrayed her with a variety of the women he dealt with in his previous cases. For them, it doesn't "figure" that a guy who has had so many women before he met Nora would suddenly go cleanly monogamous. ("Oh dear," sighs Nora, "I thought he was lying.") In the process of working this angle—which cannot work because of the special synergy between the pair—the detectives tell Nora about two of Nick's previous women about whom Nora has never heard: Bella Spruce and Letty Finhadden. Spruce was the widow of a coal yard owner who wanted to set Nick up in a detective agency, and Finhadden was a lighthouse keeper's daughter. Nora is utterly unmoved by the seductions of the police, who cannot even imagine the kind of relationship she has with Nick, but, in scenes of unique comic exuberance, she uses the information in conjunction with her glamour to counter Nick's efforts to keep her from getting into the investigation game, the premier position of control and importance in these films.

As he investigates the death of Colonel McFay, Nick tricks Nora into staying home instead of coming with him to Smitty's with the police by obnoxiously playing on her feelings for her child. He tells her he hears the baby crying, and when she goes to check, he leaves with the police. However, because Nora is at home, it is she who receives a phone call from an informant with crucial information on the McFay murder case; Nick's attempts to turn Nora's maternity into a weakness end up being counterproductive. As a result of Nick's ploy, Nora is not out of the way, but instead way ahead of him, arriving at the West Indies Club before he does, for the next clue. Interestingly, like Nick, the audience doesn't know this for a while. For a time, the audience thinks Nora *has* been relegated to the home. Her visibility becomes an issue, in fact, just when Nick appears to be at his most stereotypical, exercising his freedom to be part of the action and to remain sexually attractive to women while the "little woman" is sheltered at home.

Nick indeed makes his way to the West Indies Club without the tip to which Nora is privy, having found the usual matchbook with the crucial name on it at Smitty's. At the club, surrounded by beautiful women, he receives a mysterious note, purportedly from Bella Spruce, reading, "Sweetheart, if you still remember poor little me and my coal yard in Cleveland, won't you come over and have a drinkie for old times sake?" The tone of the note makes it clear to the audience that Nora is playing with Nick and that she is now in the game. When Nick looks up to see a crowd of men, behind which the charmer is, it would seem, invisible in the thick of her admirers, the dynamics of audience and film become intricate, making the spectator as much a part of Nora's joke as Nick is, in a lovely moment of shifting possibilities that play with the way we read mysteries. Prefigurations of the appearances of characters are often scripted this way in Hollywood movies. But here the convention is being used as part of the husband/wife charade rather than to create suspense about the main action. A role-playing game of suspense is involved here, since there is Nick's motivation to think about. Nick was not in on the conversation between Nora and the detectives, so there is an ambiguity about how many possibilities Nick is entertaining about the identity of the note sender. Weaving through this indeterminate to-ing and fro-ing between the pair is the audience's knowledge that neither Nick nor Nora could have known in advance that the other would be at the West Indies Club, and so the joke on the mechanics of the popular culture genre of detective fiction contains a second level. The result is more than a humorous set piece about jealousy, former sweethearts, marital fidelity, and insouciant teasing.

As Nick makes his way toward the throng of admirers and penetrates the crowd, moving the gents aside in a debonair, graceful manner; as Nora lifts her eyes to him from within the ring with a provocative glance that bespeaks her triumph over his attempt to sideline her, the viewer is caught up within the organic dynamic of this pair. This dynamic trumps not only the conventional definition of male and female roles but also the artificialities of plot construction.

As Nick and Nora frolic through the conventional movie-mystery landscape, in which people seem to be interchangeable cogs in gears that shift with the impetus of greed and self-advancement, the audience gets to experience through Nick and Nora the kind of spontaneous connection that stands as a salutary alternative to the way of the world. Without missing a beat, Nick, on finding himself in the presence of his wife, the universal object of desire, displayed in her most ravishing finery, shifts into a spontaneous play scenario: "Why mommie [his pet name for Nora since the birth of their child], you know better than to come to a place like this your first day out of bed. What if the health officers find you? They'll put you right back in quarantine." Spontaneously picking up the thread, Nora responds, "I won't stay in quarantine. I don't care who catches it!" The men around her politely flee the newly constructed contagion. Nick and

Nora's connection defies the limits of language, time, and place. They use language in play to create their own special meanings, here about the limits Nick seeks to impose on Nora, and the bonding meanings flow without paying dues to time and circumstance. The two pick up each other's subtext without requiring the continuity of action. No "what are you doing here" for these two. The ordinary desire evoked in men by women as attractive objects is simply blown away by the force of a kind of mutual process of indeterminate and ambiguous knowing of the other that makes use of whatever materials culture provides to find its way.

The battle continues when the two go to the Chesterfield Arms apartment house, following the trail of new clues gleaned at the club, Nick somewhat grudgingly taking Nora along, and once again seeking to ditch her when they reach the apartment house that they need to search for further information. Once again, Nora is sidelined only to pop up with a surprise for Nick. The pair constructs an approach to the search as they stand on the doorstep of the building, Nick standing back to force Nora into a position that will ultimately marginalize her. Nora, forced to take the initiative, stammers, "We would like to—" At this point Nick changes the terms of the visit, improvising a new situation. They are not together. "Go right ahead, madame; you got here first." Nora now falls into Nick's trap by improvising her intention to rent a room, so that Miss Dolley (Marjorie Main), as Nick hopes, will shove Nora into a room to inspect it, while he seductively charms Dolley into letting him search the area that has now become pertinent to the crime.

Again, their improvisational spontaneity permits them to play out the competition in their marriage—instead of being played by it—setting them into their own level of reality apart from the ordinary tangle of corrupt and isolated souls. Miss Dolley, who has the tone of a bordello madame, seeks to curry favor with Nick when he reveals that the "other party" looking at a room is mighty attractive to him. When Miss Dolley tells Nick she "will see what she can arrange," lightly dismissing Nick's polite declining of her offer because he is married, we know she has done this often, and that she fits right in with the isolated, depersonalized world of the series. Her pandering is highly comic because it contrasts so dramatically with the values that audiences, due to the many repetitions in the series films, know that Nick and Nora represent. When Nora extricates herself from the room in which she is supposedly interested and comes nosing around where Nick is searching, Dolley makes the appropriate introductions. She has seen Nick in the newspapers and knows his name, which she offers to Nora, prompting Nora to offer her name, since Dolly doesn't know it. "Finhadden," says Nora, "Letty Finhadden." Nora thus completes the gag begun in the West Indies Club, as she drops the other shoe provided her inadvertently by the police interrogation. Again, a complex relationship between audience and film surges, as Nick takes up Nora's gamut, acknowledging her talents and skills in detecting, swelling with delight and respect. He takes her face between his hands, kisses her, and walks off with her, leaving Miss Dolley completely flustered by his "fast work." Again there is a radical disjunction between the values of the culture and the world of Nick and Nora. To Dolley, this looks like a lightning-quick pickup between strangers, while it is in fact another cycle of commitment between two very connected people. Similarly, though Nora is offered by Dolley to Nick as an object, the transaction is really about Nora forcing Nick to recognize her agency. This kind of playful passing of themselves off as lovers meeting behind the back of Nick's wife occurs a number of times in the series. The police and Nick's underworld chums all are willing to wink at what they think is Nick's infidelity, as well as to believe that the glamourous Nora is a sex object. It is another of the elements in the film that creates tension between ordinary reality and that of the Synergistic Couple. Nick and Nora can see into the lack of connection in the world—a world that cannot look back perceptively at their organic wholeness—which causes a young woman to murder her father.

Shadow of the Thin Man continues the playful/serious struggle between Nick and "mommie," though the series is already sliding away from the complex negotiations of the previous films. *Shadow of the Thin Man* concerns the deaths of a jockey with a good reputation and Whitey Barrow (Alan Baxter), a reporter with a bad reputation. The first turns out to be an accidental death, but the second is crucial to the central corruption in the film: the intrusion of the racketeers into the sport of horse racing. A reporter who is a friend of the Charleses, Paul Clarke (Barry Nelson), is mistakenly charged with the murder and his girlfriend, Molly Ford (Donna Reed), is charged as an accomplice. The two younger actors are a good example of the more or less anonymous Functional Couple, not really a screen couple in terms of the working definition of this book, but rather a perfunctory story element, a cog in the machine of the plot, which allows them to come together as their ultimate union creates a conventional marker that identifies the kind of mechanical wholeness that plot guarantees for the audience. As a garden-variety Functional Couple, Molly and Paul are examples of the kind of unalloyed Nordic beauty—actually rather bland and uninteresting in the pale petiteness and symmetricality of the facial features—that is mistakenly associated with the Hollywood couple in general. They are relatively more important in this film than conventional devices had previously been in the Nick and Nora series, and bog the film down in cliche, as do the movie's ethnic cliches—a befuddled, obese black maid and a streetwise, earthy Jewish character as police lieutenant Abrams (Sam Wannamaker).

Shadow of the Thin Man is indeed a shadow of the previous films. After a jockey is murdered at the racetrack, Major Scully (Henry O'Neill), a silver-haired, upper-crust patriarch who has been hired by the state legislature to look into racketeering at the track, gets involved in the investigation, along with the police and the Charleses. The first suspects are Link Stevens (Loring Smith) and Fred Macy (Joseph Anthony), two early filmic representations of organized crime, but as soon as reporter Whitey Barrow is killed the suspicion shifts to Paul Clarke and Molly Ford, Stevens's secretary. Then, when Stevens's girlfriend, Claire Porter (Stella Adler), is found to have been a blackmail victim of Barrow's, the suspicion moves to her. But it soon moves again to a small-time bookie named Rainbow Benny, when he is discovered dead in his apartment, seemingly a suicide, with the burnt remains of Link Stevens's missing record book in his fireplace. A slip on Scully's part about where Benny's apartment is alerts Nick, finally, to the real killer: Scully has forged a partnership with Stevens—protection from investigation for a part of the illegal profits—and Whitey Barrow threatened the "sweet deal" with exposure.

During this racetrack murder mystery, no longer as playful about the devices of mystery films, no longer as playful about social mores, Nora's desires are held up to ridicule much more than they are granted validity, as previously. During the course of Nick's investigation, Nora is effectively sidelined, though she continues to exist on her own terms as a person who does not accept Nick's bullying, and certainly as a woman who is both desiring and desired. At one point, Nora insists on being taken to a wrestling match, and she wears a ridiculously inappropriate chiffon cocktail dress and a huge picture hat worn at a forty-five-degree angle on her upswept hair. The hat makes Nora the butt of a series of jokes that may make fun of glamour, but at Nora's expense rather than as part of her ludic honesty. At another point, when she wants to go with Nick to hunt for clues, he rather arrogantly sends her home to slip into an exciting negligee, adding insult to injury by sadistically suggesting that sex will not follow when he returns, but that he will see her in the morning. Nora follows Nick, regardless, and is defeated by the outsized hat, which gets in the way of her physical flexibility in hunting for clues. When Nick leaves Nora and Molly to do men's work with Lieutenant Abrams and Paul Clarke, Nora grabs Molly, as we expect her to do, and orders a cabbie to "follow that car," which he does, but without the ladies in it, a feeble joke that once again ruins the previous balances between Nick and Nora. All the clues in this film are discovered by Asta instead of Nora.

The scenes in which Nick and Nora's sublime connection is most clearly probed are scenes between Nick and Claire, Stevens's moll, in which Nora does not appear, in her apartment and in the apartment of the recently deceased Whitey Barrow. Claire is a shadow Nora, as Steven perhaps is a shadow Nick. Like Nora, Claire is always elegantly dressed in luxurious fashion, and always forced to spend her time in dingy settings with which her style contrasts. Claire, like Nora, keeps her nose in the air around her seedy male colleagues, and like Nora, she speaks with an annoyingly elite upper-class diction and tone. Like Nora, she radiates a seductive glamour that she unabashedly uses to gain influence with men. Unlike Nora, however, Claire isn't playing around. Her ability to manipulate the signs of aristocratic femininity are a deadly serious business to her. She comes from a distinctly disadvantaged background, and cultivation of the "right" style has been her means of pulling herself out of the gutter. For Stevens, an upwardly mobile lower-class man like Nick, Claire is a mask of legitimacy. There is no play between them, and no loyalty either. They are Nick and Nora as they would be if they were locked into social norms, a situation as true of criminals as of "decent folk" in this series, if the criminals use force where the decent folk use hypocrisy. When Nick comes to see Claire, she tries to take control of the interview, as Nora does, but through a calculated use of her heady perfume, her charming offer to Nick of one of her white carnations (tenderly proffered in her long, white fingers) as a boutonniere, and her flattery. Nowhere in evidence is Nora's manic appreciation of gender politics as a serious game with inferior tools. That he is immune is not a factor of his lower-class common sense (Stevens has that too) or his general desire to keep a distance between himself and women. Nick, like the spectator, is organically connected to a Nora who is available to the audience and to him as energy, not as a spectacle of stately attire and manners.

But a great deal of Nora's ability to define Claire's shoddiness is a matter of slippage from earlier films. In this film, she is not only the butt of jokes about her marginality, but even when she propels herself into the center of things, her desire to take an active part in life is more laughable than not. In the obligatory revelation scene at the end of *Shadow of the Thin Man*, in Lieutenant Abrams's office, Nora gets her chance to make fun of the cliched suspense of the mystery film convention, as Nick takes his own sweet time revealing the name of the murderer, saying, "Nickie, I can't stand it. Was it me?" However, when Nick reveals that Major Scully (Henry O'Neill) is the murderer and Scully grabs Nick's gun, Nora is ridiculed again when she throws herself at the gun-toting murderer in a seemingly brave gesture. It turns out that Nora is hysterical and later has no recollection of her behavior. Furthermore, Nick has been carrying a gun with no bullets in it. Knowing nothing of Nick's plans, she is foolish in her dithering anxiety to protect him. The balance is shifting between them toward an ominously dominant patriarchal stance on Nick's part, a shift that continues in the next film.

The dumbing down of Nora reaches its extreme in the next and fifth film, *The Thin Man Goes Home*, with which the series became temporarily an ode to the family and the bonding between father and son. In this film, Nick is given a righteous country doctor for a father, a detail that overlooks completely the conversation between Nick and Nora in the third film, *Another Thin Man*, when Nick suggests that his father was a rather shady character. In that film, when Nora says, "My father was just as honest as yours," Nick counters, "Someday, you'll find out what a hot recommendation that is." Made toward the end of World War II, *The Thin Man Goes Home* mirrors the desperation in the country to hang on to the myths of bedrock America, and alas, what Nora found was a falsification of the series in which she had participated for ten years. As befits the needs of the country, she becomes sidelined as a cheerleader for Nick, as he tries to win his father's approval, talking about the role of American men in the battle without once mentioning the war, which appears in the overt text of the film only at the end, when the weapon of death is revealed to be a Japanese gun brought back from the war by the murderer's brother, certainly an isolationist reference to the contamination America was suffering from so much foreign exposure, and a prefiguration of the Red Scare that flared up after the war.[15] The flattening of the Synergistic Couple into the same realm of reality as Nick's supposed small-town family in this disastrous part of the series proves by exception what is important about the Nick and Nora films, for they almost cease to exist here, falling to the level of George and Gracie or Dagwood and Blondie.

In the last film, *Song of the Thin Man*—the swan song, as it turned out—the couple regains some of its energy and oppositionality, but the postwar changes in Hollywood and in the country have created a new environment in which Nick and Nora have become obsolete. In the preceding Thin Man films, the solution of the crime brings the situation back to an artificial, plot-induced form of harmony, corrupting elements having been purged, that almost eradicates perception of the organic connection between Nick and Nora. At the end of the last Thin Man film, there is a kind of unease that pervaded the postwar American film noir and that renders Nick and Nora's organic connection insufficient. Moreover, Nora cannot even play off Nick's customary authority, since for a good deal of the movie, they both seem lost, adrift in a context in which they don't understand the language: the jazz lingo of the musicians among whom the murder was committed. The murder of Tommy Drake, a corrupt bandleader, occurred as the result of greed and a disloyal relationship between a husband and wife. Phyllis Talbin (Patricia Morison), wife of promoter Mitch Talbin (Leon Ames), is in love with womanizing Drake. In the standard revelation scene at the end, Nick has gathered all the suspects on the casino boat. He puts the pieces together so compellingly that Mitch confesses to having killed Tommy to keep him away from Phyllis; at this point Phyllis kills Mitch, having sworn to avenge Tommy. It is a strange scene for the series, in which two people point guns at each other, an image that has now become common. The impact is deepened because they are husband and wife, and this is a series dominated by a very different image of husband and wife.

The culminating image of Phyllis and Mitch is only the last and most intensive representation of the angst and adversarial stances we have previously seen throughout the narrative, but the extremes of murder to which Phyllis and Mitch go are not justified by the story, as we see when Nick explains the pieces of the puzzle; the logic is not compelling. There is a sense in this film of an inexplicable universe in which Nick and Nora contrast as comparatively *less ambiguous*. Their balance and relatedness seem to form a new norm in the context of a postwar image of a senseless disconnected universe, a universe embedded in another couple who are tied to the murder by the thinnest strands and yet who seem to symbolize this universe more than do the Charleses: Fran Page (Gloria Graham, strongly associated with film noir), the former singer in the Drake band, whom Mitch killed to keep his secret, and Buddy Hollis (Don Taylor), a jazz musician in Tommy's band who has declined into alcoholism and madness because Fran deserted him for Tommy. In his confused state, Hollis has been fooled by Mitch into thinking he committed the murder.

Buddy and Fran are not characters bedeviled by greed or disloyalty but by disintegration. Neither of them is coherent, or, in psychological terms, neither has a unified ego. They cannot hold together under stress, nor can they hold together for each other even though they are actually quite deeply attached. They open into the Charles universe a kind of fragmentation that obsessed the postwar West, and at the end of the film their losses remain a gaping wound in the film of the type that would be increasingly a part of the post-studio film, and that a new generation of Synergistic Couples (see Chapter Six) would be configured to deal with. In Nick and Nora's world, the malaise represented by Buddy and Fran remains intractable. Fran is killed trying to help her former lover, and Buddy remains insane, although Nick saves him from a murder prosecution. To do this Nick speaks for Buddy, though he is incapable of actually entering into Buddy's point of view. Instead, he says what Buddy "would have said" if he were whole and coherent. The ploy to catch the killer involves bringing Buddy from the sanitarium back to the jazz scene to play and then "make an announcement that's going to throw a little bombshell into the Tommy Drake murder case." Buddy plays with the band, but when he is called upon to make his announcement, he cannot speak. What Nick says as Buddy's surrogate voice explains who killed Tommy Drake; it does not explain Buddy's disintegration, nor does it explain why Fran, against her best judgment and even most powerful feelings, betrayed Buddy, for not only does the last Thin Man film spotlight the usual elements of greed and selfishness, it calls the very coherence of the self into question.

In light of the enigma of such global human disintegration, Nick and Nora's parrying no longer seems either compelling or scintillating, for their synergy presumes the inviolability of the stable self, and thus does not address the uncanny manifestations in the movie. There is now something tired about Nora noticing the pertinent clues and Nick making deductions but keeping them from her in this film. She gets off a few good lines, as for example when she notices some interesting discrepancies in Phyllis's jewelry, an observation that leads directly to ascertaining what happened to Tommy Drake. Nick looks in Phyllis's direction, ostensibly at the jewelry, and Nora remarks, "The earrings are higher up." This line was criticized by the PCA, but remained in the film, or at least is in the current videotapes in circulation. But on the whole her challenges and his defense of his authority are rather static, as is the scene in their apartment after they return from having "solved" the mystery. Nora's quip, "And to think you did it all with your own little hatchet," makes her sound more like a nagging wife than a vibrant partner negotiating for appropriate recognition. And she follows her tired remark with a cliched pat on the back for him about how proud she is. The original script had called for the film to end in their bedroom, but the PCA, empowered by the wartime desire for simpleminded, unambiguous images, was able, sadly, to prevail in its rejection of that final image, and it was replaced by a few frames in which Asta is caught by Nick and Nora in bed with Nicky Jr., and, knowing that he shouldn't be there, pretends to scurry out only to return to snuggling with Nicky Jr., as soon as Nick and "mommie" leave the room. Asta's triumph over the rules, a triumph Nick and Nora couldn't achieve, is both a pathetic last visual of this depleted series, and a sad in-joke made by the creative team about censorship and sexuality.

MOLDED!

Nevertheless, Loy and Powell, in the synergistic Thin Man series at its dimmest, embody the capacity for intimacy with a documentary vividness that compares favorably with the formulaic films Loy and Powell made together, which harness their combined charisma for idealized male and female stereotypes, idealized as mates within the terms of that society. That Loy and Powell *could*, during the same period of time, move between films that unleashed their synergy and films that domesticated it to reductive cliches substantially demonstrates how remote from the control of the involved principals is the existence of the Synergistic Couple in the mass media. We have seen that Weissmuller and O'Sullivan's combined energies were a matter of pure serendipity, unalloyed with issues of acting skill, conventional visual paradigms for pairing actors, or cleverness of plot and dialogue. What brought out their gift to the movies was plenty of screen time for pure sound and visual image that would imprint their spontaneous ability to move into the intimate space that some actors inhabit with each other. The alternative to the opening up of such a space between acting partners is the ability that other kinds of actors have to snap into a preset mode of response that is organized around their understanding of character types, a range of calculated verbal and physical gestures.[16] Of the actors who snap into a restricted range, partner work depends on the compatibility of the ranges of the individual actors. Of the actors who open up an intimate space in which to work with a partner, partner work depends on whether or not that space will open up with any given actor. Most actors are one kind or the other, in terms of their own performances and in terms of couple work; a few can shift among modes, depending on the partner. Loy and Powell are quite unique in their ability to shift between modes with the same partner, though clearly neither knew that they had two modes of pair work.[17]

Nevertheless, while the Loy/Powell non-synergistic films are generally very well acted and often smoothly and effectively directed, their characterizations are formed along clear, crisp lines. Very little in their performances is enigmatic or inexplicable. Very little leaves wiggle room for the imagination; the films are pitched toward the shallower faculties of logic. These performances very handily compliment the ordinary fictional universes in which ambiguity and indeterminacy are impediments to a world of hard-edged normality. If such ambiguity should occur in the eight non–Thin Man films, it is soon clarified, in the typical Hollywood attempt to prevent anxiety on the part of the spectator. Loy and Powell's jobs in these projects are to build clearly defined situations with each other. Their visual images in these projects are similarly unambiguous. We see nothing that cannot be explained by its relationship to the plot.

Only a representative sampling of these films is necessary to explore Loy and Powell's alternative work methods. For this purpose, I have chosen *Evelyn Prentice* (1934, Dir. William K. Howard), one of only three formulaic melodramas made by Loy and Powell; and one screwball comedy, *Double Wedding* (1937, Dir. Richard Thorpe).

Evelyn Prentice is a standard, neglected-wife courtroom melodrama. Working within the constraints of many old cliches, in this film Loy is the eponymous heroine, the virtuous wife of a prestigious and successful lawyer, John Prentice (William Powell). Neglected by her extremely busy but loving husband, Evelyn is courted by that well-known desperado, the fortune-hunting poet (!), Larry Kennard (Harvey Stephens), the philandering live-in boyfriend of Judith Wilson (Isabel Jewell). Evelyn resists his seductions until Nancy Harrison (Rosalind Russell), a wealthy, glamourous, sultry client whose life John saves, plants evidence to make Evelyn think that John is having an affair with her (a narrative ellipsis makes it unclear to what extent he encouraged Harrison's ardor). In anger, Evelyn goes to Kennard's apartment, but then thinks better of it, and despite her disappointment with her husband, tries to break off with the seducer (a narrative ellipsis makes it quite unclear as to whether or not the poet is a would-be or successful seducer). Kennard turns nasty and eventually threatens to show Evelyn's husband three innocent but compromising notes Evelyn sent him unless she gives him fifteen thousand dollars. Evelyn sees a revolver in the drawer Kennard has opened to retrieve the letters, grabs it, and threatens him if he will not give the letters to her. He complies. The scene shifts to the street door of the apartment house, where Judith Wilson, in entering the building, hears a gunshot. By the time Judith gets up the stairs, Evelyn has fled the scene, and keeps her secret for most of the movie, though guilt moves her to persuade her husband to defend Judith, who has been accused of murder in the case of Kennard's death. Just as it seems that Judith will be convicted, Evelyn confesses in court. John Prentice comprehends in a flash how lonely his wife has been, and, even beyond that, that Judith Wilson is in fact actually guilty. Cross-examining his own client, he ferrets out new evidence that Kennard was not dead when Evelyn left after the gun went off by accident, and proves that Judith then killed him in an argument over Evelyn. Now vindicated, but feeling unworthy of the love of a good man, Evelyn makes plans to sacrifice her happiness for her husband and daughter and leave forever. But John forgives her and they make plans for a six-month European vacation for the whole family.

Evelyn Prentice turns on a highly contrived plot that requires cliched characters acting out of simple motives. There is little ambiguity, aside from the question of whether Kennard and Evelyn actually had sex, which, in terms of the emphasis on resolution of the plot suspense about whether or not Evelyn will go to jail, doesn't matter much anyhow. Evelyn is a stereotypical Hollywood upper-class wife whose glamour is her natural state, not a series of effects, as it is presented in Nora Charles's situation. Marriage, stereotypically, is rightly a formal arrangement that leaves out the possibility of play: between male ambition and female household duties there is neither time nor reason for it. Any resistance to the ideal is clearly corrupt. Who is sorry that marriage has changed Evelyn from a spirited girl into a poised and proper woman? Only Evelyn's promiscuous, overly reckless, single friend Amy Drexel (Una Merkel). Amy, the unmarriageable woman, is clear proof that energy of any kind is inevitably transgressive in a woman, and Evelyn isn't "like that." Similarly, Evelyn is distinguished from Nancy Harrison, who is sexually aggressive, and also transgressive. Evelyn isn't "like that" either. Judith Wilson is also transgressive, living with a man without benefit of clergy. Evelyn isn't comparable there either. Evelyn's goodness is stereotypically equated with passivity, a portrait that Loy draws for the audience by mustering all the restraint at her command and giving an almost seamlessly static performance. Class issues are present in her inadvertent rivalry with the lower-class Judith Wilson, but in expedient Hollywood tradition the film defines Wilson as expendable, well sacrificed to the "real" upper-class family, so utterly dysfunctional in the Thin Man series, and here the paragon of American life, whose troubles come from outside.

William Powell is equally rigid as John Prentice. The conventional "good provider," he is not particularly criticized by the film for being an absentee husband and father since he is keeping his family, thereby, in the lap of luxury. Moreover, his regrettable, if undefined, lapse with Nancy Harrison, quite in keeping with the cultural double standard, is far more catastrophic for Evelyn than for him. Similarly, matching the pattern Mulvey noted, as described above, Evelyn's happiness is the end of the glamour that makes her too attractive to potential Lotharios. By the "happy ending" of the film, her evolution has taken her well beyond the diminution of her pre-marriage zip. Wearing the dowdiest outfit she has worn in the film, Evelyn is no longer the queen she was at the beginning. The film delights in a terminus in which all disruptive energy (hers) has been harmonized to the patriarchal domestic hierarchy, while the potentially disruptive lower classes are either dead or constrained in jail. Loy and Powell turn in (very good) recipe performances full of stock gestures and well-modulated line readings. Their manic energy erupts in only one scene, in which John, who has been alerted by Amy to Evelyn's knowledge of his vaguely sinister connection with Nancy Harrison, tries to make amends. His efforts are too little too late—Evelyn is already involved deeply with Kennard. John joins Evelyn and their daughter in a little exercise time that brings out briefly the wild impulses of the two actors, but this is quickly reabsorbed back into the stiffness of their standard characterizations, which facilitate the dramatic formula.

Loy and Powell also did some non-synergistic screwball comedies together. There is in these films a certain amount of tension between the couple charisma of the acting partners and the formulaic plot structures, which in the case of *Double Wedding* is a carnivalized fantasy about a repressed upper-class woman and a free-spirited man. In this, the non-synergistic film they made together that most threatens to disrupt formulaic scripts, Powell and Loy each play a single facet of the multifaceted characters they created in the Thin Man series. Powell's Bohemian Charlie Lodge is Nick Charles bereft of his more controlling, patriarchal urges, a man whose body simply has a will of its own and whose energy turns the world upside down. Loy played the rigid formality of Nora without her leavening spirit of play.

In this movie, marriage is little more than a sober responsibility in the mind of Margit Agnew (Loy), who has spent her life making a fortune as a dress designer so she could bring her younger sister Irene (Florence Rice) up properly. Margit does no living herself; instead she micromanages Irene's life to the nth degree, including picking out Waldo (John Beal) as a husband for Irene and keeping him in their house for four years until Margit herself sets the wedding day. At night, while Margit sleeps, the only time Irene has any freedom, she and Waldo sneak out to Charlie Lodge's trailer, where they rehearse his screenplay and dream of stardom in Hollywood. When Margit discovers Irene's secret, she and Charlie clash. The stage is set for love. But in a film like this, where Loy and Powell function as an Iconic Couple rather than as a Synergistic Couple, freedom is an abstract idea, not an embodied form of energy. Loy, playing a stereotypical repressed and controlling career woman, loathes Charlie's freewheeling lifestyle and lack of discipline. But Powell also plays a type, a cliche of a free spirit. They go through the motions of liberation, but there is nothing to liberate, as all the characters are equally mechanical. Charlie sees in Margit—under her buttoned-down suit, presumably—a quality that he has tried to encourage in Irene and Waldo, fruitlessly, as they read his work: "Yumph," or "IT!"—that Hollywood euphemism for sexual magnetism. Charlie finagles ways to get to know Margit better and win her love, and finally, in desperation, he stages a mock wedding to Irene in his cramped trailer, hoping that this will encourage Margit to acknowledge her desire for him and at the same time inspire Waldo to be a man—to defy Margit and make love to Irene on his own terms. In a final scene that resembles the stateroom scene in the Marx Brothers' *A Night at the Opera* (1935, Dir. Sam Wood), all hell breaks loose at the overcrowded wedding. But the raucous ending is still the predictable final link in a mechanical chain of incidents that lead inexorably to the requisite happy ending, in which Waldo finally gains his manhood and carries Irene off caveman style, as Margit and Charlie announce their love for each other and then are each knocked unconscious in a flurry of flying paint and floral tributes.

Unlike the synergistic Nick and Nora, multidimensional people who reveal the human capacity thwarted by social institutions, Charlie and Margit are as cartoonlike as all the other characters—just more energetically so. However, the film does achieve a certain amount of dimensionality through its use of Charlie's attempt to make something of his film script. As the characters work on the script, we are led to think about the contrast between the "reality" of the characters and their ability to assume roles. Charlie's screenplay is an absurd pastiche of the final scene in *Morocco* (1930, Dir. Josef von Sternberg), exaggerating the already hyperbolic finale of that film, in which Marlene Dietrich as Amy Jolly takes off her sandals and follows Gary Cooper as Tom Brown and his Foreign Legion regiment across the sand into unknown dangers and certain death. There is endless subterfuge in *Double Wedding*'s attempt to lull us into believing that *that's* what screenplays are like, artificial and ridiculous, at the same time that we are supposed to suspend disbelief about the movie that we are actually watching, *Double Wedding*. When Charlie teaches Waldo how to play a love scene with Irene, he similarly shifts from his "ordinary life," the set of cliches about Bohemians that the movie expects us to take as reality, into a set of formulaic but potent gestures (filled with Yumph). So we know that people can move into gestures of feelings that they don't actually feel. But we don't actually see any characters in the movie that go beyond mechanical impersonation.

Later in the film, Charlie reminds the audience that we also can feel what we can't show when he tries to tutor Waldo to woo Irene by learning the right gestures by which to display his desire for her. But, of course, the character of Waldo is a cliche of a Milquetoast, so his "feelings" do not exist anywhere in the movie except as an idea. So when Waldo carries Irene off in a drunken stupor that permits him to emerge from his shell, it's all part of the mechanics of the narrative, just words and contrived actions. Margit and Charlie's mutual unconsciousness at the wedding is more promising. Sinking beneath the verbal and plot level by going into the subconscious indicates another level of existence, even if it has not been shown anywhere else in the film. That the film ends in storytelling limbo is its boldest aspect regarding the representation of couples. If intimacy is to be represented, those wild surges must find some place in the movie.

The chemistry of Loy and Powell in their non-synergistic performances often facilitates a delightful use of a formulaic script by two powerhouse performers, using only a small percentage of their full range of performance techniques, resulting in a couple of star turns as an Iconic Couple that in the end support Old Hollywood cliches. However, to preserve the complications of a very interesting screen partnership, even when Loy and Powell used the acting mode of snapping into a limited range of performance gestures, they exhibited a compatibility that is quite notable in comparison to Powell's other screen ventures as a detective. Previous to his work with Loy, he had played a detective in Warner Brothers' Philo Vance series, where he portrayed the traditional lone wolf detective. Urbane, detached, and incisive, Vance is a Sherlockian sleuth for whom the world is a solvable puzzle. A male authority figure, he rights a disheveled world upset by passion, generally of the unrequited sort, as in *The Kennel Murder Case* (1933, Dir. Michael Curtiz), in which the culprit is a rejected lover driven to frenzy. The couple in this film is completely functional, an obligatory appendage, subject to imbalances that Vance rebalances through his dispassionate objectivity. Powell's performance as Vance, which was and still is highly regarded, is a mechanical display of acting virtuosity. Powell is stiff and often stentorian in comparison with his ventures with Loy, but he uses his techniques to render lengthy, pontifical speeches so that they will not put the audience to sleep.

Except for his work with Loy, Powell's detective films continued to feature mechanical performances that lacked the grace of even his non–Thin Man films with her. Powell was never cast more than once in a detective film with any other actress, and each of those experiments was clearly an attempt to imitate his work as Nick Charles. One such film is *Star of Midnight* (1935, Dir. Stephen Roberts), for which RKO borrowed William Powell from MGM to star him with Ginger Rogers in a role calculated to remind the audience of his Nick Charles image. However, even though he and Rogers had each succeeded as part of a synergistic pair with another acting confederate, their work together in that film is quite formulaic, making it a vivid example of the difference between synergistic chemistry and a professional but formulaic partnership. In *Star of Midnight*, Powell plays Clay Dalzell (Dal), a wealthy lawyer who doesn't want to get involved with detective work but is lured into it by Donna Manton (Ginger Rogers), a madcap debutante. This situation echoes the Thin Man trope of Nora's encouragement of Nick against his will to be a detective despite the cushion of her wealth, now that they are married. The story of *Star* also mechanically mimics *The Thin Man*. It begins with a disappearance, here that of an actress named Alice Markham, never seen in the film. The man who loves her wants to find her. Dalzell solves the mystery, Donna trailing after him, annoying him with both her interest in helping him solve the case—she finds clues just as Nora did—and her persistent demand that he marry her. They solve the case and he marries her. The cliched definition of Dalzell as stereotypical bon vivant and Manton as an equally stereotypical free-spirited society girl (who has none of the complexity of Nora) also discourages any enduring interest in the film. Moreover, the fact that she is young enough to be his daughter disappears, as a potential complication, into the cartoonlike characters and formulaic situation. Powell and Rogers are each snapped into that very limited band of possibilities in their acting modes and choices. They remain completely parallel to each other as performers creating a static couple out of two potentially powerful stars. A similar effect is created in *The Ex-Mrs. Bradford* (1936, Dir. Stephen Roberts), for which RKO borrowed Powell from MGM in another vain attempt to build on the Thin Man success with a reluctant detective and a debutante paramour, this time an ex-wife.

CONCLUSION

The synergistic films of the Thin Man series thus distinguish themselves from the non-series movies made by Loy and Powell and from the doomed attempts to imitate the synergy between Loy and Powell in copycat mystery films like *Star of Midnight*. The repeated Thin Man pairings of Powell and Loy evolved toward an increasingly rich and multifaceted onscreen energy. The Thin Man films as a whole, though, began to move toward a more formulaic pattern with the 1941 *Shadow of the Thin Man*. The 1942 *The Thin Man Goes Home*, in which Loy and Powell had to work with a new production team that treated the Charles family as if they were Frank Capra creations, marked the low point for the series. The flattening of the Charleses' energy reflected larger social and political changes in the country during World War II, which was probably less a matter of the ability of the PCA to enforce its code, as many think, than it was a matter of increased societal demand for war propaganda. The destructive social pressure continued after the war, when creative teams in Hollywood were intimidated by a postwar hysteria about purported Communist enemy agents—agents that could be anywhere, disguised as ordinary citizens, threatening the bedrock of American life. This frenzy coerced Hollywood into depicting life in unambiguous, hard-edged terms that simplistically polarized good and evil, hardly a fertile ground for the complexities of the Synergistic Couple, and much more suited to the bottom-line Functional Couple (see Chapter One).

The abatement of synergy under these wartime and postwar pressures is sufficiently significant that had the last two films in the series been the only ones to have been made, no one would remember Nick and Nora at all; the same might be said for Loy and Powell if all that existed of their work was their delightful but formulaic non-series comedies and melodramas, which serve as exemplars of the kind of cultural artifacts decried by Mulvey, Wexman, and others as purveyors of dominant ideology. Yet such films arguably represent only the most disposable part of what Hollywood does with couples. There is another aspect to Hollywood's mode of depicting couples, exemplified by the earlier, synergistic, Thin Man films, in which Loy and Powell as Nora and Nick created an ever-deepening organic rapport that stood in shining contrast to the mechanistic society surrounding them. These films are informed by extraordinarily subtle and complex explorations of Otherness, which distinguish them from the very large number of Hollywood couple depictions that have come to stand as the limits of possibilities for this kind of portrayal in the mass media. The best of the Thin Man series played with the perspective of a masculine norm, which narrates the relationship between male and female in terms of a hierarchy topped by white men, the exclusive relationship between language and masculinity that leaves women outside the circle of expression, the founding of the couple on the basis of trading women as property, and the gender recipe that calls for the configuration of masculine/dominant and female/submissive. Male entitlement was Nick's idea, one with which Nora, whose point of view was often given parity with Nick's, didn't agree, creating opportunities for incongruity, humor, and ludic competition that upset many assumed gender rules. More serious, the idea of "woman" as a vehicle for the exchange of goods sometimes threatened to expose a raw nerve at the core of the Charles marriage, supported almost entirely by Nora's inheritance. At the same time, the films never dealt with the harsh realities of the situation—what would happen if the money were to disappear. Did Nick's cynical humor betoken a basic and organic bond that distinguished Nick from all the opportunistic fortune hunters in their adventures? The implicit answer is a resounding yes, but an implicit mode of representation stands or falls on education. The palpable class issues could easily be glossed over by the unsophisticated spectator who wished to concentrate on the Powell/Loy charm.

While Nick and Nora may be considered melioristic from some perspectives—like Tarzan and Jane, they represented a special instance that could not be emulated by real couples in dealing with these issues—they also offered a good deal more than the seamless illusions of the non-series films made by Loy and Powell. The non-series films offered mere escape from financial depression and war. They permitted a mass audience to imagine itself as secure at the top of the class system; questioning of any kind would have ruined escapist comfort. The humor and drama in those films was nothing more than the mechanical manipulation of the details of the illusion, and illusions grow old and wear out. In contrast, the synergistic Nick and Nora films offered hope of the irrepressibility of organic human connection regardless of the repressive and alienating social pressures of depression and war. The mystery in the Thin Man movies may have been presented superficially as a standard Hollywood murder investigation, but on a subtextual level that series was about the freedom granted by synergistic intimacy to Nick and Nora and their insights into the mystery of why and how people allow themselves to be entrapped as they do. They are the ancestors of many subsequent uses of the genre of mystery as a metaphor for the enigmatic interior and exterior connections between the members of a couple.

CHAPTER

FRED ASTAIRE AND GINGER ROGERS
Music Makes Me

The luminous partnership of Astaire and Rogers was comparatively brief, from 1934 to 1939, followed by a pallid one-time-only reunion ten years later in 1949, but their work as an onscreen couple has indelibly impressed on the culture its immense erotic power. They were and remain the reference point not only of all onscreen couple dancers, but of the very concept of the pair. In our culture things go together like ham and eggs, coffee and doughnuts . . . Fred and Ginger. At the same time, many believe that the movies they made are fragile, silly excuses for their exquisite dancing interludes, a strange critical platitude since the movies could never have held up as remarkably as they have had that been the case. Indeed, a closer look reveals varying degrees of organic relationship in the Astaire/Rogers films between the plots and the dancing.[1] The more organic the relationship, the better the film, at the best a counterpoint between narrative and dance that expresses through the Astaire/Rogers mating ritual a dynamic contrast between the ordinarily invisible, interior emotional life and the all too visible—and alienating—external social conventions. Their breathtaking beauty together as dancers, the extraordinary fusion of the spontaneous and the crafted in their work, made possible movies that effectively used the genre of the musical movie to illuminate the rigidity and Alice-in-Wonderland artificiality of social conventions that bedevil human relationships.

Reading the interdependence between plot and dancing is the key to the Astaire and Rogers series and its evolution of a spectrum of representations of courtship, love, intimacy, human interconnection.

Focusing on the dynamic of how the couple emerges in the Astaire/Rogers films reveals that those among their films that endure as the most moving, beautiful, and interesting are the works in which the plots and the dances have the most organic relationship to each other and to the dynamic of the Astaire/Rogers romance. Because Astaire and Rogers did not play in a series of movies about the same characters, the evolution of the couple in their films takes a route different from those of Tarzan and Jane and Nick and Nora. Each time, Astaire and Rogers sparked a new perspective on mutuality through a different complex of characters, filmic structure, design, and theme. The films in the Astaire/Rogers series each featured a distinctive new pair of lovers: Fred and Honey (*Flying Down to Rio,* 1933, Dir. Thornton Freeland), Mimi and Guy (*The Gay Divorcee,* 1934, Dir. Mark Sandrich), Lizzie and Huck (*Roberta,* 1935, Dir. William A. Seiter), Dale and Jerry (*Top Hat,* 1935, Dir. Mark Sandrich), Bake and Sherry (*Follow the Fleet,* 1935, Dir. Mark Sandrich), Lucky and Penny (*Swing Time,* 1936, Dir. George Stevens), Petrov and Linda (*Shall We Dance,* 1937, Dir. Mark Sandrich), Tony and Amanda (*Carefree,* 1938, Dir. Mark Sandrich), Vernon and Irene (*The Story of Vernon and Irene Castle,* 1939, Dir. H. C. Potter), and finally Josh and Dinah (*The Barkleys of Broadway,* 1949, Dir. Charles Walters). If the characters vary, however, the complications faced by these lovers have a typical cast to them: the quintessential Astaire/Rogers love story tended to feature obstacles that had to do with internal confusion, miscommunication, and misperception, rather than with external impediments. With one exception, *The Story of Vernon and Irene Castle*—a movie that was not in spirit an Astaire/Rogers film despite their presence in it—body images were integral to coping with misperception and misrecognition and the general failure of ordinary verbal communication. In the masquerades typical of the Astaire/Rogers film and closely related to the dance sequences, the performers' bodies are almost literally speaking about things not being what they seem, and of the organic reality that lies behind the daffy appearances that are commonly understood as ordinary life.[2]

In this special form of "speech," music plays a crucial role and one that sets it apart from that played by music in Classical Hollywood. The studio system favored keeping music firmly subordinated to ordinary verbal speech, which found form in dialogue and in the narrative purposes of the films, establishing music as a servant of the kind of stereotype and tradition officially favored by Hollywood. The cliched impact of music increased as Hollywood became increasingly interested in underlining the emotions with music, a tendency for which David O. Selznik gave himself credit, claiming it gave more harmony and unity to a film.[3] Unfortunately, Selznik's influential style of using music in movies as a unifying element undermined that which is best about popular culture, the vitality of collaboration and heterogeneity and the liberating composition aesthetic of dissonance.

Astaire and Rogers musicals, in contrast, use music and dance as a form of cultural energy that complicates, breaks up, and shades and nuances the simplistic plots of their movies. While the typical Astaire/Rogers script tells a romantic story about the bumpy road to love through familiar stories, usually of the boy pursues girl variety, the songs and particularly the dance images create complex, multiple layers of meaning around those romances that trace the interior blocks to emotion caused by zany, yet abundantly conventional, social practices.

The Astaire/Rogers festivals of music and story fall into four categories of varying complexity: major works, minor works, transitional works, and entropic works. The major Astaire/Rogers works include the three powerhouse films in which the balances between the musically based filmic language and the verbally based language of dialogue and plot reach full interconnection and expressiveness: *The Gay Divorcee, Top Hat,* and *Swing Time.* In the three minor Astaire/Rogers works, the two levels of Astaire/Rogers reality remain parallel, juxtaposed by implication rather than by a full counterpoint within the film: *Flying Down to Rio, Roberta,* and *Follow the Fleet.* Entropy began to set in by 1937. In 1937 and 1938, Astaire and Rogers made two films that can be classified as transitional films. In them the distinct reduction of the power of the musical component of the film in favor of a heavier emphasis on plot bogged the films down as compositions, although some fascinating fragments still distinguished the movies as Astaire/Rogers works: *Shall We Dance* and *Carefree.* The last two films found the Astaire/Rogers series in a state of entropy, in which the decay of the creative impulses surrounding them were reflected in the poor fit between their synergy and their final film projects: *The Story of Vernon and Irene Castle* and *The Barkleys of Broadway.*

THE MAJOR FILMS

In the major Astaire/Rogers films—*The Gay Divorcee, Top Hat,* and *Swing Time*—character and event evolve as much because of the negotiations of the Astaire and Rogers characters through images created by music and dance as because of the negotiations through dialogue and plot. These films are, therefore, within the terms of this study, examples of truly integrated musicals, balancing the nonverbal power of music and the verbal power of story, lyrics, and dialogue. The most common definition of the integrated musical has been predicated on a model that gives priority to verbal language, favoring musicals containing songs that move the plot forward, which is actually a radical compositional imbalance that subordinates the preconscious power of music to the shallow faculty of verbal logic. The enduring power of the major Astaire/Rogers musicals is based on their resistance to such an imbalance through an ongoing dynamic in which music and scripted plot comment on and transform each other. In these films, connections that are forged, through the synergy blossoming in dance and music, are almost undone by the absurd, alienating social forces at work in the script. As the growth and development of intimacy between the Astaire/Rogers characters is restarted with each new musical eruption into the plot, however, the social forces of the plot gradually lose their power as obstructions, until music, connection, and intimacy surge triumphant in the final frames.

Clearly, nothing could have been further from the conscious intent of the creators of these mass media films than the earnest philosophical debates engendered by the modernist investigation of relativity, that uneasy anxiety typical of twentieth-century thought about the instability of language and the values that it represents—in the words of T. S. Eliot, the way they "slip, slide will not stay in place." (For details of the conscious battles among Astaire, Rogers, and Mark Sandrich, please see Appendix One: "Fred, Ginger, and RKO.") Yet the results of the battles that created the major Rogers/Astaire works are popular culture equivalents of those insights. The fractured nature of social systems is just what the major Astaire/Rogers films illuminate, though they, unlike the more pessimistic of the modernists, inhabit worlds that intuit that outside of the systems, but in tandem with them, is the inherently coherent energy of intimacy, passion, and human connection. The much-noted misrecognitions by which the romances of the Astaire and Rogers characters are typically almost blighted—used with brilliance in the major films—are external and social in nature, caused by the bad fit between perception and language or arbitrary social codes. Help arrives when social formulas are besieged by the "second language" of nonverbal filmic elements organized by the music, which give scope for the transformative powers of dance. Because of the organic relationship between dance and script, the repeated castings of Astaire and Rogers do not result in mechanical imitation, though there is a central thread of theme and variations that runs through the body of work. Though Astaire and Rogers always play a couple that would have lost their connection if not for music and dance, each encounter is unique, so that when the Astaire/Rogers films are viewed in all their complexity, as compositions, they are as different from and similar to each other as one Monet painting of water lilies is to another.

In the three major works, the Astaire/Rogers couple effects its most dazzling escapes from culturally devised sexual typecasting and a mad, mad world that makes intimacy impossible, throwing the clearest light on the nature of their synergy. The actual content of these films stands in distinct opposition to the reductive, oft-repeated bromide coined by Katharine Hepburn: "He gave her class; she gave him sex." Indeed, far from fitting the cliched gender categories within which the male guarantees status and the female provides the sensual attraction, at their best, the Astaire and Rogers figures are defined by the way they do not fit stereotypes. They oppose a farcical and manufactured culture with an organic energy that comes from their bodies but does not easily find expression within the social maze of confusion. In their abilities to intuit a bad fit between social rules and reality, the Astaire and Rogers characters tend to be almost as much like each other as they are opposites. However, in the typical Astaire/Rogers movie there is much to do before each can discover the other, since reality is much obscured by social codes. The Rogers character tends to provide the resistance, the Astaire character the instigation, though not always. Her belatedness in seeing the Astaire character as her true love is, fascinatingly, generally a function of the Rogers character's anxiety about marriage, which is generally (comically) rendered problematic as an institution in the Astaire/Rogers universe in a way that ran counter to the sanctimonious attitudes about matrimony promulgated by the Production Code Administration. Similarly, the confusion of the Astaire character about the resistance of the Rogers character tends to be related to the inability of men to understand the female predicament. The journey to love in the Astaire/Rogers film tends to be a journey toward clarity that involves dispelling cliches.

Within the context of Astaire/Rogers tradition, the glamourous image with which they are so firmly associated is actually just one more element in the maze of contradictions the lovers must negotiate. In the Astaire/Rogers films, the couple pair is always costumed and groomed according to stereotypical gender definitions, she in soft and flowing feminine glamour, he in tailored and well-defined masculine attire. Likewise, their mannerisms are conventionally gender coded. Rogers has a wide gamut of tonalities and expressions, but they are all familiarly feminine, whether they be saucy, sweet, or angry. Similarly, Astaire's presentation is generally delivered in the tonality of a masculine freedom to pronounce, demand, pursue, assert. However, these polarized tonalities maintain a healthy tension with the Astaire/Rogers psychological responses, which are androgynous. The stereotypical male-female domination/submission mode is scrambled in their films. The Astaire/Rogers characters are equally assertive, witty, spirited, and playful in pursuing their desires, speaking their minds, and asserting competency as well as sexuality. These exquisite tensions between conventional glamourous appearance and unconventional mutuality is the seminal difference between the Astaire/Rogers collaborations and the films they did with others, which were indeed stylish and entertaining, but in the final analysis merely mechanical reproductions of the Hollywood formula.

The major Astaire/Rogers films are the most satisfying in purging the world of its absurd cliches through the salutary energy of bodies set to music. Though a close reading of all three would be ideal, the need for economy forecloses that possibility. However, a comparison between *Top Hat* and *Swing Time* will demonstrate how the major works represent nuanced shadings of gender difference and the triumph of intimacy over a depersonalized culture. *Top Hat* matches Astaire and Rogers as psychological equals thrown together in zany social circumstances that are consistently confused by the way words point people in the wrong directions. *Swing Time* is motivated less by the odd fit between life and language signs and more by the comedy of clashes among the myriad of competing arbitrary limits and boundaries created by groups, communities, and even individuals.

In *Top Hat*, Jerry Travers (Fred Astaire) and Dale Tremont (Ginger Rogers) are both Americans in London. Although they seem to be in constant opposition, the adversarial elements of their relationship are increasingly revealed as situational. The two of them are remarkably similar in ways that cross the conventional gender lines drawn by Hollywood. Though the display of the body is considered essentially feminine, each is employed displaying his or her body. Jerry is an American dancing star who sometimes works in London. Dale Tremont is a young woman who is supported by dress designer Alberto Bedini (Erik Rhodes)—an early prototype of the fashion spokesperson; she shows off his clothes, and he keeps her in the style to which she wishes to be accustomed. Though assertiveness is considered essentially masculine, both Dale and Jerry are noticeably assertive. They are immediately attracted to each other when they meet in a flurry of gender crossing: he quite masculine though involved in the supposedly feminine display of body and she quite feminine though involved in the supposedly masculine display of will. Late at night, Jerry is dancing in the hotel room he shares with his friend Horace Hardwick (Edward Everett Horton) out of the sheer exuberance of being young and free to enjoy new and exciting experiences ("No Strings"). Dale, in the suite below, is wakened by the tapping and raises hell about being disturbed, turning the hotel management upside down with her complaints. When everyone else proves ineffective and Dale finds it necessary to confront the tapper herself, Jerry and Dale connect. She yells at him; he dances for her. The battle becomes one in which the alienation of words struggles with the unifying energies of the body. Attraction! From that point on, the confusions fomented by the unreliability of verbal language confront the clarity of emotion that arises when the two dance. Dance, the "second language," wins, but not before the social obstacles to intimacy do their worst.

The immediacy of dance requires time to work its way through the social maze in a ritual of deferred connection. The first problem is caused because in her spontaneous, late-night contretemps with Jerry, Dale fails to ask his name, which she doesn't learn until the end of the film. Getting Jerry's name wrong proves to be a major dislocation, because of the power of labels in society. Jerry is mislabeled the next morning in a mistaken identity comedy that makes Dale think that he is her best friend's husband and that her attraction to him is a bad impulse which she must fight. When Dale asks the hotel clerk the name of the man in the suite below her, we see that if bodies in space give rise to connection, words in time give rise to confusion. Because the hotel suite Jerry shares with Horace Hardwick, not only Jerry's best friend but also the husband of Dale's best friend Madge Hardwick (Helen Broderick), is registered in Hardwick's name, the hotel clerk misidentifies Jerry as Horace. For most of the rest of the movie, Dale, Madge, Jerry, and Horace are caught up in a linguistic comedy of errors that hinges on the way the name Horace Hardwick is continually detached from the right body and attached to the wrong body. The tendency of the name to attach to the wrong person sends Jerry, who has no idea he has been mislabeled, on a roller coaster of emotions as Dale, wanting to stay loyal to her best friend, is horrified at how passionately she is drawn to Madge's "husband." Dale is alternately carried away by Jerry in dance and abruptly seized by a need to slap him, depending on which has the upper hand: her desire or her guilt. When things become as confused as they can ever be, a blowup ensues between Horace and Madge, and, as they fight, Jerry becomes aware of Dale's misprision. By this time, Dale, in despair, has married her employer, Alberto Bedini. Jerry, undaunted, arranges to be alone with Dale. All is well when it is revealed that in yet another wild mismatch between appearance and reality Alberto and Dale were married by Horace's butler, Bates (Eric Blore), disguised as a priest. Why? Horace has been suspicious about Dale—more linguistic confusion—thinking that she is a gold digger and has had her followed by Bates. Identities and bodies are so flimsily connected in this film that Bates's disguise consists of nothing more than turning his collar around, but that is enough. He has kept Dale from really making a mistake until Dale and Jerry can finally find their way out of the cultural maze of misrecognition.

How seriously can we take a plot in which Dale does not know Horace, the husband of her best friend Madge, though both of them are twice her age and have clearly been married all of Dale's life? Not very, but how important is seriousness to the important business of making meaning? Not very, for this is a filmic universe in which carnivalized slippage, disguise, and play are the primary modes of learning. Dale's confusion about Jerry's identity is motivated by so many fascinating mismatches between words and physical circumstances that her not knowing her friend's husband works as just another misfiring of human consciousness.

The "play therapy" of this film takes off when Dale searches for Jerry's identity through his name, the label, as of course she must as a person engaged in civilized life, although only a direct apprehension of him will really reveal who he is to her, as events demonstrate.

The clerk's misinformation to Dale about Jerry's identity comes about in the form of the literal difficulties of trying to attach the label of the name to a body in the physical universe. He sees Hardwick walking along the balcony in back of Dale, with a top hat and a briefcase and cane, and points him out to Dale in an answer to her question about the name of the person in the suite below her. The clerk is right and wrong at the same time because of the complexity of the relationship of words to reality. Hardwick is the person to whom the suite is registered, but he is not the person who was in the suite when Dale made her nocturnal visit. Moreover, by the time Dale turns to look at the man to whom the clerk points, Hardwick has disappeared behind a chandelier, which obstructs her vision, where he is intercepted by Jerry, also wearing a top hat. Because Hardwick has to return to the room briefly, he hands Jerry the briefcase and cane. By the time Dale's vision is no longer obstructed, the man with the top hat, briefcase, and cane is Jerry. The wrong label has been attached to the man she loves.

These fragmented discontinuities quickly become the rule. This unstable play of signs and signification is the plot obstacle, a logical chain of misconnection. The hotel clerk, the chandelier, and the uniformity of male dress inadvertently threaten all the synergy that has been set in motion. For Dale has already danced with Jerry before her attempts to find out his name. Earlier that morning, Jerry found a way to be alone with Dale in a park gazebo by disguising himself as a London cabbie. Trapped together in a gazebo during a rainstorm, they face a conversational impasse until they move into a conversation through dance to "Isn't It a Lovely Day to Be Caught in the Rain?" Many critics have spoken of the way Jerry and Dale mirror each other in this number, but that resemblance has always been spoken of in static terms; what is most important about the mirroring is that it evolves out of a process of discovery during this dance; they are no longer separated by their previous argument by the end of the dance.[4] The powerful energy connection between Astaire and Rogers in this dance is the basis on which Jerry's illogical attraction to the very hostile Ms. Tremont now seems to have roots in a more profound reality, the embodied commonalities between them. Dale's sudden feeling that she is in love once the dance is over similarly takes its reality from the subconsciously anchored experience of their real connection, regardless of their social circumstances or petty quarrels. That love is now in the air is doubly interesting. If it opens up that second layer of experience, it also reveals how body-based levels of human interaction conflict with the plane of ordinary social logic, since this is by no means an erotic dance in the ordinary understanding of the term. Rather it is a journey of discovery that finds deeply satisfying resemblances that both cross gender lines and dissolve combative circumstances: they are both dressed in tweedy pants outfits and perform step patterns that are both conventionally masculine and feminine in tone, and they initially met over her profound irritation with him. It also transforms rain into sunshine: what a difference a dance makes.

The dance is a gossamer tissue of invitations and responses. Jerry begins the invitations and Dale not only accepts, she also begins her own overtures, to which he registers curiosity and surprise, and ultimately pleasure. After rhythmically strutting around the gazebo, hands in pockets, like two British gentlemen, they move through a series of delicate steps punctuated by moments of rest in the dance in which they test this exciting mutual perception of heretofore unknown similarities between them. At one point, the music stops, as they watch each other perform the same gesture of crossing arms over their own chests, and then the music continues as they go through more and more intricate patterns of mirrored action. The end of the dance finds them shaking hands as they discover the rain has stopped.

However, the clarity that comes to them during their dances continually faces cultural slippages of language that blunt perception and breed confusion for this developing duo once the dance is over. Immediately after "Isn't It a Lovely Day," Dale, newly tingling with desire for Jerry, is thrown for a loop by the hotel clerk and the confusion that can be caused by a hotel register, an obstructing chandelier, and the undependability of the cultural signs of masculinity: the top hat, white tie, tails, and briefcase. Unaware of the new stumbling block, Jerry, the next time he sees Dale, blissfully approaches her with memories of the gazebo in the park shining in his eyes, and is brought up short when she publicly smacks his face, causing a scandal that almost gets Horace and Jerry thrown out of the hotel in disgrace. Needless to say, Jerry is stunned and brokenhearted when he discovers that Dale has left the hotel. His mood lightens when he learns she has gone to the Lido, to visit with Madge, presenting a new way for him to find her again.

The cultural signs of masculinity by which Dale is forced to misrecognize Jerry are further rendered mysterious, problematic, undependable, and dangerous in the next musical number, "Top Hat, White Tie, and Tails," which Jerry performs in his London show before he and Horace leave for the Lido themselves. In this famous number, Astaire's Jerry dances in what seems to be a completely formulaic fashion in front of a line of chorus boys, all wearing outfits identical to his top hat, white tie, and tails. But the formula of the male tuxedo collides with the disruption that is music during the course of the dance, when Jerry elegantly uses his cane and the sound from his tap shoes as a series of guns, first single-shot weapons, then machine guns, to kill all the other men onstage, to the gleeful applause of a claque of upper-income audience members wearing outfits identical to those of the now-deceased chorus boys.

Jerry's response to their idolatry is to aim his cane at them and "fire a shot," which elicits even wilder applause. What disrupts the action of the narrative, Jerry's pursuit of Dale, continues it on another level. Jerry's dancing is about anger at the pressures of cultural appearances that efface identity. In an enigmatic continuity that is at the same time a rupture in the verbal texture, Jerry's art and commercial endeavors combine to reflect the problem that has caught Jerry and Dale in its twisting maze of illusions.

Jerry (Fred Astaire) deals with the problem of the reductiveness and confusion caused by social signs. He channels violence through dance to eliminate all the other men in top hat, white tie, and tails.

When the narrative resumes at the Lido, where Jerry and Dale will play out their courtship, it is evoked in the most fantastic, least realistic representation possible of the cliches associated with Venice. By itself, such a set would be simply a silly escapist image, but in the context of the film's elegant fabric of multiple slippages of signs and language, the glorious and enchanting obviousness of the set's artificiality becomes part of a meaningful pattern of instability of meaning.[5] This is an even more perfect setting for reflecting on the numerous ways in which such cliches of meaning beget slippages than the somewhat fantastic London in which the characters began the movie.

The mislabeling of Jerry persists because of the inability of language to make accurate references to the material world. Pointing pronouns, like "he," and floating referential words like "your husband" and "my husband" continue the mispointing of the hotel clerk for Dale, Madge, Jerry, and Horace. And as the confusion grows, each character acts appropriately to his or her misunderstandings in ways that only deepen the confusion. The contrast between living literally through words and living by looking through words to the visceral world is important in this film. Dale is stuck in the gap between the two. Her own connection to Jerry—made powerfully manifest in music—cannot be denied when Madge finally officially introduces her to Jerry and pushes her to dance cheek to cheek with him without labeling Jerry in such a way as to clear up the confusion. Thus, the film is not a critique of social structures, but a radiant vision, made possible by the Astaire/Rogers synergy through music, of how complexly social and inner realities relate to each other; it is an anatomy of the twists and turns we must go through to reach intimacy when we are caught in the tensions between the creaky mechanisms of culture and the flow of inner surges.

The "Cheek to Cheek" dance is the most erotic of the performances in the Astaire/Rogers series. As with "Isn't It a Lovely Day to Be Caught in the Rain?" this dance moves the character and situational development along by countering the effect of the script, whose words always estrange, and never connect. The dance is an oasis of synergy in a strange, conflicted landscape. The conventional grammar of masculine and feminine glamour implicated in the tuxedo and evening gown worn by Astaire and Rogers is complicated by the energies in the image. The rigidity of the white tie and black tuxedo that became so closely associated with Fred Astaire, as a result of his movies with Ginger Rogers, is contradicted by Astaire's flexible and light-footed body, as the body's natural force is both strengthened and opposed by the social authority of the upper-class uniform. Similarly, the pale evening gown worn by Rogers, unconventionally composed of billows of soft, floating feathers yet yielding the stereotypically feminine aura of fragility and yielding, is at odds with Rogers's substantial, feminine self-possession, conveyed not only in her powerful body tone but also in the smooth and precisely coifed crown of golden braids in which her hair is dressed. Underneath the chimerical glamour is a force to be reckoned with, a paradoxical combination that is almost a metaphor for female yearning in a patriarchal society.

The dance so completely represents the flow of sexual rhythms and energy partly because it is cinematically conveyed through filmic forms that permit the wild energy of the Astaire/Rogers bodies to radiate from the screen without being interrupted by a heavy editing process. The sequence, barely relying on editing, is Bazinian in character, the camera permitting the audience to see the mise-en-scène with clarity and insight, but not editorializing, an invasion that could do nothing but detract from the powerful Astaire/Rogers rapport.[6] The formulaic dance steps are balanced perfectly with the energies of the two bodies, mixing egalitarian side-by-side mirror movements featured earlier in the dance in the gazebo with male-dominated poses stereotypically associated with romance in Hollywood films. The balance creates an idealized perfection in which inner reality is revealed rather than impeded by outer signs. The erotic interface between the energies of the Astaire/Rogers bodies as they execute the steps suggests another balance as well, that between the culturally conditioned male aspiration to control, and his sensitivity to vibrant feminine energy. Similarly, there is a balance between Dale's female conditioning to submit and her experience of her own desire. She takes his arm as they dance side by side. He whirls her in ballroom position. He dips her backward in that most conventional of all dance statements about male domination of the female. She bends deeply; he holds her securely. With the echo of the words "heaven" and "can hardly speak" silently lingering in the air of the instrumental accompaniment of the dance, he lifts her at the crescendo of the music, resolving at once to a posture in which they both kneel in identical positions and rise, as Dale, on the crest of her own passion, executes an exalted back kick, leading into another set of lifts which resolve to an orgasmic dip, held for an impressive ten seconds (in contrast to previous two-second dips) in which he is almost as parallel to the floor as she is and they are both temporarily transported beyond motion. They rise from the backbend whirling tenderly to a position of rest at the stone wall of this balcony, she alighting first and he coming to rest and then gliding toward her over the intervening space along the balustrade, as if in the grip of a gently magnetic field, evoked physically by the dazzling whiteness of the set.

The breathless shimmer of the moment of bodies perfectly met in space cannot fully define this couple, however. They are also a part of the temporal world that rushes past this perfection of balance, bringing with them Dale's guilt. That moment of mislabeling is still with them. Dale tries to talk to Jerry about this troubling situation. Again, words misfire, deepening the confusion. Jerry, who has no idea that Dale thinks he is Horace, thinks that Dale is encouraging him to declare himself, and he throws caution to the winds and asks her to marry him. Under the circumstances, Dale is horrified. Slapping Jerry's face, she storms away, saying, "How could I have fallen in love with anyone as low as you?" He reels from the slap, but then caresses it, saying, "She loves me." The emotional disjunctions of this moment are conveyed filmically by a violation of the 180-degree rule, as this conversation in the aftermath of the dance is edited to reflect its contrast with the flowing communication of the dance. As Dale and Jerry misunderstand each other more with each word they speak, we as viewers are jolted by an abrupt 180-degree reversal of our perspective on this couple, as if we had mysteriously been thrown from one side of the pair to the other. At least as important as the words in the scene, then, is the filmic grammar, evoking the counterpoint between the herky-jerky starts and fits of this misfiring conversation.[7]

When Dale can no longer stand her push-pull feelings for Jerry, she marries her ridiculous patron, Alberto Bedini, in a union that is in the most absurd way nothing more than a convenient economic arrangement, and very comparable to the absurd Hardwick marriage. The romance of this film defines the couple outside of marriage, a social form that, like language, is supremely collapsible: after the wrong label is removed from Jerry, it is discovered that the wedding was performed by Hardwick's butler in disguise, so it is only a marriage in appearance, though appearance is mostly what marriage is in *Top Hat*. Removal of the wrong label from the faux marriage is, at any rate, an anticlimax. Dale has already discovered that Jerry is not Madge's husband in a scene that interestingly takes place offscreen. When Dale and Jerry are alone after the marriage to Bedini, they begin to sort things out, though the big revelations take place in the ellipsis between that scene and Dale and Jerry's celebration of their important breakthrough. Through the twists of circumstances so typical in this film, Bedini, Madge, and Horace are stranded on a Venetian canal. They lost the pole from their gondola as they were chasing Dale and Jerry. Dale and Jerry are left together on the wedding night in the hotel nightclub, where they experience their first unequivocal joy in their union in the big, communal dance number "The Piccolino." Here, society finally gets it right by abandoning its own flawed logic and becoming part of the dance language of Dale and Jerry.

"The Piccolino" is the kind of production number in which the pair is moved into relationship with the larger community, similar to dance numbers in previous films such as "The Carioca" in *Rio* and "The Continental" in *The Gay Divorcee*. However, these numbers are not interchangeable or mechanically repetitive, as many believe. There are clear distinctions between this number and previous numbers formed around the social sensation of a particular dance step. In all of them, the couple is articulated in terms of its place in its society. But in each case the articulation and integration have different emphases. In each film, the social celebration is designed specifically to fit the nature of the integration that culminates the process of intimacy that has been moving through the film in parallel with the social process of alienation (which by this time has lost the battle). In *Top Hat*, while "husband" Alberto and Madge and Horace are on a wild goose chase looking for Dale and Jerry, the couple unites with joyous negotiations of inner and outer languages. A telling aspect of this film is that the marriage that it ends with—that between Dale and Alberto—is a fraud while the union of Dale and Jerry through the Astaire/Rogers synergy in dance is authentic and abiding. The dance steps executed joyously by Dale and Jerry as the film ends signal the union that matters in this film, having nothing to do with a socially labeled formulaic transaction: marriage.

The equally important *Swing Time* features a filmic universe as fully integrated and satisfying. The musical language threads its way through the movie, altering the social constraints on Lucky and Penny, the Astaire/Rogers characters, which block them as they are drawn toward each other. However, the transformations made possible in *Swing Time* by the body states that grow from music and dance are subtly different from those in *Top Hat*. These transformations work on capriciously set boundaries that are misread as forces of natural law, but actually never truly fit the natural energies at play. Taken seriously at first by Lucky and Penny, arbitrary limits keep the lovers at arm's length. But as the music moves Lucky and Penny, these "mind forg'd" limits slide imperceptibly from absolute injunctions into absolute nonsense.[8]

The movie begins on the intended wedding day of Margaret Watson (Betty Furness), a rich young lady, to John "Lucky" Garnett (Fred Astaire), a dancer by trade, a gambler by avocation. Neither of these pursuits is acceptable to Lucky's future father-in-law, Judge Watson (Landers Stevens); at the same time the marriage is unacceptable to Lucky's all-male chorus of dancers, from whom Lucky will be separated by the impending nuptials. They trick Lucky into believing that his trousers are out of fashion because they have no cuffs on them and intimidate him into sending the offensive trousers to a tailor. This makes Lucky so late for the wedding that Margaret calls it off, but "the guys" lose Lucky anyway. In the aftermath of the ruined ceremony, Lucky just wants to get out of town, to gamble on new and strange experiences, whatever they may be, in New York. But what about his commitment to Margaret? Playing the social game, Lucky cannot just leave her flat. So, he convinces his intended father-in-law that he's going to New York as part of the game, so that he can come back to claim Margaret with a nest egg of twenty-five thousand dollars. Judge Watson respects anyone who can make money, and agrees to the deal. Setting off to pursue his fortune, Lucky hops a freight train and makes it to the big city with Pop (Victor Moore), a bungling stage magician, the oldest, most broken-down, but also the most loyal of his vaudeville cronies. In the city, Lucky has nothing more than the clothes on his back, which command a certain amount of respect since he is still wearing the formal morning suit in which he was to be married. Not sure which way to turn, he bumps into Penelope "Penny" Carroll (Ginger Rogers), a dance teacher; immediately the two are caught up in limits in the form of law, when a misrecognition causes Penny to think Lucky has cheated her of a quarter. She calls for help from a passing policeman, who immediately takes Lucky's part because he is wearing the uniform of the upper classes, and they are both in danger of being arrested.

But humor saves the day, and Penny and her best friend, Mabel (Helen Broderick), the older woman friend that was so often a part of

Penny (Rogers) and Lucky (Astaire) are caught up from the very beginning in dealing with artificial and repressive boundaries and limits.

the Astaire/Rogers formula, become a foursome with Lucky and Pop. Although Penny initially wants nothing to do with Lucky, he blunders his way into her affections, and into a dancing partnership with her. After a while, Penny is confused by Lucky's reserve about pursuing the romance beyond feelings, sighs, and gazes. Lucky too is somewhat confused. But he knows about the constraints on him because of his promise to Margaret. So he works out his own limits, an absurd compromise that typifies the absurdity forced on people by problematic social values. Carefully limiting his winnings when he gambles and his salary when he dances, so that he will never have the twenty-five thousand dollars that will force him to go home and claim Margaret, whom he no longer wants, he also holds back with Penny because of the promise he made to his fiancée. When Penny discovers Lucky's prior commitments, she loses all hope and locks herself into another set of limitations; on the rebound, she promises to marry Romero (Georges Metaxa), a bandleader and a longtime suitor, even though she still loves Lucky. Just in time, Lucky discovers that Margaret doesn't want him either, and delays Penny's wedding to his rival with the same trick his stage cronies used on him—Romero's morning suit pants are taken to the tailor for cuffing. But Penny holds fast to her absurd commitment to Romero until the energy that has escalated through dance and music through the film generates enough laughter to dissipate all the angst over promises and false obligations. Penny calls off the wedding to Romero, and Lucky and Penny unite as a couple.

The filmic articulation of these events changes the narrative from a fluffy entertainment into a rich comedy of the human condition by pitting the interior freedom to take risks, embodied in music and dance, against the sterility imposed by external social limits.[9] Lucky is tied in knots by the latter at the beginning of the film; he even has a sterile relationship to music. In *Swing Time*'s astonishing opening frames, we are shown a long shot of a stage on which seven identically dressed male dancers are performing, one in front of the other six. The distance from which the shot is taken makes it impossible to see that Fred Astaire is the dancer in front. This bold strategy, which plays against audience expectation, given Astaire's star status, dramatizes the fact that at the beginning of the film Astaire/Lucky is alienated from his own vitality, bogged down in the grind of ordinary business, indistinguishable from his identically dressed compatriots. At this point in the movie, Lucky has no true choices. He is stuck between a dead-end job and the opportunity to become a member of the stuffy, conformist Watson family, who will take him only on the condition that he fits the profile of the upper-class provider.

Lucky escapes the horns of Scylla and Charybdis because the competing sets of social limitations negate each other, like two monsters that each keep each other from devouring the humans in standard monster flicks. The dancers momentarily intimidate Lucky with a phony fashion "don't" when they draw a line on the trouser legs of a magazine illustration of a model in a morning suit like the one Lucky is going to wear for his wedding, and laugh at him until he agrees to get his trousers cuffed. But the practice of drawing absurd, meaningless lines and then investing them with social authority, in this case, has unexpectedly positive results. Lucky is prevented from making a marriage that would be based on drawing lines that are as meaningless as the penciled-in cuffs, as we see when Lucky arrives late for the wedding at the Watsons' expensive home. It is an imitation universe, so regimented by abstractions of social status that they radiate from not only the people but also the inanimate house furnishings, and even the Watson family pets.

Lucky's arrival is greeted not only by the expected displeasure of

Margaret and Judge Watson, but also, in successive close-ups, the hostility of their barking poodle and their spitting cat. Even Margaret's grandfather, enshrined as he is in an oil portrait on the wall, casts a frown of disapproval for Lucky. However, when Lucky lies and tells the judge that he was detained because he was closing a business deal for two hundred dollars—he was actually shooting craps—the mood shifts 180 degrees. Lucky's pretense of status alters all the Watsons' feelings, animate and inanimate alike. When Lucky goes further and vows to reclaim Margaret with a bank account of twenty-five thousand dollars, Margaret and Judge Watson break into smiles, the poodle becomes affectionate, the cat purrs, and the expression on the face of venerable grandfather Watson in his framed portrait changes to one of approval. In this dauntingly impersonal impersonation of a family, all emotions depend on superficial social conditions. However, even though Lucky temporarily escapes from the Watsons, he cannot escape his own allegiance to the kinds of limits they and respectable society draw, symbolized by his promise to get the twenty-five thousand dollars, which shadows the entire film. In fact, the more profound level of reality embodied by the dance numbers is haunted by the visible shadow of social obligation. The dances in this film are—atypically for the series—suffused by actual shadows, a visible image of Lucky's interior emotional paralysis. He goes toward the energy of the city, but for all his willingness to take risks, he cannot imagine a way out of the box created by the promises he has made, even though a greater reality is presented to him through the synergy he forms with Penny when they dance. Thus *Swing Time* is constructed out of a narrative of lies, denial, and evasions as the counterpoint to the vitality and direct emotion of its dances.

The first of the Astaire/Rogers dance numbers, "Pick Yourself Up, Dust Yourself Off, Start All Over Again," emerges from Lucky's pretense that he can't dance. He begs Penny to teach him to dance so that he can stay near her after their chance meeting. Lucky's false bumbling is so extreme that, in exasperation, Penny tells him that no one in the world could ever teach him to dance. Unfortunately her boss, Mr. Gordon (Erik Blore), overhears Penny and promptly fires her. In order to save Penny's job, Astaire's Lucky unleashes his real abilities. As her hero, he flies through the air, liberating himself from false social constraints, defying gravity, and physically embodying the possibility of jumping over limits. The dance is full of buoyant leaps, the preliminary whirls and parallel side-by-side step patterns like the revving up of a jet plane for takeoff, leading to a series of lifts that take the couple seemingly effortlessly across and back over and across again the small white fence that surrounds the dance floor, as they literally and figuratively romp joyously over the conventions that would confine them. Mr. Gordon not only rehires Penny, but arranges for the two to audition for a glitzy nightclub. Inner freedom breaks down artificial barriers.

But the barriers created by status consciousness still predominate. Gordon's arrangement of an audition depends on Lucky getting dinner clothes in which to dance, and Lucky doesn't tell Penny that he doesn't have any money. Pop and Lucky lose the audition for Lucky and Penny by trying to win enough money to rent dinner clothes for Lucky's audition costume. Pop thinks he has the situation under control when he brings home a drunk in dinner clothes, whom they think they are going to sucker into a card game, the stakes of which will be the drunk's clothing. The drunk makes them his patsy in a card game that ends with Lucky in his underwear, in no condition to audition at the Silver Sandal nightclub with Penny. The situation worsens. Penny now refuses to see Lucky under any circumstances, even for a second chance at an audition.

The barriers Penny sets up against Lucky dissolve only after Mabel secretly lets Lucky into the apartment and he sings "Just the Way You Look Tonight," a charming love song that celebrates spontaneous beauty as immune to time and the ravages of age. The music dissolves Penny's defenses and erases the barriers she has put between them, literally. Penny drifts out of the bathroom in the middle of washing her hair to hear him, only belatedly realizing that she has a head full of soapsuds. He thinks she's lovely anyhow. Although when the music is over, propriety takes over and Penny runs from the room, the die is cast. Lucky and Penny are, albeit uneasily, beyond appearances mandated by the social agenda.

The counterpoint between calculated tricks and the buoyancy of music continues. On the one hand the lies continue as the only way available to negotiate the limits drawn by an absurdly organized society. When Lucky and Penny finally get their audition, they need to force the bandleader, Romero, to play for them. Romero is in love with Penny and doesn't want to see her dance with another man. Lucky has to bet Raymond, the owner of the nightclub, for Romero's contract to get music for his audition. When Pop sees that Raymond is about to cheat at the card game Lucky and Raymond are playing, without telling Lucky, he cheats first. At first, it seems that cheating in a good cause saves the day, but that is only appearance, and such appearances are shadowed by an irrefutable reality.

The shadows, unsuspected by both Penny and Lucky, show up in the audition dance. Over the glow, laughter, and humor of *Swing Time* is the shadow. In the pas de deux of the "Swing Time Waltz," which is Lucky and Penny's first dance together as a public team, they forget everything else, including the shadow of Lucky's social obligations. Lucky, for the moment forgetting about Margaret, flies through this dance on the optimism of his gamble for the contract—which he doesn't know was fixed by Pop—and Penny, knowing nothing of Margaret, is floating on the apparent promise of romance and success beyond her wildest dreams. Nevertheless, there is an undercurrent of darkness in this light, optimistic dance, embodied materially in the shadow cast over the spotlight in which the bodies of Penny and Lucky dance. Such a use of shadows is unique in the Astaire/Rogers pas de deux dances. And the texture of the shadows in this most joyous of dances in their body of work is underscored when, at the end of the dance, the two whirl off behind a wall that is at first completely transparent and then becomes translucent, turning the bodies of Lucky and Penny into shadows. Exuberance alone will not be enough to free them for the intimacy they crave.

The spectre of social limits resurges when Madge, Pop, Lucky, and Penny drive up to a romantic old inn in the country for a little holiday in celebration of their professional success. Lucky intends to maintain the pose of being his own man, even though he chafes under the obligations of an engaged man. He makes a deal with Pop to give him a nudge whenever he is in danger of being "inappropriately" romantic with Penny. But Penny, knowing nothing of the real situation, brings music into their enchanted winter idyll. Penny sings "A Fine Romance," with witty impatience about this man who is "just as hard to land as the Isle de France" and about "a fine romance with no kisses." It is a charming song, and can be interpreted in the usual fashion as a segment interpellated into the script mechanically because this is how musicals operate. However, to view the song in this way would be to overlook how dynamically it works. Penny's musical expression of disappointment creates a counterpressure to his unemotional but strongly anchored social obligation to Margaret. Under this pressure, Lucky decides to throw caution to the winds and get romantic with Penny, at which point Pop takes it upon himself to police the situation; he takes Penny aside and comes clean with her about Margaret. Now the invisible social injunctions weigh on her, and now it's a puzzled Lucky's turn to sing about his "strong aged-in-the-wood woman" who doesn't glance at the orchids he sends: "no you like cactus plants." It is a scene of testing limits. Lucky wonders what he can do about his obligations, as the audience wonders about the necessity for honoring such a capriciously entered into obligation. It is a scene that pits the charm and magic of the Lucky-Penny connection forcefully against the whole civilized system of limits and boundaries. The ghost of Margaret and her set of bogus obligations seems to take control when Penny learns about the prior engagement and reacts to the absurd promise as Lucky did. This would seem to be another foolish plot ploy of the conventional musical. But in fact, it works nicely in this film as a testimony to the weight of invisible social chains, charting by indirection how difficult it is for each of us to move in the direction of inner desire when silly but powerful social demands are made on us in the name of status.

After the frustrating trip to the inn, Penny is so stung by Lucky's dishonesty that even though Mabel takes pains to point out that Lucky is not acting like a man who really loves his fiancée, she is not willing to cross that line. Mabel incites her to cross it—to go and kiss Lucky—daring Penny to just forget what is obviously a meaningless obligation. The ploy works, and Penny bowls the delighted Lucky over with a big kiss, albeit behind a door and out of sight of the audience.[10] It looks like Penny and Lucky are going to get beyond the absurd, groundless promise after all.

Again, the rapturous kiss is a premature moment of celebration, though it escalates the energy of opposition to the invisible social barriers that stand between Penny and Lucky. All such moments will be premature until the couple squarely faces what separates them. Enigmatically, this too-soon rapture is followed by a musical number in which Astaire's Lucky does homage to Bill "Bojangles" Robinson, the great African American dancer, by dancing as Robinson in "Bojangles of Harlem," in minstrel show blackface.[11] The dance number clearly wraps Lucky in the mantle of sexual potency stereotypically associated with African American men, but it also brings in the chiaroscuro of deep shadows, both in Astaire's famous dance with three huge shadows of himself, created by a special effect, and in Astaire's donning of blackface as a kind of shadow representation of himself, conveying, even more emphatically than the "Swing

Time Waltz," the premature exuberance of those who deal only in partial truths.

Much attention has already been paid to the phallic nature of this number, as Lucky originally appears propped up with huge, false legs suggestive of phallic potency. Furthermore, when a crew of chorus girls separates the fifteen-foot legs, the camera travels up between them, emphasizing Lucky's crotch in a kind of gender reversal of Busby Berkeley's famous traveling camera, whose object was invariably the female crotch. What has not been attended to is the positioning of this number within the context of the film's narrative, nor has anyone noted that during the aborted wedding at the end of the film the "Bojangles" melodic line is scored briefly under Romero's attempt to reclaim Penny, who is wearing his valet's trousers.

Some will find uncomplicated racism in these references, but if it is undeniably racist to reduce any group of people to acting as a functioning metaphor for another more socially powerful group, this is not the capricious racism of Al Jolson's horrifying blackface number in *Wonder Bar* (1934) or the gratuitous sprinkling of films of the studio era with characters that "establish" African Americans as inherently cowardly and stupid.[12] The situation is not simple. Lucky's donning of the black face is a way of establishing his difference from Margaret's patriarchal heritage, and it likens him to Romero and the Bojangles in their inability to really be part of the formidable wall of absurdity that passes for masculine authority in the mind of the patriarchal Judge Watson. Lucky, Romero, and Bojangles all lose their pants in some way; yet they do not seem to be feminized as much as they are liberated, propelled into what the film defines as a more worthwhile masculine identity, and better, if wildly comic, male bonding that points toward passion for a female partner rather than the acquisition of a desirable object. Seen in this manner, the dance is brilliant not only technically and stylistically, but also psychologically and narratively, as Lucky emerges from the giddy kiss to explore, through the delightfully entertaining conventions of musical comedy, the shadows of masculine identity, arguably a necessary prelude to his liberation from the shadowless, uninflected, absurd world of white patriarchs and their denatured cats and dogs, who bark and hiss in the service of artificial values.

A careful observation of the "Bojangles" dance suggests that it is part of the second language in the film, which enables a probing of male identity issues that the script does not. As a play of shadows and substance, it speaks of the dancer's negotiation, if not conscious discovery, of various layers of reality, going beyond the bi-polarity of shadows and bodies to a third possibility, as the "real" figure becomes translucent, superimposed over the material background as the dance ends. In addition to the representation of Lucky's assumption of a marginalized persona, which permits him to move among shadows, there is some sense of transcending the limits of male identity through the shadows as well as the ability to move among them, a deeper, more authentic sense of life than is possible in Margaret's uninflected world. Thus this sequence may be said to build on the shadows in the earlier *Swing Time* waltz, which featured a bi-polarity of shadows and brilliant spotlights, but which was oblivious to this chiaroscuro on the part of the dancers. This brief euphoria is even more intense than that exhibited in the *Swing Time* dance; and it is followed by an even deeper depression. After Lucky's performance, Margaret goes backstage to talk with him. On seeing Margaret, Lucky is overtaken by the shadows he had ignored and capitulates to his obligations to her.

Bereft, Penny accepts Romero's longstanding proposal, but this decision merely heaps false limits on top of false limits. If the barriers between Lucky and Penny proliferate, the synergy also intensifies. The bittersweet subtlety of *Swing Time*, which makes it arguably the most sophisticated and important of all the Astaire/Rogers series, brings the transformative powers of dance and the synergy of Astaire and Rogers to their zenith in "Never Gonna Dance," the number in which Lucky and Penny try to say good-bye to each other. This dance, the most passionate of all the Astaire/Rogers dances, cannot dissolve the social barriers that stand between them, adding to the film a complexity and a clear sense of the difficulty of achieving intimacy within a society so strictly governed by illusion. In fact the scene begins by evoking illusion and appearance. The films cuts to a shot in which we see Penny and Romero standing together in the empty, glittering nightclub, when suddenly we realize that we have been looking at a mirror reflection, as Lucky opens the mirrored door and enters, his heartbroken presence taking the place of the preceding mirror image. Refusing to congratulate Romero on his engagement, Lucky apologizes to Penny. He remains puzzled about what is really keeping these two apart, as does the audience. It is the moment at which the strangely tenacious limits people impose on themselves appear in their most absurd, yet most powerful, light.

Granted a moment alone, the two are trembling with love for each other, which they cannot express directly in the dialogue. However, their powerful dancing rapport bleeds into their conversation, which takes on a multi-layered tone. "Does she dance very beautifully?" asks Penny. "Who?" he replies. "The girl you're in love with," she explains. "Yes, very," he says, and it is clear to each of them as well as to the audience that he is talking about her. "The girl you're engaged to; the girl you're going to marry," Penny clarifies. To that, he answers, "I don't know." Trying to leave, Penny is drawn into a musical frame of reference that does express, and very clearly, the absurdity of the two planned marriages.

This musical segment is more intricately edited than any of their other scenes, cutting between upwardly angled shots of his point of view of Penny on a staircase against the artificially twinkling stars of the nightclub and her point of view, rendered through downwardly angled shots of Lucky at the bottom of the stairs, singing "Never Gonna Dance." The song is an interesting lyric, using, in a very unusual stroke for the Astaire/Rogers series, metaphors from the Great Depression to express Lucky's private sense of bereavement. The lyric tells us that his heart has been taken by "the wolf," a common metaphor for economic hardship at the time, as in the common expression of the time, "the wolf at the door," causing an almost uncanny set of resonances in this seeming enclave from the hard times outside of the movie theatre, since the heroine's name is Penny, and the lyric specifically says the wolf has left Lucky without his Penny. But the wolf, "being "discreet," has "left me my feet." Still Lucky will never dance again.

Except that he does. Neither can leave the other. As Lucky moves up the staircase, Penny moves down toward him and then moves around him down to the dance floor. They walk slowly, hand in hand, absolutely confused, and so in love. The parallel walking changes into a side-by-side motion in which she moves into his shoulder with a slight pressure, as if the two were connected. Penny tries again to leave, but Lucky dramatically blocks her exit; startled, she stops and they look at each other, frozen, for a moment before they move back into the euphoric *Swing Time* waltz, for the moment reliving the rapture that enfolded them previously, when they had fooled themselves into believing that the road ahead would be smooth sailing. As they move up the double staircases to an upper dance floor, they enter a glittery, starlike, Hollywood version of heaven, the perfect location for eros tormented by illusion. Each on his or her own stairway, they meet at the top, perform a frantic series of whirls that resolve to a frozen clutching of each other, and then Penny whirls away, leaving Lucky alone. The glamour of the scene, which is widely referred to in discussions of the escapism of the Astaire/Rogers films, particularly in the context of the national depression, is actually a setting that complexly melds the chilling with the seductive. Passion is a prisoner of glamour, the shill for social systems.

A release from prison for Penny and Lucky is granted, however, and in a way that might easily be interpreted as a deus ex machina, but which actually has an interior energy that brings out the primary making of meaning situated within the body, a strength which has been growing, via dance and music, among the shadowy social codes since Lucky's first meeting with Penny. Margaret, it turns out, has only come to see Lucky to tell him that she no longer wants him. She has decided to marry a man who really fits her values, Herbert, whom we never see, but who bears a name that had come to be associated with the social grind. By aligning herself with a world of pure social codes, Margaret writes herself out of a film that distinguishes itself by its necessary relationship to of opposites, social and body languages. Now it is Penny's obligation to Romero that stands in the way.

Resolution comes only when the weight of social abstractions is dissolved by laughter welling up from deep inside the body, the source of the dancing. At the end of the film, Pop and Lucky in last-ditch desperation turn the tables on social propriety through the same trick by which the all-male dancing chorus initially tried to trap Lucky into staying in harness. They take Romero's trousers away to get cuffs put on them, thus postponing his wedding to Penny. When Romero, more determined than Lucky had been at the beginning of the film, arrives wearing his valet's pants, many sizes too large, Lucky, Mabel, Pop, and finally Penny burst into laughter. Appropriately, laughter conveys the power of moving beyond whatever absurdly binds us to sterility and punishes desire and energy.

The ability to see through and laugh off conventional limits, in this filmic universe, is not a matter for the individual, or even the couple. This film makes quite clear what has been the case in all of the previous Astaire/Rogers vehicles: moving into the flow of life from the constriction of meaningless social limits requires the second language of music and dance, and indeed the end of the movie turns into an operetta, with everyone singing instead of talking. In a scene in which laughter passes from person to person, as they sing altered lyrics to the tune of "A Fine Romance," Romero enters wearing his valet's giant trousers. Music is release into laughter. Penny can no longer keep herself within the set of limits in which she has imprisoned herself. When the laughter reaches its highest crescendo, no one really needs to tell Romero that the wedding is not to be, and Penny and Lucky naturally reunite. The nothing that has been keeping them apart cannot function without communal support. In the glass dome, overlooking the big city in the falling snow, recalling both the blocked union in the earlier scene in the old inn and Romero's attempt to make Penny his, Lucky and Penny sing a cappella in counterpoint to "A Fine Romance" and "Just the Way You Look Tonight," respectively. This scene reminds the audience of how each of them, even in union, has his or her own song. When Lucky throws a deck of cards into the air, the false sets of limits have been dissolved; the real, the necessary gamble is the one they have taken with each other, and the real limits are the ones they will create out of their conjunction.

THE MINOR FILMS

The minor works were filmed during the Astaire/Rogers heyday and cannot be placed in terms of a linear falling off of the pair's partnership: major and minor works appear in alternation until 1936. Rather, the juxtaposition of the two kinds of films reflects the uncontrollable flow of energies in the studio system days. The minor works reflect spurts in which Hollywood cliche and stereotype begin to gain a stronger foothold in the Astaire/Rogers pairing. This type of Astaire/Rogers film features two separate plots, almost cleanly segregated as if there were a glass partition between them that affords visual contact between the two strains of the story, but no interpenetration of two different kinds of couple energies. In these films, Astaire and Rogers play the narratively "second" couple, but are not only the primary box office attraction of the film, but also the primary exemplars in the film of what love and human synergy is about. The "primary" couple in each film is a Functional Couple dragging through the conventional script logic, a clear demonstration of how lackluster the screen couple generally is without the wild energy of chemistry. The Functional Couple in these films is never permitted a full engagement with the Astaire/Rogers model of intimacy.

The Astaire/Rogers series began with the most minor of the minor works, *Flying Down to Rio,* in which the principal couple is played by Delores Del Rio as Belinha, a young upper-class Brazilian woman, and Gene Raymond as Roger, a brash American bandleader. It is interesting enough as the first screen appearance together of Astaire and Rogers, but the kind of dynamic between Astaire/Rogers and the film's story that it exemplifies will be amply clarified and more fruitfully explored by means of examining it in light of the later minor films: *Roberta and Follow the Fleet.* An extended discussion of *Rio* will be sacrificed here to the requirements of brevity.

Unlike in the major works, in which the Astaire/Rogers couple moves back and forth between the obstacles posed by the script and the means to surmount them in the music and dance, in Roberta, the film is bifurcated between the scripted primary couple, John (Randolph Scott) and Stephanie (Irene Dunne), thwarted unmercifully by social obstacles, and the story of the Astaire and Rogers characters, Huck Haines and Lizzie Gatz, told almost exclusively in music. As the second couple who do little more than dance and sing to each other, Huck and Lizzie have no sustained conflict, while John and Stephanie have little else. The logic of their final reunion is the unconvincing logic of the forced convention of Hollywood happy endings, whereas the persistence of Lizzie and Huck's connection is fully satisfying and organic, if somewhat nebulously grounded. The Astaire/Rogers' relationship to the film as a whole, on the other hand, is not satisfying even though it provides sporadically the pleasure of Astaire and Rogers dancing, demonstrating the importance for them as an onscreen couple of the relationship between their synergy and the formulas of narrative.

Roberta is the story of a band of American musicians called the Wabash Indianians, who get stranded in Paris without a job. Alexander Voyda (Luis Alberne), the owner of the Café Russe, cancels their contract abruptly when he learns they are not American Indians. He's not interested in Indianians. Huck, the bandleader, begs John, his best friend, a former college football player who is probably the band's manager, though we never see him doing anything remotely useful for them that Huck hasn't thought of, to get help from his Aunt Minnie (Helen Westly), who is known in Paris as Roberta. Aunt Minnie, couturier to the rich and famous, has as her spiritual daughter Stephanie, whom John meets and falls in love with when he goes to Aunt Minnie for help.[13] Unbeknownst to John, Stephanie is a Russian princess dispossessed by the Revolution. The American/

foreign nobility plot is parodied by Astaire and Rogers as the "second couple." At Roberta's, Huck reencounters Lizzie Gatz, his childhood sweetheart back home in Indiana, who is Roberta's best customer. Lizzie is using the pseudonym, Scharwenka and masquerading as a Polish countess, accent and all, because, as she says, you need a title to make it in Paris. Lizzie/Scharwenka, who is singing at Voyda's club, periodically terrorizes Stephanie with her temperamental demands. To keep Huck from spilling the beans about her real identity, Lizzie gets back his band's job at Voyda's club, where they work well together. When Aunt Minnie dies unexpectedly, John inherits the business, but knowing nothing about women's clothes and because he is in love with Stephanie, he gives her half-ownership in the establishment and all of the design responsibilities, but they don't work well together.

The primary plot of this film is an unintentional self-parody. The obstacles that threaten the romance of Stephanie and John are potentially interesting. First, John is a macho, parochial, American prude who doesn't understand "what women want" in clothing, and he threatens continually to destroy Roberta's business with his male desire for designs that will keep women's sexuality under control, here imaged as fussy, prissy dresses. Second, his parochialism keeps him from respecting Stephanie's cultural identity; everyone who isn't a Yank is a weird foreigner to him. Third, he begins the movie as a slave to status and class, so enthralled by Sophie (Claire Dodd), the spoiled American socialite who ended her romance with John because he was not her social equal, that he almost lets her get away with her attempt to effect a reconciliation when she learns he owns the fabled Roberta's. However, these script issues become entirely cartoonlike as they are handled, since there is no chemistry of any kind between Randolph Scott and Irene Dunne to embody any felt sense of what John fails to perceive about women in general and Stephanie in particular. The Randolph/Dunne affiliation rasps tediously onward, forced by the plot logic alone to grind through the movie. Because the virtually unscripted romance of the Astaire and Rogers characters has so much synergy, the film continually threatens to break in two pieces, barely held together by a subtextual suggestion that the Astaire/Rogers connection is a lesson for the primary couple in what real intimacy is, parody though it may be. Indeed, parody is necessary to achieve any actual intimate energy in this film, since the primary couple has no life. Lizzie's reencounter with Huck, in playing with the fantasies attached to mysterious foreign beauty which Dunne's character unblushingly demands that we take seriously, allows us to find the subtext of passion that may be covered up by the charade. On the other hand, Dunne's is a humorless charade of foreign nobility; she plays this role with the trumped up, almost self-mocking seriousness of the classical Hollywood style: her Stephanie has not one single ethnic Slavic characteristic. In contrast with Lizzie's outrageously silly accent and theatrical clothes, Donne speaks with the mid-Atlantic, quasi-British inflection so popular in Hollywood at the time, and she dresses like an American movie star. The primary couple comes straight off the Hollywood assembly line, a kind of inadvertent confession about the limitations of Hollywood manipulation.

By contrast, the music text with its images, sound, and negotiation of space plays with Huck's knowledge of Lizzie's real identity in Rogers's amazing "I'll Be Hard to Handle" number. The script first shows us that Lizzie is hard to handle, but that Huck is undaunted and even somewhat amused. There are no overt obstacles to their romance. They need only negotiate the distance between two different people, the otherness of male and female that exist in the human condition. After their first confrontation, in which Huck bites her hand, playfully mocking her expectation of a kiss because of her assumed identity, they just continue to move toward each other around the obstacles between John and Stephanie. The first major transition occurs at the Café Russe, during a rehearsal period with Huck's band, as Lizzie/Scharwenka practices her solo number, "I'll Be Hard to Handle," which flows into a spontaneous dance by Huck and Lizzie. Lizzie's solo is perhaps the most playful, transparently spontaneous number performed in any Astaire/Rogers film. Its megawatt sense of improvised energy is genuine, as the dance that follows which was, in Rogers's words, "the first time a number was done direct; the taps were just as we did them, with no additions. Fred's and my laughter and giggling as we got into the throes of the dance were not added either. They were real. The two of us enjoyed dancing together. The spontaneity was very real . . ."[14]

Lizzie's musical declaration of what a wildcat she is—"just ask my dad the trouble he had controlling me"; "I'm as cold as any shellfish; I tell lies; I'm mean and selfish"—is playful hyperbole. She also throws "chairs and tables and I never miss." By the end of the song, Lizzie is practically leaping out of her skin with enthusiastic endorsement of her bad temper so that the lyric is never verbally completed, but instead dissolves into Slavonically accented scat. This is the one number in the Astaire/Rogers canon in which the characters threaten to slide into the actors themselves, as the actress peaks through the character winking and blinking with an irrepressible sense of fun that contagiously envelops Huck, who watches her statement of militant female agency with a sense of delight that seems to come from Astaire as well as from Huck.

As the band continues to practice the tune, Huck and Lizzie remember the old days, for example a valentine he sent her bearing a picture of an arrow piercing the heart and dripping blood, in a conversation that screams self-consciousness about the sentimental forms of media romance. Then Hick and Lizzie noodle around the dance floor, not particularly practicing any routine that will go into a show, but just doing steps together because they like to, and because they know how to dance, and because they can dance well together. The fun continues because one pattern of steps suggests another that is a variation, and the musicians begin to play with them, giving them cues for steps, which they take up as a form of a cappella dance challenge, each trying to outdo the other, prompting Lizzie to manufacture steps in which she slaps Huck silly and then steps on his foot, a dance slugfest with which Huck cooperates in fantasy. They go on until they have driven each other to the top of their form and finally whirl each other into collapse on chairs near the dancing area. It is an evocation of shared invention that moves among the members of a group—the whole ensemble includes the invisible band—inescapably suggesting that couples are parts of larger interconnected networks that support their dynamic, which is a mutual exchange of electricity through the agency of social forms, music and dance technique being the representative constructs. It also involves the rejection of cliches about romance for something much more organic and spontaneous that could not have been verbally articulated. Fascinatingly, as they bask in the afterglow of their interconnected creation and waves of applause break from the cleaning staff at the club, eerily juxtaposing images of the characters as persons and performers and Astaire and Rogers deriving personal pleasure from their partnership before it is redefined by observing eyes into a form of entertainment.

Stephanie, narratively the "real" foreigner, throws tantrums we are supposed to take seriously, self-righteously sulking about John's puerile infatuation with Sophie while parading herself, without a hint of playfulness, in ridiculously carnivalistic, sleekly glamourous outfits often festooned at the neck with bowlike decoration, as if she were one big present for John's consumption. But she styles herself as a simple, unaffected maiden. These are simply her little "working girl" outfits. Lizzie's glamour is all presented either tongue-in-cheek as part of her made-up identity, or as part of a dance or song routine that is clearly also a costume. Stephanie, we are to believe, is that most romantic of all women, a princess, shorthand for the exaltation of women on pedestals; she even appears once in a crown. Lizzie is only a pretend countess, who gets her hand bitten in tribute. The romance between Stephanie and John is replete with cliches of visual romance such as gauzy drapes that are drawn between them, which he violates in a scene that threatens to separate them forever, as Stephanie sings "Smoke Gets in Your Eyes" when she believes that John can never be hers, an example of how music can be used to drag a script further into cliche. That these two are stuck because of all kinds of social conditioning is visually conveyed by a number of images in the film, but none so obvious as at the "happy ending," when they clear up all the misunderstandings and kiss—through the bars of the Parisian elevator in Roberta's establishment. Nothing will ever release them, though they will link up in some strangely blocked manner.

If Stephanie and John go on ad nauseam in an endless series of scripted scenes, the development of Huck and Lizzie's innate connection into full-blown romance is presented in a deliciously economical series of dances. There is not one narrative scene devoted to their falling in love; the rapport embodied in the "Hard to Handle" number just grows musically onscreen during the fashion show, at which the first post–Aunt Minnie fashion line is displayed. The last model to walk down the runway is Lizzie. Her glamourous black satin halter evening gown, decorated by a diamond clip at the decollete, is not depicted as her natural appearance, but a clearly assumed costume that is meant to sell Roberta's dresses. Huck is attired in white tie and tails not because he dresses that way either, but because he is the master of ceremonies. As such, Huck sings the song that has been playing under the runway entrances of all the models, "Lovely to Look at." Then Lizzie sings part of the lyric to him; if he finds her lovely to look at, she finds him equally so. They move off together into a dance which modulates from "Lovely to Look at" into "Smoke Gets in Your Eyes." The modulation also marks a partial slippage of the couple from the professional into the personal. They are still entertainers, but there is always some combination of innate feeling and structured dance as they move together. We have heard the lyrics to "Smoke" already, and have also seen them interpolated into the story in their literal meaning. The words speak of betrayal and loss in love, and specifically of Stephanie's feelings in connection with John. Here, the dance is constructed against the grain of the words and in harmony with the lilting but muted melodies in the composition. It is an encapsulated form of counterpoint between script and music that occurs in Roberta only in fits and starts, but in the major films is the dominant mode of composition. This is a dance of infinitely quiet discovery of the erotic exaltation of soul mates. Beginning, as Astaire liked to, with the couple walking rhythmically, the dance evolves into a series of parallel, side-by-side positions that merge into parallel face-to-face positions and back again, punctuated by face-to-face ballroom dancing position turns and one deep backward dip for Lizzie that finds Huck almost equally parallel to the floor. The aftermath of the dip is a nestled side-by-side position that makes them one before they move back again into parallel side-by-side movements that rise briefly to a crescendo as they appear to defy gravity by flying up a flight of steps in tandem and then moving off in a nestled side-by-side position. The connection of equals, bonded and yet free at the same time, both meticulously impersonal practitioners of their dancing craft and yet both erotically illuminated, is so profound that when Huck makes a comic marriage proposal to Lizzie after their dance, it is clear that language, while regarded in this universe as necessary to the couple's connection to culture, is superficial and trivial—hence the opposition between the transcendence of what has been enacted by Lizzie and Huck and the cliched literalism of what was sung by Stephanie. Huck and Lizzie have laughed the "primary couple" back to each other despite his narrow mind and her self-righteousness.

A similarly bifurcated film, *Follow the Fleet*, features Astaire and Rogers as Bake Baker and the irrepressible Sherry Martin. Again the Astaire/Rogers pair contrasts with a leaden primary couple, Sherry's sister, Connie Martin (Harriet Hilliard, who later went on to star in Ozzie and Harriet with Ozzie Nelson), and Bake's buddy, Bilge Smith (again Randolph Scott).[15] The script for this film is a great deal more accomplished and witty than that of the other two minor works, containing, as *Rio* and *Roberta* do not, some pointed awareness of the problematic nature of social stereotypes and cliches. There is a greater sense of active and productive counterpoint between the verbal text and the nonverbal text. The primary couple even gets some help from the musical subtext in complicating their formulaic romance. However, once again it is the Astaire/Rogers couple, regardless of their secondary presence in the script, who are foremost in impact, and also principal in the way they transcend the obvious cultural cliches of the supposedly primary couple.

In this story, Connie and Sherry are contrasting sisters. Sherry is a glamourous looking professional dancer who has ended up, despite her flash and dazzle, as a ten-cents-a-dance girl at the seedy Paradise (in name only) Ballroom. Connie is initially lonely, frumpy, and bespectacled, and as Bilge intuits the minute he sees her, a teacher. (We all know how frumpy teachers tend to be.) Bake Baker and Bilge Smith, both sailors in the United States Navy, are suitably contrasting friends. Bake is a former professional dancer, once Sherry's partner, who has a lively but respectful interest in women. Bilge is a sailor who aspires to be captain of his own commercial vessel, and who avoids "nice" girls and commitment like the plague in favor of garish, good-time babes. On a shore leave, Bilge and Bake wind up at the Paradise Ballroom, Bilge in search of a good time, and Bake in search of a phone with which to contact Sherry—he does not know she is working there. The same night, Connie comes to see Sherry, but is not permitted in without an escort, to which she responds with a sweet, witty sadness, "Oh, I see; women aren't even admitted to Paradise without a man." This film is aware of the ironies of the double standard. Bilge, standing nearby, is willing to allow the tweed-suited, dull-feathered Connie to buy him a ticket on the pretense that she has been waiting for him, but he soon gives her the brush-off. Backstage, the forlorn Connie is given a glamour makeover that dazzles Bilge and sets the two of them off on a romance. The pretense leads to something real when Bilge learns to appreciate true feeling in a woman after Connie goes into debt to restore the Connie Martin, a boat left to her by her father, so that Bilge can realize his dream of being captain of his own ship.

At the same time, Bake and Sherry, although happy to see each other again, run into some plot complications that keep them apart. Bake, although nowhere near the would-be macho tyrant that Bilge is, unadvisedly starts to take charge of Sherry's life and thereby gets her fired from her job. When his shore leave is so abruptly canceled that Sherry mistakenly thinks Bake has walked out on her and left her jobless to boot, it takes his return with a tiny monkey dressed up in a sailor suit to make Sherry laugh at all their troubles and to assure Sherry that Bake understands he was a "monkey" in his behavior to her. And she is committed once more to Bake. It takes Connie and Bilge a little longer to deal with his macho fantasies, which, as in *Roberta*, the Randolph Scott character will clearly never really see through. But both couples make peace as they put on a show to pay for the restoration of the Connie Martin, and in the final frame Connie, Sherry, and the monkey wave good-bye to Bilge and Bake as they go on their next mission for the Navy, each expecting marriage when the boys return.

As in *Roberta*, the plodding lead couple reenacts the domination/submission gender model, while the second couple almost entirely through music works out a much more complex couple structure. The Sherry/Bake musical numbers bestow an individual life on Sherry and Bake in their solo numbers (Bake's "We Saw the Sea" and "I'd Rather Lead a Band" and Sherry's "Let Yourself Go") and a developing mutuality of commitment to each other in their duets ("I'm Putting All My Eggs in One Basket" and "Let's Face the Music and Dance").

The climax of their growing partnership takes place in the last of these numbers, the justly celebrated "Let's Face the Music and Dance," which functions in the film as a ritual of reconnection, the resolution of Sherry's anger at Bake for what she thinks is desertion. "Let's Face the Music and Dance" is a stunning example of the possibilities for musical movies in directly interrupting yet obliquely augmenting script with musical text.[16] This musical number is presented as just a part of the show that the Martin sisters have authorized on the good ship Connie Martin to make enough money to pay for the renovation loans. However, it plays a much larger role because it indirectly speaks to Sherry and Bake's situation, and in a larger sense speaks about indirection in general.

Narratively, working-class Bake has gone AWOL from the Navy to do the show out of loyalty and love for working-class Sherry. Sherry, for her part, has forgotten about her career so she can help Connie with the show, again out of love and loyalty. If the show succeeds, Connie will be all right, but Bake and Sherry will still be in trouble. Nothing but ruin is staring them in the face, with only this moment of the show as a possible reward for all they have figuratively gambled.

The conventions of the musical comedy mean that such painful issues must be glossed over in the narrative, but those conventions also leave room for an oblique treatment in the music. The literal meaning of "Let's Face the Music and Dance" could not be further from the story; it concerns rich, glamourous people at a fashionable gambling casino. However one need not go far to see the parallels between a girl and a gob up against it and two desperate gamblers.

The song-and-dance number takes place in a fantasy version of a gambling resort frequented by the rich and frivolous. Two glamourous people, played by Bake/Astaire and Sherry/Rogers, down on their luck meet accidentally when she is about to commit suicide by drowning herself, while he, no longer a success and bereft of the funds to recoup his fortune, is contemplating shooting himself. He stops her from killing herself and then throws his pistol into the water. Whatever has driven them to hopelessness has not been changed; it still lurks. But the couple has decided to live the present moment fully, and that turns out to be enough. The emotional parallels between the fictional dancers and Bake and Sherry become obvious, as does the meaning that this seemingly escapist image potentially had for the dispossessed of the depression. It is a pristine example of how carnivalization and disguise as part of the language of the music text work to free expression for Astaire and Rogers.

The passionate "Let's Face the Music and Dance" is the most haunting of all their dances, with its music liberally utilizing the minor key, the seriousness of the dance's images of suicide, and its bittersweet tone. The pain of survival is never glossed over in this dance, despite the luxuriousness of the gown and the tux and the ravishing loveliness of the rapport the partners reach. In steps that evoke the necessary cohesion created by the mutual holding quality of links in a chain, the two become partners in survival after her initial dependence on his rescue of her. Indeed the melding of pain and triumph is burned into the filmstock by their unforgettable final dance position as they exit, a contrast as stark as anyone can imagine given the flustered rehearsals for this show that the film audience has seen previously. They bend back in dramatic sync, one of each of their legs grounded to support the rigidly angular, high-stepping, perfectly matching kick that each makes with the other leg, propelling them together into the future with dignity, style, and a measure of desperation.

This representation of the end of the dance contrasts sharply with the scripted resolution of the film. The end of the story hinges on a series of disguises as Bake orchestrates an unlikely deception during which he creates an illusion that makes Bilge believe that the flashy society woman—with whom he is cheating on Connie—is cheating on him with Bake. Only in this way can Bilge be induced to make an honest commitment to Connie—certainly not a basis for a sound intimate partnership. Thus, the last image of the film, which shows Sherry and Connie waving gayly to Bake and Bilge as they set off on ship, suppresses a host of remaining problems. Bilge will always be a boorish chauvinist. Sherry and Bake are beset by instability. What will happen to these boys on their last official mission with the Navy? Normally, this question would disappear under the waves of Bake and Bilge's boat. However, the end of the eerie musical number "Let's Face the Music and Dance" acknowledges the continuing suffering of the couple. The dance, unlike the script, creates resonances of survival of the unknown and of pain as well as triumph that will not let this film be either a simple, mindless entertainment, or an entertaining but piercingly carnivalized insight into the human condition.

Here the two never really linked languages of the film break the film's spine. The unbridgeable gap between the power and intensity of this dance (and other of the subconscious poetic text facilitated by music) and the slight and rickety narrative is the reason that *Fleet* is not one of the major works of the series. The unproductive asymmetry between the negligible narrative and its unspeakably powerful reflection in the final Astaire/Rogers dance cancels any possibility that the elements of the movie can hold together. But the collapse of *Fleet* as a structure does serve to point in a dramatic way to the role of dance in the creation of the couple in the Astaire/Rogers films. Their dancing, the essence of cinematic language with its use of time and space, visual imagery, light, dark, sound, and nonverbal articulations of emotion, required counterpoint with a very particular kind of narrative that could rise to its heights but without blocking it with verbiage or the kind of abstract conceptualization that often is mistaken for the only possible form of seriousness.

THE TRANSITIONAL WORKS

The transitional works, *Shall We Dance* and *Carefree,* both feature Astaire and Rogers as the primary pair, but in vehicles that are overly weighted toward plot. Unlike the major and minor works, in the transitional works, the destiny of the Astaire/Rogers characters is worked out primarily through the formulaic script instead of through the liberating form of music and dance. Ironically, these two transitional works became more overt in their acknowledgment of issues, but issues were reductively treated in classical Hollywood when the script was their main vehicle.

Shall We Dance is about a woman, Linda Keene, a.k.a. Linda Thompson (Rogers), and a man, Petrov, a.k.a. Peter P. Peters of Pittsburgh (Astaire), who get caught up in the snares of image.[17] He is a famous ballet star who would like to cross over into popular entertainment. She is a famous tap dance star who is on the verge of leaving show business because she is exasperated by all the men who chase her only because they have become infatuated by pictures of her. Marriage is her new goal; she assumes marriage will give her a "real" identity rather than the image of an identity. But society is not more real than the illusions her glamour generates. To her manager Arthur Miller (Jerome Cowan), Linda is an income-producing property, and he is determined to keep her. Linda's intended marriage is also more of the same illusion she loathes. The businessman also sees her as property that will bring him status. The script tells us that her only real alternative is Petrov, although it will take the entire movie for Linda to recognize that he is different from the others. Although this film contains some delightful musical inventions, for example the roller-skating dance to "Let's Call the Whole Thing Off" and their lovely (sung not danced) duet "No, No They Can't Take That Away from Me," less than seems to meet the eye is transacted in the music.[18] The problematic issues the surfaced in this film, however, are more blatantly visible in the next transitional film, *Carefree,* which will be discussed in full as the representative film of this category of Astaire/Rogers film.

The story of *Carefree* also dramatizes the problematic relationship between female desire and male authority. In portraying desire and authority it consciously delves into the clash between the two in the subconscious of the characters, featuring its protagonists and antagonists in a substantial variety of altered mental states—inebriation, dreams, waking fantasies, and hypnotic trances. And Rogers has a greater heft in the plot than usual: it is principally the Rogers character who undergoes a transformation. The plot itself depends on her access to the subconscious to determine what she really wants out of marriage and love. However, if, in this film, the subconscious contains the heroine's truth, the cure may be worse than the disease. As soon as the representation of the subconscious shifts from the musical text to the script, it is "dumbed down," gains a bad name, and loses its power to negotiate the ills of culture.

In *Carefree,* Tony Flagg (Astaire) is a psychiatrist who analyzes Amanda Cooper (Rogers), a famous radio singing star, at the request of her fiancé, Tony's best friend, businessman Stephen Arden (Ralph Bellamy). Amanda will not commit to Stephen; she has walked out on their engagement twice and is showing signs of doing the same again. Since Stephen seems to be a "good" man, the good folks who know Amanda believe she is the problem, but the film will reveal that the problem is that Stephen is not a good man. All the elements are in place for an Astaire/Rogers film, principally the menace of the mechanical world of business and the hope of the subconscious. At first, these elements start to take a familiar shape. As soon as Tony begins to analyze Amanda, her dreams reveal that she has fallen in love with Tony, who stirs her feelings as Stephen never has. But can dreams and feelings be sufficient reason for Amanda to switch from Stephen to Tony? She fears that no one will think so; and as soon as Amanda becomes aware that her dream has revealed that she is in love with Tony, she lies to him. Amanda is afraid that if she tells the truth, Tony will terminate treatment because Stephen is his friend. Instead, she plays the psychiatric game, inventing a dream that will hide her love for Tony but keep her in treatment with and therefore near Tony.

In a brilliant stroke, the script calls for Amanda to invent a dream she can tell Tony by looking around his office and playing off objects she sees. Spontaneously her eyes light on an ad for Red Riding Hood capes in a magazine, and Amanda tells Tony that she dreamed she was both Red Riding Hood and the wolf. From there she improvises wildly. Amanda invents a dream in which not only is she the little girl and the beast, but she is also a radio that people can turn on and off, then a tree, and finally the object of a concerted and furious attack by fish and squirrels, which terminates in her death. This wonderful nutty fiction spun by Amanda spontaneously actually reveals her truth; she is in a difficult situation as both object of appetite and a woman with her own desires, a radio singing star who is possessed by a public that can accept or reject her, and a woman who has been besieged by the squirrelly, fishy advances of Stephen, with whom she would be a complete mismatch. But the film loses its way. The logic of *Carefree*'s script defeats its own invention, insisting that Amanda's concocted story is the false dream. What passes for the "real" dream is a Hollywood fabrication, a cliched idea of a dream, a highly romantic idyll, to the tune of a sugary ballad expressing its all too direct sentiment by the dream figure of Tony in on-the-nose lyrics. The ballad, "Color Blind," allows as how Tony had never really seen colors until his love for her made it possible. Yes, Tony has the main point of view in Amanda's dream. The dance is turned into romance by a slow-motion camera, rather than relying fully on the chemistry between Astaire and Rogers. The setting of the dance evokes a paint-by-the-numbers eroticism: a watery garden containing huge flowers bearing an obvious female sexual symbolism. It seems that some fun will be made of this formulaic dream when Amanda arrives for the interview with Tony, in which the dream is discussed. Amanda is wittily costumed in a blouse embroidered with a heart at which numerous arrows are flying. The costume seems like a witty interpretation of her sappy dream of being overwhelmed by love, but the film does not rise to wit. Instead it plods on, too reliant on formula.

In fact, as the film becomes formulaic, it pays tribute to Hollywood's obligatory male protagonist, and Amanda's story, like her dream, ceases to feature her perspective. The film becomes a story about two men, Tony and Steven, fighting over Amanda. Suddenly, Amanda is just the territory in dispute as, alternately, Tony plants suggestions in Amanda's internal life during hypnotic sessions and Stephen uses social authority to take charge of Amanda's external and social life. First, Tony seems to be in control as he professionally hypnotizes Amanda as part of the cure, giving her permission to "do whatever she wants to do" in order to free her up for letting him into the secrets of her problem. Of course, when she does reveal her secret feelings to him and attempts to kiss him, he ignores that and leaves the room to "let her sleep." Then Stephen arrives and, disregarding the privacy of a patient in a psychiatrist's office, and unbeknownst to Tony, forces Amanda to come with him to the radio station, where she is supposed to be performing. As she tags along behind Stephen, who now seems to be in charge of her, still under the suggestion that she act on impulse, she appalls everyone by transgressing the rules of adult behavior, breaking glass in the street and announcing on the air that her sponsor makes a very inferior product. When Tony releases her from the hypnotic state, it is assumed that now she will be what she is supposed to be. But later, at the country club, when she again tries to express herself, telling Tony that she loves him and not Steven, Tony tries to take control of her inner life again when he gives her another set of hypnotic suggestions. In

As Amanda (Rogers) tries to shoot Tony (Astaire), it is clear that there is at least some danger in male attempts to take charge of female desire. Even the very controlling Stephen (Ralph Bellamy) is alarmed.

loyalty to Steven, Tony tells Amanda to think the following: (1) I love Stephen, and I will marry him; (2) Dr. Flagg is a horrible monster; men like him should be shot down like dogs; (3) I love Stephen; I don't love Tony; (4) Tony doesn't love me. There is a somewhat radical edge to this narrative element in that Tony's success in telling Amanda what she wants means his own failure. Once he overrides her real desires, he gets, not a compliant woman, but a compulsive monster who thinks she loves Stephen and actually tries to shoot Tony down like a dog.

As a result, the film slips away from formula a bit more at this point, as Tony has an altered state experience when his subconscious arises in the form of a mirror reflection and tells him that her love is real and that he loves her too. But no, it's Stephen's turn to dominate Amanda;

when he learns that Tony and Amanda are in love with each other, he uses a mutual acquaintance, Judge Travers (Clarence Kolb), to get a bench warrant forbidding Tony to come near Amanda, thus ensuring, Steven hopes, that Tony will never release Amanda from the second set of suggestions. Yes, Stephen is willing to marry Amanda at the cost of her sanity. An out-of-control Amanda remains a football as Tony tries to and finally does de-program her.

Rogers's Amanda may be the least free of all of her characters in the Astaire/Rogers series. Although the script officially designates her desires as the central focus, it de facto removes her control of her life with no music to bear her and the Astaire character above the gender wars. The film's giddy pleasure with Amanda's thralldom to male power is unpleasantly emphasized by the final frames, in which Tony and Amanda get married, the bride sporting the black eye Steven has given her. Although this is presented as a lighthearted joke, the image depicts a woman brutalized for her own good, coming uncomfortably close to winking at spouse abuse.

As is typical in the Astaire/Rogers series, the most powerful part of *Carefree* is in the musical numbers in the film. "The Yam" is the best of the Astaire/Rogers musical numbers in the movie and among the very best in their dance repertoire. A descendant of "The Carioca" (*Rio*), "The Continental" (*Divorcee*), and "The Piccolino" (*Hat*), "The Yam" is another dance being done all over America. Amanda introduces it at the country club just before she tells Tony that she loves him, and it nicely displays both Tony's reluctance to yield to the reality that Amanda's desire represents and the irresistible infectiousness of Amanda's energy. Amanda leads Tony all over the country club, bringing all the members into the fun before she is finished, but ending the dance in an ebullient circle of pas de deux lifts that Tony enters into every bit as enthusiastically as she does. When she leads the way, mutuality, not dominance, is the mode of behavior, and reality is the basis of emotion. Tony gets caught up in the good feelings into which she leads him, but will not let them carry him beyond his wrongheaded analysis of the situation until it is almost too late.

By contrast, "Change Partners," the most beautiful and evocative dance in the film, in which Tony tries but fails either to reverse the suggestion or to evade the bench warrant that separates him from Amanda, is a metaphor for the partial suppression of the expressive power of their work together by the dominance of the script over this film. The "Change Partners" number is a powerful use of negative space; it says more about what it is not there than what is. The dance itself is facilitated by a variety of scripted tricks by means of which Tony gets Amanda out from under Steven's watchful eyes and traps her against her will in his power. This is a situation otherwise unknown to the Astaire/Rogers works, in which it was always a matter of tricking authorities to get permission to dance, not each other.[19] When Tony finally gets Amanda alone in the gazebo outside the country club where they are all having dinner, the situation he has created makes it necessary to dance with her in a trance, as if he were Svengali commanding Trilby's comatose body, she responsive to his every suggestion, dutifully compliant as he moves her about or draws him to her from the distance to which he has propelled her.[20] The lifts, so very different from any other they have ever executed, find her lying across his arms as if she were being levitated under the power of his enchantment; the end of the dance finds her in a parody of the pose in which they end the "Night and Day" number in *The Gay Divorcee*, there so moved by emotion, here like nothing so much as a department store manikin.[21] Her portrayal here as his creature powerfully reminds us of how much she has always been her own woman in their dancing together. That such hyperbolic control doesn't work is in keeping with the spirit of the Astaire/Rogers film. A woman under a man's control is connected to no one, not even herself. She boomerangs back under Steven's control as soon as he finds Amanda with Tony, well before Tony can make use of the trance he has induced.

But in a sour note at the end of the film, Amanda does seem to need force for her own good. It is only when Stephen blunders in and inadvertently decks Amanda that the "true union" can take place. This deeply unpalatable, hypocritical use of a surrogate attack on the heroine to get her married stands in bald contradiction of the tone of the major Astaire/Rogers films. Mutuality was its most characteristic element, and connection much emphasized over the formalities of marriage. The contrast between Amanda's black eye as she marches down the aisle and the bouts of hysterical laughter that cleared the way for marriage in *Swing Time* strongly illustrate the prelude to entropy that appeared in the transitional films.

THE SERIES IN ENTROPY

The last two films made by Astaire and Rogers suffer so from entropy that, aside from the physical presence of Astaire/Rogers, they are not in tone or construction Astaire/Rogers musicals. They are rather melodramas decorated with music. The world of normality is not satirized in either film, as was the case in the major and even the minor and transitional works. There is little of the misperception and disguise that typically establishes the zaniness of "normality" in the Astaire/Rogers universe in *The Barkleys of Broadway* and none in *The Story of Vernon and Irene Castle*. Most debilitating, there is no tension between the music and the script. In *Castle*, there is a seam-less harmony between them, and in *Barkleys* there is almost complete dissociation between story and dancing, creating a fragmentation that makes the music almost a liability.

The weight of history in *The Story of Vernon and Irene Castle* makes it the most leaden of the Astaire/Rogers collaborations, tying them to the most cliched plot pattern in the American film canon: the biopic success story, a genre almost devoid of the elements that worked for the Astaire/Rogers representation of intimacy. This film is about the external events of the Castles' success. They meet, realize their compatibility, and, after a brief struggle, succeed. Then, Vernon is killed during the war and Irene is left with her memories. The dances are all reproductions of the Castle performance, none of which are integrated into the subtext of the couple's relationship. The movie deals not at all in terms of the inner obstacles to desire and freedom that so engaged the audience in the previous works. Nor do the external obstacles ever rise to any level of interest. There is a lot of music in *Castle*, but it is so carefully chosen for historical accuracy rather than for tone and mood that it has a stultifying effect. The story, undistinguished by any humor or interest, is further bogged down by dry factual recreations of Castle routines. The lifelessness of the film is owing to not only the pressure of history, which always takes itself seriously as truth, but also to the pressure of Irene Castle, who worked as a consultant on the film and who was uncomfortable with and somewhat contemptuous of the elements of the dances that arose from Astaire and Rogers's chemistry. She objected particularly to the gaze exchanged between the two of them, certainly one of the externalizations of their chemistry. She remarked that if she, the historical Irene Castle, had looked at her husband, the historical Vernon Castle, in that manner, he would have burst out laughing. Thus the little tension there was in this film was between the dreamlike form of cinema and the logic of history, as told by Irene Castle, which dominated the movie.[22] It is the portrait of a synergy falling into entropy, an almost complete absence of cinematic language made possible by chemistry. A complete inversion of Swing *Time*, which tells us so much about the necessity of crazy undignified laughter for permitting the life force to survive the crippling effects of the smallness of spirit that has been misrecognized by a limited society as dignity, *Castle* is entombed within the rigid walls of convention.

In *The Barkleys of Broadway*, although the narrative emphasis is on fun, music and dance are, sadly, pushed from center stage and subordinated to script and plot. This film is basically a series of allusions to the Astaire/Rogers past, but without any of its magic. The simple story details a bump in the road for Josh (Astaire) and Dinah (Rogers) Barkley, a professionally successfully though personally embattled married musical comedy team who cannot live with or without each other, though their incessant conflicts do not mean that they are not nice people.[23] They simply push each other's buttons; typically his perfectionism leads to dissatisfaction with tiny details, and her subordinate place as a singer/dancer to his writer/director creates resentment in her. Dinah bolts the team temporarily to try her hand at "straight" acting, with the encouragement of Jacques Barredout (Jacques François), a famous serious playwright who believes that Dinah has the potential to be a "great tragic actress." But his opinion is not completely unbiased; he is also romantically attracted to her. Dinah makes a success of a starring role in a play about Sarah Bernhardt, but finds she has gotten the serious acting bug out of her system. She returns to Josh and the more joyous musical comedy scene.

Oddly, the ways in which the Barkleys set each other off, despite their magical affinity for each other and their brilliance together onstage, so closely mirror the offscreen frustrations between the actual Astaire and Rogers that it is hard to believe that the movie was initially planned for Judy Garland and Astaire. However, that is the indisputable fact. Rogers was the third choice for the role of Dinah Barkley; moreover, despite the resemblance of the main characters to the offscreen Astaire and Rogers, the vehicle itself lacks most of the characteristics necessary for a truly satisfying Astaire/Rogers collaboration.[24] The music in the movie, which was chosen after the script had been written by Comden and Green to suit Astaire and Rogers, features an opening dance sequence in the main title credit sequence which shows Josh and Dinah dancing to a song called "Swing Trot," reminiscent of their film Swing Time, but updated to reflect the contemporary popularity of Swing music. This number also recalls that characteristic feature of the old Astaire/Rogers musicals, their introduction of a new dance sensation that everyone will want to do, but here it is the Swing Trot rather than the Continental. However, its position under the credits immediately tells us how perfunctory this reference to Astaire and Rogers is, and how shallowly self-conscious. Another equally pointed and equally failed reference later in the film is the song to which Astaire/Rogers dance as a reminder of Dinah and Josh's love for each other, "No, No They Can't Take That Away from Me," a song from *Shall We Dance* to which they did not dance in that film. This song was actually suggested by both Astaire and Rogers for *Barkleys* as a nostalgic salute to former days. Here the song is in a position to permit an important transaction between the characters, but its flatness sadly reflects how little transaction is possible in this film.

Sadly the film is only a series of allusions to the past that completely contradicts the spirit of the original partnership of Rogers and Astaire. The world of *Barkleys* is solidly middle class. It depicts people in the arts as quirky if charming, but certainly not solid citizens. This is a radical contrast to the worlds of the major works in which there is little as bizarre as the attempt at normality, middle-class life, or rational order. Thus while the quintessential Astaire/Rogers couple's profound, organic connection distinguishes it from the shaky structures created by a false, inauthentic culture, *Barkleys* valorizes the solidity of the world of business and logic. The intimacy that had been a bulwark of sanity and grace in a graceless, generally deranged world in the early films had become by 1949 chaos verging on insanity in the middle of middle-class stability. The script conflict is based on a premise that inverts the universe of the Astaire/Rogers film: intimacy is trouble. The very first spectacle of Josh and Dinah offered is the final fragment of their onstage performance of "Swing Trot," which is a dance, insofar as the audience sees it, that pits the two of them against each other. Each smiling the artificial performer's smile, each competes to be most ingratiating. The Barkleys' curtain speeches continue the rivalry as they battle to outdo each other in their expressions of gratitude toward the partner.

Underneath all this high show biz polish is Dinah's restlessness and Josh's impatience with her increasing tendency to slip from his control. But Dinah's ambition does not lead to a film in which female desire is at last consciously acknowledged, but rather to an increase of Josh's control over Dinah; indeed, at the end of the film a reconstructed Dinah is happy being "the little woman." What is more, the film suggests that she can never be anything else. When Dinah goes off with Barredout to star in *Young Sarah*, she is inept in her initial attempts to work in the new genre. It is only when Josh, spying on rehearsals and seeing her desperate situation, begins to call her on the telephone, disguising his voice as Barredout's (Astaire is a terrific mimic[25]) and giving her directions that are helpful to her that she begins to develop a successful approach to her new assignment. Thus script logic effectively vitiates all validity for Dinah's initial annoyance at the presumption of her artistic inferiority to Josh's.

Worse, the music that so complexly articulated the unspeakable in human longings in earlier Astaire/Rogers films is not present to support Rogers, stranding her on the bleak island of formulaic narrative. Here, irrelevant music simply makes the film diffuse. And there is no paucity of irrelevance. Astaire and Rogers have six musical numbers together in this movie, in addition to the main title dance: "You'd Be Hard to Replace," "Bouncin' the Blues"; "My One and Only Highland Fling"; "A Weekend in the Country"; "They Can't Take That Away from Me," and "Manhattan Downbeat." "Hard to Replace," their only intimate number and the best of the bunch, is performed after they come home from the fraught opening night that begins the film. It is remarkably tender, a complete contrast to the main title, all the false razzle-dazzle scraped away to reveal a depth of feeling that suggests how powerful a realistic film designed specifically for Rogers and Astaire might have been. Working under the handicaps described above with regard to the kind of world the Barkleys live in, the song nevertheless organizes a behind-the-scenes look at Josh and Dinah that radiates the kind of chemistry released through music in the early films, permitting the audience to slip beyond the script logic of their competition to the warmth that makes reconciliation valid after each of their power struggles. Unfortunately, we never see that kind of energy again in the film. The rest of the Astaire/Rogers musical numbers have no pertinence to their conflict, nor do the several musical interludes in which they do not appear together. The nadir of irrelevance is reached in the piano solos performed by Oscar Levant, as the couple's best friend and composer for their shows, Ezra Millar, and Fred Astaire's tour de force "Shoes with Wings On."[26]

The most telling of the failed Astaire/Rogers duos in this film is the purportedly erotic dance performed to "No, No They Can't Take That

Away from Me," after they are tricked into performing together. Clearly this is the moment when all the old feelings are meant to be reawakened. Potentially, it is a good moment. However, the dance is not a transformative experience, but a static compilation of old positions that we associate with the dances from the 1930s films. It is even presented as such. Rather than beginning with their characteristic transitional slow, rhythmic walk that led them from the mundane world into the dreamworld of dance, "No, No" simply starts cold and moves through the catalogue of familiar positions. The perfunctory catalogue of Astaire/Rogers's positions is ineffective in moving the audience toward desire. There is no felt reality possible when no raw documentary image of charisma or synergy infuses the plot with credibility.[27]

After Dinah's "triumph" as an actress, and her discovery that the significant direction of her acting was done by Josh impersonating Barredout over the telephone, the reunion scene is one of pure passive aggression—all that is left to Dinah if she wants to assert some dignity and self-respect. Dinah now orchestrates the misperceptions, as Josh did when he made his phone calls imitating Jacques. She rushes to the apartment they once shared and pretends that she is still planning a romance with Jacques. In self-defense, Josh pretends to be involved romantically with Dinah's understudy. Just as they appear to be calling the whole thing off, Dinah reveals she knows who made those directorial phone calls by imitating Josh imitating Jacques. He recognizes one of the lines he spoke in his telephone performance and stops pretending indifference, showing how he deeply loves her.

Despite this diminished form of masquerade, this reduction of the carnivalesque to a little role playing, when they fling themselves into each other's arms, some ineradicable remains of the physicality of the Astaire and Rogers of the early films floods the screen. It is as though the powerful rapport of their bodies is waiting for a dance to start that will channel the energy of the pair back through the camera lens. However, the dance that will free the energy again doesn't take place. Instead, their power is hidden again under a bushel basket of musical and verbal cliches in which they swear never to be serious again. There is then an abrupt dissolve out of their living room and onto the stage, so that we can leave them where they began the film, performing conventional dance steps in front of an audience. The final dance is about being a performer, not about the special form of intimacy between lovers.

CONCLUSION

With the exception of the last two films made together by Astaire and Rogers, their work made the central feature of the couple—intimacy—visible onscreen as a core of synergy that permeates, challenges, and alters rather than being created by the Hollywood-sanctioned signs of romance. Their best films, and to a significant degree even their lesser collaborations, are highly complex compositions of powerful documentary image and the formulaic codes of Hollywood entertainment that create imaginative pleasure in the perception of what are in fact troubling dislocations between inner and outer life. Language brings disorder in its faulty pointing toward the events of our lives; social limits are drawn with a capriciousness that threatens to numb us with stultifying obligations. Yet what is rigid in those systems can be supplemented by un-nameable but palpable energies that spring to life through the potency of music and movement.

As with the other synergistic series discussed here, entropy was the fate of the Astaire/Rogers collaboration. Most critics believe that the end of their onscreen partnership in the thirties was caused by a falling off at the box office and that the reason that their popularity did not take off again when they worked together in 1949 was because it was a new era, and what they did best was no longer in demand. A penetrating look at the trajectory of their work, however, suggests that the falling off in demand for what they had done best was an indicator not of their inability to work effectively but of a significant collapse of the movie musical under the pressure of increasingly conceptual entertainment. The Astaire/Rogers films ultimately were dominated by scripts burdened by social platitudes and increasingly drained of the synergy that originally flooded the Astaire/Rogers film with raw chemistry. Why? The evidence points to a problematic shift by the entertainment industry toward putting emphatic priority on simplistic plots in musical movies that depended almost completely on words and conceptually generated situations. Since the indeterminate nature of the intimacy of the couple is carried by the music and the images of dance in this film genre, this development was accompanied by a loss of respect for the emotional texture of the screen couple.[28] When we compare *Top Hat* to *The Barkleys of Broadway*, we see a complete inversion of priorities and the devaluing of couple dynamics. In *Top Hat*, the music and dancing is threaded throughout the story as a mode of making meaning that contrasts with the literalism of the plot, suggesting the interplay of organic force and logic as organizing systems in human affairs. As a result of this heterogeneity in the process of making meaning, the Astaire/Rogers characters dignify intimacy with powerful images generated by dance and music and a felt sense of the frequent absurdity of the social structures that organize the plot. In *Barkleys* the plot carries the entire burden of meaning, while the musical numbers are interruptions that are diversions, suggesting the irrelevance of the play of organic force in human affairs. As a result, Astaire/Rogers couple is used to suggest the freakishness of emotional rapport and the entertainment value of the sideshow of how lovers thrash about, while the more rational folk look on in amusement. Music in the musical had been trivialized sufficiently to impede it as a form of expression that could enable the Astaire/Rogers synergy. Though other channels for strong couple synergy have subsequently evolved in the mass media, the musical movie has not yet recovered from the blight of literalism.

CHAPTER *Five*

KATHARINE HEPBURN AND SPENCER TRACY
Much Ado about "the Little Woman"

Katharine Hepburn and Spencer Tracy made their major films together between 1942 and 1953, a time when Hollywood was besieged by dauntingly direct political influence as never before or since. Their films reflect both the politics of the period and the crisis of couple chemistry that was a central feature of their time. Hepburn and Tracy joined forces during a period in Hollywood in which there was, paradoxically, an increase in both government censorship and legal protection for freedom of expression in commercial feature films. While the Supreme Court was in the process of extending the First Amendment protection of freedom of speech to the movies, the House Un-American Activities Committee (HUAC) and Senator Joseph McCarthy were conducting separate, viciously intrusive official investigations into the Hollywood community to determine whether there was subversive Communist influence on the movies. The investigations pressured the studios for the first time to be wary not only of what was said in the movies but also of the politics of the members of the creative community. Despite the reality of a collaborative production system (which had long contained known Communists) that had never been taken over by any of the many and varied beliefs of any of its individual members, the studios did not resist the McCarthy/HUAC contentions that inevitably work created by writers, directors, and actors with private Communist beliefs would be corrupted by those opinions. The intimidating government investigations constrained the movies as the PCA never could. Ironically, however, while this caused a lot of private grief and a flood of mindless, pointless films that studio heads hoped would show the world that Hollywood was not a tool of the Communists, the fact is that a large number of pointedly thematic Hollywood films began to appear in significant numbers. Hepburn, one of the people in Hollywood who were seemingly immune to the threats of McCarthy and HUAC, was one of the Hollywood creators most committed to doctrinal movies. There is evidence to suggest that most politicians believed that the public would not credit any attack against her as a subversive, and she took advantage of her position to make, with Spencer Tracy, socially relevant, liberal films.[1]

The ideological ferment in commercial entertainment of which the Hepburn/Tracy series was a part emerged alongside a growing insistence that movies were covered by the free speech amendment of the Bill of Rights, a ferment that culminated in the so-called *Miracle* decision of the Supreme Court in 1952. This high court decision sheltered the right to free speech in commercial movies for the first time, reversing the long-standing legal existence of films as mere unprotected merchandise, as declared by the Supreme Court in 1915. *The Miracle* (1948) was a segment of a two-part film directed by Roberto Rossellini that told a story of a woman (Anna Magnani) who believes that she is pregnant with a new Christ child. Though the movie was not made in the United States, the PCA battled against its distribution to American movie theaters through the court system all the way up to the Supreme Court, which decided that its subject matter was covered by the Bill of Rights and could not be suppressed. This 1952 decision empowered Hollywood filmmakers who were strongly feeling the need to counter McCarthy and HUAC. World War II had stimulated general public interest, and the interest of commercial filmmakers, in many obvious questions about human rights that came out of the war because of Hitler's persecution of Jews, gypsies, homosexuals, and eventually Catholics and "Aryan" intellectual dissidents. Painful awareness of these Nazi policies led American politics toward a renewed interest in civil rights for ethnic minorities and women, and the mass media followed that interest, producing more overtly political and social messages covering more points on the spectrum than ever before.

HUAC and Senator McCarthy had a more devastating effect on the wild images of the second language of visual and sound image: the kind of chemistry that made possible the Synergistic Couple. Censorship, which ignored Communism as a theoretical construct and described it as a kind of possession—the reason why the investigations of Communists in various walks of American life were likened at the time to the seventeenth-century witch-hunts in Salem—made people vigilant against what could come to them through the subconscious. The expression issue, as it concerned Hollywood films, manifested itself in an emphasis on the literal aspects of movies. Literal "belief" in a movie, as focus of value and expressiveness, crowded out the more figurative elements of belief, the poetry of nerves that the modernist movement in the arts had fostered, the power that drove Synergistic Couple chemistry. Except for the sudden emergence of science fiction films as an escape valve for the ambiguity of the imagination, the value of Hollywood films of the period became contingent on the ability of the film to link itself literally to something in "the real world."[2]

The collaboration of Hepburn and Tracy, with its combination of chemistry and social relevance, illustrates the pressures of war and postwar politics on the Synergistic Couple. Their films demonstrate vividly what happened to couple synergy, chemistry, and the documentary raw images that had so vitalized the films of the 1930s as the country moved into the last half of the twentieth century, the post-studio era in the culture industry, and a time of radical swings in general public consciousness about issues that had previously only fired up political minorities: civil rights, the gender revolution, class under capitalism. While Hepburn and Tracy worked together, "real world" films were becoming split between two kinds of entertainment movies, neither of which cultivated Synergistic Couple energy. One category included formulaic propaganda films, war films committed to the patriotic cause, and postwar films doggedly committed to the normalization of postwar America. This category espoused reductive portrayals of complex political problems, using large helpings of pseudo-documentary images of urban streets and national landmarks like the White House, and war footage, manipulatively managed for meliorist story purposes. Couples were worked into stories to fit the patriotic propaganda of the film: the recipe for the Functional Couple. Eventually, the use of couples in Hollywood movies in this manner became so extreme that Hollywood began to satirize itself, as in the parodies of the "normalization" of gender relations in the three films of Rock Hudson and Doris Day: *Pillow Talk* (1959, Dir. Michael Gordon), *Lover Come Back* (1961, Dir. Delbert Mann), and *Send Me No Flowers* (1964, Dir. Norman Jewison).

Alternatively, Hollywood critiqued ordinary moral strictures, as in the angst-ridden films about sexual repression among the young (e.g., *Splendor in the Grass*, 1961, Dir. Elia Kazan).

The other category of films, those of the one day to be recognized Hollywood auteur, dealt in the ironies of Hollywood's new pseudo-realism. Alfred Hitchcock's *Psycho* (1960), for example, aside from working as a psychological thriller, portrayed the utter irrelevance of the psychiatric mumbo jumbo so favored by earnest Hollywood social problem films as a mode of commenting on the profound mysteries of the subconscious, and Douglas Sirk's surrealist use of industrial images in *Written on the Wind* (1956) ironically revealed a subconscious subtext under Hollywood's literalized representations of ordinary reality. Similarly, the onscreen couples used by Sirk and Hitchcock tended to reflect searingly on the formulaic nature of the Hollywood couple of the forties and fifties by emphasizing, through the use of patently artificial star images, the deadening role of image in human relations. It was not the chemistry of Kim Novak and James Stewart in *Vertigo* (1958) that Hitchcock utilized, for example, but the inert elements of their star images, which pointed up the barrier to organic relationships caused by formulaic gender roles.

Hepburn and Tracy, by contrast, and virtually alone, continued the tradition of the Synergistic Couple that burns through all formulas with an energy transfer of its own. They validated the possibility of representing human connection amidst all the political and social upheavals of World War II and its aftermath. They managed to negotiate the waters of ideologically torn America and its compulsions for "realism" by a complex mode of fusing their screen chemistry with socially realistic stories and generating for the public a link between their offscreen reality and what they did onscreen. Between 1942 and 1967, the period of the Hepburn/Tracy collaboration, the two of them were the last throwback to the distinctive 1930s onscreen couples. However, as a part of a later era, Tracy and Hepburn made couple movies with pointed, socially realistic portraits of society, with "reality links" to new ideas that were being debated. Five, to some effect, actively confront Fascism and sexism: *Woman of the Year* (1942, Dir. George Stevens), *Keeper of the Flame* (1942, Dir. George Cukor), *Without Love* (1945, Dir. Harold Bucquet), *Adam's Rib* (1949, Dir. George Cukor), *Pat and Mike* (1952, Dir. George Cukor). The remaining four films—*The Sea of Grass* (1946, Dir. Elia Kazan), *State of the Union* (1948, Dir. Frank Capra), *Desk Set* (1957, Dir. Walter

Lang), and *Guess Who's Coming to Dinner* (1967, Dir. Stanley Kramer)—also raise issues, albeit ineffectively, of property ownership, corruption in the American political system, the replacement of human labor by machines, and racism, respectively.

But it wasn't issues that captivated movie audiences; the fundamental reality-linked element in their films was the chemistry generated by their own off/onscreen relationship. In none of their jointly made films did the scripts, which were generally wordy and simplistic, account for the power of their collaboration. Rather, the ideological debates in their movies depended upon the perceived reflexivity of the Tracy/Hepburn onscreen relationship. The public believed that they were offscreen just what they were onscreen. And they themselves used the screen as a privileged space in which they could contest each other as they could not in real life. What they could not negotiate with each other in private they played out in their public forum. Tracy and Hepburn did not acknowledge their offscreen intimacy because it was an adulterous affair in a time when adultery was a box office offense. Tracy is quoted as saying that they were "invisible in all the right places."[3] Yet there were traces of public lore about the behind-the-scenes reality. Only a tiny fraction of the general public knew anything about Tracy's wife and children; most moviegoers simply bracketed the names of Tracy and Hepburn in a way that made their connection a fact tinged with romance and eroticism. This was a pervasive mode of thinking that was fueled both by journalistic gossip, which had the potency on this occasion of being correct, and by their powerful connection in their onscreen appearances. A complicated relationship between screen images and real life issued from this situation. The public constructed romantic fantasies about the real Hepburn and Tracy, imagining them to be in fact what they seemed to be together in their movies. But more to the point, "belief" in the characters they played, and thus in the ideological positions they espoused, depended on what the public believed about Hepburn and Tracy as private persons, an extreme form of the mass audience tendency to become confused about the line between illusion and reality with really compelling screen couples.

Public response to the women that Hepburn played in her films with Tracy was heavily conditioned by a belief that there was some documentary truth about Hepburn in the free-spirited, rebellious, liberal, and assertive women that she played. Some slippage between life and the movies was always an issue in Hollywood, but more with

Hepburn than was usual. That Hepburn was actually free and forthright is less important than that public belief in her image was so extremely germane to the imaginative experience of her performances. The slippage of the images from Hepburn's previous films and her public image onto the films she made with Tracy was at the core of audience engagement. By the time Hepburn began to work with Tracy, the audience had rejected her films after an early enthusiasm for her, because of what was widely considered her overly abrasive femininity. Yet in hindsight, that popular rejection created the climate for her triumphant resurgence in the Tracy/Hepburn film series.[4] Hepburn's movies with Tracy were intentionally engineered by her to save her career by showing the public a Hepburn who was ultimately submissive to the right man—Tracy. In *Lion's Roar*, a lavishly produced in-house MGM publicity pamphlet that was issued regularly to promote the latest releases, the studio quite blatantly spun her new image when it promoted *Woman of the Year,* the first Tracy/Hepburn film to be released. The new image was not an inversion of the old one—the studio continued to promote Hepburn as a firebrand—but they added a qualification; hers became a refurbished image of a firebrand who could be contained. The pamphlet promotes her as "a stick of dynamite with a very short fuse. Usually the fuse is sputtering. This causes most people to back away fearfully, and seek shelter. It's the worst thing they could do either with a stick of dynamite, or Miss Hepburn. The bold thing to do with a lit stick of dynamite is to walk up firmly and snuff it out before anybody's hurt. This works with Miss Hepburn, too. Admittedly, in both cases, this is easier said than done." Clearly, Tracy is the chosen snuffer. In the description of the picture, we learn that "Tracy is of the 'treat 'em rough' school and Hepburn is the 'hard to get gal.' And in the end the man of the sports world teaches the woman of the year that love conquers even notoriety."[5] Ironically, despite the obvious manipulation of the public relations, the new image reflected an actual change that had taken place in her life because of her liaison with Tracy, toward whom she was uncharacteristically submissive. Thus the conviction Hepburn brought to her roles with Tracy was conditioned by an authentic interpersonal relationship, while at the same time the conviction experienced by the audience was partially created by Hepburn's intensity and partially by a public belief in the authenticity of the personal relationship.

Tracy's offscreen need for Hepburn, as a career strategy, was different in kind but not in degree. Tracy did not have a potentially fatal public image problem when he teamed up with Hepburn. His image was excellent. Rather, Tracy had a potentially terminal problem with his relationship to the studio. Although Tracy had played many offbeat characters, like Dr. Jekyll and Mr. Hyde, he was perceived as a "decent average Joe" whose ordinary common sense and compassion might lift him to heroic heights, and the audience assumed that he was in fact that kind of man. However, he was, in fact, a destructive, and self-destructive, womanizing alcoholic. Prone to long alcoholic binges, Tracy engaged in epic rampages in hotels and bars when he was inebriated, which were, with difficulty, kept out of the newspapers, as were his many compulsive affairs with his co-stars.[6] But there were leaks to the press, which threatened to break the dam of studio damage control until Hepburn came into his life. MGM had lost patience with his disreputable behavior and had come to feel that he was more trouble than he was worth. When this behavior diminished somewhat after he began his association with Hepburn, MGM, satisfied that Hepburn could manage him, no longer thought of letting him go. Furthermore, the studio was pleased with the evolution of his public image through his work with Hepburn—basically a much-glorified version of his earlier Good Joe image. *Lion's Roar* punches home his Hepburnified "good guy" image:

> It isn't often that Spencer Tracy gets to play straight. For one thing, his rare ability to create the difficult and out-of-the ordinary character roles no one else can do has more of less tied him down to parts off the beaten path. In this category were his Father Edward J. Flannagan, Thomas A. Edison, Dr. Jekyll and Mr. Hyde, Major Rogers, Manuel, Father Tim and a long list of others.
>
> Playing straight simply means that in "Woman of the Year," Tracy could be himself, a normal, average guy, who was nobody in particular. His character of a sports writer on a big New York daily gave full scope to Tracy's most important asset, his complete naturalness. He could wear the same comfortable, unassuming clothes he selects for his own personal wardrobe, plain blue and grey suits, blue neckties, shirts with soft collars and a battered felt hat. He didn't have to be bothered with make-up, which he detests, or the tedious job of working out a characterization. He could, in other words, be himself.[7]

This blatantly mendacious publicity campaign constructed a public image for Tracy that was the mirror image of the actual man. Perhaps his portrayal of Hyde had called for makeup, but it was closer by far to Tracy's nature than Sam Craig in *Woman of the Year*, for whom Tracy invented a life lie character. Riddled until the end of his life with debilitating guilt and doubt that made him violent, through the Tracy/Hepburn series, onscreen Tracy became "living proof" of the extraordinary decency of the ordinary man, strong with the confidence of masculine entitlement and dependably authoritative enough to effectively battle social evil: a man's man with a soft spot for a woman, tender but tough, equitable but never self-righteous.

The eerie slippages between the private and professional lives of Hepburn and Tracy, the enigmatic interconnections between their evolution as people in relationship to each other and their evolutions as screen personas, made each onscreen appearance together part of a life-changing growth as an offscreen couple, and infused the urgency, immediacy, and spontaneity into the film that karmic experiences infuse into our lives. What the camera sees and what the sound equipment hears of the work of a Synergistic Couple is always in some sense as pure a form of documentary cinema as Hollywood can manage. In the case of Hepburn and Tracy, the density of the documentary elements, or wild energies, was especially ambiguous and abundant. The mass audience did not see the Tracy that raged with alcoholic fury or the fiercely indomitable, overly aggressive Hepburn, but rather the truths that each permitted the other to manufacture in their own imaginations, and that each believed and clung to, a mutually induced belief system that played out onscreen what Tracy and Hepburn could not play out in their real connection to each other. Tracy/Hepburn movies complicated the literalistic, ideologically motivated Hollywood storytelling mode of the forties and fifties and the concomitant reductiveness of the discourse about intimacy.[8]

COUPLE OF THE YEAR

Their first Tracy/Hepburn film, *Woman of the Year*, set the tone for the rest of their collaboration. *Woman* is the story of a romance between sports columnist Sam Craig (Tracy) and political commentator Tess Harding (Hepburn), a feminist following in the footsteps of her beloved Aunt Ellen (Fay Bainter). Both reporters for the same newspaper, *The Chronicle*, Sam and Tess are drawn into conflict before they meet each other through the mutual exceptions they take to each other's publicly stated opinions. However, when they meet, for all their differences, they fall in love so instantly and so completely that it is not long before they are married. The marriage turns into a push and pull between sexual attraction and career competition. The movie shows Sam trying to deal with it honestly and Tess, egged on by her arrogant, gay (very homophobically presented) assistant, Gerald (Dan Tobin), maintaining a self-centered obliviousness to Sam's needs that soon threatens the marriage.[9] Sam puts up with her self-importance until Tess gets carried away by her public liberal persona and, without prior discussion, adopts Christopher (George Kezas), a young Greek war orphan. As events unfold, it becomes clear that Tess's glamourous independence causes her to neglect both Sam and the child. On the night she is to be awarded the title of Woman of the Year, she blithely plans to go off to the award dinner believing that it will be all right to leave Chris home alone to take care of himself for a few hours. Sam starts making his own unilateral decisions. First he returns Chris to the orphanage, and then he leaves Tess. A shaken Tess wants Sam back, especially after attending the marriage of feminist Aunt Ellen to her father (Minor Watson), at which Ellen shatters all Tess's fantasies about her role model by confessing that her years of success and independence have masked a lonely craving for the bliss of ordinary domesticity. Tess drives straight from the ceremony to Sam's new apartment, where she tricks the superintendent into letting her in. Unable to make even a simple breakfast for Sam, she despairs of being able to be a good wife. But he saves the situation by telling her that he does not want a domestic "little woman" any more than he wants a world conqueror wife. Agreeing to be more moderate in her approach to a two-career marriage, Tess is confronted with her first challenge when Gerald appears to whisk her off to a boat launching. She passes the test with flying colors, as she permits Sam to kick Gerald out of the house, and the boat launching commitment along with him. Her reward is Sam's protective embrace.

Just as this story summary reveals an overt attention to ideology that we have seen in none of the films of the previously discussed Synergistic Couples, it also reveals the kind of relentless undermining of the bold advances in discussion of gender issues that seemed possible at the beginning of the story. It is the embodiment of the paradoxical increase in both censorship and freedom of expression in the Hollywood of the time. It is also the embodiment of the reflexive nature of the Hepburn/Tracy phenomenon, as, under the women's issues–oriented plot is the issue of Hepburn's relationship to the audience and to Tracy. If Hepburn succeeded in bringing to the screen a powerful, dazzling woman writ large—much as she was in life—that woman onscreen became the target of a savage attack by the narrative—much as Hepburn had been attacked by the public. Yes, this film wants to assure the audience, it is perfectly true that without a man to set limits for her, the Woman of the Year "is not a woman at all," as Sam tells Tess at the climactic moment when she plans to leave Chris alone at home. When Tess finally submits to his leadership, that leadership is presented as more than fair in that it is willing to grant her a moderate amount of freedom to use her talent. She becomes Hollywood's candidate for the replacement for the old stereotype of the "little woman" with the "medium-sized" woman.

The film was a calculated ritual by which Hepburn accepted public chastisement for her former very outspoken refusal to operate within the parameters of what society defined as feminine, and as a result she was rewarded with the renewed embrace of the public in the form of box office receipts. Paradoxically, in the very act of submission, Hepburn assumed unprecedented female control both over her career and over the American image of manhood.[10] For this film, Hepburn maneuvered Louis B. Mayer into letting her choose the script, the director, and her co-star. Mayer was a little overwhelmed by her success at managing both him and Tracy, who, uncharacteristically, was not out of control on the set while Hepburn was there to defuse potentially disruptive situations. But what was more impressive than her ability to significantly reduce Tracy's lapses of control was her ability to make him into the image of the moderate American hero. Offscreen she was, and for the rest of his life continued to be, the external surrogate for the self-control that he could not summon up in his own interior life. Onscreen, she used him as the image of dependable masculine control over her uppity femininity. At the same time, as she adored him onscreen, she also sat at his feet, literally, in life.[11] The Byzantine tensions between submission and control embedded in Hepburn's inspired conflation of illusion and reality mark the mood and textures of the Hepburn/Tracy films in a way that complicates mass media discourse about intimacy and the social discourse of gender.

That complexity is eminently notable in the notorious closure of

Woman of the Year, which was blatantly designed, by producer Frank Mankiewicz's admission, to pander to audience prejudices against Hepburn as a powerful woman.[12] Yet, although today it is widely discussed as the fatal flaw in an otherwise delightful and progressive film, the closure of *Woman* is not as straightforward as it may seem. It is a vivid example of how the indeterminate relationship between the Tracy/Hepburn onscreen characters and offscreen public personas created a second language in the Hepburn/Tracy text that opened the movie up beyond studio intentions. The proof of the complexity of what happened in the film, despite the rather simple studio plan to punish Hepburn onscreen, is how visibly inappropriate the closure of the film is. The end of *Woman* creates a physical discomfort in the spectator, not the pure feeling of content at the diminution of a powerful woman with which the studio sought to placate the public. In this film, pleasure at her subjugation by Sam is purchased by the pain of watching Tess ridiculed, a pain created by the chemistry of Tracy and Hepburn.

The pleasure and power of the Tracy/Hepburn chemistry is in unalterable conflict with the cliched politics of the script. The dissonance between the two is the source of the enduring fascination of the film, and what separates it from the numerous comedies of the time, for example Rosalind Russell's endless onscreen falls from proud independence into the role of the little woman in films like *His Girl Friday* (1940, Dir. Howard Hawks), *Take a Letter, Darling* (1942, Dir. Mitchell Leisen), and *Picnic* (1955, Dir. Joshua Logan).[13] By contrast, the synergistic relationship between Tracy and Hepburn makes that easy kind of public sadism toward women all but impossible. Beginning with one of the great onscreen first couple encounters of cinematic history, the film is informed by such a satisfyingly startling documentary image of male-female attraction/repulsion and mutuality, as Hepburn and Tracy conspired to give to the camera their real feelings for each other, that any ideological betrayal of that synergy cost an emotional price.

The big first meeting takes place when Sam and Tess are called to the office of the editor of *The Chronicle* (Reginald Owen) so he can mediate the in-print feud between them. The nonverbal energy in this scene, infused with the ambiguous innate power of the Hepburn/Tracy pairing, so challenges the information-bearing dialogue spoken by the editor that the pleasure of the story and the dialogue becomes negligible in relation to the pleasure of the ungovernable energy in images and undomesticated sounds. In this scene, few words are spoken by Sam and Tess, while the editor drones on about their public feud and the need for collegiality. We are adrift in their synergy without any manipulated information to direct our emotions. There is no non-diegetic music to tell us how to feel about the monotonous dialogue or the thrilling energy passing between Hepburn and Tracy; all that is heard above the editor is the rustle of paper and the click of shoes as Sam walks into the office. The editor's perfunctory verbal introductions vaporize under the heat of Sam's visual introduction to Tess in a POV shot that tracks across the floor to her legs as she stretches them and smooths her stockings. If Tess's legs are objects of Sam's gaze, however, Tess is no object. As the camera moves up to her face, we see not a woman looked at but a woman looking in response, as her eyes imitate the previous camera movements by tracking from Sam's face down to his legs and back up. The film then cuts to Sam's face. He responds as a man who is being looked at; he retreats from the office and would have foreclosed the possibilities of this scene but for being called back by the editor.

The editor remains the embodiment of the necessary (he keeps

The mutual gaze that created the onscreen Tracy/Hepburn legend.

Sam in the office) but hollow omnipresent verbal communication throughout this scene, relegated to the background while Tess and Sam's nonverbal communication is foregrounded. The role of culture in Tess and Sam's life is fully acknowledged. While the editor launches into a clichéd speech about competition and cooperation among colleagues, the camera records the potent visceral embodiment of the paradoxical presence of both in Sam and Tess. A pair of POV close-ups depicts Tess's seductive gaze at Sam, answered by his return of the seductive gaze, a shot pattern that yields to another two-shot of mutual gazing that is both combative and yearning. This moment establishes a parity between the two of them that continues throughout the film and works in tension against the descending spiral of the narrative, which proposes Sam's necessary dominance over her. The unquenchable chemistry of Sam and Tess's first meeting blocks the triumphant narrative from satisfying the audience as it ties Tess into the social definition of "woman's place."

The battle between social definitions carried by the script and the much more profound energies that pass between Sam and Tess reaches its climax at the end of the film in the juxtaposition between the marriage of Aunt Ellen to William Harding, Tess's father, and the infamous taming of Tess in Sam's kitchen as the movie closes. The marriage scene is an impeccably rendered cliche of manipulated stock emotions and Hollywood illusions about marriage, while the final scene in the kitchen is, like the scene in the editor's office, a scene driven by sensory aspects of sight and sound that challenges the viewer to look beyond Hollywood illusions. Ellen and Tess's father are married with all the Hollywood trimmings. The ceremony is scored by the kind of non-diegetic music associated with the worst excesses of sentimentality in some radio soap operas. The words of the ceremony describing marriage as a submission of individuals to a union in which there are no more separate experiences or emotions are spoken in full in the sonorous movie voice of movie priests. The images of the scene are summed up by the rhetoric of the vows; marriage is, in the words of the priest, "the final truth." There are many close-up reaction shots of a tearful Tess during the ceremony framed in soft focus, rendering her a Hollywood-manipulated image of Katharine Hepburn, rather than the vital woman we have seen throughout the film.

By contrast, in the kitchen scene, words are even more negligible than they were in the editor's office during the fateful first meeting; they are virtually missing, as is the non-diegetic music that battered the previous wedding scene into submission to conventional ideological purposes. The kitchen scene is a stark expanse of time and space filled with the domestic equivalent of the pain and violence of a highway disaster. Visually, the spectator is regaled with Tess uneasily negotiating the kitchen in a mink coat, in harsh three-point lighting; there are no shadows in this home hearth. The contrast between the mink and the Formica counters creates a teeth-clenching dissonance that is not palliated by Hollywood's conventional softening lighting effects or non-diegetic music. The sudden cessation of manipulative soundtrack music is another source of the eeriness of this scene, in which the kitchen becomes a truly nightmarish setting for Tess, supervised by Sam's invisible mother, who here becomes the instrument of Tess's punishment. The few words that are in this scene, which appear in a cookbook once given as a wedding present by Sam's mother, turn against Tess. As she breezes by the open book, the page to which she has opened, unbeknownst to her, flips over; she has no idea that she has slipped from one recipe into another with quite different structural demands. The second recipe, for some unknown food calling for yeast, sends the materials of the original recipe for waffles into a ballooning distension, creating a critical temptation to see a kind of metaphor here for the slippage of the film itself at the end. This segment of the closure, structured by almost pure cinematic language of sight and sound, ends when an egg slips onto Tess's expensive, chic shoe, and Sam walks in to find her thus. Now that Tess has been defeated on the most profound level cinema can offer, she is ready for the verbal coup de grace from Sam, who makes her "his woman" in the final dialogue.

The contrast between the two scenes is deeply ambiguous in nature. On the one hand, the manipulated image of Hepburn at Ellen's wedding could be read by an audience weaned on Hollywood manipulation as a heightened, glorified moment for Tess. The hyperbolic images of priest and religious sentiment could be read as a sudden inspiration by some divine moment of truth. However, the contrast between the deliberately heightened, arguably treacly, tone of Ellen and William Harding's wedding and the relentlessly deflated, satiric tone of the rest of the film could also be read in the opposite way, as an intentionally subtextual subversive jab at the culturally sponsored fantasy that overcomes both Ellen and Tess in the movie and that overcame Hepburn outside of the movie. There is significant interior evidence to support this position.

This film is energized by a tension between the cinematic chemistry proclaiming the mutuality of Sam and Tess and the manipulated intentions of the narrative closure that firmly positions the woman according to cultural ideology as the submissive dependent of the man. This tension is not resolved by the final image of capitulation. There is a certain pleasure in the final embrace, but it is not without reservations, coming as it does on the heels of farce, which continues to leave highly inconclusive the fit between wifely domesticity and hobnobbing with the president of the United States. *Woman* is a fascinating study in the power relations between narrative and raw chemistry, between logos and cinematic language, relations that cannot be reduced to simple polarities. The narrative is not the simple enemy of chemistry; it is important in setting the stage with Tess's grandeur, which is borne out by the chemistry. If ultimately the narrative does pull the rug out from under Tess, it also makes possible a glimpse of a modern wonder woman as a part of its reality. What is more, Hepburn's personal charisma and her synergy with Tracy impacts complexly one of the main features of the film's narrative—its use of real-world figures in the lives of Tess and Sam.[14]

Tess sails into the film at great heights that are evoked in part by allusion to real-world figures: Tess herself was based on Dorothy Thompson, an outspoken anti-Hitler journalist during World War II.[15] She is identified through the evocation of other real-world figures, as a confidante of the historical Franklin Delano Roosevelt, as a woman who can get General Battista, the historical dictator of Cuba, on the phone at will. In part, her eminence is also marked by her relationship to a fictional political figure evoked within a real political context, Czech freedom fighter Martin Lubeck (Ludwig Stoessel), who turns to Tess first after he escapes from a Nazi concentration camp to the United States. This blurring of the lines between historical fact and fiction is more important than it might at first seem, for it marks a great transition in narrative strategies in Hollywood presentation of Synergistic Couples, one that bends to the pressures toward literalization and the importance of historical labeling but at the same time uses the labeling process to enhance couple energy.

The use of such historical conflation between the evening news and the fictional story of two reporters is like the conflation of Tess and Katharine Hepburn. It allows the audience to play with reality through fiction in a kind of carnivalization that takes the pressure off deadly serious political power by turning it into play: entertainment. Carnivalization contains within itself the double potential of being a steam valve so that people can continue to live in a repressive culture and of being a refreshed way of looking at reality that brings with it real forms of freedom from cultural repression. *Woman* is both. This way of bemusing audience belief in what was taking place on the screen worked to transfer onto the historical image of Spencer Tracy the fictional image of Sam that then made Sam more believable to the audience. This is a powerful repression of truth. Yet it might also be said that the carnivalization in *Woman* put a few dents into seamless Hollywood illusion. Carnivalization here can also function to break the illusion, exposing the seams and rendering the audience free to use fantasy in its healthiest form, as a way of returning with more zest and insight to reality. For example, the film blurs the lines among cultures in Tess's soirees of the international set, when her sophisticated friends mix with Sam's down-to-earth sports fans. And the alliance between Tess and Sam blends polar oppositions through the topsy-turvy effects of eros. Other instances of this carnivalization occur in all the scenes in Pinky's (William Bendix) sports bar, where director Cukor plays with the differences between illusion and reality, what we see when we look at our surroundings and what we don't, even though they are there. Carnivalization also occurs in a key scene in which Tess goes back to the orphanage to reclaim Chris and he tells her in no uncertain terms that she is not his idea of a mother, but says it in Greek sentences that are never translated for the audience. The compound presence of commercial manipulation and the liberating slippages, inversions, and ellipses created by elements of the carnivalesque, like the undeniable wild energies of the partner chemistry between Hepburn and Tracy, account for why this film is still watchable, and fascinating, if not completely satisfactory.

Intertextuality is another carnivalistic feature of this synergistic series that challenges the dominant power of the simplistic scripts. The Hepburn/Tracy series is full of reflexive references to previous work done by the stars, particularly by Tracy, but also to some extent Hepburn. For example, Tracy's characters are frequently involved in acting business concerning a hat. In *Woman*, much is made of Sam Craig's hat, which he leaves in Tess's apartment and which gets returned ceremoniously to him by her. The original ending of the film planned to focus on it in the last shot, sailing across a sports stadium. But hats had already been a major prop in Tracy's comic films. The selection and wearing of a hat occupies much screen space in Tracy's early starring role as a feisty policeman in *Me and My Gal* (1932, Dir. Raoul Walsh). Similarly, there is much comic business with a hat in *Without Love*, *Adam's Rib*, and *Pat and Mike*. Other elements repeat, such as Pat Jamieson's (Tracy) dog Dizzy in *Without Love*; a similar-looking dog, also named Dizzy, appeared with Tracy in *Fury*. Stage set cartoons are used as the themes in the main titles of both *Without Love* and *Adam's Rib*. There are also some recurring names in the series. Hepburn plays a woman named Christine in *Guess Who's Coming to Dinner* and one named Christina in *Keeper of the Flame*. Tracy plays a man named Pat in *Without Love* and Hepburn plays a woman named Pat in *Pat and Mike*. In *Woman of the Year*, Hepburn plays a reporter named Tess Harding. In the next picture, *Keeper of the Flame*, a close friend of reporter Steven O'Malley, the Tracy character, is a woman named Janie Harding (Audrey Christie). In the very next film, *Without Love*, Hepburn plays a widow named Jamie. In this film, the name is interestingly doubled: she's Jamie; he's Jamieson. To a great extent, this synergistic series lives on the pattern of intertextuality and carnivalism established by *Woman*, a tradition that was emphasized in some of the films more than others, particularly in the most complexly and buoyantly carnivalesque films: the third film, *Without Love*; and the sixth and seventh films, *Adam's Rib* and *Pat and Mike*. These intertextual echoes both give the series the feeling of being its own universe and call attention to the fictionality of the series.

FIGHTING FASCISM AND SEXISM

The second Tracy/Hepburn film, *Keeper of the Flame*, continues to work the reflexivity of the Hepburn/Tracy collaboration. A consideration of Fascism, it could not have been more topical in 1942.[16] The film also alluded to Douglas MacArthur, who was the inspiration for the film's villain, a seeming patriot named Robert Forest who turned out to represent an American brand of Fascist.[17] *Keeper*, in making reference to the contemporary Fascist menace, used pseudo-documentary images of newspapers and radio stations as well as some anonymous long-shot newsreel footage of street crowds juxtaposed with scenes of extras that have a similar appearance. But it was also heavily larded with a richly emotional, manipulative melodic line arranged for an orchestra heavy with strings. This kind of music, along with the staples of melodramatic imagery and performances, was typical of the forties and fifties in Hollywood, and precluded anything resembling a real documentary examination of World War II United States. This confluence of pressures—the patriotic PCA calling for simplistic, sugary melodrama, on the one hand, and the audience insisting on serious treatment of "real" issues, on the other—produced a strange hybrid of social realism and melodrama.

In spite of *Keeper's* sugarcoated score and simplistic script, it is truly provocative in that it was one of Hollywood's few forays into imagining the possibility of homegrown American Fascism and the crucial damage that can be done to individual rights when inhumane and tyrannous ideas sweep a society through a charismatic leader. The film directly warns the American public that Fascism *can* happen here and that we should be on our guard against our own secret evil as well as against the outright evil in Europe. The story concerns Christine Forest (Hepburn) and Steven O'Malley (Tracy), two individuals who embody the profound beauty of the individual spirit that needs to be protected from the kind of social discourse that arrogates all loyalty to itself—in a word, totalitarianism. Since the public saw Hepburn and Tracy as embodying exactly that kind of individual spirit, conflation of the star synergy of Hepburn and Tracy with their characters is crucial to direct audience desire, belief, and outrage concerning the destinies of Christine and Steven.

Steven O'Malley is a distinguished war correspondent who approaches Christine Forest, widow of a recently deceased national hero, Robert Forest, for her help. Forest's death, which occurred when a bridge he was driving on gave way, was especially ill-timed, as O'Malley sees it, since Forest stood as an inspirational figure for Americans fighting in Europe. O'Malley asks Christine to make available to him the family papers and especially her memories about Forest so that he can tell the hero's life story to a grieving nation, to keep national spirits up. After an initial refusal to cooperate, Christine is coerced by Forest's private secretary into changing her mind so as not to make O'Malley suspicious about what might be hidden by her silence. Christine is to show O'Malley enough to satisfy him and send him on his way, but not enough to let him into Forest's real goals. As he works with Christine, O'Malley, the perennial bachelor, begins to fall in love with her.

Their collaboration involves them in a process of seeing what has been hidden under a powerful image, for at first O'Malley is deceived by circumstantial evidence. Initially, he believes that Christine's glamour is the false image. As they grow closer, circumstantial evidence begins to accrue that leads him to a second mistake, his belief that she killed his hero to facilitate an adulterous sexual affair with her cousin, Geoffrey Mitford (Forest Tucker). Confronting her with his characteristic blunt honesty, O'Malley discovers that he is partially right. Christine did not actively kill Robert Forest, but by withholding information about the weakened bridge, she intentionally failed to prevent his death. However, O'Malley is wrong about her motivation, and the truth shocks him as he is forced to confront her valid reasons behind her (in)action. There was no affair; Christine permitted her husband to die as an act of patriotism. Marrying him as a worshipful young woman, Christine gradually witnessed a change in the charismatic hero, who, she discovered, was evolving into an American version of the Fascist menace that had precipitated World War II. Steven has already had a whiff of this possibility—by chance, he found Robert Forest's carefully hidden mother, a madwoman who once exhorted her son to rise as a superman over the puny herd of ordinary mortals and now hears her son speaking in the thunder of a sudden storm. At first the mad old woman only seems to provide Steven with more circumstantial evidence about Christine's guilt in Forest's death. But finally O'Malley discovers that she is only parroting Forest's own Hitlerian ideas and that Christine has been bearing the burden of her knowledge of her husband's Fascism. This validates Christine's decision to maintain her silence about the bridge.

Weighed down by guilt about Forest's death, Christine has also continued to suppress the evidence of his Fascism because she is still beset by her own illusions. She fears that the American public will be spiritually devastated by the truth and lose the heart to fight against Hitler and Mussolini. With her confession, Steven finds his true mission, not to lionize Forest in print but to reveal him to America for what he was. As Christine has removed the blinders from his eyes, he removes hers, convincing her that truth makes societies free. But truth is purchased at a high cost: Christine's life. Illusions die hard. When Forest's secretary, Clive Kerndon (Richard Whorf), a coldhearted right-wing fanatic, realizes that Christine is moving toward making some revelations, he takes upon his shoulders the mantle of keeper of the flame and tries to kill both Steven and Christine. He succeeds in killing Christine, but death only empowers her. She rises again, her image in every bookstore and newspaper in the country, memorialized as a national heroine in Steven's exposé of the Robert

Forest movement, as a previously deluded country follows Steven in shedding false gods.

The complexities of the Hepburn/Tracy fusion of image and life stand behind the film's brilliant use of intimacy and the couple. It is, after all, their star images that make the movie possible, although this is a reflexivity that the movie does not deal with. Rather, the movie uses star images to reassure the public that good images chase bad images out. But the film also uses star images to make a most un-Hollywoodlike assertion, which took it way beyond PCA limits. *Keeper* implies, by means of the pervasiveness of the pseudo-heroic Robert Forest image, a dark rottenness at the heart of American society that makes it vulnerable to immoral suggestions. The PCA explicitly forbade any implications that there was something corrupt about the whole social framework, but because *Keeper* channeled its exploration of such wholesale corruption through a couple dynamic, the PCA failed to police this representation of a tendency in social discourse to lock the country into a blind acceptance of lies told by the power structure.

Keeper explores the power of "The Big Lie" that can be told by whatever government—not just Hitler's—when it is buried beneath layers of emotionally charged but hollow images that pass for reality. Writer Donald Ogden Stewart conveys this by faithfully following the novel on which the film was based in representing Forest by only a heroic portrait hung in his palatial home, and keeping Forest the man invisible. A lesser writer might have made him visible for the film audience through flashbacks, but the decision to avoid that cliche beautifully opened the possibility for using negative space to depict Forest as pure illusion. Cukor took full advantage of this opportunity by featuring prominently in the mise-en-scène in Forest's mansion an oil painting of Forest that is of no actual person, but of a white-haired, dark-browed patriarchal ideal somewhat resembling the image of Lorne Greene later popularized as patriarch of the ranch in *Bonanza*. Similarly, Forest again appears as an invisible force when his mother talks to him as the lightning and thunder of a rainstorm. This image is devastating because of its ineffability. One cannot get hold of it sufficiently to peel it away to its evil core. What can be peeled away are the delusions about him held by both Christine and Steven, and this process is possible only when intimacy is established between them. More specifically, in this Christine/Steven intimacy, the peeling away of the gender cliches that Steven holds about Christine is the visible process by which the invisible Forest is unmasked. To make things even more rich and complex, it is the slippage of the manipulated images of Hepburn and Tracy onto Christine and Steven that gives a special force to the audience's experience of how delusions are unmasked.

As distant strangers, Steven and Christine view each other through erotically coded male and female positions, while the audience views the characters through the actors' star images. Steven's investigation of Forest through Christine is swaddled in gender implications. Christine is the bearer of a secret he must penetrate, an action irradiated by the glamour of Hepburn the star and the star image of Tracy's honest straightforwardness. First, O'Malley sees Christine as the repository of information about his hero; he is an objective researcher. On her part, she understands her role as an object of research but defends herself from penetration so that she can guard the secret she believes she must keep. However, Steven's growing love for her changes objectivity into subjective desire and fear about his intuition that she contains disturbing information for him about Forest. Christine's growing love for O'Malley, as she begins to see in him the hero she once thought Forest was, fills her with a desire to open up to him, a typically gendered female erotic dynamic as much as it is a plot-driven issue about whether on not to blow the whistle on her late husband. At the climactic moment, the political truth emerges simultaneously with real intimacy, when male fear of female interiority and female fear of penetration yield a mutual comfort with giving and taking.

The Hepburn/Tracy documentary energy inheres in the dynamic evolution of the paired star images. At first, Steven is isolated from Christine in his Tracy image, as she is isolated from him in the Hepburn image. When they meet, there is only distance between them. They are each armored in clearly manipulated versions of the star images that the public associates with the actors. This moment is exquisitely lit, as Steven/Tracy, who has broken into the Forest mansion, stands in the shadows of one of the now darkened rooms used to receive guests, illuminated only by one or two area lights. The chiaroscuro of shadow and radiance bathes Christine, dressed in a softly draped white gown, bearing flowers for the altarlike display under the portrait of her late husband. As she is a recent widow, it is odd that she wears white, but it suits the subtext of the film. Christine's authority comes from Hepburn, the screen goddess; the qualities of the Hepburn persona emphasized here are purity and integrity. When she sees him and identifies him as an intruder, his authority comes from Tracy's screen persona, the decent, average Joe. Steven is not invading privacy, for he has the right of the ordinary Joe to know what is being hidden.

The camera does not let their eyes be our eyes. We watch them watching. As much for them as for us, she is the female secret because she is Katharine Hepburn; he is the male quester because he is Spencer Tracy. These two spectacles contrast with the anonymous spectacle of the oil painting of Robert Forest, who is a generic masculine image. The evil Clive Kerndon inadvertently starts the process by which the illusion of Robert Forest and gender illusions will be dissipated when he pressures Christine to cooperate with O'Malley, on the premise that cooperation will create a control on the reporter and keep him from getting to the truth. As he takes a closer look, O'Malley sees beyond the goddess to the lady and finally to the woman. As she watches him watching her, she sees beyond the celebrity newsman to the human being to the man. With each alteration, each comes closer to shucking his or her illusions about image, a new aspect of each star persona appears, and, most vital, more of the energy of their real connection gets released onscreen. It is the force of that connection that breaks this film out of the category of routine melodrama and anchors the suspense story in something that can make claims to reality.

In their most charged, naked moments, the film dispenses with the melodramatic non-diegetic music that has scored their previous scenes. The climax of the movie, when Christine "tells all," is appropriately starkly bare of the emotionally controlling music. It depends completely on the Tracy/Hepburn synergy for the power behind its diatribe about what men and women are, and why the hero image can never be about being human, and certainly not about intimacy. In a long, passionate speech about her disillusionment with the hero that takes its ideas from Donald Ogden Stewart but its force from what the audience believed about the real Katharine Hepburn, Christine tells Steven: "When Robert began to change, I saw the face of Fascism in my own home, hatred, arrogance, cruelty. I saw what German women were facing. I saw the enemy.... And he held me in his arms and I knew that it was no longer a wife that he wanted but sons, and his eyes told me that I was a poor creature who couldn't give him sons." Womanly openness and masculine determination are also political acts of courage that are believable because the audience believes that Hepburn and Tracy are really "like that." And because Hepburn and Tracy themselves believed in each other's power to ennoble. If Tracy was not really the good scout American who would brook no viciousness in high places, he really wanted to be that for Hepburn, and she wanted to believe in his integrity. When O'Malley tells Christine that he no longer cares why she killed her husband because he loves her, now understands love and what it can do, and only wants to help her, Tracy the man was speaking to Hepburn in the context of their hidden affair, in which he really did discover what their connection could "do to a man." Onscreen, they made it so for themselves and for the movie audience.

But their star images as a couple—the very thing that made it possible to drive home the thesis of the film—took with one hand what they gave with the other. How far is the star image from the image of the dictator in manipulating the public? This question, of course, is not addressed by the film, in which the image of Christine takes the place of the image of Robert Forest in the movie, ultimately evading the question of whether any object of national hero worship is potentially a way of corrupting public understanding and discourse. Must one use fire to fight fire? Similarly, if the star image reminds us of the dangers of totalitarianism, is this a release for the mass public or a new form of delusion: is the star image, particularly the powerful star couple synergy, a totalitarian image in its own way? The reflexivity of Hepburn/Tracy synergy in *Keeper* brings to the surface this troubling question about compelling screen couple imagery.

The next Hepburn/Tracy movie did, however, take a sharper bite out of the problem of image and glamour, though in a personal, not a political, context. Their third film, *Without Love,* deals directly with the pernicious effects of Hollywood glamour on the relationship that ordinary people have to their bodies and to the passion rooted in it.[18] In this movie, scientist Pat Jamieson (Tracy), who is working on an oxygen mask that will make it possible for jet pilots to fly at high altitudes, arrives in Washington with his dog, Dizzy, but cannot find a place to live. By accident, he runs into Quentin Ladd (Keenan Wynn), who is, as usual, drunk. Quentin catches a ride in the cab in which Pat is cruising Washington in search of lodgings and invites Pat to stay the night at the vacant home of his cousin, Jamie Rowan (Hepburn). After a comedy of mistaken identities, Pat convinces Jamie to let him live and pursue his scientific research in her house. Jamie is a widow who has determined never again to become romantically involved because she believes no relationship can equal the perfection that she had with her late husband. Pat has sworn off romantic love because of a bad experience with a coquette named Lila Vine. Pat prefers books because their beauty is in their logic and dependability. Neither of them wants to recognize their attraction. Denial, however, is a complicated process. In the name of avoiding love, Jamie astounds Pat with a proposition that they embark on a Shavian marriage, in which each will support the other and provide companionship that will protect both of them from the romantic entanglements they both wish to avoid: they will maintain strictly separate bedrooms. He accepts. Their denial of their mutual attraction buries it under a facade of their devotion to Pat's work.

Jamie's intelligence makes her an indispensable workmate as Pat develops a mask that the army wants to test. But yearning grows as they spend intimate time together, fanned by jealousy when Paul Carrell (Carl Esmond), an experienced womanizer, senses what is missing in Pat and Jamie's marriage and courts Jamie. Paul's courtship fans Jamie's yearning for romance, which threatens Pat and Jamie's mutual system of denial. When Pat is called to Chicago to test the mask, Jamie makes romantic overtures toward him, which the smitten Pat rejects, but not because he doesn't love her. He is simply slower at making the transition. Hurt, Jamie goes back home and throws herself into Paul's arms on the rebound. Pat, now ready to answer Jamie's affection, readies to do combat with Paul for Jamie. Barging into Paul's apartment, he finds what may be traces of her recent presence there, but wills himself to believe that Paul is bluffing, and goes home to find her. At home, Jamie is waiting to put on an act imitating Lila Vine, for whom she mistakenly believes Pat still carries a torch. Pat finally lets her know he loves her, not Lila, and they head upstairs to the bedroom to redraft their marriage arrangement.

Without Love, which features a lighter touch than their two previous films, uses the Tracy/Hepburn chemistry to create a body language that tells Jamie and Pat what they really feel when ordinary conceptualization through verbal language is blocked by rationalizations and denials. Again, the Hepburn/Tracy star synergy is used to deal with the way social codes and illusions thwart intimacy. *Without Love* uses the compatible energies in the bodies of Hepburn and Tracy as Pat and Jamie to express an interior layer of rebellion against the rational plans of the characters they play. Pat, who has had a lifelong tendency to sleepwalk and expects Dizzy, his dog, to wake him before he does something outrageous, expresses his conflicted feelings about his "marriage" only in the sleeping state, when his waking faculties do not hinder him. The first night of their marriage, in a somnolent state he overcomes all the obstacles he has placed in front of the door in his waking state to keep him from nocturnal wandering. In a nice touch, Dizzy does not impede him as he goes into Jamie's room and gets into her bed before she discovers him and wakes him with aggrieved shrieks. Jamie embraces the boundaries vigorously instead of embracing Pat; indeed, she has been a partner in drafting them and, like a good partner, picks up the slack when it is necessary to keep the pact in order.

Intriguingly, just as collision between society and energy is a necessary feature for the synergistic screen couple, so Pat's scientific development of an oxygen mask for jet pilots as part of a government project becomes a vehicle for his discovery of his subjective feelings, as well as a vehicle for the audience's insight into Jamie and Pat's marriage. The project is a metaphor for the challenge posed by the conflicting cultural and psychological elements in romance, the need to maintain stability while being made dizzy at spectacular heights. The work on the protective oxygen mask is full of sexual references wordlessly embedded in the film's body language, which charts the readiness of each of them for taking the big plunge into the more destabilizing aspects of intimacy, love, and marriage. The first of these takes place when Jamie is working in Pat's laboratory to help him with a test, donning an initial, and flawed, as it turns out, version of the device. The test is meant to make sure that the mask doesn't over-oxygenate the pilot so he will become woozy and thus unable to fly the plane. The test is conducted with scientific objectivity; however, it is erotically contextualized. The initial shot is a close-up of the mask, which is juxtaposed by the editorial cut with tentative kisses exchanged between Jamie and Pat, as they decide to get married. He kisses her affectionately but non-seductively on the cheek, as her face begins to show signs of alarm, and then he presents his cheek to her to be kissed. She acquiesces with a similar kind of kiss, and her alarm turns into a shy pleasure. Abruptly the film cuts to the mask. It is a cylindrical, transparent plastic device, meant to enclose the entire head with about nine inches of headroom to spare, much like the astronaut's helmets. It is an image of isolation that conflicts with and opposes the pleasure of the kiss.

Moreover, the test is taking place right after their wedding, on what is technically their wedding night. The mask and the test, rather slyly, are made into the focus of the displacement of the erotic encounter that should be, but is not taking place, since this is a union "without love." After the rather interesting juxtaposition of kisses and static mask, during the test, when too much oxygen is delivered to her by the mask, Jamie becomes giddy, her clipped report of the statistics on the simulated control panel in the test chamber turning into orgasmic babbling. "Oxygen intake—oooooh, I feel so uptake, intake, outtake I take, you take, we all take," she dithers, as she turns somersaults. This halts the experiment, the mask being a scientific failure. Cinematically, it is anything but, marking without benefit of reductive dialogue or cliched visual symbols in the most filmic manner the inability of the mask of practical union, the scientific objectivity with which they have imposed on themselves, to deal with the uncontainable exuberance of the body. But we also see that neither is ready to alter objectivity to something more inclusive. Jamie still remains that image of feminine loss of control that has driven Pat into celibacy.

His release into orgasmic freedom comes later as Pat is testing the mask in Chicago in a military lab. This scene follows the scene in their hotel suite, when Jamie attempts romance. Pat flees, only to be confronted by it in a displaced manner when the test becomes a virtual orgasm. The testing of the mask requires Pat to endure a simulation of a pilot's experience at an altitude of fifty thousand feet. Whirling in a simulated cockpit in a centrifugal motion chamber, his breathing labored, his pulse rising, his head pumping back and forth, Pat blacks out in his moment of "scientific" success, as he involuntarily whispers her name. Everything brings Pat and Jamie back to the bodies they have abandoned, and the audience is along for a ride into the return of the mind to its physical moorings.

When Pat follows Jamie back to their home in Washington, ready to declare his love, he is greeted by a Jamie who has horribly transformed herself into Lila Vine, the reason he gave up on love. Jamie, in despair, thinking that Pat rebuffed her because he is only attracted to women like Lila Vine, tries to become that woman in a last effort to win his love. We never see the actual Lila, only Jamie's parody of the cliched, bubble-headed mantrap, clad in swansdown and chiffon, who flings herself into Pat's bedroom murmuring meaningless, seductive phrases of endearment and playing the piano while singing French songs. The performance stuns Pat and the audience with its ambiguities. Wonderfully, Jamie's desperation to become what she thinks is Pat's idea of a "real" woman has catapulted her body into a disavowal of itself, a substitution for itself of a series of Hollywood gestures that are supposed to constitute the desirable woman. The spectacle of Katharine Hepburn going through these contortions has a particular documentary intensity for the audience; the woman who cannot be made to compromise is demeaning herself for love. The resonances are complex, summoning up, as in the last scene of *Woman of the Year,* her situation as a rebel against Hollywood illusions. Lovably, Hepburn will go "that far" for love, at the same time making us feel that no woman should ever have to stoop this low. Her painful, but funny, absurdity redefines the Hollywood glamour pretense of normal female conduct.

Tracy's Pat must now endow the ordinary man with a very non-Hollywood rejection of its claptrap about female glamour. Playing against the stock movie hero, who gasps with delight at the transformed heroine, particularly an intellectual one like Jamie—remember the stock scene in which the bookish girl takes off her glasses?—Pat rejects the sham image of the Lila Vine femme fatale persona, but this time without rejecting the non-rationalism of the male/female connection. The conviction with which Pat accepts Jamie once he clears away the rubbish of Lila Vine is rooted in the documentary conviction with which Tracy accepts the controversial Hepburn. First this manifests itself as the two play out a fantasy scenario. In the graceful flow of the final scene of *Without Love,* a film that is absurdly undervalued by film historians and critics, the minuteness of attention the partners give each other makes possible the necessary language of indirection about love. Throughout the whole picture there is a quality of attention to each other, typical of their collaboration, that differs from the quality of attention they each had when they worked with others. Other than in their synergistic series, each paid intense attention to his or her own performance, achieving magisterial performances on occasion through the power of acutely crafted vocal, physical, and emotional representation. In the scenes at the end of *Without Love* the quality of that attention reaches a synergistic crescendo.

When the false fantasy of Lila Vine is laid to rest, the real power of fantasy is invoked. All of the eroticism of play that has been squelched by Pat and Jamie rises for the final encounter in which they express their love for each other. The transformation takes the form of play-acting, a real catharsis for two far too earnest people, indicating their liberation by love. When Pat realizes that Jamie thinks he's still in love with Lila, instead of putting her straight in the blunt fashion that has been his hallmark in the movie, he plays a musical game with her in which each follows each other's lead in creating a fantasy that will indirectly channel all the energy that science has isolated in each lonely orgasmic experience we have already seen. Pat, playing fragments on the piano to form a cliched "movie score," tells Jamie the story of a woman who thinks her husband wants a divorce, but he is actually "mad about her." They each play a number of characters during this make-believe journey to the apocryphal Metropole Hotel in Reno. A sweetly whimsical indirect confession that makes its mark as a real turnabout for Pat by flouting all audience expectation of the meat-and-potatoes image Tracy projected, it is also Tracy's mask for expressing sentiments he could not express in life, and probably never wanted to, yet knew Hepburn craved. This scene is a Chinese puzzle box of reflexivity. Tracy and Hepburn play roles of lovers playing roles in order to express their strong connection to each other. It is the power of the reality of those layers of mediation that makes *Without Love* a fascinating filmic experience in which the reality of the role playing of lovers is rendered through the special mode Tracy/Hepburn had of interpenetrating the filmic fiction and documentary image.

Through pretending to be Lila Vine, Jamie (Katharine Hepburn) helps herself as well as Pat (Spencer Tracy) see through constructed femininity.

FIGHTING HOLLYWOOD TRENDS

The next two films, *The Sea of Grass* and *State of the Union*, sound the alarm about the use of Synergistic Couple image in movies. More topical, more literally "realistic," these films are casualties of the trend in postwar Hollywood toward a confining script, co-opting the Tracy/Hepburn synergy for depressingly formulaic projects. *The Sea of Grass* follows the story of the novel of the same name about the troubled marriage between a bullying land baron of the New Mexico prairie named Jim Brewton (Tracy) and a compassionate idealist from urban St. Louis named Lutie Cameron (Hepburn).[19] They are united by passionate attraction (which barely finds its way into the film as a felt presence) and divided by politics: she liberal and populist, he conservative and individualistic. Their differences pressure Lutie into an affair with Brice Chamberlain (Melvyn Douglas), a liberal lawyer whom Lutie can respect politically. Their sexual encounter leaves Lutie pregnant with a son, but she will not leave Brewton because she loves him hopelessly, against her better judgment. The son's illegitimacy leads Brewton to exile Lutie from their family. It also leads to the profound anger of the son, Brock (Robert Walker), and the feeling of abandonment of the daughter, Sarah Beth (Phyllis Thaxter). Ultimately, Brock kills a man who taunts him about his paternity and is killed in a shoot-out with the sheriff before Lutie can get to town to try to save him. Brewton emerges from this tragedy with new humility and forgiveness. He and Lutie reunite, and he finally looks at her with the passion he once reserved only for the grass.

Only a fraction of the story's fascinating social, emotional, and psychological issues are played out cinematically; the rest stagnates under a static, unproductive script that neither the visual and sound images nor Tracy and Hepburn can bring to life. There is a certain fascination in the failure of this film to live. The failure of the director and writer to provide onscreen transitions and evocative imagery should not be counted out, nor should the terrible miscasting of Robert Walker as Brock; but the trouble is primarily with the performances asked of Hepburn and Tracy. There is substantial difficulty with some emotional transitions in *Woman*, overwritten speeches in *Keeper*, and a rather lightweight approach to the subject in *Without Love*—yet the conviction brought to the movies by the enigmatic Hepburn/Tracy on/offscreen relationship animated those films powerfully and suggestively. They can find nothing to play in the impasse between Lutie and Brewton. Perhaps the roles ran too close to aspects of their relationship about Tracy's bullying style that they preferred not to acknowledge or were too painful to transform. Perhaps Hepburn made safe choices in depicting Lutie so that she would not run afoul of the public as a female firebrand, as she had previously done. The question of slippage and what can be transformed in that process has its limits. Enigmatic and powerful though couple energy may be, it is not without its limits, including those created by the blockages in the people involved.

The same can be said for *State of the Union,* despite its timely representation of political conflict in the American process, and wonderful performances by Angela Lansbury and Van Johnson in supporting roles. In this film, the Hepburn wife figure is very much the little woman—a role her previous characters had openly disparaged. Perhaps worse, she played the "little woman" behind the great man. *Union* is a film that questions the viability of women in positions of power as none of the other Hepburn/Tracy collaborations did, strongly suggesting that only an irredeemably and savagely masculinized woman could or would attempt such a thing. Apparently, it gratified Hepburn, who believed it was a fundamentally liberal picture because her character got to harangue Adolf Menjou's character about the nature of democracy when offscreen Menjou was collaborating with HUAC's often procedurally suspect attempts to identify Communists in Hollywood. But, so far as gender is concerned, the picture is actually a conservative, possibly reactionary film that simultaneously works against the onscreen/offscreen chemistry of Hepburn and Tracy and attacks Hepburn's rich reserve of female energy.

Union, based on the play of the same name by Howard Lindsay and Russel Crouse, is about a clash between mistress Kay Thorndyke (Angela Lansbury) and wife Mary Matthews (Hepburn) over Grant Matthews (Tracy). Thorndyke wishes to propel her lover into the presidency of the United States in order to further her own lust for power, and so never takes into consideration the question of integrity in the political process. Mary, too, would like to see Grant as president, but only to further the good of the country, because she believes in her man as the best person to lead the nation. Thus the contest is resonant with topical social and ethical issues as the country was choosing its postwar direction. But there is a more pressing, if subtextual, gender issue that really drives the film. This time the concern is not the struggle between men and women but the definition of true womanhood.

The film asserts that there is but one true woman and that she is the wife/mother (Mary), not the working woman (Kay Thorndyke).[20] If Mary is a virginal fount of innocence in this film, Ms. Thorndyke, whose name says it all, is presented through the cliche of the evil proto-lesbian. Kay walks into this film grasping for control, wearing an oddly frightening version of masculine raingear as she moves to clear the way for her father's suicide once he has passed his stick—literally—on to her. Telling her that he hated her for not being a boy, Father Thorndyke conflates competence with masculinity when he tells Kay that he has changed his mind; she's better than any son because she has the sexuality of a woman and the abilities of a man. The film makes such a conflation too. In the contrast between lovely Mary and loveless Kay, the script logic in this film, directed by the conservative Frank Capra, cleanly establishes a barrier between sexuality and capability, making them mutually exclusive in women, as they were not in *Woman of the Year*. This logic also blames Kay, not her father, for blurring the lines. In Kay's twisted relationship with her father—he exhorts her to rise as a superwoman over the herd of puny ordinary men—we have echoes of the unholy alliance between mother and son in *Keeper of the Flame,* and, as in that film, questions about the capacity of the American public to deal with the truth are raised. But the bi-polar structure of this film is far more reductive than the representation in the earlier film, which leaves us with a mystery of how Forest became a parody of his early promise.

There is no mystery here; Kay is innately bad. She's a poster girl for popularized theories about Freudian penis envy. Kay begins her "manly" quest by joining forces with Jim Conover (Adolph Menjou), a notorious Republican power broker, and Spike MacManus (Van Johnson), a charming but hack publicist, to convince Grant to allow himself to be put up as the Republican candidate for president. Grant's psychological seduction is presented as a process that resembles simplistic Christian allegory in medieval morality plays: virtuous Mr. Good Man is seduced by loathsome Madame Ambition. Clearly, female sexuality is to blame. But Kay's diabolical cleverness defeats her. Wearing away at his resistance against using his estranged wife and children to woo the voters, Kay convinces Grant to reunite with Mary for the sake of appearances. Kay neatly overcomes an early surprise when Grant and Mary threaten to really reunite. But Kay only seems to have won. Her escalating manipulations show Grant that his family is in danger, and Grant completely destroys Kay's plans when he uses an important radio address to confess that he has sold out to what are now called "the special interests." It's a crisply written script, but its logic, lacking the vitality of image, renders the film too reductive to merit praise as cinema.

One of the few places in the film that uses the visual field to a powerful advantage is the scene in which Kay turns Grant away from Mary's growing influence during a campaign stop in Detroit. The scene begins with Grant and Mary flushed with emotion for each other and thrilled with the popular response to Grant's hard-hitting honesty. It ends with an estrangement between them, Grant going off to make a canned speech and Mary asking in vain for some clue as to what has changed. In the interim, Grant has gone off-camera, ostensibly to see someone from one of the major political constituencies, but the meeting is invisible to us and to Mary. There is a mystery and a power to that which happens in the blind space beyond the film frame, and when Kay saunters into the room after Grant and Mary have left for the auditorium where Grant will make his address, we know who was in the blind space, but not what happened, and that blind space is filled with evil sexuality. Ironically, the power of this moment was brought to film audiences courtesy of the PCA, which censored any attempt to show a sexual relationship between Kay and Grant; otherwise director Frank Capra certainly would have shown this scene, as he tried to film explicit evidence of the sexual liaison between Kay and Grant in early scenes. However, the film is filled with a sense that the sexuality is there but that we can't see it, and that makes for a much more dynamic sense of its overwhelming influence on Grant.[21]

The conflict between the definition of Mary's character and public perception of Hepburn thwarts to a substantial degree the slippage between actor and role that usually worked to leaven the Tracy/Hepburn films regardless of any formulaic heaviness in the narrative. Hepburn's Mary is a trivialized form of everything Hepburn was not and, more important, what the audience thought she was not. The film almost becomes a self-parody when it rams Mary's domesticity down the throat of the audience by depicting her immediately reaching for a needle and thread to sew on a loose button when she and Tracy's Grant have their first reunion moment. It is an example of how playing against Hepburn's public image might work to destroy any energy in a film. Similarly, casting Tracy as a man led around by his zipper is both a problematic contradiction of his image and, possibly, too close to his actual compulsions, and to his problem with intimacy, to permit him to deal with it in the flexible spirit in which he played the role of Pat. Perhaps it takes a picture as bad as this one to illuminate the complex of limitations and force involved in the way this pair made cinematic history as a Synergistic Couple. Tracy and Hepburn are being used here in an Iconic fashion, two stars plugged into recipe characterizations and plot.

THE COUPLE AT ITS ZENITH

In the next two films, *Adam's Rib* (1949) and *Pat and Mike* (1952), with the help of a sympathetic writing-directing team of Ruth Gordon/Garson Kanin and George Cukor, Hepburn and Tracy recovered their lost ground and enjoyed their two finest collaborations. These two films are Hepburn and Tracy at their best, not only because their synergy is unleashed but also because these films are reflexive about the use of star image in the movies. *Adam's Rib*, the very best film of the series, involves the richest mining of the offscreen lives and relationships of the two stars and is the most richly reflexive of all the films they made together. The script appears to bear all the topicality of the movie. But the obvious story about Adam (Tracy) and Amanda (Hepburn) Bonner, a married pair of attorneys who fight each other in court over a case of women's rights, also serves the purposes of a powerful reflexive look, way ahead of its time, at how the movies portray men and women. Returning to the theme of image and reality—ambiguously explored in *Keeper* and apolitically discussed in *Without*—*Rib* deals openly, completely, and politically with the lure of the image in the way it externally addresses both the Hollywood audience and gender politics under the law.

On opposite sides of the aisle at the trial of Doris Attinger (Judy Holliday), who has broken into the apartment of her husband's mistress and intentionally broken up one of their trysts with a gun, Adam and Amanda struggle with the law's definition of Doris's act. Will she be convicted of attempted murder, as Adam charges, or acquitted for defending her home, as Amanda contends? The film, although somewhat more sympathetic to Adam, virtually grants these two positions equal standing, and in so doing takes Hollywood for the first time to the portal of direct acknowledgment of multiple perceptions of the gender situation and the role that image plays in gender definition.

The film begins its exploration of the power of images by playing with them. It gives us an almost dialogueless set of opening frames that are shaped into a parody of film noir. We see Doris Attinger lie in wait for her husband, Warren Attinger (Tom Ewell), follow him to his mistress's apartment, and then break into it as she whips out a pistol, shooting wildly in all directions. The injured wife wears the uniform of the dangerous noir femme fatale, a large hat and a slinky dress. In this case, however, both are gauche verging on the absurd, and the femme is hungry, not fatale, munching nervously on a chocolate bar to keep herself from being paralyzed by fear. The dumbshow proceeds through the urban setting common to noir, but here comically rather than enigmatically seedy, to the moment of high drama, which climaxes in shots fired by, not the noir ice queen, but a flailing, bumbling hausfrau who collapses like a rag doll on the body of her wounded husband. Here we seem to see the crime in all its details, but the film makes us aware of what is missing. Despite our belief that we have witnessed the action, what we have missed is the invisible issue of perspective. We have seen the crime as a failed film noir, in which the femme fatale is guilty, but the rest of the film will question how audiences attach value to what they see.

Perspective is the guiding issue in the film, which becomes increasingly insistent about the way that social situations are more a chaos of individual universes than a seamless society with a dominant set of values. Amanda and Adam are at odds, but lawyer and client are not necessarily on the same page either. Amanda and Doris have varying points of view, as do Adam and Warren. Then there is the difference between the professional Amanda and the professional Adam, on the one hand, and the personal Adam and Amanda on the other. The boundaries among these perspectives are fragile, and the lines blur. Amanda's challenges in court to conventional gender perspectives begin to bleed into the Bonners' personal space. Adam wants to keep the trial within conventional social discourse that asks only whether or not Doris tried to kill her husband and his mistress and objects when Amanda gains the court's permission to refuse jurors who are ideologically committed to women as secondary citizens. This is the beginning of the end for clear categories, fact, and formulas, both for the trial and for the Bonners as a couple.

Amanda insists that gender decisions that have been misperceived as logical and just in the courtroom have actually been made on the basis of irrationally unjust images. The powerful role of images in thwarting justice for women begins to seep into the Bonner home in a moment that severely tests their relationship, during the massages that Amanda and Adam give each other when they return from court in the evenings. As Amanda massages Adam, she slaps his bottom "to test" whether he can feel, as they banter about his ability to relax, a gesture that neither seems to mind. But when Adam massages Amanda, she claims that he has punched her and objects strenuously when he hits *her* bottom. Was there any difference between the two slaps? The scene is ambiguous, left as a matter of their divergent perceptions because, although suggestions of underlying hostilities are built into the interchanges, the visualizations of the slaps make it impossible to determine whether these indisputable hostilities have been displaced into the physical contact. The slap Amanda gives Adam takes place in the generalized atmosphere of tension generated by the trial. But Adam's slap of Amanda occurs when Adam is *also* angered by jealousy. Adam is jealous of Kip (David Wayne), their neighbor, a client of Amanda's who has written a song for her entitled "Farewell Amanda" as part of his continuing flirtation with her. The song comes on the radio as Adam begins his massage and Adam turns the radio off in annoyance. Adam loathes the song as a reminder of Kip's endless teasing, and Kip's effeminate quality—an indirect representation of Hollywood homophobia. After the radio is off, Amanda continues to sing the song. It's a very silly song and Amanda knows it, so there is a certain ambiguity about whether she does this because of her innocent pleasure with the tribute or because she is deliberately provoking Adam. Adam slaps her behind in annoyance.

What is extraordinary in this scene is the ambiguity of the representation of the points of view. Was Adam's slap really a "slug," as Amanda thinks, one he felt entitled to as the possessor of her body? Was it different from her slap on his buttocks? There is some sense that Amanda is manipulating Adam with her tears and that Adam is playing dumb about the nature of the slap. But it is impossible to separate these strands. The scene does not reflect Adam's simple view of a world of right and wrong but rather Amanda's view of a world of competing definitions.

She wants to define the massage incident and the courtroom debate in terms of the problems of masculine entitlements. He wants to define the intertwining issues in terms of feminine irrationality: a

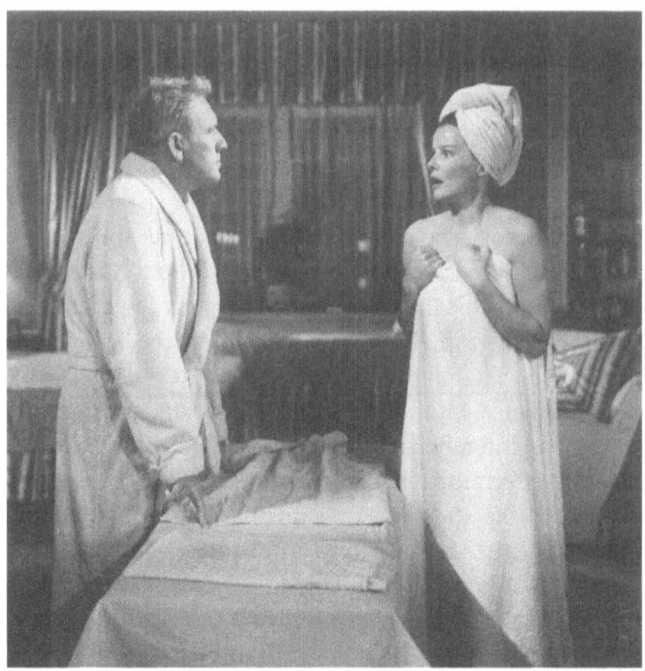

Even visually, the script's balanced representation of competing gender definitions of Adam's (Tracy) slap on Amanda's (Hepburn) bottom are suggested in this image of balanced bodies in Adam's Rib.

contempt for law, which he doesn't see as a gendered instrument of control, but rather as a neutral assertion of rational limits. The debate becomes cinematic as it plays itself out on their bodies, their star bodies, and comes to a head when Amanda cries, a new version of Hepburn's physicality for audiences who have not seen her do this before. Here is where Adam seemingly vents his most damaging charge against Amanda: female tears, he says, stronger than acid, but it won't work on him. He seems to be drawing the line between male and female along conventional gender definitions. But the film goes on to blur that boundary too.

The slippage between court and home comes to a crisis, provoking Adam to leave Amanda, when in her quest to prove that Doris is being tried for murder only because she is a woman, that the same act performed by a man would be perceived differently by society as an attempt to protect the home, she calls a group of women to testify to specifically destabilize the image of the little woman. These women include a scientist, a factory foreperson, and an acrobat who can lift as many as five men off the floor at the same time. When the acrobat, Olympia de Pere (Hope Emerson), lifts Adam helplessly above the ground in the middle of the courtroom, it is the last straw for him, and he leaves Amanda, saying she has become a competitor, as if she had committed an obscenity, when in fact the legal system is by nature adversarial. Her unacceptable competition has led her to make fun of the law, Adam charges, and undermine the dignity of the courtroom. It is no coincidence that his position is the very position of the PCA on what is permissible in depiction of the law in American movies.

The chasm between Adam and Amanda seems to become impassable with Amanda's closing speech to the jury. In terms of its language, the speech is somewhat dated, but in terms of its embedding of the conflict in the body, it could not be more contemporary, with its funny but eerie demonstration of the power of images over the mind. In Amanda's closing statement, she requests that the jury imagine the principals in the case as if their sexual identities were reversed—one of the truly delightful and important comic approaches to gender construction in the history of commercial movies. During the speech, we become the jury's imagination as, there on the screen, the female image of Doris Attinger lap dissolves into that of Doris Attinger as a man—Judy Holliday in male drag. Similar dissolves transform mistress Beryl Caighn into a man and philandering husband Warren Attinger into a woman. Once Warren is imagined as the sexually promiscuous woman—Tom Ewell performs a masterful silent mime of a "wayward broad"—his sexual promiscuity suddenly seems culpable to the jury, rather than the acceptable male philandering it had originally seemed. Doris is acquitted. Amanda and the film have subverted the iron law of gender cliche.

Adam's rage at the blurring of boundaries leads him to "threaten" to kill Amanda and Kip with what appears to be a real gun but is actually made of licorice. His intent is to shock Amanda into admitting that no one has the right to behave in this manner, regardless of intent, which is what happens, seeming to reverse Amanda's victory on appeal. But if reversal of Amanda's triumph were the point of the film, it would end here, and it doesn't. The film cleverly evades the grip of the PCA by seeming to undermine Amanda's victory. In fact, it validates Amanda's theory about perception when, in a brilliant ironic twist, Adam himself reveals that regardless of his determination to keep male entitlements, he knows full well that much that is ascribed to sexual difference is nothing but social custom. As Adam and Amanda meet in their accountant's office, ostensibly one last time as a couple, Adam starts to cry when the accountant makes reference to the last mortgage check for their country home, which they now own "free and clear." The tears look suspiciously like a performance, but Amanda is so affected by the sight of them that all hostility between them ceases instantly. Reminiscent of the meeting between Sam and Tess in *Woman*, where emotional dynamite in the visual text of the film counterpointed with the droning of the editor, this scene takes place over the droning of the accountant, as Amanda assures Adam they can get to the country if they start immediately and arrive in time to see the dogs. Leaving the accountant with instructions to spend their money any way he sees fit, Amanda bundles Adam out of the office, only to discover after they arrive at the farm that what the audience suspected all along is true. As she watches, Adam demonstrates how he turned on the tears intentionally to win her back: "Us boys can do it too, you know, it's just that we never think to.... Oh yes, there ain't any of us don't have our little tricks, you know."

Here, implicit in the denouement is a powerful implication that it is men and not women who hold the other sex in a double bind through gender cliches. When the movie ends with Adam saying "Vive la difference!" as he closes the hangings around their four-poster bed, it is not quite the same difference as it seemed at the beginning of the film. The complexity of this moment, which preserves difference without defending a number of the most basic social conventions of gender difference, is extraordinary: how many commercial films in our supposedly liberated times can say the same?

More than any of their other films, *Rib* directly acknowledges the complexity of the Hepburn/Tracy synergy and its reflexive base in the offscreen Hepburn and Tracy. The home movie the Bonners show at the beginning of the film, which depicts the day they made their last payment on the country home in Connecticut, illustrates this element of the film. This film within a film, however—with its artfully arranged discontinuities, handwritten intertitles, jumping frames, and informal shots—makes explicit the slippages discussed above relative to their previous films. It seems like a strange intrusion into a Hollywood film because of its rather long duration and minuscule relationship to the plot. We certainly need to know about the existence of this place in order to receive the denouement of the film as part of a well-made plot, but the slowest audience member does not need four minutes of screen time watching the Bonners' friends reacting to it at a dinner party to absorb that information. Rather, the purported home movie forces our awareness that we are watching a movie, a process never encouraged by the mass media, by telling us three things that Hollywood never wants to tell us. First, we learn through Kip's arch questions that films are made products involving many people we never see; second, our resistance to knowing about that is embedded in the film through Adam's increasing anger at Kip's deconstruction of the filmic experience. Third, in highlighting a difference between a home movie and the commercial movie we are watching, the film makes the audience conscious of its tendency to think of Tracy and Hepburn as an onscreen/offscreen couple.

The made aspect of films is introduced at the beginning of the home movie, when Amanda explains what we are looking at, saying it is the main house; the cottage, she says, is where the camera is. "I can't see it," complains Kip, leaving open whether he wants to see the camera or the cottage. When the mortgage check is presented to the banker onscreen, the banker, who is also in the Bonners' apartment as they screen the movie, reveals that this was all acted out after the actual event, to which Kip replies, "All right, big mouth, settle down." Kip finally asks the question that needn't have been asked and is never answered, "Who took these pictures?" Movies are artificial illusions of continuity. The fragmentary nature of the home movie highlights how much has been done to *Adam's Rib* to make it seem continuous. Th home movie is more or less a collection of random scenes of the Bonners lounging around: Adam zipping up his trousers when woken from a nap, Amanda playing tennis, Adam with his two dogs. Narrative forms around the stage-managed scenes of the paying of the mortgage. Adam and Amanda ham it up in a hyperbolically melodramatic way to express their glee once the mortgage is paid. To celebrate, after Adam locks Amanda in the barn, from which she emerges with hay in her mouth, like a cow, he mock-leeringly shoves her back into the barn, clowning gestures of sexual intent. This stylized "sex scene" continues to evoke movie conventions when it is followed by an intertitle card reading, "*Censored!*"

Adam, who resists Amanda's attempt to puncture false images at the trial, also resists Kip's attempt to puncture false images during the scenes in which the Bonners and their banker pretend to exchange and receive the final payment, and those scenes that are posed or reveal more than they are intended to. Amanda enjoys the satire. This set of responses to the movie-within-a-movie plays interestingly off Tracy and Hepburn's screen personas in ways that knock his Rock of Gibraltar manhood a little bit off center in an overt fashion uncommon in the Hollywood discourse and give more approbation than usual to her liberal image. More, the home movie mobilizes their real feelings for each other in an interesting and powerful way that reveals that a straight-arrow image may hide dishonest elements, while a hell-raiser image may hide a fundamental commitment to truth.

Some of this brilliance continues to operate in their next film, *Pat and Mike,* which reopens the exploration of star bodies and their chemistry by setting the action in the world of sports. *Pat and Mike* is a movie oddly conflicted in tone. It has the visual texture of a sitcom but incorporates real-world sports figures into the narrative as themselves. Using cliched shot patterns predominantly, it breaks into surreal imagery at two crucial points. Positing a world dominated by conventional gender stereotypes, it depicts a couple that moves not only past gender cliches, but somewhat into experimental probing of androgyny.

The story concerns widow Pat Pemberton (Hepburn), a gym instructor at Pacific Technical College in California, who excels in a variety of sports but is unable to perform well when under the scrutiny of her fiancé, Collier Weld (William Ching), the assistant administrative vice president of Pacific Technical. Pat is propelled into a golf tournament by the country club pro, Charlie (Jim Backus). Out from under Collier's male medusan eye, Pat makes it to the finals of the women's national tournament and is about to defeat real-world champion Babe Didrikson when Collier arrives and blows her a kiss. She loses her self-confidence and loses the tournament.

Meanwhile, Pat is spotted by the slick sports promoter Mike Conovan (Tracy). In desperation to escape from Collier, she decides to let Mike become her manager. Their chemistry surprises her. Mike —a "dese, dems, and dose" Runyonesque character, just this side of the law—empowers her where white-bread, preppie Collier undermines her (despite his Asian-sounding name, William Ching is central casting WASP—verging on Nazi in appearance). Mike builds Pat a professional tennis career that moves her into the highest level of competitive play. Hepburn as Pat is shown playing tennis with real-world tennis champion Gorgeous Gussie Moran, when again Collier shows up and Pat defeats herself. The vicious cycle is broken when Pat realizes she is in love with Mike, but the problem of the competent woman resurfaces when Mike is threatened by a couple of his mobster pals and Pat saves him, inadvertently bruising his male ego in the process. Mike, who has been proposing a 50–50 relationship with Pat all along, is now not so sure that he likes everything about female equality, but he recovers his enthusiasm for her. At the end, Pat wins a golf tournament despite Weld's debilitating presence, and Mike is free from his fears about a real partnership with this formidable and capable woman.

Here is a movie passionately full of class and gender issues that are punched home for the audience not only by Tracy/Hepburn synergy but also by an interesting examination of the power of movie images. Non-diegetically scored by overly cheerful "merrily we roll along" music reminiscent of the scores of 1950s sitcoms, it is often as flat in appearance as the cartoon images of Hepburn and Tracy in the film's main title. The flatness soon emerges, however, as an aesthetic choice. Several of the featured cast members, including William Ching and Jim Backus, *were* sitcom performers. Many of the narrative scenes employ the brightly lit close-ups and the two-shots of television. The sets are like the department store mockups used in television shows, lacking the dreaminess, shadows, and angles of the Classical Hollywood movie, many of which were created by director George Cukor. Seeming as though it is pitched to the lowest possible degree of style, *Pat and Mike* sinks one octave lower in the scenes that depict the sports competitions Pat enter. The textureless but overprocessed television show/backlot look and feel of the fictional scenes are counterpointed with a substantial amount of seemingly under-processed mock-documentary footage of tennis and golf games actually involving Katharine Hepburn, who was an excellent athlete, and important women in the world of sports who are shown in the blandest possible depersonalizing long shots, and sometimes even in the kind of slightly overexposed film frames that result from using uncontrolled available light, as in newsreel coverage.

Though both styles suggest a plodding kind of artlessness, they are carefully constructed by Cukor to look prosaic. The visual surface of *Pat and Mike* is intentionally flattened, Cukor's intimation of the postmodern aesthetic to come, a structurally reflexive comment on the shallow cheerfulness of the mimesis of ordinary reality in the media of the fifties. The dimensionality of Pat and Mike as characters is distinguished from the straitjacket implied by the visualization of life in the mainstream when their psychological makeups are rendered through small, interesting touches of surrealism, and by the chemistry and ambiguous slippages of Hepburn and Tracy.

The most famous of the surreal eruptions in the Ozzie and Harriet landscape of *Pat and Mike* occurs well after Pat has thrown in with Mike, when she has reached the top of her tennis form and is a finalist in the championship matches. Keeping her opponent, the famous Gorgeous Gussie Moran, on the defensive in a contest that requires two sets out of three for victory, Pat wins the first set and is about to take the second when Collier enters his box with a party of five other people who represent the very range of patrician white Protestant society with which the offscreen Hepburn is associated. The two young women, an older couple, and a young man unsettle Pat as soon as they walk in. The sight of them laughing, and Pat's correct assumption that Collier is belittling her, turns the pressure of the "cheerful" norm, represented by Collier and party, into a menace that dissociates Pat from external and then internal reality. As she plays, she experiences sensory distortions that the movie spectator experiences with her: the net seems literally to grow taller in front of our eyes until neither Pat nor the spectator can see over it. At the same time, the size of Pat's racket seems to shrink in size until she is holding something no larger than a Ping-Pong paddle, while Moran's racket appears to double in size. Every man she can see suddenly morphs into Collier, and the voice of the referee becomes distorted so that his words are an incomprehensible murmur. Frenzied, Pat loses all control, and ultimately her consciousness as well, when she is helpless to move out of the way of the tennis ball slammed at her from the opposite side of the net. The ball morphs for Pat and the spectator of the film into a cartoon of a bubbling substance that fills the screen momentarily when it hits Pat, to be followed by a complicated series of shots that move the spectator's point of view between an objective observation of Pat's reaction to being hit and a subjective perspective that permits us to share her point of view as she falls.

This segment is cool and intellectual, in keeping with the rhetoric of a film that has emotionally distanced us from itself from the beginning. It is a segment to be read, very much unlike the emotionally engaging moments of the other Cukor collaborations with Hepburn and Tracy, and indeed any of the other films in the series shepherded by other directors, which also aimed for emotional effects. The shadowless, zero-degree style mise-en-scène of the WASP world evoked by Classical Hollywood as the locus of happiness turns, before the spectator's eyes, into the domain of hysterical paralysis, the negation of human energy and aspiration.

It requires the rough edges of Mike Conovan (and Spencer Tracy) to cut holes into the hermetically sealed WASP world. If Hepburn's Pat is threatened with spiritual destruction by the "normality" of her WASP heritage, Tracy's Mike offers her a déclassé possibility, but only a possibility, for Mike offers Pat breathing room but not a complete vacation from the male ego. The scene immediately following the debacle at the tennis match pits Collier and Mike directly against each other. Seeing each other for the first time in Pat's dressing room at the tennis stadium, each struggles to be the man to comfort and control Pat in her moment of weakness.

This film boldly assumes that every man to some degree wants a "little woman" as his woman. What's a woman to do? Well, whereas each preceding film, and each of the two that came after *Pat and Mike*, depended heavily on the evocation of a sexualized attraction between the two that cannot be denied, this film depends on our belief, unheard of in a Hollywood film, that the bond between them will not be denied for the very opposite reason, that it is *not* eroticized in the usual Hollywood sense of the term. This bond concerns feelings, mutual respect, and a policy of full disclosure. Boldly the film casts in a negative light the typical male-female bonding in Classical Hollywood films, in which, like Collier's relationship to Pat, we find erotic energy devoid of feelings and a place for the little woman that is maintained by unexamined gender assumptions.

Pat takes another step toward consolidating her freedom from Collier when, at their training camp, she and Mike have to deal with the feelings that complicate their professional relationship. In a matched pair of surreal images, each sees his or her feelings projected onto the outside world. Pat sees Mike's head take the place of Collier's head in a photo she keeps by her bed that shows her looking adoringly at Collier, now Mike. More ironically, but characteristically of Mike, he goes to feed a snack to Little Nell, his beloved racehorse, and sees Pat's face reflected on the horse's muzzle. Indeed, these reflections accurately suggest that they are moving toward becoming more than a professionally allied couple, but the images do not predict the form that new relationship will take; rather, they suggest the opposite, for each is simply plugging the other into an existing pattern of behavior, and the nature of their bond is so radical a departure for each that business as usual simply will not do. Pat cannot simply plug Mike into the position of domination to her submission, and Mike cannot simply make Pat another of his professional possessions.

An event tests them, as is the case in so many of the Hepburn/Tracy films, and when they pass the test, Collier's hold over Pat is definitively snapped, catapulting her into a new relationship to men and to herself and permitting Mike to achieve with her his ideal of equality in relating to women. The event, interesting in itself, is doubled in force because it is a startling variation on one of the most typical of Tracy/Hepburn scenes in previous films, particularly from *Woman of the Year* and *Adam's Rib*; it is a repetition of that scene in which the Tracy character suddenly sees the independence and competence of the Hepburn character as a threat. In this film, the event takes place as Mike is about to be beaten up by two of his underworld business partners, who have "bought a piece" of Pat and are angry that Mike won't force her to throw her matches so that they can amass large gambling profits. In prescribed Classical Hollywood heroic fashion, Mike pushes Pat out of the way so that she won't be hurt, but she, afraid for Mike, and forgetting about "woman's place," does not stay out of the way. Quite calmly, she proceeds to defuse the threat by incapacitating both gangsters with deft, workmanlike physical defense tactics, in the process taking possession of the blackjack wielded by one of them. Pat holds the weapon in her hand after administering a sharp blow to one of the assailants, puzzling over what it might be, asking in almost so many words, "Ever seen anything like this before?"—the question associated with pornographic images, and indeed she holds in her hand a weapon that inescapably evokes the image of a penis.

Castration is what Mike feels, despite all his previous assertions that men and women have to be equal partners, "Five-Oh-Five-Oh" (50–50). However, this event is unlike those of previous films, which validate the Tracy character's uncanny experience of the Hepburn character stepping over the line appropriate to feminine behavior. This film balances the spectator between Mike's understandable embarrassment in front of "the boys" and Pat's understandable bewilderment that she should be abandoned by Mike for demonstrating her concern for him. The multiple perspective here approaches that concerning the Attinger case in *Rib*. The androgyny that has been lurking since the beginning of their series, but which has previously been rejected, rises to the surface here in a benign form, as the film suggests that it's time for Mike to do a little reality testing of his ideals.

Ironically, just at this time of gender confusion, Collier begins to suspect a sexual relationship between Pat and Mike, suspicions that Pat uses to make Collier's worst fears a reality. Reverting to stereotype, Pat tries to create a situation in which Mike will rescue her from Collier, going so far as to say that he has been her knight in shining armor, when he knows that she needs nothing of the kind. He laughs off her lady-in-distress act until it becomes clear that she is offering him intimacy with her. If Pat's ploy is straight out of Classical Hollywood, so is his response that he doesn't know if she can lick him or he can lick her, but he is sure that between the two of them they can lick the world. But the film pushes the envelope when the love scene arrives at that moment usually reserved for the Big Kiss. Hepburn's Pat offers up her lips breathlessly, in the prescribed Hollywood fashion, and Mike holds that familiar mutual gaze that has often passed between them to precede some erotic overture, but the kiss doesn't happen. Instead, Mike jumps up giddily, saying, "O.K. kid, you've got yourself a deal." A puzzled Pat receives an androgynous handshake.

The absent kiss leads some to read the relationship between Pat and Mike as the kind of non-sexual relationship that *Without Love* narratively "proved" wouldn't work. But it can also be argued that the sexuality that Pat and Mike exemplify is not absent but simply unrepresentable by virtue of the discourse of eroticism in Hollywood, a discourse that can only depict the rejected, sinister relationship between Collier and Pat, which in the last shot is given the coup de grace. As Pat is preparing to sink her final putt of the game, she glances up to see Collier looking malevolently at her. This differs radically from previous moments when he ruined her game with a look of not-proud-but-anxious love. Now Collier is unmasked for the chilling force he is. In contrast, she sees Mike wink, and the spell is broken. The lack of sexual domination pays off for Pat. In the last montage of the film that follows, she happily wins her golf tournament, looks adoringly at him, and the film is over. Perhaps that wink says as much about the picture as it does about the final frame, as the two represent what is unrepresentable at that time and place in commercial cinema. Moreover, there is embedded here the sly suggestion that we have never before really seen Hepburn and Tracy as they are in real life because of the mediation by Hollywood conventions, but that we are beginning to see them onscreen as they really are for the first time. This too adds to the power of the film.

ENTROPY

After *Pat and Mike,* however, the reflexivity of the Tracy/Hepburn pairing lost its way irretrievably in a mechanical repetition of formulas that had previously worked for them, but that had also previously been vivified by their onscreen energy of connection with each other. If their reflexive qualities had once proven to be a stunningly successful solution to the false documentary literalism of the practices of Classical Hollywood in the forties and fifties, they succumbed to those practices in their final films. *Desk Set,* their next film, seems oblivious to the new lifting of the constraints of literalism that were on their way out, and the end of the PCA. *Desk Set* features a thematic concern of a potentially serious nature, the impact of the computer on the American workforce. Bunny Watson (Hepburn) is the head of reference for the Federal Broadcasting Company, and computer genius Richard Sumner (Tracy) appears to threaten her job and those of her staff when he constructs (EMERAC), a computer that can also do research. But Sumner and Bunny are, as no previous characters in their series have been, a species of formulaic versions of the Tracy character and the Hepburn character. There is little more to be said about this film than that it contains a patchwork of recycled routines from previous movies, the conversation of non sequiturs patterned after one in *Adam's Rib,* and an office Christmas party in full swing at the end of the film, when Hepburn repeats her performance as a mock Lila Vine from *Without Love. Desk Set* is a hypocritical pretense as a film about social issues and a tedious recycling of old images. The two go together.

Similarly, just as *Desk Set* is a dehumanized film about the need to humanize the workplace, *Guess* is a racist and sexist film about the need to fight racism and sexism. Manifesting the atavistic filmmaking of *Desk Set,* it is also oddly behind the times despite its attempt to present itself as a groundbreaker. Sidney Poitier, Hepburn and Tracy's co-star in their last film, had already made a dozen or more highly nuanced movies dealing with racism, including his very first film, *No Way Out,* made seventeen years previously, in 1950. He had also had a more subtly depicted onscreen interracial romance in *Patch of Blue,* two years previously in 1965. And if *Guess* featured an interracial kiss as a first, there was no particular advance in representation that wouldn't have been served by the next interracial kiss, in the "Plato's Stepchildren" episode of *Star Trek* that appeared on television the next year, on November 22, 1968, in a much more imaginatively provocative framing. Worst of all, the once expressive tensions in the Hepburn/Tracy film were in a state of full dissociation.

The story of the film concerns a liberal crusading newspaper editor, Matthew Drayton (Tracy) and his equally liberal wife, Christina (Hepburn), who are tested by their daughter, Joey (Katharine Houghton), when she announces that she is going to marry an African American doctor, John Prentice (Sidney Poitier). Following her announcement, the Prentice and Drayton families have twenty-four hours to deal with their objections; after that John and Joey have to leave for Geneva. Alarmingly, the big narrative moment is little more than an affirmation of the crotch of the white patriarch. The dramatic tension hinges on whether Matthew Drayton (not John's father) will give permission for the wedding. It resolves to a spectacularly eccentric racist and sexist inversion of conventional racist opposition to integration and intermarriage because of its threat to white, male sexual dominance. This film creates its own form of racism by tacitly asserting that *failing to integrate and intermarry is the real threat to white, male sexual potency.* Matthew is turned around by Mrs. Prentice (Beah Richards) when she accuses him of having forgotten what it is like to have sexual desire. She scores with him when she says, "I believe that men grow old and when sexual things no longer matter to them, they forget it all, forget what true passion means . . ." Matthew remembers his passion and gives consent. Then everything falls into place.

Guess Who's Coming to Dinner is a senseless non-discussion of an important social issue. If it has any actual power, its force lies in its transfer to the screen the last scene of the story of Spencer Tracy and Katharine Hepburn's odd fusion of life and movies. The only free energy in the film is their use of it as a challenge to Tracy's approaching death, which they, correctly as it turned out, believed to be imminent. These moments are few and far between, but they are undeniable and eerie. There is a frightening chasm between the nonsense of Drayton's final speech in the film and the powerful rapport between Hepburn and Tracy when Drayton refutes Mrs. Prentice's claim that he doesn't remember passion: "And there is nothing, absolutely nothing that your son feels for my daughter that I didn't feel for Christina. Old, yes, burned out, certainly. But I can tell you the memories are still there. Clear, intact, indestructible. And they'll live there if I live to be a hundred and ten." Further nullifying the purported subject of the film, the camera gazes primarily on Tracy and Hepburn during this part of the speech, through two-shots and shot-reverse shot patterns that catch the light glancing off the tears in Christina's eyes, which have been fabricated so often by Hollywood that they would no longer have any effect were it not for the naked expression of love and gratitude exposed in the faces of the actors. The role of the Tracy and Hepburn chemistry in the film is dissociated from the lifeless, simplistic narrative, but in its isolation it became Tracy's last chance to tell Hepburn what, by her testimony, he never told her in private life, and Hepburn's last chance to hear it.[22] There is an odd and terrible voyeurism here, which makes Hepburn and Tracy complicit in using synergistic chemistry for its least valid purposes. What had originally been a fascinating source of authentic expression ended as perhaps worse than the nightmare of all critics who mistrust the mass media: the film is an inauthentic escapist fantasy not only for the audience but also for the actors, for whom it has become a surrogate for private expression.

CONCLUSION

In the forties and early fifties, the Synergistic Couple made its final significant appearances, at least in its Classical, Old Hollywood form, in the films of Hepburn and Tracy. In this time of political upheaval, anxiety was attached to the flow of ideas through the subconscious, which seemed to present a vulnerable portal of invasion of undesirable thoughts and impulses to a popular audience frightened and confused by dangers associated by governmental watchdog committees with Communism. Thus the major vehicle of couple chemistry became an alien aspect of filmmaking, apparently avoided by commercial filmmakers of all political perspectives in favor of either an earnest literal realism or an ironic commentary on the pedestrian simplemindedness of the earnest. The onscreen partnership of Hepburn and Tracy, arising from an offscreen synergy, offered the last hope for the Synergistic Couple.

Until 1952, with their work on *Pat and Mike*, they created conditions for their work in an otherwise strangled industry that were free enough to use the filmic image unconstrainedly with all its ambiguities to make compelling screen couple movies. They challenged gender stereotypes on a more profound level with their chemistry than they could with the scripts of their films, which made various accommodations with the public perception of the place of "the little woman." After 1952, however, their work went into decline, showing the ravages of a weakened studio system no longer nourished by the freewheeling heterogeneity of the 1930s that they had kept alive for a while between them and some of their frequent artistic co-collaborators.

However, the precedent that they established as an onscreen/offscreen couple had a vibrant influence on actors in the late years of the studio system and has taken powerful hold in the post-studio fin de siècle mass culture industry. Arguably, Hepburn and Tracy are behind the bizarre acting out of their private lives on the public screen by Elizabeth Taylor and Richard Burton in the 1960s and 1970s and of the similar behavior of Roseanne Barr and Tom Arnold in the 1990s. On the more positive side, they may also have influenced the extremely fruitful collaboration of Paul Newman and Joanne Woodward, who also fell in love while they were playing lovers in their first film together, *The Long, Hot Summer,* and of Woody Allen and Diane Keaton, though their offscreen romance had evolved into a friendship by the time they worked together in Allen's independent films. Although political intimidation of the media is now a pale shadow of what it was in the forties and fifties, the mass audience is still so much impressed by the seriousness of films and television that can claim to be based on a "real story" and still so wary of the imaginative experience that filmmakers even resort to false claims of that sort to make an impression on the mass audience. Think of the false claims of both the film *Fargo* (1996, Dir. Joel Coen) and the television series *The X-Files* (in its first episode) to a basis in a factual incident. As a result, imaginative screen productions continue to use the cover of an aura of reality provided by a spillover from what the audience imagines about the lives of offscreen couples onto the onscreen pairs that they play.

CHAPTER

THE POST-STUDIO SYNERGISTIC COUPLE
The Thin Aliens

Looking back, we can see the footprints of a great couple tradition containing a rich body of work, a number of principal creators, a relatively well-defined economic and social relationship to the Hollywood studio system, a number of generic characteristics and thematic concerns, and a complex relationship to ideology. In Old Hollywood, the screen couple could be either a conservative or a radical figure. It was conservative in that all media couples suggested that we would find who we are through the beloved. Thus it favored a notion of fixed rather than socially constructed identity. Nevertheless, it could be comparatively radical when it complicated fixed notions of identity with intimations of constructed cliches. Among the various categories of screen couples, Functional and Iconic Couples were the most conservative, reinforcing identities rigorously defined by social values. But the iconoclastic Synergistic Couple evaded many social definitions.

Today the media continue to present audiences with both conservative and iconoclastic versions of the screen couple; however, the categories survive in significantly translated form. First, the great couple tradition no longer has the central economic relationship to the entertainment industry it once had. Second, and as a result of the economic marginalizing of the screen couple, the number of principal creators is much decreased and the population is transient, for the most part—a far cry from the large number of studio-era actors who worked in pairs and who generally did so for the largest part of their careers, even if not with the same partner. Moreover, while the obligatory romance is every bit as obligatory in contemporary movies and television as it was under the studio system, there are fewer instances of screen couples with heft and a place of central focus in the screen story. Third, although some of the generic characteristics and thematic concerns of films and television shows associated with post-studio era screen couples are directly continuous with the established great tradition, important changes in social philosophies and realities have made their mark.

Today's contemporary extension of the great couple tradition continues to focus on the dynamics of intimacy and to displace emotional anxieties and opportunities onto the surroundings in which the couple operates. That is, the mystery story, the exotic/fantasy location, the musical, and the melodrama continue to embed indirect images of onscreen intimacy and a general preoccupation with ways in which the body disturbs rational concepts of limits in physical processes like sports, dancing, and physical illness. These images and generic types of stories evoke the breathless uncertainties about limits, the sense of elevated reality, and the heightened awareness of bodily sensations that most people associate with intimacy. However, today's couples are placed into narratives that shift away from older definitions of intimacy as an interior stability that constitutes an ultimate form of security. Today's media couples imply a new definition of intimacy that more poignantly recognizes its interior forms of confusion, which verge on terror. The new Synergistic Couples, in particular, radiate a highly unstable as well as an indeterminate core, and even the more conventional contemporary media couples reflect fin de siècle crises in social and personal identity.

NEW INDUSTRIAL ECONOMICS

The fascinations of the onscreen couple are a permanent feature of popular entertainment, but because of the profound alterations in the structure of the electronic media and the way they deliver entertainment to the mass audience, there is no longer a lock fit between those fascinations and the economic basis of film production. The screen couple was a natural result of the multifunction studios of the old system. In the landscape of the new Hollywood studio, there are no contract studio actors, directors, writers, designers, or even technicians. The studio is a financial entity that employs staff acquisitions personnel and development personnel, to whom scripts, production packages, and even complete movies can be brought for development or distribution. Sound stages and movie equipment can be used by the packagers, who generate movies with the studio development people. The studio forms pacts with producers, who operate as if they were development or distribution personnel. The almost complete split between production and the finance of distribution means that, in most cases, little heterogeneous collaboration occurs, as it did in the old system, which housed a relatively stable group of people with differing points of view. Instead, freelance writers, producers, and directors who are unlikely to have an ongoing, evolving relationship with the development and distribution personnel who make demands on them put together packages. Instead of a continuous, comparatively long-term collegial dialogue, ad hoc, short-term politics now structure the entertainment industry. Overall, this structure is not conducive to the ongoing pairing of screen couples.

The talent agency, another modern institution that has filled the vacuum left by the termination of the roster of studio contract players, does have organized access to a somewhat stable group of creative personnel and is often instrumental in putting together movie packages because of its contracts with creative clients. However, the talent agency works on commission, not with a talent pool on regular salary, and so the talent agency is not motivated, as was the old Hollywood studio, to foster acting teams so that contract stars would not languish while drawing weekly checks. Their thinking is a little more long term than that of most packagers, but not long term enough to experiment with repeat casting of the same stars. In addition, whether the package is put together by a producer, a part of the creative team (writer, director, or actor), or a talent agency, the coalitions that put together film packages cannot be sure that their efforts will meet with success. Deals fall through regularly after months and even years of negotiations, and even deals that are brought to fruition are typically so fraught with delay and instability that the initial casting of stars that was part of the package is likely to change many times as the process works through. Such volatility, like the decentralization of moviemaking, is not promising for the fostering of onscreen couples in repeat pairings.[1]

Repeated screen pairs are more feasible on television, where the economic structure is more conducive to continuity. While networks do not have stable talent pools, many individual television series do maintain long-term contract writers, producers, directors, actors, designers, editors, and composers of music. Because they are on salary, it is to the advantage of the series to deploy these creators in as many interesting combinations as possible in the various episodes, and so in television something like the fostering of couple talent can be financially advantageous.[2]

The increased power of the actor, another feature of the post-studio media, has also proven to be, in some ways, a force that works against the great tradition of screen couples. Working as part of a screen couple, especially one that involves intense synergy, is frustrating and irritating for actors. Individual restiveness within the grip of the intense energy sharing of this kind of collaboration can be as frustrating and alarming as the tensions of real emotional intimacy. Screen couple partners today often openly express dissatisfactions that were kept under wraps by publicity directors during the days of the studio system. Many of these expressions identify the pressure that couple work puts on individual identity, a pressure that might be paraphrased in this way: when a space of that kind of intimacy is opened between two actors in a work situation, so much energy is created that they either want to punch or kiss each other.[3] Under the conditions of the studio system, actors were often forced to work through the pressure; they can now avoid being caught in the grip of synergy because in the new decentralized structure, they can sometimes take on the power of the producer. With less heterogeneous collaborative energy involved in the creative process, there is less counterpressure to contain personal frictions with onscreen partners. At the same time, actors who enjoy working together cannot count on doing so unless they become producers. In the current environment, even a pairing like William Powell and Myrna Loy would not be likely; there is no studio entity to ensure repeat castings or make the arrangements. Further, the evidence suggests that very few actor/producers show any interest in persisting in couple projects, even with those they enjoy as professional partners.

Actors who do not become producers may demand many perks for themselves, but they do not demand specific co-stars with the idea of building a compelling couple. Actors have more freedom than they did in the old system, but even with that, many leading men either have little interest in the couple aspect of their screen projects or pointedly prefer to overshadow their co-stars. This combination of factors—a lack of interest on the part of actors and industry decentralization—has resulted in the disappearance of the once abundantly used star Iconic Couple, at least in the form that it once took. Today, a star will often be teamed with an attractive, stereotypically compatible central casting type, a situation virtually unheard of under the studio system, which had no reason to pair a star with an actor of lesser status. Today, even the pairing of stars no longer creates the distinctive energy of the Iconic Couple. Instead, packaged films create a screen couple that, except for the presence of stars, is indistinguishable in its effect on the movie from the old Functional Couple, doing little more than meeting the minimum business and storytelling requirements. Movie packagers for the big studios, whether the packagers be primarily talent agencies working with their clients, individual writers and directors seeking to make a movie initiated by them, or pact producers seeking projects, still use the Gable Plus One pattern of casting discussed in Chapter One to build couples. But, because today's casting decisions are not influenced by the availability of stars already paid for, the packagers may not wish to incur the expense of two star actors. Today's economics favor packages created around a charismatic star like Al Pacino, filling in the female role with this or that stereotypically interchangeable attractive female actor, who will be less expensive than a star. This practice has made common a new asymmetrical pattern that devalues the partner and the role of the couple—as, for example, in the string of films in which the completely forgettable Penelope Ann Miller starred with some of the most important actors in the industry—making the couple an obligatory aspect of the plot, but one that doesn't carry very much of the interest of the film.[4] Since the post-studio version of the iconic screen pair has become a cliche to such an extent that it is virtually devoid of pair chemistry, I will have little to say about the perfunctory, uninteresting, and abortive partnerships that they have become in major motion picture Hollywood releases.

The exception to actor disinterest in the energy of the screen couple relates to the situation of the onscreen/offscreen pair. Actor producers may now insist on collaborating professionally with their offscreen partners, whereas actors under the studio system rarely had such freedom. Occasionally this produces the special kind of energy of the Hepburn/Tracy partnership, an early instance of such actor initiative. But often the results are not interesting—for example, the onscreen/offscreen partnership of Tom Cruise and Nicole Kidman, whose only work of enduring interest has been their assignment to Stanley Kubrick's *Eyes Wide Shut* (1999), and in that case their lack of screen chemistry was compensated for by Kubrick's brilliant auteur vision.[5] Similarly, without the studio structure to override personal ruptures, potentially compelling screen partnerships, for example Steve Martin's partnership with Bernadette Peters, whose two films together gave every evidence of the kind of greatness of the synergistic quartet in earlier chapters, collapsed with the failure of their offscreen relationship. Much the same can be said of Warren Beatty and Julie Christie (three films) and Jack Nicholson and Anjelica Huston (two films).[6]

However, the combination of the end of the Production Code, the rise of the small independent commercial film producer, and the new freedom of actors to choose and even direct their own projects has had some positive influence on the screen couple. The distinctly small and independent production organization has yielded a Synergistic Couple or two, and has been part of the trend toward the development of the Thematic Couple, a new kind of mass media couple. The Thematic Couple is a category of screen pairing that reflects the freedom of expression in post-code media by shifting the emphasis in the creating of complex meanings. Under the studio system, shared energy was the most fruitful generator of non-cliched meanings in popular entertainment. The current environment makes possible a shared interpretation between a couple and a relatively provocative script that goes significantly beyond the limits once imposed by the PCA. Merchant-Ivory, for example, has been willing to take chances with the kind of script that permits the emergence of a Thematic Couple. At the same time, in today's less restricted media, the shared energy of a dynamic Synergistic Couple may also be enhanced by the possibility of a more provocative script, as in the Woody Allen production. Allen's experimental interests, coupled with his desire to assemble a group of actors who work together repeatedly and his great fortune in procuring funding that does not tie him to casting formulas, create ideal conditions for the emergence of a new version of the Synergistic Couple.

Nevertheless, even in the category of independent commercial film, which is also a phenomenon of the post-studio/post-code era, I have had few choices to make using the original criterion that a significant screen couple must have worked together in at least six films. Using this criterion, I have identified only one Synergistic Couple, Woody Allen and Diane Keaton. In some ways an onscreen/offscreen couple (they had ceased to be personally involved by the time they made their first film together), their working relationship fortunately survived the termination of their personal relationship. The volatility of the current media situation for the screen couple is apparent in the disparity between the Keaton/Allen partnership and Allen's many screen collaborations with Mia Farrow, to whom he was personally connected while they worked together, which worked only in the context of films that were not dependent on their shared energy. Allen and Farrow neither emerged as a Synergistic Couple nor professionally survived the collapse of their personal relationship.[7]

Another powerful onscreen/offscreen couple with synergistic chemistry that emerged in the 1970s in independent commercial movies is John Cassavetes and Gena Rowlands, but their work, while well worth examining, does not have the quantitative heft needed for this study. Cassavetes and Rowlands acted in six pictures together, and he directed her in three more, but in only two did they play a screen couple.[8] Cassavetes and Rowlands are not generally known to the mass movie audience, but Rowlands's smoky sensuality and Cassavetes's world-weary cynicism combined onscreen to create powerful cinematic experiences of intimacy in a number of delicately shaded, complex, and ambiguous portrayals of human emotional rapport. Their work should not go unremarked in the context of this exploration.

The onscreen collaboration between the offscreen couple of Paul Newman and Joanne Woodward suggests another positive opportunity the current situation offers for onscreen/offscreen pairs that are stable, or for professional collaborations that can discipline themselves to rise above personal irritation. The Newman/Woodward collaboration is a primary example of the new Thematic Couple that has been made possible by augmented freedom of expression in the post-PCA environment. Such pairs can work to consciously articulate a commercial script comparatively complex in its text about human relationships. Newman and Woodward do not produce their own films, but they are interested in working together and they have attracted independent producers as a team, as well as individually. They began working together just as the studio system was falling apart, but they were still under pressure to conform to studio cliches (*The Long Hot Summer*, 1958, Dir. Martin Ritt). They have grown into an acting pair willing and able to successfully explore a wider range of human interrelationships than had previously been possible when the code was still in force (*Mr. and Mrs. Bridge*, 1990, Dir. James Ivory). While Newman and Woodward are exceptional as actors who work as a Thematic Couple because of the large number of films they have made together, they are part of a fairly extensive new couple category, if we count the numerous one-shot thematic pairings of actors hazarded by high-quality, independent production packagers. But because of their partnership in repeated films, Newman and Woodward stand out in this group, distinguished by the richness that repetition gives their work together, a richness lacking in the majority of single-assignment Thematic Couples.

Predictably, the scarcity of screen couples with heft in post–studio era movies contrasts with a relative abundance of important screen couples within the venue of the television network, and to a certain extent among the packagers of serial programs for cable television, where both Synergistic and Thematic Couples are, comparatively, thriving. Television networks have found that they attract audience loyalty through the development of compelling couples in their serialized entertainment: daytime television network soap operas and nighttime network television dramatic series and sitcoms. Thus they foster synergistic chemistry when ratings predict profits from keeping a couple pair together. Television has also been prolific in developing Thematic Couples in high-concept serialized television that reflects some of the tentative breaking of old taboos in society at large.

Time has not yet tested the value of Synergistic and Thematic Couples produced by television, and therefore my choices of pairs to discuss at length in this review of contemporary televisual inheritors of the mantle of Astaire/Rogers, Weissmuller/O'Sullivan, Loy/Powell, and Tracy/Hepburn have been made on a somewhat personal basis, at least with respect to my evaluation of their value. However, all the television couples I have chosen have created major impacts on audiences for a period of at least four years. Among the many possible contenders, I will make claims for three onscreen couples as demonstrating the enduring power of the great couple tradition. Among these pairs, from the venue of television, I have distinguished the following as the most significant Synergistic Couples: David Duchovny and Gillian Anderson, who have played Mulder and Scully on the Fox Network series *The X-Files* since 1993; and Anthony Geary and Genie Francis, who have played Luke and Laura on the daytime soap opera *General Hospital*, with breaks in their participation in the show, since

1980. As the most significant Thematic Couples produced by television I have chosen Bill Cosby and Phylicia Rashad, who worked together in the nighttime television network sitcom *The Cosby Show* from 1984 to 1992, and Bruce Willis and Cybill Shepherd, who worked together on the nighttime network television series *Moonlighting* from 1985 to 1989.

The rigorous selection process at work here in the highlighting of six couples—three synergistic and three thematic—from among the hundreds of possible pairs who have worked in the post-studio media has been necessary in order to accommodate the comparative brevity of the space allotted for this part of the discussion. But my selections also reflect a judgment about importance to the American media. Despite their less-than-serious reputations among critics, and despite their association with series labeled cult, at best, Duchovny and Anderson, Geary and Francis, and Allen and Keaton, whom I identify as post-studio Synergistic Couples, demand a second look in the context of any exploration about the onscreen couple. Their work, as full of surprises as that of Weissmuller and O'Sullivan and Astaire and Rogers—all of whom were misrecognized as lightweights in their day—alerts us to the ongoing potent role of chemistry in making the mass entertainment industry a vehicle of expression and value. At the same time, Cosby and Rashad, Willis and Shepherd, and Woodward and Newman, whom I identify as Thematic Couples, alert us to changes in the industry that have made way for better texts that deal openly with racial issues, or with a reasonably wide range of sexual issues, or experiments with nonlinear narrative structure. As with the quartet generated by the studio system, however, they all also point up the expressive limits of the mass media as well as its possibilities.

THE NEW SYNERGISTIC COUPLE

While both old and new Synergistic Couples are replete with staggering screen chemistry that informs the screen story through the prominence of the energies of their paired bodies, the uses of the chemistry of new Synergistic Couple differ from those of the couples that formed the great tradition. For the couples of the grand tradition, chemistry was a form of rootedness in a large, universal harmony that opposed the undependable, capricious aspects of traditional social values and exposed those flaws despite social claims to order and solidity. The old Synergistic Couple comforted audiences beset by social inequities with an assurance that the universe was an ordered place. By contrast, the chemistry of the new Synergistic Couple heavily qualifies the hope it offers. By its very nature the richness of energy in screen chemistry implies some generous universal force that exists independently of narrow social mores, and so the strong chemistry of the new Synergistic Couple ipso facto implies some cosmic human freedom from cultural institutions. Yet at the same time, the possibilities offered by the universe of the new Synergistic Couple have become as questionable as those offered by the society in which they live, making the entertainment industry a vehicle by which questions are raised about the possibility of human freedom. Existentialism, or at least cosmic indeterminacy, has found the commercial media.

The contemporary iffiness of the hope generated by chemistry is compounded by the nonlinear elements in the contemporary Synergistic Couple narrative. The compelling raw synergy of the studio-fostered Synergistic Couple contrasted with a predictably formulaic plot and dialogue in order to put conventional ideas in a more fruitful new perspective, but the indeterminacy of the new, post-studio Synergistic Couple is amplified by the instability of a modified type of commercial narrative newly freed from the constraints of linearity. The new Synergistic Couple lives in a narrative in which incompatible multiple perspectives are the rule in place of the one comparatively harmonious dominant angle of vision of the old movie stories. In part this is the result of the rise of television, which tends toward the serial narrative as entertainment. The television series, by virtue of its form, tells its stories through narrative discontinuities, something that Old Hollywood avoided as potentially too disturbing to the public. The more imaginative series, like *The X-Files* and *General Hospital*, have learned to use the inherent discontinuity of the medium to create mysterious and interesting ellipses, another storytelling element that was discouraged in Old Hollywood. And indeed, while the television audience has learned how to read and enjoy the series form, it still howls with frustration at some of the built-in complexities of the genre. Although these two series have a strong, devoted following, audiences for *The X-Files* regularly express discomfort with the elliptical narrative discontinuity of the series, while audiences for *General Hospital* show an equal amount of impatience when the daytime serial takes a few too many twists and turns.[9]

In part the new liberation of the media story from linearity is also a result of post-code film production. The current freedom in film has meant that many commercial independents can elect to use discontinuity and ellipsis, emphasizing the inherent discontinuity of the editing process of film, which was disguised in Old Hollywood by smooth continuity editing. Woody Allen has been very active in defying Hollywood's linear narrative conventions through disruption of the flow of plot events by the interjection of direct commentary by the characters on the situation, temporal discontinuity, and elliptical omissions. The modern sense of destabilization pervades the world of the new mass culture Synergistic Couple because the new media are discontinuous by nature and because auteurs can choose to emphasize the ruptures in the filmic process.

For these reasons, the new Synergistic Couple provides a more overtly uncanny experience than the old one, with fewer built-in reassurances. The flow of life in the narratives of Scully and Mulder, Keaton and Allen, and Luke and Laura proposes a bittersweetness in the couple stories. Unlike the sense that the older mass media Synergistic Couples provided—that while the path of true love might be arduous, such love would conquer all—the new mass media Synergistic Couples haunt us with the possibility that love, though the strongest bond we know, may not be enough given the centrifugal forces of the universe and our repressive culture.

SCULLY AND MULDER

A new Synergistic Couple that clearly exemplifies both changes from and continuity with the great couple tradition is the team of Fox Mulder (David Duchovny) and Dana Scully (Gillian Anderson), a pair of FBI agents in the weekly nighttime television serial *The X-Files*. Mulder and Scully were originally conceived by series creator Chris Carter as part of a high-concept series about adventures in the paranormal created "to scare the pants" off his audience. Carter conceptualized Mulder, his hero, as the kind of gadfly figure within the government bureaucracy that was made extremely popular in another genre by Clint Eastwood's *Dirty Harry* series of movies, and by Eastwood imitators. However, Carter was principally influenced by a specialized science fiction gadfly, the cult figure Kolchak, who appeared in the television series *Kolchak: The Night Stalker* (1974–1975), a favorite of Carter's when he was a child. Kolchak (Darren McGavin), an independent gumshoe with a twist, was a self-styled gadfly, outside "the system," who insisted on the reality of the paranormal. The concept of *The X-Files* is that Mulder, a Kolchak-like pariah at the FBI, is the guardian of the X-Files, the record of cases suggesting paranormal activity that the bureau would prefer to sweep under the rug. The concept immediately sets up a contradiction at the heart of the show that was not present in *Kolchak*. Kolchak pursued his own obsessions on his own, while Mulder is paid by the system to investigate what it does not want investigated. Why? Carter's *X-Files* further complicates the old formula by adding a woman partner, Scully, a scientist distinctly skeptical of paranormality. In concept, Scully was intended to function on the show as part of the narrative formula. Her skepticism sharpens the inner contradictions of *The X-Files*, as she enters the picture because she has been sent to work with Mulder by the FBI administration as an in-house spy who will subvert his inquiries. This is an inexplicable, never to be explained, administrative choice on the part of the FBI. Why can't this powerful arm of the government just fire Mulder instead of instituting surveillance to prove their unbelief?

The series has evolved a highly convoluted plot in response to the logical flaw in its foundation, implying ambiguous powerful forces within the bureaucracy detailed below determined to protect Mulder. However, the logical flaw in the series is one of its major strengths, creating a dreamlike ellipsis in reason and granting appropriate power to the accident of casting that created the chemistry between Duchovny and Anderson. Perhaps this series does deal in storytelling that "scares the pants off" some viewers. But what is really eerie, what carries the show unerringly forward from week to week, is the intimacy that the Duchovny/Anderson chemistry made possible between Scully and Mulder. If the fantastic plots about paranormal phenomena and aliens challenged the concept of the normal and the comforting security of limits, that concept ultimately became the setting for the drama of the Mulder/Scully synergy and the ultimate challenge to certainty: intimacy.[10]

The compelling gravity of the Scully/Mulder connection—and the ability of the show to convince viewers of their effective resistance to the powers that be—is more a function of the Anderson/Duchovny chemistry than of the early scripts modeled on the Kolchak idea, which were competent but standard fare about individuals with peculiar powers. Those scripts, of course, provide the ideal context for the representation of the modern, troubled path to intimacy, but, all appearances to the contrary, stories about things that go bump in the night are a vehicle, not the main energy of the series. The moment of truth came in the second season of the series when Anderson became pregnant and had to be written out of the shows for a few episodes. Under the pressure to create Scullyless adventures for Mulder, Carter and his associates came up with a whole new direction for the show, a storyline about a conspiracy between important men in high places and alien invaders. With this new direction, suddenly the seemingly unconnected incidents of the paranormal became vaguely associated with a long-term story about an unofficial FBI conspiracy with an alien civilization interested in colonizing Earth. The conspiracy mythology, which has become very complex and rich, began with an alien abduction of Scully, purportedly as a practical measure to give Anderson a very brief maternity leave. It evolved into an umbrella story about a power struggle within the FBI between collaborators with the aliens and those who opposed collaboration. It turned into an attempt at a logical rationale for Mulder's place as the guardian of the institutionally rejected X-Files.

However, the very decision to take this route because Anderson needed a brief hiatus from work confessed to the real priority of the series—which was not the Byzantine narrative. As a weekly show devoted to new paranormal mysteries in each episode, *The X-Files* should theoretically not have needed any special tinkering if one of two agents had to be out of the story for a week or two. That Scully's absence made such a momentous difference suggests that the real priorities of the series were making themselves known in this serendipitous way. The nature of Scully's abduction is also telling since it resulted in experiments by aliens involving her reproductive organs. From that point on, the story content, whether it was a stand-alone paranormal mystery episode or an episode connected with the mythology of the conspiracy, became increasingly pointed toward intimate places in Scully's body and Mulder's connection with them. The powerful synergy between Duchovny and Anderson increasingly filled the verbal silences about the erotic subtext of Mulder and Scully's adventures. Carter's avowed determination to avoid a love affair between the two, because, in his words, that would impede the mystery adventure, did not prevent him from following the trajectory of the show where it led him. But it did make "love" the name that could be neither spoken nor ignored, the unacknowledged central mystery and adventure in the series.

The disparity between the original concept and the elements that have ultimately been important to the popularity of this series is deep and dramatically evocative of the fear and murkiness that surrounds the representation of intimacy in the current media, which are far more comfortable with unmotivated sex than with tender passion. Carter's repeated assertions that he conceptualized the series as a descendant of *Kolchak: The Night Stalker,* a truly non-erotic action series, deftly avoids acknowledgment of the centrality of the intimacy of Scully and Mulder to *The X-Files,* with Carter simply (officially) ignoring the fact that Kolchak, though a loner like Mulder, never developed any connection with anyone but an elderly woman who stayed in his office as a confidante rather than accompanying him into the ghoul-haunted field.[11] Carter explicitly focuses, instead, on the inspiration that he took from the tantalizing lack of resolution in *Kolchak's* discontinuous investigations of different monsters each week, which had the distinction of bringing into television's realm of quick fixes and easy solutions a breath of indeterminacy and continuing mystery that Carter has made a hallmark of his show. However, the inspiration for the show is far more complex, certainly demanding acknowledgment of the influence of *Twin Peaks,* the breakthrough series about unexpressed tenderness, mystery, violence, and multiple levels of reality. Even more important are the images of Duchovny and Anderson, whose casting was a matter of instant recognition for Carter and whose synergy is the fulcrum that moves the series.

From the first episode, the investigation of the paranormal and the hostility of the FBI hierarchy toward the quest have been a displacement of the mystery of the Mulder/Duchovny-Scully/Anderson intimacy, just as mystery was a displacement in the Thin Man series for the synergy of Nick/Powell-Nora/Loy. The casting process for *The X-Files,* in all its complexity, is the story of how image led the way, all concepts to the contrary, for the series to be a contemporary milieu for an important Synergistic Couple. As Carter tells the story, the casting of Duchovny was an early and easy decision. His cool, witty, attractive presence made him a natural for Mulder. The Scully figure involved dialogue and debate between Carter and the Fox network producers, who very much wanted a big-breasted blonde of the Pamela Anderson Lee (*Barb Wire*) type. Such a casting would have suffused the series with an aura of standard, leering, *Playboy* soft porn that would have suited the current formulaic Functional Couple, which is sexual but not erotic, physically but not emotionally or spiritually intimate.

Carter fought the standard casting formula, primarily on the strength of the impression made on him by Gillian Anderson, and by her rapport with Duchovny during the audition. Carter has said that Anderson brought a seriousness to the character that was right. But this is hardly the kind of image for which one enters the bruising creative media wars. Again, Carter's statement is disingenuous, or he himself is unable to verbalize his motivations. The brilliance of this casting coup, evident immediately in the pilot episode, suggests that what Carter saw was the kind of eroticism that compels viewers with its uncanny, unclassifiable force. From the very beginning, the synergy of the two actors led the series away from flat concept and toward an organic relationship between uncanny events, uncanny authorities, and uncanny couple bonding. Carter and his creative team have de facto gone along with the energy of actor chemistry, to their credit and despite their disclaimers. As a result, the genuine allure of *The X-Files* is based neither on Grand Guignol chills and thrills nor on a sustained argument about corruption and deceit in high places indicting the patriarchal hierarchy of Western democracies. Rather, both the thrills and the conspiracy story sustain a fantasy environment through which its two bonded questers can indirectly explore concerns about the fate of shared humanity in a terrain that reflects a radical cultural fin de siècle uncertainty about our bodies and our institutions.

The pilot episode, which concerns a series of abductions of high school students in the town of Bellefleur, Oregon, establishes the triple-ringed *X-Files* pattern of eeriness in events, authority, and couple synergy. The abductions involve young people being "called" to the forest by a mysterious force visualized as a brilliant white light that concealed more than it revealed. The abductions sounded the first note of the oft-repeated strains in the series of disruption of time and magnetic fields, alien invasions of the mind and body, and the fleetingly glimpsed alien body, here (as often) a corpse mysteriously stolen.

Then, in an second ring of disquieting presences, the show introduces the FBI hierarchy, which is almost as eerie as the extraterrestrials and just as alien. The episode begins with the assignment of Scully to Mulder by a man in authority whose conversation with her evokes that disconcerting silence that lurks beneath the manipulative words of those in charge. Power is rendered uncanny, as words, like the light that accompanies alien abductions, seem to hide rather than to express, and to hide a devious intent, at that. The FBI authorities will not directly ask Scully to spy on Mulder. They simply trust that she will "make the proper scientific analysis." To augment the aura of discomfort associated with the purported keepers of national security there lurks a silent man, tall, slim, in appearance a cross between the patrician literary scholar Mark Van Doren and a central casting Nazi, smoking a cigarette, to be known in future shows as The Cigarette Smoking Man, Cancer Man, and finally C. G. B. Spender (William B. Davis). He is not immediately visible when Scully enters the office where her instructions will be issued. We see that he was behind the door only after she enters. He observes, but does not speak. He does the same at the end of the episode, when one of the briefly abducted students is being interrogated by the FBI, as Scully, Mulder, and the higher-ups look through a two-way mirror. When he whispers something to the man ostensibly in charge, it becomes clear who *is* in charge. Similarly, Scully is nonplussed to see him enter the office immediately after she has been debriefed. For good reason. This shadowy man emerges, once the conspiracy mythology kicks in, as the éminence grise behind official authority that has compromised our government by selling it out to alien forces.

In this landscape of bodies that cannot defend their boundaries and government officials who may well be facilitating alien invasiveness, Scully and Mulder take root as unexpressed (or inexpressible?) desire for the integrity of human life in its spiritual and erotic aspects. In the pilot episode, the two spar about the nature of the universe, as they meet in a ritual of initiation that resembles nothing so much as two cranky librarians bickering over cataloguing procedures. They are each encyclopedic storehouses of data for their own ways of sorting out experience: her classification system files grant significance and weight to human events through the scientific method, while his mandate "thinking outside of the box" when science fails. The emotional edge is sharpened by the political situation. The scientifically minded Scully is understandably wary of working with a man whose nickname at the FBI Academy, Spooky Mulder, has raised him to celebrity as a strange fanatic, while Mulder is understandably hostile to a woman he knows has been brought in to spy on him. But the traits for which Scully has been assigned to Mulder as a spy—her cool, balanced objectivity—also, complexly, render her incapable of being used. Similarly, Mulder's unconventional ability to move beyond rational categories by fishing the waters of the subcon-

From the first gaze in The X-Files *pilot episode, the truth sought by Scully (Gillian Anderson) and Mulder (David Duchovny) was not "out there" but in them.*

scious leaves room for him to see through Scully's official assignment and standardized training to the woman who negotiates her deep passion to know, understand, and help through her conventional means. The pilot episode inaugurates the series rhythms in its evocation of the tension between a paranoid and inconclusive narrative and the Scully/Mulder relationship created by the chemistry of Duchovny and Anderson.[12] While the legal authorities in both Bellefleur, Oregon, and Washington, D.C., are up to their eyeballs in obstructive, illegal activities, Scully and Mulder are caught up in a process by which their synergy will unite them despite the most adverse of social conditions.

Once they are in the field, after their initial sparring in Mulder's basement office at the FBI, Scully and Mulder find themselves oscillating between philosophical debates when they are alone and exchanging knowing looks when they are among hostile authorities who try to block their work. The comically irritable, multisyllabic intensity of their debates contrasts tantalizingly with the profoundly emotional silent rapport of the gazes. The two exchange their first special Scully/Mulder gaze in a state psychiatric hospital in the pilot episode, when they both see the welts Mulder has associated with a group of unexplained murders on the back of one of the patients, a symptom overlooked by the institution's doctors. The empathy of the gaze causes a small explosion between Scully and Mulder that shakes both Scully's skepticism and Mulder's suspicions about her. Its unexpected and completely unique power adds a layer beneath their rather snippy delivery of dialogue in the car as they approach the "crime scene." After the initial gaze, there is a transformation of the verbal repartee to something collegial, verging on intimate. Although the debates continue, they cease to take the form of cranky, defensive speeches and begin to take the shape of a complex dialogue shared on two levels.[13]

There is a fascinating counterpointed tension between Scully and Mulder thinking through both their bodies (gaze, touch, energy) and Scully and Mulder thinking through the drone of their mental processes. On the physical level of the gaze, there is a touching and tender trust between them, implicitly but not explicitly erotic, that piquantly coexists with their almost totally antithetical conceptual positions. From the pilot episode onward, the counterpoint between dialogue and gaze quickly escalates into a powerful and unsettling mind/body link between them in which physical energy embraces and mental energy is locked into opposition. There are moments, however, in which mind and body suddenly achieve an unpredictable balance. This pattern of the sudden emergence of a momentary balance makes itself manifest immediately in the series, just past the midpoint in the first episode. When Scully disrobes to take a shower, she sees marks on her back that so closely resemble the marks on the murder victims that she is sufficiently panicked to go to Mulder's motel room and reveal herself to him in her bra and panties, asking him to examine them. The scene, potentially a cynically commercial display of skin, is nuanced delicately, full of the shy hesitation of strangers on the verge of deep involvement accidentally brought into an intimate moment by a completely clinical question. There is a convention in mass culture fiction in which the woman is accidentally seen by the dark stranger in a state of undress in ways that absolve each of responsibility for the striptease. In complete contrast, although there is an official reason for Scully to strip, both actors create this as a moment in which each takes responsibility for the unexpressed pleasure that accompanies official duty and for the hesitation that each feels. The composition of the shot as Mulder slowly lowers himself to examine Scully's lower back places him between the curve of her exposed arm and the curve of her all but naked back. Holding a candle in the darkness—the electricity has gone off—Mulder's examination takes on the mood of a religious devotion. Part of the conceptualization of Mulder's characterization is that he likes pornography, a trait revealed in later episodes, but this moment, preceding the more schematically devised characterization, deeply imprints Mulder's wonder-filled tenderness about Scully's body, and his concern that it not be violated, which forms the basis of his future agony about her abduction. This first scene of a complete Scully/Mulder rapport is a triumph of subtlety on the parts of the actors and the production team, who palpably show the respect that is elicited by the presence of a charmed collaboration.[14] The two relax when Mulder discovers the marks to be mosquito bites, not the dreaded "abduction welts." An elliptical time cut from this moment discovers Mulder confiding in Scully about the trauma in his life that started his quest, his inability to save his sister when she screamed out to him as she was being abducted, presumably by aliens.[15] The sequence of tension, relaxation, and pillow talk links Scully and Mulder erotically in an intercourse in its most literal and metaphorical conflation: wanting intellectual knowing and wanting carnal knowing simultaneously.

The unconsummated Scully/Mulder relationship, which became a long-lived feature of the series, is consistently juxtaposed with the inconclusive paranoid narrative structure of the episodes. No connection between these two incomplete processes is made explicit, but their persistent, fevered juxtaposition expresses a modern angst about intimacy caught up in institutional chicanery and a scientific form of "original sin" that rivals the darkest, most apocalyptic medieval vision of the inherent corruption of humanity. In the *X-Files* conspiracy mythology, that which is alien is represented as devouring and implacable in its desires, but the alien is the hidden aspect of being human. The aliens in this series are almost certainly the ancestors of either the entire human race or some part of it. First, they were clearly here before the advent of human beings on Earth. Second, the series constantly suggests the relationship between the human and the alien by a conflation of human and alien bodies.

Frighteningly represented as shape-shifters without definite limits, the aliens come in at least two races, the best-articulated one of which reproduces the human cycle of maturation. Its three-stage life cycle begins as a virus transmitted as black oil, mutates into a monstrous devouring beast, and finally reaches maturity as a gray, humanoid creature. The disconcerting fantasy, nevertheless, oddly mirrors, as if in a distorting reflection, the progress of human maturation: the inert chemical beginnings of life, the turbulence of adolescence, the flat competence of adulthood. The other reasonably well-defined race is more elliptically presented and makes more sporadic appearances. We don't know its life cycle; we only know that, looking like the mature gray alien but lacking any facial features, it does not want to colonize Earth and is actively opposing the invasion strategy. Both are humanoid figures that in a blinding light or camouflaging shadow often provoke suspense about whether the creature is human or alien.

The ability of the aliens to morph into replicas of known characters adds to this visual indeterminacy. A further ambiguity is added by the most prominent alien shape-shifter, a character known as the Bounty Hunter (Brian Thompson) who shows up at most of the abductions and accomplishes his task by taking on the appearance of a person trusted by the character to be taken away. Although he is clearly an alien, his transition between human and alien appearance is more intensely fraught with mystery, as it is not entirely clear which group of aliens he is working for.[16]

Narratively the threat of conflating the alien and the human is worked into the details of the conspiracy, which is essentially a scandalous secret permission given the aliens by powerful political authorities to experiment on humans—this is why Scully was abducted—to create an alien/human hybrid that will facilitate their takeover of Earth. Conflation of the alien and the human is also narratively underlined by the stand-alone episodes, which are permeated by a fear that we ourselves contain some kind of larger abilities that do not conform to the recognizably human, and that there is no clear boundary between these two aspects of ourselves and no defense against the slippery and uncontrollable powers that roil around within us.

When push comes to shove, however, all the human/alien confusions serve to force the issue of what it is to be human, which comes down to the difference between the ability to love and dream that defines the human on the show, and the reduction to nothing more than a basic survival organism, which defines the alien.[17] Scully and Mulder emerge as the representatives of the fully human—they dream and they love—not only in distinction with the "grays" (mature aliens), but also in opposition to the loveless pragmatism of their supposedly human opponents, the ruthless and/or ruthlessly literal authorities, who are suffused with the aura of the less than human in the way they reflect the alien qualities in their makeup. The investigation of the human/alien mysteries at the core of *The X-Files* is a fantasy landscape that facilitates the central issue of the show: Scully and Mulder's fight for intimacy as a couple. They are, in this way, the inheritors of Hollywood's great couple tradition, in which fantasy contrasts allow couples to define themselves for the audience and to entertain us as they evolve toward higher levels of humanity than the world around them.

The late-season episodes have been increasingly explicit about the distinction of the human capacity to love and its distillation in the Scully/Mulder synergy, for example in "Milagros" and "The Unnatural," the sixteenth (April 18, 1999) and eighteenth (April 25, 1999) shows of the sixth season, respectively. "Milagros" is a purely stand-alone episode. "The Unnatural" is a strange and unique blend of the stand-alone and conspiracy arc episode. As parts of the same narrative they represent the spectrum of bittersweet depiction of shared humanity on *The X-Files*. "Milagros" emphasizes the vulnerability of the Mulder/Scully synergy, whereas "The Unnatural" underlines its strength.

The stand-alone, "Milagros," asks whether love is enough and comes up negative. It concerns a writer named Phillip Padgett (John Hawkes), whose lonely, alienated attempts at fiction release into the world a mysterious character who uses psychic surgery to remove the hearts of unwilling strangers as stimuli to Padgett's creative process. As the area becomes littered with corpses whose hearts have been extracted, Mulder and Scully take up the case, and, as they investigate, Scully becomes the object of Padgett's passion, and almost his victim. Padgett never means harm to Scully, but his involvement in the murders depends on paranormal processes that run amok—that cold, impersonal force of the slippage into the alien.

As a writer and a voyager in the subconscious, Padgett has an alien-like, deadly inability to remain within normal physical and mental limits. His creative impulses as a storyteller have led him to evoke a psychic familiar, Ken Nasciemento (Nestor Serrano), a former "self-proclaimed" psychic surgeon, who, now dead, has been resurrected by Padgett to perform fatal psychic surgery while Padgett remains at home with his typewriter, his 3 x 5 file cards, and his cigarettes. An instance in which slippage between the human and the alien sucks the life out of living beings, this episode exemplifies how the stand-alone episodes are doppelgangers of the alien invasion plot in exploring through the couple the problems of human connection in a world in which secure limits have collapsed.

By the end of the episode, Padgett is almost unable to stop his familiar, Nasciemento, from extracting Scully's heart because of the vampiric relationship between the energies of the humanizing subconscious and the abstract (alien-like) conceptualization that knows no bounds. When Mulder finally confronts Padgett about the relationship between his novel and the murders, Padgett disclaims responsibility. He even believes what he says—at least at that moment. His experience with Scully will teach him otherwise. The show brings him and the audience toward an understanding of how empty, loveless words can cut the heart out of life, figuratively and literally, when a creator seeks to replace the unlabeled energies of organic existence with formulated concepts.

The indelibly human Mulder/Scully mind/body connection is juxtaposed with Padgett's obsession with Scully. Theirs is an organic passion rooted in the body; his is a conceptual passion that assaults the life energy that comes from the human body (like the aliens). The deadliness of Padgett's conceptual approach to life is evident in his first encounter with Scully, which occurs in an elevator as she goes to visit Mulder to talk about the death of one of Padgett's young victims. Representing Padgett's gaze, the camera crawls over Scully/Anderson's face while she is briefly isolated with him in the elevator. The shot-reverse shot pattern openly and unexpectedly makes the audience complicit in the invasiveness of this gaze, as Scully squirms under the extreme close-ups of Anderson's lips and eyes. The lips, particularly, are photographed as soft and vulnerable, the lipstick applied without liner so as to avoid the hard-edged definition so common in screen makeup. The eyes are also soft and undefined by liner or shadow, the eyelashes very lightly coated with mascara. Scully, the character, squirms visibly under the oppressively fragmenting and microscrutinizing gaze.

The episode continues to make the audience complicit with Padgett, daringly setting up an identification crisis for the viewer between the ingrained identification with the chemistry/intimacy of Mulder and Scully and Padgett's alienating perspective. And Padgett, having taken an apartment next door to Mulder, is in a position to assert his perspective repeatedly. While Mulder plies his usual trade of enlightening a closed-minded world about psychic surgery, Padgett continues to impose his personal narrative on Scully and the viewer, as we again are drawn into his conceptually based fantasy world by the technology of visual storytelling. Scully finds a pendant delivered to Mulder's apartment anonymously but meant for her. Padgett's voice-over describes his fantasy of her reaction to finding the charm with a running commentary on her gestures, her thoughts, her moods that blurs the boundaries between his thoughts and Scully's reality as the camera actually reveals Scully's replication of Padgett's text. Scully is lured into Padgett's apartment, where he has had a fantasy of sex with her, which we see, as we have never seen sexual contact between Scully and Mulder, a fantasy so insistently supported by illustrative images that the audience does not know whether or not it has taken place until Scully enters Padgett's apartment in the "real" time/space of the episode to return the pendant. The conceptual fantasy threat becomes acute when Scully is maneuvered into drinking a cup of coffee he has prepared (the palpable threat of drugs) and sitting on Padgett's bed with him because he has no other furniture in the apartment besides the desk and chair, but the threat is abated when Mulder, apprehensive about Scully's well-being, breaks into the apartment.

Mulder's synergy with Scully is the only defense against the deleterious effects of a false concept of reality that finds words manipulating body instead of body as the foundation for words. Their synergy ultimately inflicts a fatal trauma on Padgett's confusion of art and reality and leaves him with a tragic knowledge of his own evil. During one of Mulder's interrogations of Padgett, Padgett is stunned by a brief, subtle, but powerful physical sign of the bond between Scully and Mulder when Scully, hoping to extricate Mulder from a pointless battle with Padgett, lightly presses her fingers on Mulder's arm. This fragile-seeming gesture has the impact of a cannon on Padgett and on the viewer. The camera, which has been teasing the audience with identification with Padgett, sharply jolts us with this moment, when our real allegiances are recalled. The camera records it with a visual exclamation point, foregrounding Scully's hand momentarily resting on Mulder's arm, while in the background of the image Padgett is riveted by the sight. The power of the moment is reinforced by Scully's merest whisper of Mulder's name. Padgett's shadow self, projected into the dead Nasciemento, cannot abide the sign of the power of organic life distilled in that touch, and from then on, while Padgett is in conflict with his shadow, the audience is fully in league with the Scully/Mulder chemistry. However, it is the tragic Padgett, not Mulder, who saves Scully from having her heart gouged out. Her life depends on the burning of the manuscript, since only by the destruction of the concept that seeks to control life can it be prevented from turning her into a reflection of itself: void at the core. Mulder doesn't know what to do in this situation and almost dooms Scully by mistakenly trying to stop Padgett, who understands that it is necessary to commit the manuscript to fire. Only by chance does Mulder become distracted in time to let the necessary destruction take place. As his manuscript burns, Padgett dies, his heart literally in his hand, as the human in him wins out mysteriously, and for the first time his lovelessness knows itself for the empty destroyer that it is.

The burning manuscript returns an extinguished Scully to life after Mulder finds her blood-soaked and lifeless. Only with the destruction of the text and the writer do life and their synergy fully reassert themselves. Scully snaps back into life spasmodically. As she does so, she moves toward Mulder, who, bending wretchedly over what he thinks is her corpse, completes the synergistic process she has started by moving toward her into a fascinatingly articulated embrace. Mulder meets the spasm of Scully's gasping reentry into life by holding her arms securely, keeping her at a distance to look at her. The look is a moment completely apart from the invasive look to which Scully was subjected by Padgett. Mulder responds to rather than assaulting her body with his eyes, a gesture of such organic passion that when the two enfold each other, the emotion that wells up fills his face with a nonverbal new knowledge of the ache and sorrow of profoundly shared feeling that again contrasts with the web of conceptual utterances that Padgett spun around Scully in the elevator. There are no words for Mulder's agonized joy. For her part, Scully's revival is also a return to the indescribable pain and suffering of such organic connectedness. She kneads the flesh of his back and shoulders with hands that pull him to her with an eloquence that explicit declarations will never achieve. What is between them is beyond concept, but not safely beyond its hollowing powers, as *The*

X-Files recognizes its own (potential) tragic weakness as a cultural product to kill the very energy that feeds its desire.

"Milagros" contrasts two ways of organizing human life, one via concepts, which contain a devouring black hole at the center, and the other a life-affirming existence centered on the integrity of body-based energies. The implications of this episode for the series narrative are enormous, since Scully's methodology is arguably identical with or closely related to Padgett's, as is the conspiracy story. Since the episode represents Mulder's helplessness, it fortifies the series-long questioning of Mulder's role as a hero. On another level, the episode questions the unspoken core of the series, the relationship between Scully and Mulder. Their bond may be powerful enough to show false concepts up for what they are, but is it sufficient to prevail? Only barely, this time. Here is the pessimism that shadows the new Synergistic Couple, that sense of the invasiveness of undependable and even uncannily treasonous cultural structures like language. In this instance, there is a sudden act of generosity on the part of the writer because he is struck by the sudden recognition, as he contemplates what he has unleashed on Scully, that he is a destroyer, not a creator. The source of this insight is not clear, nor is it clear that such insights will always motivate the positive act of destruction—Padgett's incineration of his manuscript—in time to save the human condition. What is unequivocal here is that the organic mind-body connection between Mulder and Scully is life and that their adventures pit the forces of organic life against the death-suffused destabilizations inherent in modern indeterminacy about boundaries and culture. Equally clear is the essential role of the screen chemistry of Duchovny and Anderson in representing what is organic. The acting choices made during their final embrace radiate from their synergy; had they been deliberate acting choices, they could not have created the moment of unlabeled feeling without which there can be no contrast with the word-haunted world of Phillip Padgett.

"The Unnatural," in contrast, narrates a story of the joy of the Mulder/Scully connectedness and the comic implications of Mulder's inability to defeat the forces of evil that he so painfully perceives. The episode, written and directed by Duchovny, is a part of the series' alien mythology arc, which has relentlessly painted a picture of the degeneration of the human body by alien experimentation. However, in "The Unnatural," for the first time, the series suggests the existence of a regenerative organic process whereby the alien may become fully human. It is no coincidence that the episode also for the first time portrays Scully and Mulder in rapturous celebration of their bodies.

Scully and Mulder frame the episode, which concerns a flashback to 1947 and to a (fictional) young black baseball player named Josh Exley (Jesse L. Martin), certainly a pun on *The X-Files*. Exley is one of the greats in the Negro League who does not wish to follow Jackie Robinson in breaking the color barrier. The reason is that Exley is an alien who has shape-shifted into the form of an African American so he can pursue his passion for baseball and remain hidden from the rest of his alien kind by the anonymity of the league. He's a lover, not a fighter. He doesn't want to be part of the invasion team. He forms a friendship with a young white sheriff named Arthur Dales (Fredric Lane in the flashback) in Roswell, New Mexico, assigned to protect Exley from the Ku Klux Klan, led by a white supremacist who turns out to be an alien Bounty Hunter, a sort of alien MP sent to punish the AWOL Exley. The friendship is severely tested but survives Dales's inadvertent discovery of Exley's alien body, to which Exley shape-shifts at night. When the Klan finally catches up with Exley, the executioner demands that Exley "show his true face"—shift back to his alien body—before he is killed, and Exley refuses. But as he dies in the arms of Arthur Dales, who arrives too late to save him, it turns out that Exley is now fully human. The blood oozing from his wounds—which should be a form of green acid, and indeed is such in a previous scene in which Exley is accidentally hit by a ball and injured—is nothing but red, noncorrosive human blood. Exley's alien body has miraculously slid over the great divide into the purely human. Ostensibly, the transformation derives from love—the brotherly love between Exley and Dales, and Exley's love of baseball—but its pro-foundly optimistic tone is the deep sense of the capacity of the organic to heal itself, a capacity not at all present in "Milagros."

The prominence of starry sky vistas, which *The X-Files* has always associated with invasion, is in this bittersweet episode associated with a radiance that the literary minded can connect with a Dantesque ecstasy of salvation, and the less literary with a romantic image of rapture. Mulder's part during most of this episode is as the audience for the tale of Exley as told by Arthur Dales (M. Emmet Walsh in the present), now an old cynical ex-sheriff. The tale is instructional for Mulder, as the old boy seems to be educating him to understand that, as Dales says, Mulder should be concerned less about the "heart of the mystery" of the aliens and more about the "mystery of the heart."[18]

Exley's tale of universal love (in the form of his passion for baseball) as a transformative power is clearly juxtaposed with the transformation of Mulder and Scully. At the beginning of the show, Mulder is led to Dales by an article in a yellowed 1947 newspaper, where he is not only looking for X-Files material but also enjoying the conceptual brilliance of the box score, which "distills all the chaos and action of any game in the history of all baseball games into one tiny, perfect rectangular sequence of numbers..." Holed up in a dusty archive on a gorgeous baseball day, Mulder is, by the end of the show, out under the stars with Scully, the Platonic abstraction of perfection having been supplanted by the organic.[19]

In a state of euphoria after having heard Exley's story from Dales, Mulder lures Scully to a baseball field where he has provided a batting cage and a pitcher, and where director Duchovny has provided a sound track of evangelical spirituals evoking the salvation theme over the romance visual. Encircling her in his arms, Mulder coaxes Scully into a little four-handed batting practice on one bat. "Not a bad piece of ash," he says to her, emphasizing that he's talking about the bat. He then murmurs into her ear what might be the most sexual batting instructions ever proffered, his hands moving her hips along the arc of the ideal batting swing. "We're just going to make contact," he says, nuzzling her ear. "We're not going to think. We're just going to let it fly." In a completely physical moment, their bodies are rhythmically mated as together they pop one "scoring" hit after another, until the baseballs begin disappearing into the heavens among the stars and the spiritual becomes more audible on the sound track as "Come and Go with Me to That Land." Coming and going together, Scully and Mulder transform the image of baseball from one that evokes the individualist hero both of and apart from the team into the crucible of love, as surely as the Astaire/Rogers dance was. But what is crucial here is that a parable of the potential for the alien to become human is the foreplay for the potential for the connection between the two individual agents thwarted by a dysfunctional social organization. The chemistry of Duchovny and Anderson is celebrated here, as Scully and Mulder see past the confusions and betrayals for the first time, in a joyous prefiguration of the Power of 2 that the Synergistic Couples in the studio system took for granted.

Duchovny's contribution to the series through this and other episodes that he has written and/or directed is an example of what the new freedom of post-studio entertainment industry can mean to the couple tradition beyond actors' power as producers. With the liberation of actors from their position as bargaining chips, children of the paternal studio, or cattle—all viable descriptions of the actor in the studio system—both Duchovny and Anderson have been able to go further than pouring their enigmatically paired energy into the series. They have also been permitted by Chris Carter to let their profound connections with the characters shape the scripts of the episodes to the major advantage of the show. "The Unnatural" is an exquisite rendition of the elements of the series rendered through a sensibility that understands it on a profound level from inside the mythology. Similarly "all things" [sic], an episode written and directed by Gillian Anderson for the seventh season, balances the Duchovny/Mulder insight with the Anderson/Scully insight. "all things" is a sensuous, passionate voyage into Scully's sensibility that, in the tradition of the series' elliptical indeterminacy, may mark the inception of a sexual relationship between Scully and Mulder. Seized by an epiphany, Scully is led to Mulder in a train of events glowing with karma and destiny. The episode places her in his apartment for the entire night in two scene fragments that show the couple's warmth and rapport but leave open the question of what events transpired between late night and morning, when Scully quietly leaves a sleeping, naked Mulder. Nothing is made of this event in the immediately subsequent shows, but in the last minutes of the seventh season, Scully reveals that she is pregnant, after Mulder has been abducted by aliens, in a cliff-hanging season finale. She connects her pregnancy with an emotional need to find Mulder, all pretense of professional camaraderie shucked, suggesting strongly that the baby is Mulder's and leaving the audience to make its own guesses about previous episodes, a process complicated by our never having seen any onscreen sexual activity between them.

The arrival of Scully and Mulder at this new bend in the road casts their powerful synergy as paradoxically fragile in a slippery universe, the new bittersweetness of modern love embodied by a new kind of collaborative synergy, the lifeblood of the popular culture industry, made even more potent by the sharing of responsibility among actors and creative team.[20] Yet by the end of the eighth season, the last episode of *The X-Files* as a chronicle of Scully and Mulder, before its resurrection with a new central couple, John Doggett (Robert Patrick) and Monica Reyes (Annabeth Gish), what has seemed fragile is redefined as miraculously enduring. With the closure of the eighth season, the series confesses that its core has been the couple connection between Scully and Mulder, and what a connection it is. The last scene contains no action, monsters, or world leaders. It is focused on the birth of Scully and Mulder's baby boy, who has been threatened by alien beings that want to kill him for no discernible reason, and after the birth abandon their murderous quest equally mysteriously. As the aliens dissipate, seemingly of their own lack of endurance, the Scully/Mulder pairing bumps the alien/monster elements from the center of *The X-Files* and permits the core meaning of the show to emerge in the final moments of their adventures with as much clarity as anything ever can have within this fictional universe. As the two tremble on the brink of their last scene on the show together, Scully and Mulder pursue a conversation about fear, truth, and the baby in her arms. It culminates in their first onscreen purely sexual and romantic kiss. This, says Mulder, is "the truth we both know." *The X-Files* points a way past the existential panics of the post-studio Synergistic Couple. After nearly a decade of tracking down events that push the limits of ordinary logic, fearing that that search would force them to face the extinction of the human race at the hands of aliens, Scully and Mulder reach a distinctly different closure, their regeneration of the human race with a new life.

KEATON AND ALLEN

Synergy of this power but not this optimism is also present in five of the six major filmic collaborations between Woody Allen and Diane Keaton, five in the 1970s and the last in 1993. This does not count *Radio Days* (1987), written and directed by Allen but featuring Keaton only in a cameo appearance. This does count the first film in which they worked together, *Play It Again, Sam* (1972, Dir. Herbert Ross), which will not be discussed in detail because it is immaterial to this study; it is a conventional film project that adapted a Woody Allen stage play for the screen, using Allen and Keaton as a Functional Couple. The films created by the rich synergy between Allen and Keaton are not high-concept projects, as was *Play It Again, Sam*, with its one-joke structure based on the idea of what would happen if a man had the great Humphrey Bogart to coach him in his "treat 'em rough" strategies with women. The other five films are fundamentally different kinds of projects that employ Allen and Keaton as a Synergistic Couple, and as co-creators who work together on developing their films. In these, Allen paints moving canvases in which the alien qualities of the Jew, the outlaw, and the misfit place the couple in all kinds of farcical social dislocations. As is typical of the post-studio Synergistic Couple, the Allen/Keaton duo evades the repression of society through various forms of intimacy, but in this case the satisfactions are generally no more than fleeting, leaving behind little but memory. Paranoia, another staple in the post-studio Synergistic Couple project, is the terrain on which the alien characters in the five Allen/Keaton collaborations play out the comedy/drama of intimacy and connection.

Sleeper (1973) and *Love and Death* (1975) both contain overtly dramatized repressive governments, a futuristic tyranny and a historical tyranny, respectively, which form the context of the paranoia of the Allen/Keaton couple. In both cases, the couple is associated with an alienness that is interchangeable with being an outlaw. In both cases, absurd images, often distorted slapstick images of the bodies of Allen and Keaton, belie the potency of the tyrannies, but these images also suggest an instability that undermines the permanence of the couple in a way that conflicts mysteriously with the felt power of the bond between the two actors, forged by their screen chemistry. In *Annie Hall* (1977), *Manhattan* (1979), and *Manhattan Murder Mystery* (1993), more complex and less purely slapstick films, being alien is a condition of life, not a political situation. These movies even more bittersweetly evoke the lack of hospitality for human relationships in the cultures we have built and in the universe beyond them, and create interesting polarities between existential flux and the odd permanence of the chemistry, in itself strange, as the relationship may not endure. *Manhattan Murder Mystery*, the happiest of the films made by Allen and Keaton, displaces the usual Allen melancholy away from the Allen/Keaton couple and closes with a testimony to a process of rejuvenation that inverts the attenuation of chemistry by urban anonymity.

In most of the Allen/Keaton films, people are aliens on this planet. Oblique references to strains of the alien in daily life in *The X-Files* are present here, in a more ironic and comic form, but there is a remarkably similar layering of couple synergy, institutional images, cosmic images, and language. The images of our alienation are, as in *The X-Files*, constructed of juxtapositions between raw couple chemistry and a contemporary world that lacks physical and spiritual limits and coherence, and in which love is not enough, though it does sometimes bungle its way into permanence. Within this context, conceptualization, language, and logic are buffeted on the oceanic energies represented in human form by the Allen/Keaton couple. Whether perceptive, self-deceived, foolish, or strangely incongruous, the prevalent voice-overs and dialogues in the Allen/Keaton films become enigmatically irrelevant before the forces unleashed by images of intimacy. At first in these films, language presents itself, simply in terms of volume, as a major force in the lives of the characters, but it diminishes to a whimper by the end of the film, where the real priorities—the energies embodied in the Allen/Keaton couple—are finally confirmed.

Sleeper and *Love and Death* both juxtapose, through farce fantasy, the personal intimacy of the couple with the insanity and repressiveness of social systems. *Sleeper* is a futuristic pastiche in which Miles Monroe (Allen) is frozen cryobiogenetically in 1973 and resuscitated in 2173, a post-nuclear holocaust world organized by Our Leader, a Big Brother figure who closely resembles Franklin D. Roosevelt. Monroe (like Mulder) is always fighting for his humanity against a culture that keeps threatening to turn him into inert matter. When he comes out of the freezer, he is wrapped in silver foil like a package of hamburger, and almost immediately he is forced to disguise himself as a household robot in order to evade a police dragnet; the resuscitated are considered aliens in 2173. As with Mulder, Miles's only human contact is with a potential partner in intimacy, Luna (Diane Keaton), a pretty, pampered citizen of the brave new world into which Miles awakens. She winds up joining him in his resistance to the sterile, techno-paradise she once called home, closing the film in Miles's embrace after having successfully worked with him to assassinate Our Leader. But having rejected political solutions and science, the two are in limbo, which renders their final embrace only a hiatus in a cycle of boom-and-bust governmental oppression, relying tenuously for their happiness on sex and death, two experiences that Miles reassures Luna come only once in our lives (the difference being that you aren't nauseous after death).

Love and Death is *Sleeper* set in nineteenth-century Russia. In a parody of Tolstoy's *War and Peace*, Allen sets Boris Grushenko (Allen) the task of maintaining his humanity in a world wracked by the Napoleonic wars, started because of the egocentricity of a small man who spends a lot of time designing the pastry that will be named for him. The Russians are told they are fighting so they won't be forced

Luna (Diane Keaton) and Miles (Woody Allen) caught trying to masquerade as famous doctors. The image of the couple fleeing from the pursuing power elite epitomizes the position of the Keaton/Allen pair as aliens in a repressive society.

to eat soufflé. Again, the Allen figure finds his only human bonding with a potential partner in intimacy, Sonia (Keaton). But intimacy is more complex here. Sonia doesn't recognize Boris as the love of her life until she has worked her way through half the men in Moscow, and after they have married, in the midst of their domestic bliss, Boris becomes suicidal for no discoverable reason and then just as abruptly recovers his will to live. Ultimately, however, social insanity drives them both crazy. When war interrupts their plans to start a family, Sonia bullies Boris into assassinating Napoleon to make the world safe again for lovers. Boris is caught and executed. As in *Sleeper*, love is the only salvation on the horizon, and it doesn't really work. After he is dead, Boris visits Sonia, but there is still no complete union. Talking at cross purposes, she rhapsodizes that he was her "one great love," while he fulminates about the injustice of his early death.

Both films gain their manic comedy from the same kinds of slippages that make *The X-Files* uncanny and eerie. But in the Allen/Keaton movies we laugh instead of hyperventilate when slippages define the unreliability and incoherence of the world that intimacy promises to redress but to which it falls victim. *Sleeper* oscillates between the tyranny of the government and the tyranny of the underground resistance. Each group seeks to transform Miles through procedures that send him careening across gender lines. When Miles is caught by the government they reprogram him to fit into society by brainwashing. They connect him to a machine by electrodes and take him through a Miss America pageant in which he is Miss Montana, the winner of the contest. As Our Leader's reprogammers invade Miles's body, he slips into a falsetto voice and hyperfeminine gestures as a Miss America contestant. When he is captured by the underground, the radical leader deprograms him using hypnotic suggestion through a drug-induced trance. The underground radicals intend to return him to his Jewish roots by taking him through what they think might have been a Passover dinner with his immigrant parents. But in the middle of amusingly deformed yiddishisms performed by Anglo-Saxon Protestant types, Miles—even further removed from his ethnic roots by a severely damaged cultural memory—slips into the identity of Blanche Dubois from Tennessee Williams's *Streetcar Named Desire*. More falsetto voice and hyperfeminine mannerisms. The slippage snowballs as Luna is forced to take on the role of Stanley Kowalski, assuming the masculine body language of Marlon Brando, to bring Miles out of it. Quite clearly the aliens themselves, Allen and Keaton blatantly experience the indeterminacy that has been forced on them by social institutions. On the run from both the government and the underground at the end of the movie, Miles and Luna are grounded in an unassailable rapport with each other, but the film gives us no way to imagine them staying outside of the organized domains of conformity and rebellion. While *Love and Death* is less pronounced in its gender shifts, Boris is clearly framed in a feminine position frequently in the context of the virile, war-crazed world. But *Love and Death* concentrates primarily on other slippages, for example those between interior and exterior reality. What is inside is worn on the outside in hilarious monologues in which Sonia and Boris, and other characters as well, speak their thoughts directly to the camera, unheard by those standing inches from them. The boundaries between life and death also become tenuous as corpses farcically rise to finish up the business details of their earthly lives. The line between the human and the divine is crossed when Death speaks to Boris, in a funny parody of the meeting between the Knight and Death in Ingmar Bergman's *The Seventh Seal*

(1957), and when Boris, in jail, has a visitation from an angel. All these slippages make life very uncertain, particularly the angelic prophecy that Boris will not be executed. After he is shot by the firing squad, Boris still cannot figure out why the angel lied to him. We laugh at his plight, but the fact remains that we are laughing to avoid crying at the thought of a perverse cosmos in which all that we may depend on is death. Love has ceased to become important to Boris, and Sonia's memory of him as the love of her life is superseded by his dance with the figure of Death as he leaves her.

The chemistry of Allen and Keaton makes the comedy important. The depth and richness it gives to the relationship between their characters adds layers of meaning to what otherwise would be nothing more than a flat set of parodic jokes (as in earlier Allen movies). That these characters have a connection cannot be established in opposition to the superficial alliances in society any other way. In addition, the Allen/Keaton chemistry works so well as a comic version of the socially alien position that tends toward pathos in *The X-Files* because the body energy is anchored in bodies so clearly alien to the Hollywood imperative to grant sexuality (and intimacy) only to exaggeratedly Nordic styles of beauty. The men whom society (either the mainstream society or the rebel society) in *Sleeper* deem appropriate for Luna are all tall, blond, blue-eyed, Nordic mesomorphs, while Allen is not only skinny, balding, and Semitic in appearance, but so much shorter than Keaton that he has to reach up to kiss her, the obligatory feminine position for the Hollywood kiss. The chemistry between Allen and Keaton that validates this strikingly counter-media eroticism demonstrates the degree to which chemistry can overwhelm the formulas for physical attractiveness in the entertainment industry.[21]

Allen's delight in silent film comedy also adds to the texture of the Allen/Keaton collaborations. The nonverbal quality of their couple chemistry is reinforced by the presence in both *Sleeper* and *Love and Death* of action in the style of the visual comedy of Buster Keaton and Charlie Chaplin. In *Sleeper*, the reawakening of Miles is visually recorded in the style of the large comic gestures of the old films, accompanied by the syncopated music we associate with them. Similarly, the state police squads, whose raids punctuate the film at regular intervals, are modern Keystone Cops. In *Love and Death*, of the many references to silent comedies, one that stands out is a sequence in which Boris and Sonia hijack the clothes of emissaries to Napoleon. As Boris is caught in the act of trying to knock one of them unconscious with a bottle, he and Sonia pretend that they are playing a game with each other, Boris hitting Sonia on the head numerous times until the intended target of the bottle is distracted enough for Boris to hit him. By this time, of course, Sonia is out cold. There is no sound at all during this sequence, except for the sound of the impact of the bottle on Sonia's head, followed by the thud when it hits the emissary. This sort of play with the texture of the film complements the powerful element of image in the Synergistic Couple. The bottle scene and others similarly reminiscent of silent comedy complicate the tone of the film. The strength of the image in this scene supports the powerful chemistry of Allen and Keaton; at the same time the content of the image makes us see the unstable world through laughter as well as tears; this doubleness makes Boris's death and his separation from Sonia melancholy and funny at the same time.

But above all, the Allen/Keaton synergy is released because of Allen's refusal to let concept dictate the film. Allen has been quoted as saying that he is too tied to words, unable to make visually based films with ease, but his films say otherwise, suggesting that when he is at his best, as with Keaton, he lets nonverbal inspiration lead him.[22] Another indication that this is true is his rapid work mode. Working with as few takes as possible, casting his actors with barely a minute or two of interview or audition, forecloses the possibility that cliches or even the limits imposed by verbal frameworks will take over the image.[23] Such a mode of working is crucial to the release of synergy. Allen's early years as a stand-up comedian dominated his first films, in which images were cartoonlike illustrations for extremely funny jokes, for example the image at the end of *Bananas* of the notoriously verbose and insensitive sportscaster Howard Cosell trying to interview an assassinated dictator as he lies dying. However, that kind of image gave way, arguably because of the impact of the films of Ingmar Bergman and Federico Fellini on Allen, to increased liberation of the image from the job of mere illustration. The extraordinary image of Allen's thin, nervously tense body literally dancing with Death down an avenue of symmetrically placed trees is certainly part of a conceptual comic idea, but the image goes well beyond the limits of the idea, radiant in its delicate depiction of the human spirit rising above even the finality of death, ebullient even in a universe in which the emissaries of God have betrayed it. Such images are the necessary companions of the Synergistic Couple. Allen's willed freedom from concept is also displayed in his later film, *Annie Hall,* as he abandoned the earlier concept of making a murder mystery with Keaton and let the creative process take him toward a much less plot-structured examination of human relationships.[24]

Annie Hall (1977) and *Manhattan* (1979) use the Allen/Keaton chemistry to propose even bleaker representations of comic-horrific slippages in a world in which emotions are turned into aliens beset by the juggernaut logic of society. *Annie Hall* is about the brief but vivid romance between Alvy Singer (Allen), a New York Jew, and Annie Hall (Keaton), a WASP Midwesterner from Chippewa Falls, Wisconsin. They eventually go their separate ways, leaving each other subtly changed after they work through the interlocking neuroses of her feelings of intellectual inferiority and his pleasure at dominating a woman to whom he can feel superior. *Manhattan* is about the complicated love lives of five New Yorkers: Yale and Emily (Michael Murphy and Anne Byrne), Isaac and Tracy (Woody Allen and Mariel Hemingway), and Mary (Diane Keaton). Mary, a single, neurotic, intellectual social climber, turns the lives of the other two couples upside down in a series of betrayals that result from the human inability to cope with the promptings of passionate urges. After she leaves an affair she is having with Yale, because she doesn't want to be a marriage wrecker, Mary breaks up Isaac and Tracy when she turns to Isaac. When Mary and Yale decide that they can't live without each other, Emily is left on her own, and Isaac finds that he cannot return to Tracy. In this movie, no one is able to mesh ethical principles with desire. As a result, no neuroses get worked through, as a sense of impermanence in human relationships comes to seem the rule. Both *Annie Hall* and *Manhattan* are more realistic in visual design than either *Sleeper* or *Love and Death*; they are shot on real locations on the real island of Manhattan, making short excursions to real locations in Westchester and Long Island. This realism makes the undependability of the language and the institutions in which we trust, as well as the shifts that seem to ignore all established limits, more (comically) harrowing than in the earlier, more fantastic Allen/Keaton films.

Annie Hall is full of complex and elegantly executed shifts of all kinds. The film itself shifts its relationship to the audience continually, beginning with Woody Allen, who speaks directly to the camera, and moving back and forth between direct address and traditional voyeuristic presentation of scenes for the audience to look at. The film's willful violation of movie "reality" is striking in the famous scene in which Alvy drags Marshall McLuhan out from behind an advertising poster in the lobby of a movie theater as an expert witness to Alvy's argument with another movie patron about McLuhan's ideas. The film later transforms Annie and Alvy into cartoon characters as they rehash their continual differences. It executes some more filmic acrobatics when it collapses time barriers, allowing Annie and Alvy to visit Alvy's childhood home and "see" the past taking place as they stand there. Similarly, Alvy is able to walk into his elementary school and talk directly to his old teachers as they were when he was a child, and to his schoolmates as they were then. The children, in turn, say directly to the camera where they are now as adults. Spatial barriers are broken in a split screen that juxtaposes Alvy and Annie at their separate therapy sessions.

The comic freedom taken with time, space, and the barrier between fiction and reality makes us laugh as it empties the world of its parameters and of its immanent core of values, whereas *The X-Files* seeks to make us shudder at the same situation—two processes that are physiologically similar to each other and to sexual activity. These freedoms reveal how the attempt at creating a story of intimacy, a humanizing gesture through which we pretend there is a shape to our lives, is a pretense without which we could not survive. But in the end, the way Allen uses images reveals that our gestures are like rocks thrown into water. *Annie Hall* begins and ends with Allen doing a stand-up monologue about how contradictory life is; it is funny, but it introduces a film in which the viewer makes a journey from fullness to emptiness. The film frame in the opening monologue is full of Allen/Alvy and the closing monologue is a voice over an empty film frame that has just been emptied of Annie and Alvy, who are now separated. Indeed, right after the opening monologue, we see an empty frame that will soon be populated by Alvy and a friend. The words are a brave attempt to give the characters control over the impermanence of life. But filmic representation, with the Synergistic Couple as its vehicle, reveals what the words cannot conceal. Like life, the film frame is empty by nature; Annie and Alvy only populate it briefly and then are gone.

Manhattan even more complexly and more sorrowfully uses the Allen/Keaton chemistry as a vehicle for portraying the complex contradictions of the fullness and emptiness of life. The film opens with a New York montage framed by a voice over narrative by the protagonist, writer Isaac Davis (Allen), who is revising one draft after another in an unsuccessful attempt to derive a satisfactory narrative for the protagonist of his novel about living in Manhattan. There is a notable contrast between the cliched words and the evocative, energetic, beautiful images of the montage, so full of the New York setting and so empty of the protagonists, whom we do not see for a good five minutes while the montage rolls by. When Isaac and Tracy, and Emily and Yale enter the frame, they are at Elaine's, one of Allen's favorite New York watering holes at the time, in mid-discussion about the value of art. At the same time, Allen's camera is moving around the table creating discontinuities by doing away with eyeline match editing, which creates the illusion of orientation in time and space.[25] It is hard to tell where these characters are in physical relation to each other, which turns out to be the underlying emotional and psychological truth of the film as well. By the end of the film their words about wanting to find meaning through art will be hollowed out by their impulsive betrayals of the people they say and believe they love. Yale will betray his wife and his best friend for an affair with Mary that, given the inability of each to commit to anything but their personal desires, will not last. Isaac will selfishly ask Tracy to give up a major educational opportunity in London to satisfy his own needs, although he has not seen or spoken to her for months since abruptly discarding her for Mary. Emily will martyr herself to the betrayal without a fight. The absent Mary will discard Isaac and be a party to the breakup of Yale's marriage because she worships her impulses and will not think through the consequences of her actions.

The most emblematic use of the Allen/Keaton chemistry in *Manhattan* is in the planetarium at the moment when Isaac and Mary are beginning to feel an attraction to each other. At first we see them walking into the planetarium exhibit, where the man-made models of the planets are clearly artifacts manufactured for the purpose, but then the tone shifts. The camera loses itself in the illusions of the displays of the Milky Way, the moon, Saturn, and the stars, as the relationship between Mary and Isaac starts to propel them into "outer space," a metaphor for the rapture of attraction. As they talk about Mary's troubled relationship with a married man, Yale, and debate whether reason or intuition is the primary source of knowledge, they are exquisitely envisioned as walking on the moon, and adumbrated in profile as they look at each other against the stars by a thin, glowing halo of light.[26] They are the center of emotional gravity in the film, by virtue of their chemistry, while complex references to the limitlessness of the universe and the artificiality of the models by which it is envisioned confer a troubling set of contradictions on their blossoming relationship. It is too fraught with contrary elements to mark it as the saving connection in a chaotic world. At the same time, the chemistry is too powerful to designate it as just one more transitory fling.

If the Allen and Keaton characters are the paradigm of the human propensity to impose stories on the fragmented flux of life, they are not alone; all the adult characters in the Allen/Keaton series behave this way to some extent. Nevertheless, because of the Allen/Keaton chemistry, the films are not just so many tumbles into the void. From the moment Keaton joins Allen on the screen, the energy between them ricochets from all directions. Towering over Allen physically in a way that immediately slashes all cliched romantic images, Keaton yells, cries, coos, argues, and placates with no thought to formulaic, romantic, "feminine" poses. Allen characters, for all their ridiculous demands that life comply with their preordained script, are completely free of any stipulations about conventional femininity. He and Keaton indulge in pure energy exchange, which remains an interface between the masculine and feminine though, unlike the more conventionally male and female characters who surround them, rather extensively stripped of the ordinary identifying marks of heterosexual man- and womanhood. The Keaton women look down on the Allen characters, wearing men's clothes or mouthing intimidating pronouncements about life, the universe, and everything. The physical shapes of Allen and Keaton are more alike than different, both flat-chested, both with minimal muscular development in arms and legs. Yet there is never any trauma to their heterosexuality because of the absence of traditional physical distinctions between male and female. There is rather a high degree of freedom in the comic Allen/Keaton rapport that overcomes the widespread anxiety usually elicited by a blurring of the line between male and female, as designated by the culture. Through the Allen/Keaton chemistry, the artificial gender-related external requirements for feminine and masculine appearance and behavior fall away, leaving the dialogue of male and female energy solidly in place.

In the last film made by Allen and Keaton, *Manhattan Murder Mystery* (1993), there are no signs of the entropy that was evident in the later collaborations of the quartet of studio-era Synergistic Couples discussed in Chapters One through Five. The chemistry between Allen and Keaton remains strong and lively. If the disturbing aspect of their synergy is downplayed in a project that offers a more optimistic prospect for the couple bonding represented by their kind of onscreen connection than any of the previous films, there remains their jointly manic energy, an energy so easy to distinguish from that in his non-Keaton films. In general, without Keaton, Allen has resorted to using multiple couples in order to achieve complexity in the depiction of relationships, doing so most effectively in *Hannah and Her Sisters* (1986) and *Crimes and Misdemeanors* (1989), and to a lesser extent in films like *Midsummer Night's Sex Comedy* (1982) and *Husbands and Wives* (1992). In his touching film *The Purple Rose of Cairo* (1985), the central couple, one a human being and one a Hollywood image, played by Mia Farrow and Jeff Daniels, the pathos and comedy derive from a concept rather than from the rapport between the actors. Only in the synergistic Allen/Keaton collaborations is he able to achieve through a story focused on one couple a rich and layered view of the indeterminacy of life and the contradictions of the human heart. The concentrated form made possible by his shared energy with Keaton is more powerful than any of his other films in using the medium for their serio-comic ventures in the mystery of the human condition.

LUKE AND LAURA

Scully and Mulder of *The X-Files* and the Allen/Keaton partnership are acting collaborations that baffle the simplistic labels usually deployed in commercial entertainment, that stun the camera into producing raw documentary image, and that empower complex explorations of modern themes of paranoia, alienation, and being alien. These hallmarks of the post–studio era Synergistic Couple are also to be found, surprising as it may seem to some, in daytime serial television. Around 1980, Tony Geary and Genie Frances, as Luke and Laura on the daytime serial *General Hospital*, broke the mold of Functional Couples on soap opera, ushering in a new phenomenon on soap opera called by the media press the Supercouple, which is, in the terms of this study, the Synergistic Couple.[27] Their richly improvisational acting energy, their capacity to generate compelling images of intimacy, and their story of the paranoia within the normal community all have revealed the capacity for soap opera, because of its structural ability to incorporate spontaneous ideas as its endless plot is developed, to deal just as complexly with intimacy as entertainment generated by the more respected auteurist creations and nighttime serials with intellectual and conceptual credentials.

The Luke and Laura phenomenon began on *General Hospital* with the meeting of Laura, a golden girl from the best part of the society of the town of Port Charles, and Luke, a street kid living on the edge, excluded from "normal" society and surviving as a petty hoodlum. Their story makes of the ideal small town a candy-coated nightmare, revealing the power behind the pretty, polite surfaces of Frank Smith, one of its leading citizens, who hides his command of organized crime behind his credentials as a social lion. The story also draws on the tortuous history of the golden girl. Having been sexually molested by David Hamilton (Jerry Ayres), one of the good citizens of the town, Laura killed him in self-defense, provoking a crisis in soap opera that changed its perspective on ingenue heroines forever. Situated on the boundary between respectability and the social underbelly, Smith's and Hamilton's effect on Luke and Laura made for a paranoid vision of the soap opera small town, where good and bad now became indeterminate.

At the same time, Tony Geary and Genie Francis defied the physical typing of media heroes. Geary was atypical in appearance. Much like the Woody Allen persona, Geary was clownish, manic, hair either limp and lanky or curled tightly through the technology of the permanent wave associated almost exclusively with women, his skinny body prone to the asymmetrical comic position rather than the symmetrical, classical, balanced stance of the hero, prone to the farcical mischief of Harpo Marx. Francis was a classical, young, blonde media beauty in the style of Betty Grable, with a similar blonde glowy exuberance, but her looks were openly nuanced by the conventionally ignored darker side of this familiar Hollywood type. Whereas the Hollywood musicals of the 1940s of which Grable was queen suppressed the aspect of Grable's image that suggested an underlying sense of banked fires that could erupt, threatening her straight-white-toothed-smile ideal of all-American wholesomeness, *General Hospital* let that double aspect of Francis emerge.[28] Thus Francis's image candidly disturbs and allures at the same time. The powerful chemistry of her fraught image was the reason for the success of Laura's first story arc on the show, one in which she was sexually molested by her mother's would-be lover, out of frustrated vindictiveness at being refused by the mother. Francis's embodiment both of the American object of desire and of the otherwise invisible torment of being desired but having no freedom to negotiate her own desires achieved a sensation among soap opera watchers not just because it was the first story of its kind, but because Francis's chemistry brought home the truly disturbing aspects of her first story. Geary's addition to the action turned star chemistry into Synergistic Couple chemistry, which saved their story from functioning as a quasi-pornographic form of titillation in which an underaged actress was used for the pleasure of the audience by being actually sexually handled by an older actor.

Important to the Geary/Francis chemistry is its emergence spontaneously on the show, its sudden appearance dynamiting away all planned traditional story arcs in the serial in which Luke was originally just a blip on the screen intended to cause trouble between Laura and her establishment boyfriend, Scotty Baldwin (Kin Shriner). The Luke and Laura scenes generated such interest that Scotty became the blip. The chemistry between Geary and Francis took the *GH* creative team so by surprise that, like the RKO creative community's understanding that the purported second couple of Astaire and Rogers was actually a primary couple in the making, they took their cue from the onscreen image to move the story away from Scotty and Laura, at the time a very popular soap couple, toward a story for Luke and Laura.[29] As a result, even in purely narrative terms, Luke's alienness became more important and desirable than Scotty's normality. Synergistic chemistry born of image rather than concept led, as it will, to a more complex and troubling vision of intimacy. Laura did marry Scotty, but the marriage dissolved in her experience of increasing confusion about her conventional situation, which, when it did not leave room for her struggle for self-determination, made of the princess an alien who set out straight for Luke. As a man alienated from socially based masculine entitlement, he understood and supported Laura's desire.

The confluence of the image-led mass culture story with the image of the alien is the key issue here, a part of the new direction of screen couple synergy that reveals the problems of female glamour and male violence in erotic relationships, problems previously suppressed by the veneer of "normality" in the conventional soap couple. Geary's alienness brought out the eccentricity of the norm in more than one way. Francis's golden beauty, one of the major coded images of the entitled class, became visibly goofy in her conversations with Luke, in her emerging sense of her own alien needs to separate herself from the demands of the establishment. But the chemistry of the actors did not inspire the creative team, to their credit, to a sweetly romanticized story of the rebel boy and the respectable girl. Rather, the team followed the profound elements in the story to suggest Laura's inherent problems in turning to the wild outlaw world for support of her dissatisfaction with normal social rules for girls. When a turn in his relationship to the mob boss Frank Smith made Luke understand that his next assignment was to be a suicide mission, it became clear that Luke's disregard of social norms was part of a pattern of violence that didn't stop at the water's edge. Trapped by Smith, Luke exploded at what was nearest, dearest, and most vulnerable. Impotent in his anger at his destiny, Luke turned against Laura in the form of rape, when he couldn't turn against the powerful Smith. His mortal thoughts exploded all his class hatred, and in a torturous, deglamourized rape scene he took his frustrations out on Laura sexually. This turn in the plot created, on the basis of the Francis/Geary synergy, one of the hardest looks at human intimacy in commercial entertainment.[30]

The onscreen rape of Laura by Luke, the catalyst for feminist cries of rage against the glamourizing of rape by a "love your rapist" story, is anything but.[31] It is rather a highly complex set of texts and images that was misused by overeager critics in search of a way of talking about the then almost impossible situation of the raped woman. Anything but tempting, the scene itself is a model of feminist representation of rape, conveying the ugliness of such violation, even if committed by a man who actually loves the woman; love is no justification for such violence, nor is male suffering. Standing as a model of the possible representation of the complexity of human life, Luke's rape of his beloved Laura recognized that the convolutions and involutions of human erotic relations are such that acquaintance rape is frequently a fraught situation in which genuine feeling is frighteningly mixed with misunderstood fantasies of male entitlement. The story of Luke and Laura, in all its comedy, fantasy, melodrama, and pathos, is not a "love your rapist" lie, but a story of the human capacity to move away from the damage that has been done to it by false expectations, to grow, to change, to achieve self-knowledge and to forgive self and the other.

As a matter of chemistry, however, the rape scene accelerated a complex and troubling shared energy that released the actors into a fully flowered synergy. Begun in 1980, it still surges twenty years and a new century later in reconsiderations of this trauma to both of their lives.[32] Both original event and reconsiderations work because of the Francis/Geary chemistry, which expresses itself in the interface between them on the profound level of a mutual wounding that forms a deep, invisible expression as a Synergistic Couple. Using the mystery, the isolation in a fantasy/exotic setting, and physical representations that were commonplace in the narrative trappings of the Old Hollywood Synergistic Couple, but had never before been used on soap opera—including dance and action stories—Luke and Laura explored the indeterminacy, anxieties, and euphoria of intimacy. Fleeing Frank Smith, after Luke's involvement with Laura stopped him from completing his suicide mission, the couple found who they were by moving around on the confusing boundaries between the legitimate and the criminal in a story arc that emphasized confusions about friend and foe, and even male and female. After Smith disappeared from their lives, another paranoid plot sprang up to contextualize anew their unclassifiable complexity as a couple and to permit them to grow even richer in their exploration of feelings and connections. With even more intense paranoia, the second big Luke and Laura story arc was a fantasy plot, the Ice Princess caper, which, in its use of the paranormal, both broke new ground on soap opera and prefigured the more overt paranoia of *The X-Files* as the milieu of the current Synergistic Couple. As its conflated villain/authority, the Ice Princess caper featured a fabulously rich and ruthless family, the dangerous Cassadines, seeking world domination through a formula by means of which they could create subfreezing temperatures at will in any place in the world. As with the plots of *The X-Files*, the Ice Princess arc failed as a coherent story, but functioned well as a metaphor for the murky slippages that fuse living-on-the-edgeness (alienness) with the normal, a boundary-line experience within which human beings in pairs can come to know each other and themselves as they cannot when they are pigeonholed within an illusionary social framework.

Luke and Laura's disturbing/ecstatic image speaks to us profoundly about human interrelationship. This disturbing/ecstatic image, which I have been calling documentary or raw, led the *GH* creative community away from previously formed story plans and continues to define the partnership of Francis and Geary to this day. The collaboration between Francis and Geary relies on their ability to open each other to an uncontrollable state of emotion during a rehearsal process which then becomes the energy source for their technical accomplishment of a scene.

Luke (Tony Geary) and Laura (Genie Francis), the boy-man and the woman-girl. The complexity of these actors generates a powerful, raw, but radiant chemistry.

The rehearsal and taping process of a scene between Luke and Laura—taped on May 14, 1999 and aired on June 7, 1999—richly illustrates this point.[33] The scene in question finds Luke and Laura, twenty years after their agonizing negotiation of the rape, separated again by Luke's paranoid alienness. Laura has learned autonomy from the process of their negotiations but remains threatened by Luke's tendency to blur the boundaries of civil behavior, which she has always known can be deadly (for example, the rape) as well as life-giving (for example, his support of her self-determination). Luke has suffered a serious paranoid break with reality, crossing once again into a twilight realm of physiological male entitlement that has caused him to actually plot (albeit unsuccessfully) the murder of an enemy. This has made Laura feel that she can no longer stay with him. (Appropriately, this plot turn inverts the situation in which they first came together as Luke unwillingly felt compelled to carry out a contract murder and was saved from following Smith's orders by Laura.)[34] As a form of retaliation, the intended victim, a Cassadine, kidnaps their son and makes it appear that he is dead, causing Laura to suffer a nervous breakdown. Their mutual devastation brings Luke to Laura's hospital bedside, as much to seek his own healing as hers. Textually, their encounter is a formulaic piece in the soap opera tradition, following a single emotional line that focuses on the concerns of the moment. Rendered by Francis and Geary, however, it is an exquisite study in the nuances of the kind of human connection that endures all vicissitudes.

In conventional soap opera style, the writing and taping of the scene is partitioned into four beats (segments) that will be seen by the audience distributed over the introductory teaser (or prologue) and three of the six acts that make up the day's episode. The teaser beat is about thirty seconds in length. None of the other three beats runs for more than two minutes. However, also in conventional soap opera production style, the four beats are taped in succession in a session that lasts about forty-five minutes. Typically, there is a run-through and then a taping for each segment. In this case, Geary, on behalf of himself and Francis, requested after the teaser taping that there be no run-through, that they tape almost without pause all of the segments. What resulted was a finely shaded, emotional encounter with a finely honed series of rising and falling intensities.

What the audience saw when the show aired was a sequence fragmented by its juxtaposition with other storylines but which had a richly continuous developmental flow. The flow begins with the underlying layers of banked emotional energy, the pain and pleasure of seeing each other destabilized by the now superseding anguish of the loss, as they think, of their son, represented textually by a very low key verbal interchange. Laura wakes to discover Luke leaving her room and asks him to stay. In the second beat, the quiet dialogue concerns his revelation to her that he knows the circumstances of her breakdown and her exploration of feelings: does he feel as "half alive" as she does? She recounts her imagining of the life their son did not live to have, evoking the stereotypical scenes of marriage and parenthood, to which Luke replies in a complex moment typical of their dynamic that he imagines teaching his son, Lucky, to cheat at cards. The evocation of Luke's alien perspective breaks the cliches, as Luke always breaks the cliches of Laura's "normality." But it is only a small pressure release. The grieving seems endless. The small respite only frees up their powerful rapport with each other, and Laura plunges into sorrow, tearfully pulling Luke after her. They sob in each other's arms. In the third beat, they pull into a calmer moment, each trying to stabilize the other, as they take turns stumbling emotionally but fully engaged in each other until Luke asks if Laura has made plans to get away, and her expression reveals that it will be with the new man. They draw away from each other slightly, poised on the edge of mourning for the moment. In the fourth beat, they begin with a kind of stiff yet gently understanding composure, seemingly drained of all capacity for petty jealousies or even self-involvement. The quiet dialogue reveals their concern for each other, their mutual refusal to burden the other with their own concerns. But when Luke rises to leave her to rest and bends to kiss her, their individual reserves are shattered. The gentle kiss on the mouth is prolonged, not into an erotic contact but rather into the physical equivalent of their declarations of tenderness, which elicits from Laura both smiles and sobs. Luke respectfully draws back from labial contact and presses his lips to her cheek, hiding his face from the camera but revealing through the muscle tension of his back and shoulders the depth of emotion in the embrace. She arches her back in what resembles an erotic surrender, such as we have seen in their sexual love scenes, but here it is an epic motion of release of pain that appears to be facilitated by his body.

The minute articulation of their physicality bespeaks the alien outrageousness of his separation from social norms impacting on the codes of social boundaries that hold her in check. The nuanced moments of transformation speak the text beyond the capacity of its words because words never express either their mutual sadness or their ecstasy. These are the hallmarks of the Geary/Francis collaboration. Their mode of tapping into the rich reserve of their synergy in preparing for this scene was to rehearse on the set, a decision very unusual for soap opera actors, who typically rehearse in private and put the final touches on in the tape run-through that precedes the actual taping.

As they rehearsed, Geary and Francis used the lines from the script, but improvised physical contact that never appeared in the taped version, not because the director suggested other blocking, but because it clearly was never intended as a literal rehearsal. Instead, it seemed clear that Francis was using the improvisation to rouse an intense emotionality in Geary. As she spoke, she sat up in the bed, as she never was intended to do during the taping, took his face between her hands and covered his face with tiny but intensely impressed kisses, at which he began sobbing so uncontrollably that he had to excuse himself from the set. When he returned, they then discussed the emotional motivations of the scene with the director, about which

Francis was the most vocal. During the taping, the emotions freed by Francis's improvisation never got out of control, but instead seemed to move as if along an emotional equivalent of musical notes moving up and down a scale. Moments available to them during the respites between beats were used in calm, methodical clearing of their noses and drying their eyes, though both actors were unquestionably in the grip of emotions very much larger than their capacity to exert conscious control. Quite clearly, Geary's last contact with Francis, when he moved from her mouth to her cheek in the last beat of their scene together on that day, was his return to her of what she had given him in pretaping. She responded with an uncontrollable fit of sobbing on camera. The rapt silence on the set of even the jaded camera and sound crew reflected the awe-inspiring technical and emotional fusion of talent, technique, and chemistry of which Francis/Geary are capable. The scene over, Geary left the set in character as Luke, as per the script, but returned to Francis as Geary, and they enfolded each other in a long, tender embrace and kiss, and then quietly left the soundstage separately.

In order to appreciate the mystery of the fusion between the deliberate and the involuntary in their working methods, the Francis/Geary synergy must be understood in the context of a fraught and complex interpersonal relationship between these two actors, who are not and never have been in love in the usual meaning of the term. Personally, they are separated by different lifestyles, if repeated and sustained rumor is correct. It has been for more than twenty years "common knowledge" in the soap community that Geary is a gay man of many social contacts, and that Francis fears his lifestyle, not his gayness, which she fears could make her vulnerable to AIDS. What is certain is that Francis has made it clear that the writers are never to write a kiss on the mouth between Luke and Laura into the script, a demand she has enforced by angry rages when the writers tested her resolve. However, Francis reserves the right to kiss Geary when she chooses, which she did in this scene, a decision unquestionably made on the spur of the moment and almost certainly on the basis of the same kind of involuntary emotion that she released in herself while releasing powerful feelings in him before the taping. Every one of their mouth-to-mouth kisses in the scene in question and all scenes within recent memory are preceded by a moment in which they gaze at each other, a moment in which, almost certainly, a signal passes from her to him about whether or not there is to be labial contact.[35]

CONCLUSION

The availability of the working process of Geary and Francis brings to the surface and makes visible the way Synergistic Couples, both contemporary and in the great tradition, mobilize voluntary and involuntary forces to produce screen chemistry, though the evidence suggests a much more ritualized process for Geary and Francis. In the case of Astaire and Rogers, the actors' statements focus on the painstaking work their collaboration involved; Loy speaks of her chemistry with Powell as a given; Hepburn refers to her chemistry with Tracy as a function of his power; O'Sullivan simply acknowledges that Jane was her most memorable role. The fusion of energy and work was apparently never intentionally summoned, nor was there much articulation of its existence. Present-day actors, freed from both the restrictions and the protection of the old studio, do appear to be aware of the synergistic processes involved in their work, though certainly there is no pretense of analysis for the purposes of control or theorization.

While Francis and Geary are involved in "practical magic" that arises from a spontaneous sensitivity to each other and a practiced mode of working together with that sensitivity, Duchovny and Anderson evidence no comparable rituals but rather a more thoughtful awareness that their connection is grounded in subconscious forces with a life of their own. In an interview for *USA Weekend*, Anderson asked Duchovny how he perceived their relationship, and he said, "It's like the roots of a tree. It's very twisted, but it's growing. You know the tree is alive, and it works in its own treelike way, yet you couldn't untangle it. You could, but you'd need the help of a gifted professional."[36] The humorous suggestion by Chris Carter, creator and often writer and director of the show, that they go to a "gifted professional" for counseling was discussed by the two of them in the interview subsequent to this comment. Generally confirming widespread rumors that their relationship is a volatile one, Carter's joke also confirms their group understanding of its subconscious roots in the same forces that make their collaboration a special one. Allen and Keaton also support this generalization, beginning as lovers, moving into a very intimate friendship that involves dependence on each other's opinions about their work.[37]

There is a genre gulf between the work of Anderson/Duchovny,

Allen/Keaton, and Geary/Francis. However, the clarification of the role of chemistry in the great couple tradition from the studio days makes clear the many commonalities that underlie the dynamics of their separate enterprises. In their fictions of horror, comedy, and melodrama, the partnerships of Duchovny/Anderson, Allen/Keaton, and Geary/Francis mirror the state of intimacy. Their images reflect a capacity for human endurance and even fleeting joy in the face of fear and death. The nature of these creations also tells us something about the endurance of human creativity within a culture industry that is mechanized to program rather than to follow the lead of inspiration.

CHAPTER Seven
THE THEMATIC COUPLE
A Post-Studio Innovation

Our last look—at the latest bend in the road for the onscreen couple—is at its newest category: the Thematic Couple. A product of acting technique rather than the summoning of wild, wildly connected energies of an acting pair, the Thematic Couple is a descendant of the Iconic Couple, but it is fully a consequence of the heightened freedom of the post-code era. The new parameters permit mass culture to deal more searchingly and explicitly with couple issues once taboo in the media, but which have always been part of the conceptual agenda of high culture. Thus, the Thematic Couple negotiates some narrowing of the gap between the high culture venues of the stage and print fiction and the mass culture venues of movies and television. However, the expanded popcult articulation of ideas evident in the Thematic Couple reveals not only the achievements but also the limits of mass culture in achieving linguistic and conceptual complexity. Thematic Couple depictions of intimacy and human connection remind us that the popular media are still not able to verbally construct the kind of luminosity that is radiated by the chemistry of the Synergistic Couple, old or new. Some Thematic Couples break into new representations that could not have existed at all in Old Hollywood. But, in their challenges to couple conventions, today's Thematic Couples preserve the dominance of cultural codes, adding not very much more than a nonthreatening edge of controversy to the iconic prototypes that appeared in the days of the studio system.

Crucial to the Thematic Couple is that whether it is a new version of familiar pairings or a new couple figure entirely, it is more tentatively influenced by contemporary anxieties and identity crises than are the new Synergistic Couples. The disturbing comic and dramatic figures of the alien and alienated that characterize the new Synergistic Couple are muted in the representations of the Thematic Couple, a more bland and reassuring approach to the social issues of difference that are always at the heart of couple representation in the media. Like the Iconic Couple of Old Hollywood, the new Thematic Couple represents a compromise with audience sensibilities, generating new and genuinely improved formulas that mark out territory at the border of what is considered acceptable, but at the conservative side of the border. If Phylicia Rashad and Bill Cosby, as Cliff and Claire Huxtable on *The Cosby Show* (1984–1992) became a Thematic Couple in their groundbreaking representation of the African American couple, the representation comfortingly presents its forms of originality and complexity in a manner that filters out most of the alien-ation and marginalization of people of color in our society. Intelligent, stylish, and charming, Cliff and Claire seem to suggest that personal excellence is all it would take to break the glass wall of prejudice. Similarly, Cybill Shepherd and Bruce Willis, as Maddie Hayes and David Addison, in *Moonlighting* became a Thematic Couple in their moderately original, direct portrayal of gender problems that make men and women aliens to each other—problems once much more obliquely represented. However, they made the gender war cute, by and large, only rarely hazarding a central place for the underlying pain that did lurk under many of their episodes in what could have been a real challenge to the limited understanding of gender under the status quo. Paul Newman and Joanne Woodward, as India and Walter Bridge in *Mr. and Mrs. Bridge*, galvanized the energy of the Thematic Couple by embracing a script that depicted the solid middle class as a powerful social group almost completely alien to its own emotions and desires. At the same time, the film is quite conservative in its suggestion of the viability of this hollowed-out approach to life, a far cry from "Milagros" on *The X-Files*, which depicts the impossibility of living without one's heart. (Please see Chapter Six for an extended discussion of "Milagros.")

With the Thematic Couple, television again plays a major role. Post-studio film can boast of the partnership of Joanne Woodward and Paul Newman, who acted together in ten films and made five others in which Newman directed Woodward, but there are few other Thematic Couples in post-studio film production of this richness and longevity. The small group of collaborations of cinematic Thematic Couples tends toward one-shot pairings, like the one between Katharine Hepburn and Peter O'Toole in *The Lion in Winter* (1968, Dir. Anthony Harvey) or the much more recent collaboration of Joseph Fiennes and Gwyneth Paltrow in *Shakespeare in Love* (1998, Dir. John Madden), both of which feature skilled, well-matched actors working technically toward intelligent, nuanced, or at least inventive, explorations into intimacy issues without really disturbing audience equilibrium. By contrast, in television, the thematic collaborations of Cybill Shepherd and Bruce Willis in *Moonlighting* and Phylicia Rashad and Bill Cosby in *The Cosby Show* were chosen from a large number of potential candidates, including Jean Stapleton and Carroll O'Connor in *All in the Family* (1971–1979); Barbara Bain and Martin Landau in *Space 1999* (1975–1977); Ted Danson and Shelley Long in *Cheers* (1982–1987); Janine Turner and Rob Morrow in *Northern Exposure* (1990–1995); Roseanne Barr and John Goodman in *Roseanne* (1988–1997); Julie Kavner and Dan Castellaneta in *The Simpsons* (1989–); Kyle MacLachlan and Sherilyn Fenn in *Twin Peaks* (1990); and Sarah Michelle Gellar and David Boreanaz in *Buffy the Vampire Slayer* (1997–1999). Lucille Ball and Desi Arnaz in *I Love Lucy* (1951–1957), and Jackie Gleason and Audrey Meadows in *The Honeymooners* (1955–1956) might also be considered in this group, even though they emerged during the last gasp of the studio system environment; they paved the way in many respects for the category of media pair that I have labeled the Thematic Couple.

The Thematic Couple resembles the Iconic Couples that were harnessed together by the studios in that its charisma does not spontaneously erupt through the cultural structure, as is the case with the Synergistic Couple. However, the Thematic Couple differs from the conventional Iconic Couple in that it inhabits a script that is less formulaic than the ordinary mass media script used to be, a script that may in fact *rationally* challenge some of the conventions of storytelling. Unlike the Iconic Couple, which lends energy to cliche through adoption of formulaic poses and through established acting techniques, then, the Thematic Couple lends energy through some idiosyncratic poses and some established acting techniques to mass media attempts to tell more dynamic, more realistic stories about human life. The other major defining characteristic of the Thematic Couple is its relationship to image. All image engages the spectator on two levels, the conscious and the subconscious. All image relates in some way to the linguistic aspects of the film or television program: the dialogue and the plot/story. Unlike the old and new Synergistic Couples associated with wild images, the new Thematic Couple is involved in screen projects in which image is subordinated to somewhat liberated rational purposes, and only minimally related to the subconscious.

THE COSBY SHOW

The collaboration of Bill Cosby and Phylicia Rashad in *The Cosby Show* is a defining example of the Thematic Couple in part because it could not have existed in the studio era. Cosby and Rashad, as Cliff and Claire Huxtable, exist as part of an ongoing story that offers a highly radical concept in the American mass media, the centrality of an upper-middle-class couple of color. While Oscar Micheaux, the only successful black, independent moviemaker during the studio era, depicted ordinary middle-class life for segregated black audiences, the mainstream media severely marginalized black characters as either peripheral or as members of the lower working class. Cosby's emphatically mainstream show, even at this writing, remains a pioneering standard in orchestrating images that support an underlying set of stereotype-shattering ideas.[1] First, the show proposes a family of color who have a lifestyle that resembles those of the professionals in the audience. Cliff and Claire Huxtable are attractive, personable professionals—he a doctor and she a lawyer—who evidence elegant taste both in the furnishing of their house and in their personal presentation.

Cliff and Claire resemble Loy and Powell's Nick and Nora in the tone of their relationship, though not in the substance of their adventures, which are always literally domestic, whereas Nick and Nora implicate the darker side of domesticity through the metaphor of mystery. Like Nick and Nora, Cliff and Claire have a wonderfully eccentric, playful, and erotic relationship, which involves—generally because of their eccentric resistance to the mistakes of conformist citizens—a very high standard of ethical and moral behavior. In the progeny department, the Huxtables go Nick and Nora four better with their five children, all more interestingly drawn than the cliched Nicky Jr., but all as hopeful, well spoken, attractive, and in possession of the full range of choices and opportunities offered to the privileged American upper-middle class that Nick, Nora, and Nicky Jr. repre-

The Huxtables (Bill Cosby and Phylicia Rashad): shattering stereotypes with their intelligent, sophisticated, and exuberant pride in their ethnic heritage.

sented. In short, they fulfill Cosby's stated desire that the Huxtables resemble the viewers, not what they imagine to be the lives of their "servants," which Cosby understands as the appeal of the numerous sitcoms featuring African American characters with ghetto mannerisms and lifestyles.

The barrier-breaking nature of the high concept that motivates *The Cosby Show* is primarily what determines Cosby and Rashad's collaboration as a Thematic Couple. Their success in animating dozens of scripts through conscious attempts to counter—with their abundant good looks, charm, and comic talents—the conventional media presentations of people of color as comic at best, primitive and ignorant at worst, defines their success as an American media Thematic Couple. He reverses the media and sociological cliche of the parentally delinquent, hustling, sexually uncontrolled, often drug-addicted African American man. She reverses the cliche of the "mammy," the physically large, sexually neuter servant who lives to assure the spiritual and physical comfort of the white upper classes. He is a highly responsible parent, husband, and professional; she is a very attractive woman whose energies are directed toward her own goals, her own husband, and her own children. Yet in following the ideas built into the script, this acting pair cannot be considered as iconic because there is little standard cliche either in the textual depiction of the family and the couple or in the acting style through which Cosby and Rashad complement their scripts.

Cosby and Rashad are technique actors; they do not succeed because of a synergy which throws the audience into contact with the subconscious. Rather, they create a renewed audience awareness about ideas of ethnic images. But their technique, greatly involved in well-coordinated physical comedy, energizes the relative complexity of the script. The guiding conception of the show is saved by them and by the many playful scripts from being a dry replication of socioeconomic idealizations. And although the physical comedy has its roots in the *best* elements of the traditions of comic film acting by African Americans pioneered by "Stepin Fetchit"—the professional name of Lincoln Theodore Monroe Andrew Perry, the actor who created the character—*The Cosby Show* has none of the minstrel show "darky" stereotypes that are associated with the more unfortunate aspects of that character.[2] Indeed, Rashad and Cosby have been so creative in bringing their idealized father and mother figures to life that it is no simple thing to discuss in what way these characters are ethnically flavored, although it is clearly impossible to relegate them to that generic sitcom heaven occupied by hundreds of media characters played by white actors.

By and large, Claire and Cliff do not loom as large in the episodes as do the other couples under discussion in this chapter in their respective stories. Part of this is a result of Bill Cosby's atypical ideas about dramatic storytelling, ideas that fly in the face of established media directives on this matter. Primarily, the difference lies in Cosby's lack of interest in conflict as a dramatic principle. Though he clearly supports fragmented moments of conflict in each show, he cautioned his writers to avoid a through conflict line that controls the shape of the entire show.[3] Post–studio era freedom allowed Cosby to realize his ideas on a major television network. A *Cosby Show* episode tends to be a flowing representation of family life in which a variety of individual conflicts surface and submerge. The total design is one in which open-ended issues render daily life indeterminate, while a strong parental presence stabilizes the family by stressing the permanence of their bonding, regardless of whether actual solutions to problems can be found. The structure of *The Cosby Show,* thus, provides Cosby and Rashad with a script more complex than is traditional in American television sitcom. While retaining the reassuring aspect of that tradition, a *Cosby Show* episode rejects the cliche of the family as a machine that can erase all the troublesome places in our lives, in favor of a more complicated picture of a unit that can endure even if the rough edges cannot be smoothed.

In another departure from media practice in general and American television sitcom practice in particular, *The Cosby Show* made eroticism an integral element in Cliff and Claire's strong parental presence. The scripted combination of commitment and sexuality between Cliff and Claire flavors every episode whether or not they are central to its preoccupations, creating a positive model of African American family life that may serve in the larger sphere as a positive model for all family life.[4] A typical episode depicts Cliff and Claire playing out the battle of the sexes, suffused with the culturally specific details of African American life, but reflecting pan-cultural, centuries-long traditions of male-female combat. Cosby and Rashad's high spirits keep the warfare lively and suspenseful while attending to the details of Cliff and Claire's obviously strong marital devotion, thus limiting the adversarial action to that which will not rupture the parameters of family love.

An example of such a typical *Cosby Show* episode begins as Claire sits in the living room working on a legal brief but listening to "An Evening in Paradise," performed sensually by African American singer Jimmy Scott. Cliff walks in to discover her surrounded by the lush melody and initiates a wordless flirtation with his wife that is both a real sensual invitation and a joke on the first flush of romance: the dance is a wittily playful parody of coy smiles and seductive posturing. Claire at first withstands temptation, but Cliff is too playful to resist, and she rises to join him in a dance that is again both authentically sensual and a witty comment on the erotic impact of young love. In the final "dip," Claire comically bends Cliff over her knee and drops him.

Their momentary euphoria quickly turns into a traditional battle of the sexes wager over a difference of opinion about the date that Jimmy Scott recorded "An Evening in Paradise." The terms are set by Cliff, who is sure he will win, and the penalties for the loser are significant: the loser cooks the evening meal and cleans up, then serves breakfast in bed the next morning, and finally washes the winner's car. Cliff loses, but resists paying the penalty for a while. However, this conflict does not become the central issue of the episode, which soon moves on to the decision of their daughter Denise (Lisa Bonet) about which college she will attend out of all those that have accepted her, as the men in the family pressure her to attend Spelman College, the traditional Huxtable alma mater. Simultaneously, Cliff helps the other children in the family deal with what Denise's departure will mean to them. At dinner, Denise announces her decision to attend Spelman because she wants to continue in the family footsteps, and there is an affectionate ritual of family celebration that includes the Huxtables' children and Cliff's parents. The collage-like structure of the episode defines the African American family as an organic unit in which the friendly/erotic/adversarial parental relationship does not preclude a stable set of relationships among generations.

However, there are occasional shows about Cliff and Claire which focus from beginning to end on their emotional dynamic as the essential family core. One of these episodes involves Claire's invitation to Cliff for an anniversary celebration of the day he proposed to her. It begins with the almost obligatory repartee between husband who has forgotten and wife who has remembered the anniversary date. But it soon moves into an established tradition of African American storytelling, the verbal bragging contest, chronicled so deliciously by Zora Neale Hurston in her stories of African American lives. Despite the fact that both Claire and Cliff use standard American pronunciation, they often move into riffs of dialect identified with black characters in the media. This and the bragging repartee brings a new flavor to the television screen, one that has its roots in a highly specific tradition that has not yet become part of the standard media baggage. It perfumes the appearance of ordinary American affluence, creating a dynamic to the text of the affluent American couple that both is and is not familiar as a battle of the sexes.

The dialogue escalates in an exuberant trajectory. Claire lures Cliff away from watching television to settle him on the elegant sofa in an embrace, cooing that she is going to take him to the Golden Dove, an exclusive and expensive restaurant. He raises the stakes. Suitably appreciative of her generosity, he makes the evening a contest of who will look the best, since a dinner at the Golden Dove deserves a stellar appearance. Claire assures Cliff that she will be gorgeous. He counters. He will be "gorgeouser." The script itself disrupts the gender cliches by giving male and female an equal interest in the body. It has also set in play an African American tradition of verbal play. Cosby and Rashad give it exactly the body language necessary to bring it to life. Unlike the bland, happily married partners of generic sitcoms, which have historically focused on the lives of white Americans, Cosby and Rashad create a happily married couple that is full of ginger. In white sitcoms, ginger is reserved for the unhappily married, and single parents. By contrast, Cliff and Claire escalate the debate with panache, continuing to hug and caress each other, laughing with enormous energy of togetherness, while at the same time asserting dominance as the spectacle, the someone to look at:

Claire: I'm going to stop the people in their tracks.
Cliff: And I will be looking so good that the man will put me at a table in the center of the restaurant by myself and put the spotlight on me.
Claire: . . . when the people look they're going to say, "Who is that smooth, gorgeous woman sitting next to that pitiful man in the spotlight?"

The bragging contest leads to their agreement to compete in a "Smooth Contest" for the evening, to be judged by their children.

Cosby and Rashad create a complex fiction in which ordinary life is structured at its deep, inner core by ethnic traditions. Textually organized, it nevertheless takes the cliched competition of husband and wife of the American media into new places, emotionally and ethnically, and in terms of physical comedy as well. Cosby and Rashad use their bodies and faces in fresh ways. Dazzling smiles and grotesque grimaces come into play, alluding to set comic facial expressions like the double take, but formed by the unique talents and comic insights of the acting pair. Similarly, the "Smooth Contest" generated by the bragging contest of African American folktales, complicated by Claire breaking her ankle, generates a second wave of physical humor when Claire vows to look smooth (and does) despite an injury that forces her to hobble. A very funny segment in which Cliff tries to dominate Claire by showing her the right way to walk with a cane, which works on the dynamic typical of their relationship, ends when she trumps him by letting it fall and hopping up the stairs on her good leg.

Each situation on *The Cosby Show* tends to open up opportunities for highly inventive comic exploitation of physical situations on the part of Rashad and Cosby that is reminiscent of the great comedy of silent films. Although that comedy more often than not had its primary link to the subconscious part of the mind in films that bore the most tenuous connection to story and none to dialogue, in an innovative variation on silent film legacy, Cosby and Rashad employ that kind of body comedy in a manner that is subordinate to the linguistic aspects of the media, dialogue and conceptually motivated story. The same can, in fact, be said of other televisual Thematic Couples in sociologically inspired sitcoms, as for example Carroll O'Connor and Jean Stapleton in *All in the Family*. Cosby/Rashad broke new ground for the onscreen couple using the energy of the comedy of the body within a structure, highly disciplined by Cosby and determined by his strong ideas about the kind of representation he wanted to convey.[5]

MOONLIGHTING

Inevitably, the Thematic Couple is not as truly disruptive as the Synergistic Couple, even though it may break some cliches and break them more obviously for the audience. It opens up stereotypes but never really makes the audience uncomfortable with the indeterminacy it may suggest. In fact, Rashad and Cosby make the audience more comfortable than do most sitcoms by assuaging cultural guilt about injustice through an ethnicity that is depicted with dignity and grace. Similarly, while Cosby and Rashad use their bodies and voices innovatively, there is, in typical sitcom style, no compelling visual language that challenges easy ideas about the harmony of being a couple. The show uses a typical three-point lighting and zero degree style format in "showing" the persons and settings in the scenes, the kind of visual that is characteristic of Thematic Couple vehicles. However, if the Thematic Couple is never associated with powerful, unsettling images, it is sometimes associated with moderately inventive visual style, as is the case with Cybill Shepherd as Maddie Hayes and Bruce Willis as David Addison in *Moonlighting*, which may have been intended to break gender cliches and which did involve a more interesting visual language than is typical of American television.

Received opinion regards Shepherd and Willis as an acting couple with abundant chemistry. However, close examination of their work together suggests that while they have high energy in their ensemble work, they do not have synergy in the sense that it is explored in this study, as is the case with Anderson/Duchovny, Francis/Geary, and Allen/Keaton. Much of the seeming chemistry is a result of how well they energize a script that is more innovative in its comedy than the usual television sitcom script. *Moonlighting* scripts are self-aware, giving Willis and Shepherd scope to play a savvy version of the "fire and ice" couple cliche, she the cool, upper-class blonde and he the sensual, no-holds-barred, streetwise hustler. But in significant ways, Willis and Shepherd suggest how very little headway has been made by the new freedom for the mass media. There is a poseur quality to the self-consciousness the show flaunts. Having reached a parting of the ways toward the middle of the series, Shepherd and producer Glenn Gordon Caron each look back on *Moonlighting* with a different take on what kind of gender portraits the show was intended to paint. Shepherd's expectation of a feminist series left her generally unsatisfied with the treatment of gender issues on the show.[6] According to Shepherd, Caron originally created the show specifically for her, and Caron was influenced by her feminist ideas as well as her certainty about casting Willis as her co-star. However, Caron's current claims about the show's genesis couldn't be more different. He asserts that he created the series looking for a "real man" to stand up to a headstrong woman, as a reaction against the "sensitive" men of the 1980s. Caron also claims that it was his wife, the one woman at the top of the ABC hierarchy, who was responsible for the casting of Bruce Willis, whom he claims the network initially rejected. In the Caron/Willis version, Caron's wife kept him centered by supporting his position about Willis, which the network's male executives rejected with the assertion that Willis is not the kind of man "that women like" until the sole female executive—who was not consulted about what women like—piped up with her contribution that Willis looked like "one dangerous fuck" to her.[7]

How much revisionism these diverging accounts reflect is impossible to determine at this point; Caron and Shepherd remain alienated today after a long period of antagonism during the middle and later part of the series, forcing Caron to leave the show he created. But the episodes themselves support Shepherd's complaints about the distortion of Maddie's character midway and late in the show in ways that exploit her and reintroduce patriarchal biases with a vengeance.[8] In terms of this study, however, the significant point is that the show, with mixed results, based its creation of the couple on ideas; it was not a spontaneous development of story based on charismatic image. Caron and Willis have made contradictory claims for both the spontaneity of the show and for its literary quality. Shepherd too speaks of being attracted to the show initially for its superior writing. The episodes speak more loudly than either of these warring parties of spontaneity within a very strictly defined set of ideas about men and women, marking it as a vehicle for a Thematic and not a Synergistic Couple.[9]

Moonlighting was, from the very first, more style (albeit a charming and refreshing one) than substance. Maddie and David were, from the get-go, scripted with a fresh approach to television that had a mildly postmodern, self-mocking edge, and was, by Shepherd's account (and Caron concurs with this), considerably influenced by the innovative gendering of the Hollywood screwball comedies of the thirties, which she introduced to Caron. But concept-generated entertainment is always bound by the limits of someone's ideas, and David and Maddie were always drawn within comparatively conservative gender limits, considering the feminist issues that had already been raised by society in general when it was created. The feminist "angle" is embedded in the show's promising concept: Maddie is a model-turned-businesswoman, trying to run the ramshackle Blue Moon Detective Agency. Woman as eroticized object/spectacle turns into woman as action hero. But the concept is weighted down by the ghosts of some old cliches. Maddie is never quite an action hero. A cool (emotionally reserved) upper-class blonde beauty, Maddie remains the spectacle of the gaze of David, the cool (emotionally hip), streetwise angler. Shepherd was photographed in close-up with a lens that gave her a diffuse, romantic, hazy appearance—a lens used only for her and never for Willis—to make her look "prettier."[10] She is always off base in her handling of business situations, and although she is given some unusual perks for a cool blonde—the right to lose her temper and speak her mind—she is quite frequently penalized, or even demonized, by the show for taking care of business. The association between *Moonlighting* and the old screwball comedies does give Maddie a good deal of the latitude of the screwball heroine, but the narrative arcs of the show's episodes are much more closely related to the 1940s working-women comedies in which female success in business is linked with repression and unhappiness, and true feminine bliss is always reached only when the woman stops asserting what the script happily assures us are masculine prerogatives.[11]

The ideas in *Moonlighting* keep slipping back to the taming of the woman executive in 1940s comedies. In general, Maddie's demand of David that he act professionally in the office is regarded as a stuffiness on her part, a sign of the repression that David is there to cure by releasing her sweet, feminine side. All sympathy is given to her fun-loving partner's desire to "humanize" the office, generally by doing things like throwing limbo parties during working hours. (Ah, yes, an office diversion much recommended by all male executives.) Maddie's insistence on a work ethic, a quality that would be applauded in a male character, is "scroogified" frequently. One Christmas show, "It's a Wonderful Job," a parody of *It's a Wonderful Life* (1946, Dir. Frank Capra), is devoted to Maddie's rethinking of her demand that her staff work Christmas week (not Christmas Day) so that Blue Moon can honor its contract with a client who needs paperwork so he can go to court.[12] The upshot is that she is applauded when she gives in to emotionality and sentimentality, deciding to give the staff the time off although we know that this means leaving the client to go to court without the necessary papers. Because IT'S CHRISTMAS. Maddie is de facto moved back into the position of "the little woman" who happens to own a business, and the episode depicts her desire to be an effective and competent businessperson as aberrant. The woman-bashing aspect of these episodes is disguised by snappy dialogue and the breaking of the fourth wall, when they address the audience. Tellingly, however, it is almost always Willis who breaks the wall.

This said, Willis and Shepherd, for all the masked conventionality in their show, produced a number of episodes that merit their reputation for having had a special collaboration. In picking up the energy of the innovative pacing of the show, and playful riffs on the conventions of sitcom structure, they produced work worthy of note as occupying the Thematic Couple's midway position between the stereotypical Iconic Couple and the disruptive Synergistic Couple. Perhaps the best of the *Moonlighting* episodes, and the most fruitful example of Shepherd and Willis's work as a Thematic Couple is "The Dream Sequence Always Rings Twice."

In this episode, *Moonlighting* daringly eschews plot and daringly promotes a fully nonlinear, multi-perspective angle of vision. It consists almost wholly of the contrast between Maddie and David's parallel dreams, stimulated by the unsatisfying termination of one of their cases. The actual case they are working on terminates within the first ten minutes of the show. Following the wife of a man who is anxious to find evidence of infidelity so that he can divorce her and avoid sharing his wealth with her, Hayes and Addison find that she is blameless. They meet him at the wreck of an old nightclub where all the jazz greats of the forties played—and where Judy Garland is said to have had her first drink—the Flamingo Cove. When the client is forced to face his wife's innocence and the refusal of Hayes and Addison to doctor the evidence, he shuts down his negotiations for the Flamingo Cove, which, in keeping with his remorseless boorishness, he was planning to level and turn into a parking lot. Maddie and David are off the case. However, they continue to be struck by the romance of the old place, and particularly of a famous unsolved murder that took place there all those decades ago.

A kind of "legend of Los Angeles," the Flamingo Cove murder case involved the history of the Sloan orchestra (fictitious), which played at the club (also fictitious). The singer, Rita Adams, married to the band's clarinet player Jerry Adams, got involved in an affair with Zack McCoy, a new cornet player, and Jerry soon turned up dead. Both Rita and Zack were executed for the crime, but doubts remained about which one was guilty. Each died declaring his or her innocence and blaming the other. Maddie and David quickly embark on one of their characteristic gender battles, she unreasonably and rigidly positive that Rita, used and abused by Zack, was innocent; he more flexibly, playfully, but decidedly inclined to believe in Zack as the victim of a "femme fatale." Their debate identifies their strategies of argumentation with pretty familiar gender categories: Maddie is shown to be too emotional to think straight or do anything but attack wildly during a difference of opinion, while David can be trusted to deal even with issues to which he is passionately committed with a sense of fair play and poise. (Poor Maddie is doomed by *Moonlighting* to be rational and emotional at all the wrong moments, while David gets the cushy assignment of being both more rationally poised and more emotionally liberated than she is.) The characteristic staccato, rhythmically repetitive dialogue of their tiff puts a polish on these old cliches, but they remain cliches. However, the dream sequences which arise from this dispute are scripted in a way that uses this couple to play with witty, stylish comments on old film genres, and to acknowledge, to some degree, a multi-perspectival reality and a more sophisticated understanding of the indeterminacy in human affairs than is ordinarily found on American television.

Both dreams are shot in black and white, reminding the viewer of the beauty of the old films, by using film noir lighting, expressionist shadows, and interesting angles, all of which are generally lacking in the color stock on which the episodes of *Moonlighting* (like all contemporary sitcoms) are shot. Caron made a concerted effort to play with the aesthetics of black-and-white movies, using two kinds of stock—what he calls a glossy MGM-style stock for Maddie's dream and a Warner Brothers grainy stock for David's dream.[13] Shockingly, however, the episode makes us aware of how few people in television know how to use black and white today. *Moonlighting*'s quotation of the black-and-white photography of the forties movies is generally aesthetically inept, with no authentic feel for the spectrum of whites, grays, and blacks that once enabled Hollywood to make original use of the screen medium. Thus the dream sequences are a succession of uninspired stock shots and lighting patterns that do nothing more than strike the chords of memory about the older glamour of black-and-white film. The fun is the generalized pleasure of seeing a reminder of glorious black on television and the particular frisson of seeing Shepherd and Willis through the lens as it once looked at Barbara Stanwyck and Fred MacMurray.

Similarly, the plots of each dream are parodies of the older films, with no innovation that would actually enable the *Moonlighting* team to be as potentially disruptive of television cliches as film noir was of film cliches in the late forties. Shepherd and Willis are merely dressed up in the clothes of their "cinematic parents," playing "old movies." Nevertheless, there is a certain complexity to the intentional, self-conscious playing with the older forms that permits the show to adopt a truly multi-perspectival approach to gender difference. Maddie's dream is first and it depicts the victimization of women. In it, she visualizes Rita (played by Shepherd) as a fresh-faced, Alice Fay-like "sweet kid" clad in demure, light-colored forties feminine glamourwear, who sings a chastely romantic version of "Blue Moon."

Married to a nebbishy dormat of a Jerry (Frank Bannon), Rita is overwhelmed by the seductions of Zack (Willis), a coldly predatory hipster done up with the look of Robert Montgomery as Philip

This dream reconstruction of 1940s movies on Moonlighting *gives Maddie's (Cybill Shepherd) inner life a rare parity with David's (Bruce Willis).*

Marlowe and imbued with the ruthless spirit of the kinds of characters typically played by Robert Ryan.

Rita's inability to resist Zack's sexual advances, like a rabbit transfixed by a snake, reflects Maddie's sexual frustration in her non-dream relationship to David, whom she obviously desires, but to whom she cannot give herself freely. Imagining herself with no will of her own—not a feature of her waking life—permits her to indulge in a fantasy of sexual abandonment. It also reflects the series' belief that underneath Maddie's assertive surface lurks a sexual victim. Tellingly, Rita, the fantasy character, pays the price of betrayal and death for her transgressive pleasures, a clever evocation of Maddie's profound feeling that sexuality itself is transgressive. This is a cleverly nuanced clarification of her paralytic inability to have the affair with David that she wants. The earnestness of her reproduction of the 1940s woman's picture/melodrama in her dream also nicely reflects Maddie's straitlaced attitudes.

David's dream of the Flamingo Cove murder articulates his psychology, particularly his fear of victimization by women. He imagines Rita as a tough vamp, seductively dressed in low-cut, high-slit black dresses. David's fantasy of Rita as a performer is an homage to Rita Hayworth's raunchy performance of "Put the Blame on Mame" in *Gilda* (1946, Dir.

Charles Vidor). In David's fantasy, Shepherd gives a hard-edged, hair-tossing rendition of "I Told You I Love You, Now Get Out," and then schemes á la the noir femmes fatales in *Double Indemnity* and *The Postman Always Rings Twice* to use Zack to get rid of Jerry for her. David's Zack is an innocent hipster, much like Humphrey Bogart's Sam Spade in *The Maltese Falcon,* putty in Rita's hands, particularly when his noble nature is enflamed by the physical abuse Rita receives from her husband; in this dream sequence Jerry (again Frank Bannon) is a cold, hard-drinking philanderer. From the first minute Jerry sees Rita, she draws him into her web, tantalizing him with double entendres. While in Maddie's dream Zack thrusts his presence into her life with an aggressive intrusion of his horn into her musical numbers, in David's dream, Zack stands silent, holding his horn until Maddie taunts him, "Just going to watch or are you planning to use that thing?" They wisecrack each other into an affair that, unlike the affair in Maddie's earnestly melodramatic fantasy, is a highly parodic, zany pastiche of film noir, reflecting David's humorous approach to the problems life puts in his way. For example, just as Rita explicitly attempts to get Zack to agree to murder Jerry, standing seductively in her slip holding an ice cube she is using to bring down the heat of a scorching evening, she drops the cube, and they hilariously chase it across the floor as they debate the issue of murder. Zack refuses to kill Jerry in a speech so convoluted that Rita is forced to ask, "Does that mean the answer is no?" "Yes," says Zack solemnly. Parodying the Hayes/Addison incessant banter in the series, and at the same time satirizing film noir repartee, Rita retorts, "You mean 'yes' the answer is 'yes' or 'yes' the answer is 'no'?" This leaves Zack to wonder, "What was the question?" When Zack is finally manipulated by Rita into agreeing to murder Jerry, David's fantasy becomes a 180-degree inversion on Maddie's fantasy of the murder. Whereas in Maddie's dream a coldhearted Zack bashes Jerry while Rita looks on in helpless panic, in David's dream, Zack loses his nerve and a castrating Rita grabs Jerry's clarinet to beat him to death with his own instrument. Whereas in Maddie's dream a treacherous Zack turns her in to the police, in David's fantasy, Rita pulls the switch for Zack's execution by electric chair in a silly parody of the "last mile" scenes of executions in old-time gangster movies. David's dream cleverly reflects *his* fears of sexuality as a form of transgression. Sexually aggressive as David may be, he makes no move on Maddie, and the fantasy shows why. She represents a danger to him from which he fears he may never recover, complete with oedipal scenario, that closeness to her involves the murder of the father, and castration—the loss of his horn. (Unfortunately, while in this episode the dreams are given parity, David's dream came increasingly to represent a single series point of view, that Maddie is a destructive woman who uses her sexuality to hurt David.)

The sharp-witted script of "The Dream Sequence Always Rings Twice" demonstrates the formative role of the text in the success of the Shepherd/Willis collaboration, and also the role of creative use of old gender cliches, interestingly packaged though only partially reexamined. This episode begs the gender question in numerous ways by giving Maddie and David fairly standard male/female traits. However, it does end by emphasizing the indeterminacy of male-female differences. The script doesn't obliterate stereotype uproariously, as do Keaton and Allen, but it does contain enough material to open them up to contemplation by humor, rather than simply reproducing them in all their formulaic glory.

The last scene of "The Dream Sequence Always Rings Twice," which depicts Maddie and David arriving at the office the next day, turns the show's cliches in a somewhat more complex direction. Neither will admit to obsessive dreams about the dispute over the Flamingo Cove murder. Both pretend that they never gave the story another thought. Then, as they prepare to go back to work, Maddie and David hold a mutual gaze; during their interior musings, conveyed by voice-over (a technique characteristic of film noir, which the show has just parodied), each spits a final imprecation at the other: "Animal," snarls Maddie wordlessly. "Sexist," snorts David silently. The odd balance of the work of the Thematic Couple between cliche and innovation shimmers here. Stereotypically, the show frames Maddie's final appearance in the episode in a soft-focus close-up image, to make her a better object of contemplation, despite the fact that Shepherd is extremely beautiful in any focus and that soft focus is generally reserved for aging women stars. Each character is standing on a conventionally gendered viewpoint. Yet something like parity is achieved by the scripting of the last few minutes, an evolution from the establishing argument of the show as David and Maddie leave the old Flamingo Cove Club, giving David a clear advantage over the out-of-control Maddie. Here they are equally adamant, equally narcissistic in their commitment to their self-involvement in their opinions. Here, the series plays with ideas about male and female as equally inscrutable, dishonest, and hampered from using the past to learn creative lessons about couple connections.

The innovative balance between gendered points of view tickles spectator stereotypes, but David's inevitable return in future episodes to his pace-setting reflections on Maddie's inability to deal with her desires for self-definition do little to really restructure audience ideas about sexual politics.

MR. AND MRS. BRIDGE

New ideas about couples are more elegantly and *somewhat* more unsettlingly presented in the Thematic Couple partnership of Joanne Woodward and Paul Newman, particularly in their very late collaboration in *Mr. and Mrs. Bridge* (1990, Dir. James Ivory). Beginning in the fifties, still nominally under the studio system and thus within the parameters of the production code, Woodward and Newman exemplify, in the way their film projects changed over time, the widening opportunities in the media for couple projects to deal explicitly with social issues regarding love and marriage. Woodward and Newman, through well-honed acting techniques, were an Iconic Couple at the beginning of their professional collaboration, animating cliches mandated by code parameters, but in the developing freedom of the post-studio era have taken new opportunities to grow into a Thematic Couple.

Early in their careers, as an onscreen couple, Newman and Woodward lent their charisma and craft as an iconic star pair to such standard melodramas as *The Long Hot Summer* (1958, Dir. Martin Ritt), *From the Terrace* (1960, Dir. Mark Robson), and other works typical of the "prodigal son melodramas" of the 1950s and early 1960s. These self-righteous films heralded themselves as hard-hitting explorations of family and society, but were in fact self-congratulatory patriarchal daydreams that simplistically and disingenuously portrayed imaginary men who beat the system on their own terms, purportedly flouting social pressures to conform while reaping all the rewards usually offered only to those who are obedient to a conformist society. In these projects, the women were inescapably reduced to accessories of conformity or liberation, which the hero acquired depending on the stage of his quest. The limitations of the late studio-era Newman/Woodward collaborations are even clearer in projects that purported to be about independent women, as in the mediocre comedy *A New Kind of Love* (1963, Dir. Melville Shavelson). Woodward chose the project because she felt that it offered more opportunities than the more typical sidekick role. It is a story about the transformation of a heroine, seemingly an advance for Woodward over their previous projects, in which only the hero had a stake in the dramatic conflict. However, the movie is built around a formulaic script that stereotypically requires her to shuck her competence to find herself sexually as a woman. Steve Sherman (Newman), a sports reporter, and Samantha "Sam" Blake, a fashion buyer, find themselves in Paris at the same time. They raise each other's hackles, he finding her in her boyish clothes, her black-rimmed glasses, and her unsubmissive attitudes unappealing and she finding him a male chauvinist. She plans to "fix" him by dressing up in exaggeratedly and garishly feminine clothes and posing (without her glasses) as a Parisian call girl named "Mimi." As in all Hollywood movies of the time, taking off the spectacles does amazing things: he falls for her, unaware of who she really is. But instead of taking her revenge on his sexism through his new vulnerability to her, as she had planned, she finds herself falling for him. By the time he learns her identity, he is too far gone to care as much as he once would have about her deceit. As a pair—she newly womanized and he newly liberalized—they marry. All throughout, Maurice Chevalier sings, "You Brought a New Kind of Love to Me."

Woodward and Newman both struggle to eke a character out of their assigned roles. But the screenplay is brittle and riddled with liberal cliches. Both Sam and Steve are cartoon figures, drawn without a shade of complexity between them. The course of their romance is completely predictable, so relentlessly recipe-like, that *A New Kind of Love* is representative of the lowering of standards for the iconic coupling that was pervasive in Hollywood in the late studio period. For all its verbal acquaintance with feminism, *A New Kind of Love* compares unfavorably to the pre-feminist Iconic Couple in *The Shop around the Corner* (1940, Dir. Ernst Lubitsch), which features a far more nuanced recipe for a movie about the metamorphosis of enemies into lovers through disguise.[14]

As the studio system crumbled, Newman and Woodward found much improved script opportunities, the best of which, arguably, has been *Mr. and Mrs. Bridge*, a highly nuanced film in which, although Woodward plays a woman completely dominated by her husband, dignity and compassionate insight are granted to the partner of the patriarch. *Mr. and Mrs. Bridge* features a script full of complex ideas about patriarchal marriage through a loose collection of important incidents in the lives of Walter and India Bridge, their three children, and some of their close friends during the late 1930s and 1940s in Kansas City. An independent film that was mass marketed successfully, it was given its commercial patina by Newman and Woodward's Hollywood cache.[15] Newman as Walter Bridge conveys with multifaceted richness the simultaneous contempt and tenderness in which he holds his submissive wife. Newman is masterful in many fascinating scenes, for example one in which he exerts a rigid control of his sexuality, which unacceptably finds stimulation at the spectacle of his very attractive older daughter, by channeling his forbidden lust toward a wife whose sexual charms are laughable to him. Playing against type, the beautiful Newman, exploited for decades by recipe Hollywood adventure scripts as male cheesecake, uses his looks intelligently in this role as a visual reminder of the possibilities Walter would have had for adultery had he not chosen to adhere scrupulously to the bourgeois cliches of righteous "family values." Playing the essence of the self-righteous man—Walter Bridge is a phenomenon of rigidity even among the class of rigid Kansas patriarchs to which he belongs—Newman animates the man behind the idea in the script, forbidding the audience from dismissing him in a flurry of liberal cliches about the male domination and racism which Walter exhibits freely. The actor finds in this patriarch a pragmatic righteousness born of a shrewd and conservative estimation of what will work in the society in which he finds himself, triumphant at a historical moment at which all he stands for is about to be challenged. The challenge is clearly prefigured in his freewheeling daughter, who will evade her father's authority as a harbinger of the feminism that will sweep away the automatic social approval of Walter's paternal tyranny, on which his entitlement rests. At the same time, Woodward, as India Bridge, uses her acting skills to convey the idea of the wife's macerated sense of herself combined with a yearning sensibility. India's glowing satisfaction as a completely sheltered spouse coexists fascinatingly with her tormented sense of the impotence of her position, which assails her periodically. She is particularly torn when she must watch her best friend, stultified by middle-class life, drift toward suicide, and when she must endure her husband's cold dismissal of the tragedy as the act of an unstable woman whose husband "gave her everything a woman could want." Woodward, whose acting techniques provoke a subtlety to match Newman's, prevents us from feeling Walter's contempt for this woman, whose

The wedding of the younger Bridge daughter (Margaret Welsh) promotes images entirely faithful to Hollywood's glorified stereotypes of "ordinary life," yet contains a subtle, troubling visual subtext of smug shallowness.

weak, deferential behavior is the creation of a particular historical period.

Compelling visual image plays a role in the brilliance of the Woodward and Newman partnership in Mr. and Mrs. Bridge. Unlike the uncanny images created by the Synergistic Couple, however, the images of India and Walter Bridge, as well as the images of the sets and characters around them, are meticulously mimetic. Far from being rapturously unsettling, disquieting, or disturbing, as are the images of the Synergistic Couples we have attended to, these thematic images are breathtakingly recognizable in their comfortingly faithful, rational reproduction of ordinary life in all its nuance.

In scene after scene, Newman's face and body are translucent displays of the internal workings of Walter Bridge's psychology, making film seem a mode that is capable of rendering reality almost totally knowable. Newman's face and anatomy convey the rigidity with which Walter holds himself, as fugitive emotions visibly swirl through Bridge's iron frame of will and discipline only to be palpably immobilized by Newman's re-creation of Bridge's years of social rectitude. For her part, in a performance that daringly flaunts the Hollywood imperative for women to refuse any sign of aging, Woodward conveys India's malleability in a face and body slackened by middle age and tractability. Her very bones appear to lose calcium before our eyes, taking on a spongy appearance along with the rounded curves of her belly, breasts, and hips; as if, were we to push down hard on her head, India Bridge would reveal herself to be foam rubber, devoid of skeletal resistance. In scene after scene, Woodward's taut and model-like face is transformed into a soft, fleshy, yielding mass of conciliation, permanently equipped with a desperately hopeful smile under which ripples a coherent, but permanently stymied, understanding that she is being unreasonably immobilized as an individual.

The encounter of these two perfectly melded visual and textually formed characterizations creates not a synergy but an interlocking pair of performances conveying what conscious artistry can understand of the domination/submission pattern in conventional middle-class marriage. Among the multitude of scenes that demonstrate the Woodward/Newman artistry, the most dramatically and comically spectacular is the scene during which a seventy-five-mile-an-hour typhoon approaches the country club in which the Bridges are dining. While the other patrons, at the request of the management, retreat into the storm cellar, Walter, in a successful display of determination to be superior to any force of nature, wills India to remain at the table until the storm has passed. The physiology assumed by each of them by means of their craft, behind which their star images have disappeared as if the flesh were being covered by a material mask, as well as their rendering of the text, interplay elegantly: he anchored to the spot by determination, she tangibly on the verge of jumping out of her skin and already half in flight emotionally toward safety. Their teamwork—as Walter, without touching India, moors her while the storm buffets trees, awnings, lawn furniture—is the essence of the relationship between the Bridges and of the deliberate Newman/Woodward filmic acting partnership. While rational understanding dominates the audience's reading of the scene, Newman and Woodward's chameleon ability to assume characteristic physical shape dictated by a mimetic imitation of social reality brings the subconscious into play as a subordinate element, creating an imaginative experience of a sociological perspective on male dominance in marriage. Never do we feel the uncanny, inexplicable, rationally frustrating, unnameable insights generated by Scully and Mulder, Luke and Laura, and Allen and Keaton. Rather, reason glows with the satisfaction of a perfectly labeled, albeit fully complex, portrait of a marriage.

Aside from the performances, another element that prevents the precision from hardening into cliche is the film's narrative structure. *Mr. and Mrs. Bridge* fragments its story into a mosaic of a multitude of events rather than organizing the moments of family life around a conventional story, as did the generic, formulaic family movies of the forties, like *Life with Father* (1947, Dir. Michael Curtiz). In this way, the creative team of *Mr. and Mrs. Bridge* produces a multi-perspectival view of the Bridge family. Although this modernist narrative fragmentation does not invite a trip into the subconscious, as with the fragmentations in the texts of the Synergistic Couple, it does leave room for India's point of view, and those of the Bridge children. This contrasts with movies like *Life with Father*, which were structured by the patriarch's point of view, his family little more than a comic set of annoyances and trivial correctives to his dominant authority. With its fragmented perspective, *Mr. and Mrs. Bridge* renders conventional socialization problematic. But because it never allows the higher energies of the subconscious to carry it away, the film never really challenges the status quo. Rather, it anchors itself in a critical yet greatly affectionate admiration for Mr. Bridge's command, authority, and sense of responsibility. Walter is delineated as a sexist and racist, as well as a man unable to experience joy and passion, but those flaws are somewhat trivialized in a film that admires Bridge too much for almost always being right about the way things really work, not so very far away from *Life with Father*, at that. In the typhoon scene, the film celebrates Walter's exuberant defiance of the elements, as it crowns him with success. Moreover, in the title cards at the end of the film we learn that Walter turned out to be right in his seemingly snobbish objections to the marriage of his younger daughter Carolyn (Margaret Welsh) to a working-class boy, who ultimately abuses her and whom she leaves to marry into her own class. We also learn that he is the eventual role model for his son and grandson. His son, Douglas (Sean Robert Leonard), returns to the fold after sowing his wild oats with working-class women and enters his father's law firm, as does Douglas's son after him, creating the dynastic law firm of Bridge, Bridge, and Bridge. Indicative of the film's not so secret love affair with Mr. Bridge is that the title cards say nothing further about India. In the end, the Thematic Couple in all the cases examined here supports the status quo, regardless of the mimetic or witty brilliance with which it portrays the couple.

CONCLUSION

The pairs in the sextet of post–studio era couples discussed here—three synergistic and three thematic—tell an interesting story about the best-case scenarios for portraying couples in the contemporary media. They show, as did the couples created by Old Hollywood, that conceptualization of the story and script are only part of the defining difference between innovative mass media representation of the couple and mass media representation of the couple that spits out tired stereotypes. They show that another crucial factor determining the difference between cliche and complexity remains the degree to which intimacy is represented through image as a process rather than through script as a labeled thing. Hence the continuing importance to the representation of the onscreen couple of serialization and repetition, which creates dramatic spaces for ellipsis, indeterminacy, and undomesticated energies. Hence also the continuing importance of the raw image, with its ungovernable energies, to the flexibility and range of media couple representation. The weightiness of serialization and repetition has made television a medium of rich resources for the onscreen couple, granting the sitcom, the weekly adventure show, and even the humble and poorly regarded soap opera the cultural space needed for representing the layered nuances of human erotic bonding. The economics of the current culture industry has almost completely disabled the movies as such a venue. Thus the scarcity of exciting couples also speaks to the losses incurred in a culture industry that no longer has the heterogeneity in collaboration once enforced by the studio system.

At the same time, audience and popular media discourse about screen couples today reveals how the ghost of the Production Code lingers on, in unofficial production preferences for mind and eye candy, showing the old in-house Hollywood censors to have been rooted in a pretty acute perception of the limits of popular tolerance for complexity, indeterminacy, and truth. Even without the code, most media efforts are kept within relatively narrow guidelines by the way audiences vote with their dollars, or at least by the way movie packagers and television officials think they will, for the most cliched of the commercial offerings unless they are lured away from their timidity and intellectual laziness by obliqueness and fantasy in depicting intimacy.[16] With the exception of a comparatively few examples, the screen couple has fallen on evil times. In the popular press, the abundance of inexpressive representations of couples and intimacy is supported by the mislabeling of contemporary Functional Couples who work together in two or three movies as having chemistry. In comparison with the great Synergistic Couples of the golden age, or with Scully and Mulder, it is hard to see Functional Couples like Richard Gere and Julia Roberts (two films) and Tom Hanks and Meg Ryan (three films) as anything but pale imitations of intimacy. Similarly, Thematic Couples are misperceived as daring when they in fact do no more than attempt the most cautious of editorial changes to old formulas. As in the old days, real synergy, with its challenges to old thinking, only becomes commercially viable when it speaks to the more educated part of the mass audience, as in the Keaton/Allen collaboration, or when it enters mass culture in a highly fantastic form, as in *The X-Files* or *General Hospital*. But there is less of it, and it is generally labeled as part of a cult phenomenon, apparently the pigeonhole these days for anything that might disturb the general slumber of media audiences. In the short run, the pleasure of the security of the familiar is confused with the pleasure of genuine and perhaps enduring innovation. At the same time, the industry grinds on, rarely understanding, as in Old Hollywood, any distinction in the quality of what it is producing.

So, none of the preceding paragraphs and chapters should be taken as apologist praise of the culture industry. What has been creatively and meaningfully disturbing about couples in mass entertainment is still disturbing when strong heterogeneous production conditions allow for spontaneity or the rare burst of intelligence. However, the couples created by film and television who mindlessly and, worse, passionlessly reproduce tired old cliches about men and women far outnumber the wonderful creations that have been the subject of this study. This will be eternally true in an industry devoted to profit and fearful of either offending or provoking potential customers. Yet that is no reason for serious thought about the media to overlook the more adventurous manifestations of the screen couple. In the history of mass entertainment, the screen couple has taken many interesting forms, including that of the alluring formulaic fantasy that is the Iconic Couple, the disturbing yet fascinating representation that is the Synergistic Couple, and the moderately exploratory vehicle for ideas that is the Thematic Couple.

Certainly in the most pedestrian of screen couples, the ever and increasingly present Functional Couple, we see reflected tiresome old ideas that we have been conditioned to accept as normal; they reflect our platitudes, easily expressed, and give us the false comfort that the world is a stable place. In the Iconic Couple, we often see received standard-issue gender ideas tediously dressed up and unimaginatively glamourized. In Thematic Couples, however, we see a tentative scrutiny of society and its mores that make widely accessible some more innovative thinking: Cosby and Rashad, Willis and Shepherd, Newman and Woodward offer vivid performances of edited but nevertheless moderately expanded ideas on racism, sexism, and social power. And in the most impressive of the screen couples, the Synergistic Couples, we see reflected our inner, often inexpressible, understanding of the limitations of our ideas about intimacy and the consequent problems attendant on its fit with society. Implicating the unnameable subconscious resonances set off by sound and visual image with the logic of plot and dialogue, the screen couple at its best, in the form of the Synergistic Couple, pulsates with chemistry and forges for the mass audience and in the mass audience a contemplative and passionate experience of the paradoxes of human connection. At the same time, we see reflected our often inexpressible faith in the enduring, unlabeled intimate energies that cluster about the bizarre structures we call civilization. This is fascination, and we don't tire of such couples, hoping for more movies and series episodes, and granting all of them multiple viewings that in many cases transcend the time in which they were produced. The fascination is our deepest selves set before us in all their loveliness, ineffability, and tantalizingly oxymoronic qualities, mysteries regained both because of and in spite of all the limits, obstacles, and detours created by culture.

Once, in the films of the studio system era, the most expressive couple figures suggested that intimacy functioned in society as a regenerative force. The uncanny power of the dancing of Astaire and Rogers, of the natural links forged between Tarzan and Jane, of the ability of Nick and Nora to dispel mysteries of avarice and inhumanity, and of the courage of Tracy and Hepburn in the face of social injustice all mitigated the effects of culturally and subconsciously instigated greed, rigidity, and rapacious self-interest. Today, the couple figure at its most expressive still speaks to large audiences about the part that intimacy plays in society, but depicts it as part of an ongoing, possibly unresolvable struggle. The Allen/Keaton, Scully/Mulder, and Luke/Laura figures are part of a persistent dialogue, disguised as fantasy, with a universe of swerves, paradoxes, and inexplicable distortions, in which the momentum shifts dramatically all the time. They are part of the dialogue between the creative community of the mass media and the mass media audience in which the larger unfathomable forces that move the collaborative media creative process meet with the unknown desires of the public (which does not know what it wants until it finds itself compelled), and they are caught up in two blind, struggling, interlocking aspects of the same search for truth. Popular fantasy can be one genuine kind of mediator of these forces and desires.

In a general statement about the link between identity and economics, Jacques Attali has proposed the following paradox: "No organized society can exist without structuring differences at its core. No market economy can develop without erasing the differences in mass production."[17] He might have been talking about the paradox of the chemistry of the movie couple. The American media conceal and reveal.

APPENDIX One
FRED, GINGER, AND RKO

The production history of the Astaire/Rogers series tested the limits of collaborative heterogeneity under the studio system. It is one of the major tributes to the polyphony of that system, which made major contributions to mass culture by fostering the creative warfare of difference such that the deadening influences of control by the conventional ideas of any one faction was rarely an option. Astaire and Rogers were two uneasily paired actors who had, paradoxically, both indelible professional conflicts and uncanny professional affinities, as each struggled with volcanic ambition, imbalances caused in great part by their asymmetrical positions of power both within the production team and within the studio, and fierce mutual pride-in-work and perfectionism.

The details of the early lives of Astaire and Rogers, well documented in their separate autobiographies, reveal the disjunctions and parallels from which their complicated relationship arose. Both Astaire and Rogers came from working-class families, both were swept by their mothers into show business careers, both left behind fathers who could not be included in their mothers' ambitious dreams, Rogers's father because he was an abusive alcoholic, and Astaire's father because, according to the diary of Astaire's sister Adele, although he wanted to go on stage too, his wife, Ann, forced him to take a more dependable job to support the family. But the relationships of the two to their mothers were tellingly divergent.[1] Astaire was always under pressure to please his demanding mother and satisfy her desire for social status, while Rogers was the focus of her mother's ambitious adoration. Rogers's mother, Lela McMath Rogers, as self-appointed guardian of her daughter, hurled herself against whatever powers might be with such ferocity that even the fact of her lack of official leverage did not stop her from shielding Rogers to an impressive extent. She taught Rogers to be resilient, persistent, and proud, as an individual, but not in terms of social and economic class. Astaire's mother, Ann Austerlitz (Astaire's birth name), on the other hand, drove her son to break the waves *for her,* which required not only commercial success but also a rise in social status. She arranged for a valet for him when he was quite young and made clear to him that other actors and dancers were not suitable company. In response, he learned to dress himself according to standards of English haberdashery, which he acquired in part by befriending Edward VII, Prince of Wales, and married a very proper English girl.

Perhaps the most erotic Synergistic Couple brought to the screen by Hollywood, Astaire and Rogers each had unsettled sexual lives that were much involved with maternal pressures. As a young man, Astaire had to cope with his mother's burdensome emotional demands. In a letter to Adele, he voices in confidence the anguish to which he never gave public voice, not even in his memoirs. The letter refers to Phyllis Potter, the Englishwoman he eventually married:

> Damn it—it's all so difficult and unfair Delly—and I *don't want to lose* this *girl.* If she gets away for a time anything can happen. All the girls that I've liked in the past have gone off and married—one can't expect them to wait forever—not that I want [sic] any of those in the past. 'Cause I never asked any girl to marry me until *this one* and I mean it. . . . Mother is so difficult at times—she'll have a fit I suppose if I get married to anybody within the next ten years. I don't know what she expects me to do—keep a couple of tarts or play with myself . . .[2]

The complexity of the situation becomes clearer in an early letter from Astaire to Adele, and from Adele's later diary entries. In a letter written in 1933, probably just before Astaire married Phyllis Potter, he fends off his sister's possessiveness: "Freddie is doing alright babe—please don't try to inject an inferiority complex into me by suggesting I cannot get *along without* [double underline] mother. . . . Lord knows I miss her terribly Delly but I know it's not good for her and *for me* [double underline] to think that ma *has to be with me in these shows* . . ."³ In later diary entries after the death of her husband, Adele makes it clear how ingrained her possessiveness of her brother remains. She still wants to have Astaire all to herself, wishing that he were homosexual—a "faggot," as she phrases it—so that she would never have had to share him with another woman. Adele's comments, facetious and rooted in her profound loneliness, touch on one of Astaire's early fears, of which she knew. But Astaire took the gamble and succeeded, probably because of the class issue. In many ways, Rogers never broke away from her mother, although she became sexually active early and remained so. Rogers continually asserted her independence from her mother in sporadic liaisons with men, but either her choices made her mother's disapproval of Ginger's forays into matrimony self-fulfilling predictions, or Lela's powerful connection with her daughter left no real opportunity for a strong, permanent alliance with a husband.

The onscreen chemistry of Astaire and Rogers had some anchor in a brief offscreen romantic reality. They met in New York City when Rogers was working in *Girl Crazy* in 1930, and Astaire, helping out with the choreography, dated her. Rogers's autobiography, the only documentation of this period in their lives, is provocatively vague. It is hard to determine how often they saw each other and how intense they became, but her own giddy excitement about dating him is clear. That they were sexually attracted and involved is also clear; probably they were lovers. Certainly they had an asymmetrical view of each other. Rogers, oblivious to class and status, believed that had she not left New York to make movies in Hollywood, they could have been "a serious item." Astaire's book omits any speculation about romance and any reference to its intermittent appearance in their lives. The brutal probability is that this suppression had its roots in his class consciousness; he probably thought of Rogers as the kind of girl he mentioned in his letter to Adele, who would do as a "tart" he might keep in order to satisfy both his needs and his mother's refusal to let go of him. Rogers was not of the class his family ordained him to marry into. This kind of attitude was betrayed by Astaire when he and Rogers met again in Hollywood. "Fred looked the same but acted differently. He was not as open, far more formal. I felt I didn't even know him. As if to explain his behavior, he said, 'I'm a married man now.'"⁴ The subtext of a sexual history seems clear here; it's unlikely that he would have made such a point had they shared nothing more than a kiss. With marriage came the end of his need for side dishes.

The most brutal fact about their partnership, however, is that only the fraught stalemate enforced by the collaborative studio structure made possible the continued teamwork of Astaire and Rogers. Had either of them had the final say, they would have gone their separate ways. Astaire/Rogers was always in danger of fragmenting, primarily because Astaire resisted it strenuously, but ultimately also because Rogers got fed up with a constant lack of appreciation. When Astaire heard that *Rio* had been a hit and that RKO was contemplating a new film of which he would be the star along with Ginger Rogers, he roared angrily in a letter to his agent Leland Hayward:

> What's all this talk about me being teamed with Ginger Rogers? I will *not* have it Leland—I did not go into pictures to be *teamed* with her or anyone else, and if that is the program in mind for me I will not stand for it. I don't mind doing another picture with her but as for this *team* idea it's *out*! I've just managed to live down one partnership and I don't want to be bothered with any more. I'd rather not make any more pictures for Radio [RKO] if I have to be teamed up with one of those "movie queens." This is no flash of temperament on my part Leland. . . . I'm just against the idea—that's all and feel that if I'm to get anywhere on the screen it will be as one not two.[5]

Astaire's reference to Rogers as a "movie queen" is odd because she was hardly that in 1933. She was a workhorse who was sent from production to production to maximize her cost-effectiveness to RKO, with barely a moment to breathe between projects. But Astaire was not just letting off steam in expressing his reluctance to work with her. Three days later he instructed his agent, Leland Hayward, to "*squelch* the idea of *teaming* me with Rogers."[6] Neither the studio nor Astaire's agent was impressed with his emphatic tone. Hayward lied to him quite blatantly, reassuring him that

> I don't think R.K.O. [has] any intention of teaming you with Ginger Rogers. When Pandro Berman came through New York on his way West from Europe . . . I talked to him several times about "The Gay Divorcee" which they were negotiating for at that time, and told him you were not terribly keen to play forever and ever with Ginger Rogers. Pandro said there was nothing obligatory

about having you do same. . . . if you felt so vehemently about not having her with you, they probably would not use her. However, they have no intention of making it a permanent team.[7]

Hayward did wire Berman about Astaire's objections, but the return telegram is unequivocal. The studio wanted Astaire and Rogers together for as long as the customers would pay to see them. "Tell Astaire to hold his water with regard to teaming. He is not yet ready to be a star in his own right and if we want to bolster him with good support for next few pictures think he should thank us. Ginger Rogers seems to go rather well with him and there is no need to assume we will be making permanent team of this pair except if we can all clean up lot of money by keeping them together would be foolish not to."[8] In *Steps in Time*, Astaire suppresses the entire incident, saying that when Leland Hayward told him he was going to work with Rogers in *The Gay Divorcee* "the plan seemed very good to me and I waited Berman's arrival anxiously."[9] However, RKO was only able to keep Astaire with Rogers by promising him a percentage of the profits from the Astaire/Rogers films, while she remained on her featured-player—the second step on the studio ladder and just above a contract player—salary.[10]

Even on the Astaire/Rogers set, Rogers did not receive the kind of respect given to Astaire. Rogers had to contend with a good deal of humiliation and abuse from Mark Sandrich, who directed five of the ten Astaire/Rogers musicals. Sandrich was in awe of Astaire, but, in Rogers's words, regarded her as a "clothes hanger who could dance sometimes, sing upon occasion, and perhaps make the leading man smile at me."[11]

Yet there is nothing simple about Astaire's enormous influence on the professional achievements of the team. He was not the paragon of self-confidence he appeared to be. And this further complicated his fraught relationship with Rogers. He seems to have been deeply wounded by his first professional experiences, as a very young dancer, and then as a young man, when he was regarded as "only" Adele Astaire's younger brother, who at first did not live up to his mother's high expectations as the subordinate member of the dancing team into which she had organized them. Adele was the main attraction, and when Adele married into the British aristocracy, he faced a crisis in his career, which his careful cultivation of calm insouciance hid, for the American press vocally mourned the absence of his sister. Despite the outright praise, the unusual creative control, and the substantial financial remuneration he received in Hollywood, astonishingly, Astaire gave evidence that some part of him always felt like a second-rate dancer. Vincente Minnelli phrased it this way: "He lacks confidence to the most enormous degree. . . . He will not even go to see his rushes. He'll stay out in the alley and pace up and down and worry and collar you when you come out and say, 'How was so and so?' . . . It would be much simpler if he would go and look at them himself, you know, but he always thinks he is not good."[12] Alan Jay Lerner recalls a time when Astaire came over to him, "threw a heavy arm around my shoulder and said: 'Oh Alan, why doesn't someone tell me I cannot dance?' The tormented illogic of his question made any answer insipid, and all I could do was walk with him in silence."[13]

These insecurities, as well as the economic and managerial instability of RKO, compounded the complexity of Astaire and Rogers's personal feelings and threatened the continuity of their partnership during the entire time they danced together. Given any creative control, neither would have attained the creative heights they attained together. Certainly when Astaire finally forced RKO to give him casting approval of his leading lady, the results were unfortunate. For *Damsel in Distress*, he chose Joan Fontaine, who had the requisite delicate looks and demeanor of the English lady, exactly the sort of woman he would have chosen for *The Gay Divorcee*, even though she could neither sing nor dance, exactly the sort of woman whom his mother regarded as the right sort of person. Right for mama, but wrong for the screen: the two had no screen chemistry and the film was a patent failure for Astaire. Yet this was the kind of lifeless choice he continued to make. Though in his future partnerships he chose actresses who could dance and sing, he continually opted for women whom he could control as he could not control Rogers, suggesting the frightening quality of the chemistry he had with Rogers, which he never again dared to engage once he was unconstrained by studio authority. Never again did Rogers risk such emotional danger either. And never again did either do anything that went very far beyond transcended cliche, despite their enduring talents and skills.

As long as they could be held together, however, the actual development of the material for the Astaire/Rogers films was fraught with creative clashes, buoyed by the extraordinary vitality of spontaneity, planning, and the role of the many voices of the Hollywood creative community. Astaire did the pre-production work on the

Astaire/Rogers dances. He recalls having about a month before Rogers came on board to work out ideas. His work method was improvisational: "For a couple of days we'd [Astaire, Rogers, and Hermes Pan] stand in front of a mirror and fool around.... Then suddenly I'd get an idea ... or one of them would get an idea.... So then we'd get started."[14] Rogers recalls six weeks of rehearsal for about eight hours a day of preparation that neither producer Berman nor director Sandrich monitored.[15] Atypically for dancers, but typically for Astaire, he even gave instructions to the songwriters about what kind of music he wanted to choreograph in a given narrative situation. For the "Swing Time Waltz" in *Swing Time*, Jerome Kern asked "Freddie what he wanted."[16] He even called the shots about how he and Rogers were to be photographed. As Astaire tells it, "for a while" he used three cameras that were to shoot simultaneously from different angles, "... but I gave that up. I'm instrumental in making them give it up, because I just didn't like the way it works out that way. It's much better to come over and get it all fresh from another angle."[17] In order to facilitate the single camera strategy, a special mechanism was developed called the Astaire Dolly:

> It was on tiny wheels with a mount for the camera that put the lens about two feet above the ground. On it rode the camera operator and the assistant who changed the focus ... Fred always wanted to keep the camera in as tight as possible, and they used to shoot with a 40 millimeter lens, which doesn't give you too much leeway. So every time Fred and Ginger moved toward us, the camera had to go back, and every time they moved back, the camera went in. The head grip who was in charge of pushing this thing was a joy to watch. He would maintain a consistent distance, and when they were in the middle of a hectic dance that was quite a stunt.[18]

Later, Astaire's fastidiousness led to inflexible, virtuosic dancing and pedestrian dancing partnerships, but with respect to his work with Rogers, Astaire's attention to detail worked well with her spontaneity. Rogers might have chafed under Astaire's protective veneer of personal superiority, but her 1936 account of his perfectionism is full of respect: "I thought I knew what concentrated work was before I met Fred, but he's the limit.... He may get a hunch in the middle of the night.... Ask the boys around the studio. They never know what time of night he'll call up and start ranting enthusiastically about a fresh idea."[19] He demanded perfection of himself and his coworkers, chewing them out immediately and then rushing to smooth things out. Working on the number "Top Hat, White Tie, and Tails," he snapped a cane in half with frustration about a mistake, throwing the props people into a panic, because they had only one extra. Perhaps, however, the key to his brilliance was not simple, unadorned perfectionism but the unlikely, exciting combination of perfectionism and what he called his "outlaw style." Rather than being the conventional perfectionist dedicated to pure forms of dance, he was wildly eclectic, producing what John Mueller has eloquently described as "an odd and singularly unpredictable blend of tap (making use, however, of the entire body) and ballroom with elements from other dance forms worked in." His mercurial use of transitions in his choreography are described even more trenchantly—and admiringly—by Rogers from the point of view of a partner who was involved in joining him in his terpsichorean flights: "Just try and keep up with those feet of his sometime! Try and look graceful while thinking where your right hand should be, how your head should be held, and which foot you end the next eight bars on. . . . Not to mention those Astaire rhythms. Did you ever count the different tempos he can think up in three minutes?"[20]

On his part, he was receptive to her spontaneous ideas, though he does not credit her in his public statements for all she contributed. She helped director George Stevens out when she came up with the idea of using whipped cream to simulate shampoo when Astaire sang "Just the Way You Look Tonight" in *Swing Time*. She came up with a number of the most famous touches for the dances that Astaire embraced and used. She thought up a comic routine for the two of them during "I'm Putting All My Eggs in One Basket" in *Follow the Fleet* in which Rogers would get stuck doing a dance step and Astaire would try to snap her out of it. She came up with the idea of doing the dance to roller skates during "Let's Call the Whole Thing Off" in *Shall We Dance*. She thought up the delicious climax of "The Yam" in *Carefree*. To fill in sixteen bars of music at the end of the number she suggested, "We could put the tables in close enough together to form a semicircle, I can execute a series of leaps [over Astaire's leg propped in succession on each table] and it will fill the sixteen bars with a flying-in-the air routine." She suggested that they dance to "No, No They Can't Take That Away from Me" in *The Barkleys of Broadway*.[21]

Outright warfare did break out between this fastidious man and this exuberantly intuitive woman, particularly about her costumes, which Rogers supervised to the nth detail. The brilliance that her dresses has added to the onscreen image of the pair validates her willingness to realize her ideas in ways that very nearly called for her to step over Astaire's (or someone's) dead body.[22] The most famous of these face-offs was over the feathered dress she wore for "Cheek to Cheek" in *Top Hat*. In his autobiography, Astaire records the clash in his characteristically low-key manner, while in hers Rogers is characteristically more vivid on the subject. Astaire retells the story as an amusing incident in which he was somewhat inconvenienced by the feathers floating off the dress, linting his dark tux and, he feared, littering the dance floor. "It got to be funny after a while. The news went all over the lot that there was a blizzard on the *Top Hat* set." That night, according to Astaire, he and Hermes Pan playfully parodied "Cheek to Cheek" to commemorate the incident:

Feathers—I hate feathers—
And I hate them so that I can hardly speak,
And I never find the happiness I seek
With those chicken feathers dancing
Cheek to cheek.[23]

In her book, Rogers comments, "Instead of 'Cheek to Cheek,' the song should have been called 'Horns to Horns.'"[24] Yet only four days after the extraordinarily beautiful rushes were screened, perhaps because his immaculate professionalism forced him to recognize the texture added to the dance by the contested dress, perhaps simply to regain a modicum of peace on the set, or perhaps for both reasons, he gave her a gold charm in the shape of a feather for her bracelet with a note that read: "Dear Feathers, I love ya! Fred."[25] This indeterminate respect-rivalry never really ended.

Beyond personal, studio, and creative disputes, the PCA loomed from the first as another obstacle to making the first film co-starring Astaire/Rogers, *The Gay Divorcee,* which almost died before it was born when the PCA objected to the premise of the film and the original title, which although comic in nature violated the prime directive of the PCA that never was the sanctity of marriage to be mocked. The PCA file on *The Gay Divorcee* reveals that in addition to the objections to the title, the Hays office had three major issues with the film: the plot premise of what they called a "fixed divorce"; the lyrics of the song "Let's K-knock K-knees"; and the stereotypical Italian represented as the professional correspondent. The PCA was initially adamant that the musical made fun of the institution of marriage by basing its entire plot on the fun of watching a woman fake a basis for divorce, and its threats to withhold approval delayed production. The obvious light-heartedness of the fantasy eventually protected the film from the PCA's objections, but not before an extraordinary number of memos were exchanged and a series of negotiations were carried out within which producer Pandro S. Berman finally was able to convince Jason Joy, Joe Breen, and Will Hays of what had been obvious from the beginning. The case against the plot premise was stated in a memo that now seems ludicrous for its stern, serious despair regarding the making of such a movie. The premise of the movie, according to the memo, presents "grave difficulties." "While admittedly a broad farce comedy, the theme of this play, as well as its particular incidents and lines seem [sic] to me to make it impossible of picturization [sic]." Not long after this memo Berman requested permission to speak with the PCA about this matter: "In reference to our conversation regarding *Gay Divorcee* I would appreciate it if you would allow me to tell somebody in your organization exactly why I should be able to make this. I consider it perfectly beyond reproach from both our angle and yours, and I am sure you would feel likewise had you seen the play and the lightness of handling this theme." Apparently, Berman was able to make his point, because on February 1, 1934, Joe Breen wrote to Merrian C. Cooper at RKO to clear the picture for production, since "it is your plan to treat this play as a broad comedy, and to exercise your usual great care in the writing of the dialogue." The speed with which the impossible became possible is telling. The PCA must have seemed formidable initially as it spewed forth its memos, but in the final analysis, it did not have bigger teeth than Astaire, or Berman, or Rogers, or the writing staff in this instance. It was only one force, and not an indomitable one in the negotiations by which popular culture was created.

That impression is only strengthened by a brouhaha almost as hilarious as the misrecognitions in the movie that lasted several weeks when the PCA became nervous about the lyrics of a song in the movie that was actually called "Let's K-knock K-knees" but that had somehow been misspelled in the documents they had, or misread, as "Pets Knock Knees." In a series of perfectly serious memos, the PCA dunned the production team of *The Gay Divorcee* with requests to see the lyrics of "Pets Knock Knees," which they claimed they couldn't find in the script pages that had been sent to them. The lengthy fuss made over the song is hard to understand in any other way than that the principals at the PCA did not actually read what was sent to them. The song was placed in the seaside resort in which almost all of the action of the movie takes place and was meant to define the atmosphere of freewheeling flirtation of the place. Sung by Betty Grable as an invitation to Edward Everett Horton to join her in the merrymaking going on, there was not a pet anywhere in sight, and it should have been clear to anyone reading the script that "pets" had to be a misspelling. The failure of the PCA to understand that they were dealing with a typo rather than a moral scandal produced a farcical self-satire that just about summed up the ineptitude of the PCA stewardship over the values of the movies. The memos grew increasingly irate about having the requested lyrics "withheld" from the PCA until they discovered their error. Without missing a beat, or acknowledging their misreading, on discovering the true title, and perusing the lyrics, the following telegram signed by a J.K. informed the liaisons between the PCA and RKO that "WE HAVE DEFINITELY REJECTED RKO'S SONG TITLE LETS KNOCK KNEES [sic] WILL YOU KINDLY INFORM MR. BREEN DR. WINGATE OR ANYONE ELSE IN THE OFFICE THERE WHO SHOULD KNOW REGARDS JK." But by August 4, 1934, the lyrics had been approved by the PCA, with several changes. The following constitutes the offensive language that was excised from the film:

> You are so unforgettable
> Oh tell me are you pettable
> Do take some liberties
> And let's k-knock k-knees.

as well as the following:

> Here's my address—here's my keys
> Let's k-knock k-knees.

The PCA, however much annoyance they caused for Pandro Berman, who had to field all their objections, may have taken out a line here and there, but had almost no effect on the collaboration of Astaire and Rogers.

APPENDIX Two
THEORIZING CHEMISTRY IN ENTERTAINMENT VIA NEUROSCIENCE

Many neuroscientists are offering strong proof that in our daily lives the healthy, functioning mind makes meaning by a process anchored in the sensuous image produced by collaboration between the subconscious and the body. According to these theories, it is this collaboration that enables us to make judgments and decisions repeatedly during the day. Neuroscientists warn us that our erroneous belief that reason is dominant in the making and receiving of meaning has skewed our understanding of reality. If these theoreticians are correct, then they provide, among many other things, a framework for separating the healthy from the moribund in mass culture. Commercial entertainment that emerges from a fully collaborative process energized by an all-out struggle among competing viewpoints would be, by these lights, a wholesome form of popular representation, a healthy source of popular explorations of ordinary life, as opposed to the sterile, escapist popular fantasy that emerges when formula controls the process. The question of what "fully collaborative" means using these theories of neuroscience hinges on the role of formula in the composition process of mass entertainment. Surprisingly, the issue is not whether rationalized formula enters the process, but at what point and in what capacity. The latest neuroscience theories propose that conflict between some form of logos and the emotional energy or image, not control by reason (which is always some form of convention or cliche) is the necessary precondition for intelligent thought and conduct; according to these theories, lacking that conflict, the perceiver is in a mental state comparable to that produced by a lobotomy. Applying this idea to the movies, we can explore the irritant of formula at the most productive end of the creation process as a catalyst for authentic expression, while intrusion of formula at the wrong end of the process can be explored as a lobotomization of popular culture.

A clarification of the relationship between formula and energy in mass culture can be gained by the theoretical discussion of a seminal relationship between non-rational image and rational logic in effective thinking, the formation of judgments, and the ability to implement plans in the work of neuroscientist Antonio R. Damasio. In his two book-length studies, *Descartes' Error: Emotion, Reason, and the Human Brain* and *The Feeling of What Happens: Body and Emotion in the Making of Consciousness*, Damasio constructs a portrait of the human mind, the logic of which demands that we understand that although we process image and logic separately, their integration through complex, diffuse (rather than hierarchical) interfaces is the ground of intelligibility. The model proposed by Damasio merits further exploration here, as it is intended as a reference point for understanding the relationship between Synergistic Couple chemistry and Hollywood formulas in the production of meaningful portraits of intimacy, courtship, love, and marriage.

Damasio's work is germane to the way we understand Hollywood film because Hollywood's powerful images have routinely been castigated as forms of destructive seduction. Damasio suggests that compelling image may well be the foundation of healthy thinking. According to neuroscientists like Damasio, the biological process by which thinking takes place is *facilitated*—not seduced—by images that are based in an internal experience of body state.[1] In fact, Damasio likens the working of the healthy, productive mind to a movie, in which the many tracks of image, sound, logic (augmented by the senses of touch, smell, and taste, which are not part of the film) interface to make meaning.[2] It may be that at least as central to the making of meaning in the cinematic experience is the role for image explored by neuroscientists, who have come to the conclusion that rationality is impotent and incoherent without the collaboration of a pre-verbal, emotional, image-based part of the brain. This is not to say that we need to feel after we think, or that pleasure experienced in pre-cortical faculties accompanies thinking, but that human logic is *incapable* of coming to conclusions, judgments, or decisions to act without the constant, simultaneous interplay between reason and the images produced by the pre-cortical, emotional part of the brain. The crucial issue seems to be the part of the cycle of thinking in which image plays a role. Image that precedes reason and generates logic seems to create healthy possibilities (as in the case of the Synergistic Couple) while the primacy of logos and reason seems to guarantee frustration and meaninglessness (as in the case of the Iconic Couple).

The seminal case for the interdependence of image and logos in the thought process and the primacy of image is the dramatic industrial accident that destroyed the life of Phineas Gage in 1848. Phineas Gage, a twenty-five-year-old foreman for the Rutland and Burlington Railroad, was supervising a gang of men laying track across Vermont when a charge of explosive powder he had planted to blast away rock from the path of the track blew up in his face, sending an iron rod through his left cheek, piercing the base of his skull from the front of his brain through the top of his head.[3] Gage walked away from the accident and appeared to be cured in less than two months. However, where he had formerly been a pleasant, temperate man, he was now brutal and bad-tempered, unable to form judgments, unable to follow through on plans: he was unable to hold a job or to marry and start a family. This case has become evidence that is in the process of rocking the foundation of the Western traditions regarding human intelligence. His social conduct had been affected so devastatingly by a trauma that had not affected the reasoning part of the brain but instead had affected that part of the brain associated with image making and feeling. The accident had caused no damage to the cortical part of the brain, the part responsible for language, memory, perception, and attention. It had ravaged the frontal lobes, part of the pre-cortical system associated with the "lesser" functions, which were thought to be expendable in the serious business of making meaning.[4] In hindsight, we now know he had undergone a horrible, inadvertent lobotomy. Since then, similar accidents causing similar trauma have been examined, and it is clear that lobotomy is a permanent foreclosure of rational, not irrational, behavior.

Working from this and many subsequent cases in which damage to the frontal lobes appears, Damasio has concluded the following: "Basically in the high reason view you take different scenarios apart and to use current parlance you perform a cost/benefit analysis of each of them. Keeping in mind 'subjective expected utility,' which is the thing you want to maximize, you infer logically what is good and what is bad. . . . Now, let me submit that if this strategy is the only one you have available, rationality, as described above, is not going to work..."[5] While attention and working memory are limited in their capacity, the "key components unfold in our minds instantly, sketchily, and virtually simultaneously, too fast for the details to be clearly defined."[6] From his research, Damasio has concluded that it is the somatic elements (feeling, emotion, body) in us, thought to be solely pre-cortical and thus below thought, that actually engage the cortical processes effectively by marking out details for our attention. Thus Damasio claims that "in the end, if purely rational calculation is how your mind normally operates, you might choose incorrectly and live to regret the error, or simply give up trying, or simply give up trying in frustration."[7] In sum, no normal mind does operate in a purely rational way. The pre-cortical part of the brain containing the potential for feeling and emotion, long assumed to be inferior to the cortical functions, must be activated before thinking can become effective.

Perhaps even more radical is the role that the body plays in the functions of the well-ordered mind. Damasio proposes that the ability of the mind to continually ground itself in body state is a crucial part of the activation of pre-cortical faculties in the process of making meaning. Body awareness has long been evaluated as an impediment to the life of the mind. Damasio maintains the converse, postulating the body as the source of the capacity to create image, the buttress of logical thought. Within this framework, image is a true part of consciousness, the loam of intelligent consideration, and the sign of the wholeness of body and mind, since it is image that makes the conclusions of mind possible. The imaging energies of the body, says Damasio, "when represented back to the brain, constitute what I see as the bedrock of the sense of being alive."[8] Further, "Developing a mind... really means developing representations of which one can be made conscious as images..."[9]

Theoretically, then, neuroscience provides a framework within which the powerful onscreen chemistry of the Synergistic Couple in counterpoint with the formulaic studio system plot can be examined as the necessary conditions for the creation of meaning, conditions lacking in the Iconic, and certainly in the Functional Couple, where the power of image is so deadened as to threaten the viewer with a range of ersatz experiences that can, in the worst instances, replicate the lobotomized frustrations caused by Phineas Gage's wounds.

NOTES

CHAPTER ONE. AN INTRODUCTION TO THE IMPORTANCE OF COUPLE CHEMISTRY UNDER THE STUDIO SYSTEM

1. David Bordwell, Janet Staiger, and Kristin Thompson, *The Classical Hollywood Cinema* (New York: Columbia University Press, 1985), p. 16.

2. Richard Dyer, "Charisma," in *Stardom: Industry of Desire*, edited by Christine Gledhill (London: Routledge, 1991), pp. 57–60. Dyer, a leading theorist of stardom, provides an important example of earlier thinking about the fascination of the star. He discusses it in terms of charisma, a function of the personality. Using the work of Max Weber and E. A. Shills as his theoretical foundation, Dyer explores the star personality as one "set apart from ordinary men" and as having connection with "some *very central* feature [sic] of man's existence." Dyer links the extraordinary and the central to social ideology—the star's representation, in his or her exceptional person, of "specific instabilities, ambiguities and contradictions in the culture..." By contrast, I am not speaking of charisma in Dyer's sense, but of *chemistry,* an aspect of energy that is not essentially related to personality, but to the synergy between two actors as it is conveyed by camera image. This synergy is not a function of an actual social relationship, nor of ideology. It impacts the audience as an intensity of image. Its relationship to ideology varies, depending on how image is used in a particular film.

3. While most leading men in Old Hollywood were able to eke out at least some screen partnership(s) with co-stars, Gable was extremely adept in this area. He earned his title of The King, making his mark with equal success in all his co-starring assignments with the reigning Hollywood screen queens. He played with Claudette Colbert in only two films—*It Happened One Night* (1934, Dir. Frank Capra) and *Boom Town* (1940, Dir. Jack Conway)—but his partnership with her in the Capra film became a Hollywood romantic classic. Similarly, he was identified as Loretta Young's co-star on the basis of only two films: *Call of the Wild* (1935, Dir. William A. Wellman) and *Key to the City* (1950, Dir.

George Sidney). In his four repeat partnerships in movie series of four films or more—with Joan Crawford, Lana Turner, Jean Harlow, and Myrna Loy—he was able to make the audiences, at least for a time, identify him with each co-star as if they were each an exclusive Hollywood screen couple. The films he made with Joan Crawford are as follows: *Dance, Fools, Dance* (1931, Dir. Harry Beaumont), *Laughing Sinners* (1931, Dir. Harry Beaumont), *Possessed* (1931, Dir. Clarence Brown), *Dancing Lady* (1933, Dir. Robert Z. Leonard), *Chained* (1934, Dir. Clarence Brown), *Forsaking All Others* (1934, Dir. W. S. Van Dyke), *Love on the Run* (1936, Dir. W. S. Van Dyke), *Strange Cargo* (1940, Dir. Frank Borzage). The films he made with Lana Turner are as follows: *Honky Tonk* (1941, Dir. Jack Conway), *Somewhere I'll Find You* (1942, Dir. Wesley Ruggles), *Homecoming* (1948, Dir. Mervyn LeRoy), *Betrayed* (1954, Dir. Gottfried Reinhardt). The films he made with Myrna Loy are *Men in White* (1934, Dir. Richard Boleslawski), *Manhattan Melodrama* (1934, Dir. W. S. Van Dyke), *Wife vs. Secretary* (1936, Dir. Clarence Brown), *Parnell* (1937, Dir. John M. Stahl), *Test Pilot* (1938, Dir. Victor Fleming), *Too Hot to Handle* (1938, Dir. Jack Conway). The films he made with Jean Harlow are *The Secret Six* (1931, Dir. George Hill), *Red Dust* (1932, Dir. Victor Fleming), *Hold Your Man* (1933, Dir. Sam Wood), *China Seas* (1935, Dir. Tay Garnett), *Wife vs. Secretary* (1936, Dir. Clarence Brown), *Saratoga* (1937, Dir. Jack Conway).

4. Gilberto Perez, *The Material Ghost* (Baltimore: Johns Hopkins University Press, 1998). For a superb discussion of the complexity of the documentary aspects of the photographic image see pp. 29–49.

5. David Sterritt, *The Films of Jean-Luc Godard: Seeing the Invisible* (Cambridge: Cambridge University Press, 1999). Sterritt perceptively characterizes Godard as a prime example of a filmmaker for whom actor chemistry is only one more kind of energy, not a special counterpoint to studio-processed images. Godard's aesthetic is so formed by a love of spontaneity that all his images betray the artifice of the narrative he uses: "His work can be understood as a sort of dialectical wrestling match between documentary and fiction, setting fabricated plots and characters against vivid real-world backgrounds" (p. 17). In Hollywood, the chemistry permitted in the film because of the commercial value of the star couple image instigates a comparable kind of violence, albeit not as a function of auteur vision.

6. Charles Affron and Mirella Jona Affron, *Sets in Motion: Art Direction and Film Narrative* (New Brunswick, N.J.: Rutgers University Press, 1995). Affron and Affron document the kinds of questions asked by the set designers in Old Hollywood that led to the inspired visual artifice of the studio system set.

7. The following bibliography of neuroscientific investigations of the connections among emotion, body, image, and reason should prove useful to those interested in this topic: Bernard Baars, *In the Theatre of Consciousness: The Workspace of the Mind* (Oxford: Oxford University Press, 1997); Antonio R. Damasio, *Descartes' Error: Emotion, Reason, and the Human Brain* (New York: G. P. Putnam's Sons, 1994); Gerald Edelman, *Bright Air, Brilliant Fire: On the Matter of Mind* (New York: Basic Books, 1993); Oliver Koenig and Stephen Michael Kosslyn, *Wet Mind: The New Cognitive Neuroscience* (New York: Free Press, 1995); Joseph LeDoux, *The Emotional Brain: The Mysterious Underpin-*

nings of Emotional Life (New York: Simon and Schuster, 1996). Of these, Damasio has been most useful for this study and is discussed in detail in Appendix Two.

8. Gregory Black, *Hollywood Censored* (Cambridge: Cambridge University Press, 1994), pp. 4–5.

9. Jeanette MacDonald and Nelson Eddy made the following eight films together: *Naughty Marietta* (1935, Dir. W. S. Van Dyke), *Rose Marie* (1936, Dir. W. S. Van Dyke), *Maytime* (1937, Dir. Robert Z. Leonard), *Sweethearts* (1938, Dir. W. S. Van Dyke), *The Girl of the Golden West* (1938, Dir. Robert Z. Leonard), *Bitter Sweet* (1940, Dir. W. S. Van Dyke), *New Moon* (1940, W. S. Van Dyke), *I Married an Angel* (1942, Dir. W. S. Van Dyke).

10. Some camp couples in the grand couple tradition—like Ruby Keeler and Dick Powell, and Maria Montez and Jon Hall—live in cultural memory because their repeated collaborations made their exaggerations of formula and stereotype hilarious by dint of sheer re-iteration. Other camp screen couples, like Mae West and W. C. Fields, and Rock Hudson and Doris Day, have commanded their place in film history with absurdly few movies between them. Mae West and W. C. Fields indelibly stamped themselves on public memory with only one film! The Keeler/Powell films are as follows: *42nd Street* (1933, Dir. Lloyd Bacon), *Gold Diggers of 1933* (1933, Dir. Mervyn LeRoy), *Footlight Parade* (1933, Dir. Lloyd Bacon), *Dames* (1934, Dir. Ray Enright), *Flirtation Walk* (1934, Dir. Frank Borzage), *Shipmates Forever* (1935, Dir. Frank Borzage), *Colleen* (1936, Dir. Alfred E. Green). The Montez/Hall films are *Arabian Nights* (1942, Dir. John Rawlins), *White Savage* (1943, Dir. Arthur Lubin), *Ali Baba and the Forty Thieves* (1944, Dir. Arthur Lubin), *Cobra Woman* (1944, Dir. Robert Siodmak), *Gypsy Wildcat* (1944, Dir. Roy William Neill), *Sudan* (1945, Dir. John Rawlins). The West/Fields film is *My Little Chickadee* (1940, Dir. Edward F. Cline). The Day/Hudson films are as follows: *Pillow Talk* (1959, Dir. Michael Gordon), *Lover Come Back* (1961, Dir. Delbert Mann), *Send Me No Flowers* (1964, Dir. Norman Jewison). Cary Grant/Mae West, Jeanette MacDonald/ Maurice Chevalier, and Gene Kelly/Judy Garland—tantalizingly indeterminate in category although extremely popular in their day—are all but forgotten except by aficionados. (Perhaps this applies somewhat less to Kelly/Garland.) However, there is enough interesting disturbance of standard gender roles and standard formulaic stories in the works of all of them to merit detailed analysis, if not enough collaboration to establish them as determining forces in the great couple tradition. The films of Grant/West are *I'm No Angel* (1933, Dir. Wesley Ruggles) and *She Done Him Wrong* (1933, Dir. Lowell Sherman). The films of MacDonald/Chevalier are *The Love Parade* (1929, Dir. Ernst Lubitsch), *Love Me Tonight* (1932, Dir. Rouben Mamoulian), *One Hour with You* (1932, Dir. Ernst Lubitsch), *The Merry Widow* (1934, Dir. Ernst Lubitsch). The films of Kelly/ Garland are *For Me and My Gal* (1942, Dir. Busby Berkeley), *The Pirate* (1948, Dir. Vincente Minnelli), *Summer Stock* (1950, Dir. Charles Walters).

11. Acting teams with heft and historical importance, Groucho Marx/ Margaret Dumont and Judy Garland/Mickey Rooney are well remembered today. Somewhere on the border of camp and iconic, these pairs arguably are so eccentric in nature—particularly Marx/Dumont, who were also integrally

related to the tripartite team of the Marx Brothers—that they have not had the kind of formative influence on the great couple tradition that demands consideration in the present study, though as presences in the history of mass entertainment they are eminently worthy of exploration. The Marx/Dumont collaborations are *The Cocoanuts* (1929, Dir. Robert Florey), *Animal Crackers* (1930, Dir. Victor Heerman), *Duck Soup* (1933, Dir. Leo McCarey), *A Night at the Opera* (1935, Dir. Sam Wood), *A Day at the Races* (1937, Dir. Sam Wood), *At the Circus* (1939, Dir. Edward Buzzell), *The Big Store* (1941, Dir. Charles Reisner). The collaborations of Garland/Rooney are *Thoroughbreds Don't Cry* (1937, Dir. Alfred E. Green), *Love Finds Andy Hardy* (1938, Dir. George B. Seitz), *Babes in Arms* (1939, Dir. Busby Berkeley), *Andy Hardy Meets Debutante* (1940, Dir. George B. Seitz), *Strike Up the Band* (1940, Dir. Busby Berkeley), *Babes on Broadway* (1941, Dir. Busby Berkeley), *Life Begins for Andy Hardy* (1941, Dir. George B. Seitz), *Girl Crazy* (1943, Dir. Norman Taurog).

12. The Hildegarde Withers series is an anomaly in American commercial entertainment, putting its trust in a reversal of fortunes for that most patronized, sentimentalized, and marginalized of characters, the old person. In the Edna May Oliver/James Gleason collaborations, Hildegarde Withers, a scarecrow of a teacher with an Eleanor Roosevelt voice and a Groucho Marx wit, and Oscar Piper, a stringy, knob-kneed old codger of a policeman, play detective games with an enviable lust for life and an unsentimentalized interest in each other that lays waste Hollywood's "old person" cliches and wrests the spotlight from the obligatory, young, glamourous Functional Couple. The films never become quite as iconoclastic as they might in dealing with intimacy in the "golden years," but they are light-years ahead of more recent efforts like *Driving Miss Daisy* (1989, Dir. Bruce Beresford) in suggesting the potentially enduring joie de vivre in the human condition. (Oliver and Gleason were only in their mid-forties when they made the Hildegarde Withers movies, but they appear to be "sixty-something," certainly according to today's expectations about aging.) The Oliver/Gleason collaborations are *The Penguin Pool Murders* (1932, Dir. George Archainbaud), *Murder on the Blackboard* (1934, Dir. George Archainbaud), *Murder on a Honeymoon* (1935, Dir. Lloyd Corrigan). The Pitts/Gleason collaborations are *The Plot Thickens* (1936, Dir. Ben Holmes), *Forty Naughty Girls* (1937, Dir. Edward Cline). The Broderick/Gleason collaboration is *Murder on a Bridle Path* (1936, Dir. Edward Killy).

13. Virginia Wright Wexman, *Creating the Couple: Love, Marriage, and Hollywood Performance* (Princeton: Princeton University Press, 1993). I do not see Hollywood couples as patterns that audience members directly apply to their lives, but rather as images and narratives that are influential by indirection, as mass audiences are stimulated by them to meditate on intimacy. I also believe that Functional, Iconic, and Synergistic Couples have distinctly different effects on their audiences. In contrast, Wexman understands images of romance and intimacy as directly responsible for romantic behavior. "Hollywood film, which has traditionally been addressed primarily to young people, can be seen as an institution that aids in the formation of such [romantic] habits by modeling appropriate courtship behavior" (p. 5). Nor does she differentiate among categories of screen couples. Rather, she assumes that the influences differ

depending on the ideological messages in narrative and image. Primarily, Wexman believes that Hollywood distracts its audiences from the economic implications of marriage by clouding the picture with sexual allusions. Her reading of *Rear Window* (1954, Dir. Alfred Hitchcock) exemplifies her approach. She decries the failure of critics to "establish that the narrative complications that problematize the creation of the couple are sexual rather than economic in nature. In the absence of such a connection Hitchcock's teasing allusions to sexual trauma must be regarded as at best playful titillations and at worst as an attempt to mystify the cultural issues at stake by distracting the audience with provocative hints about sexual complications which sophisticated movie goers will be only too eager to seize upon" (p. 16). The star presence in a romance, according to Wexman, only intensifies the distraction from real cultural issues (pp. 16–19). I am, in contrast, establishing a distinction between the iconic star couple image as distraction and the synergistic star couple image as a force that cuts through narrative cliche.

CHAPTER TWO. JOHNNY WEISSMULLER AND MAUREEN O'SULLIVAN

1. The script conference notes for *Tarzan, the Ape Man* detail W. S. Van Dyke's desire for Jane to be a sophisticated, gutsy heroine and not a typical ingenue. The notes for these conferences can be found in the USC Special Collections and in *W. S. Van Dyke's Journal*, edited and annotated by Rudy Behlmer (Filmmakers, no. 46. Lanham, Md.: Scarecrow Press, 1996), p. 80.

2. Rudy Behlmer, "Johnny Weissmuller: Olympics to Tarzan," *Films in Review* (July–August 1996), p. 26.

3. Ray Nielson, "A Final Interview with Maureen O'Sullivan (1911–1998)," *Classic Images*, no. 278 (August 1998), p. C-12.

4. Behlmer, "Johnny Weissmuller," p. 27.

5. Ibid., p. 24.

6. Nielson, "Interview," p. C-12.

7. Behlmer, "Johnny Weissmuller," p. 30.

8. This information comes from an internet source, as well as from my personal e-mail correspondence with Sheffield in October and November of 1998. winans@ix.netcom.com, October 17, 1998.

9. Esther Williams, *The Million Dollar Mermaid* (New York: Simon and Schuster, 1999), pp. 47–48.

10. Ibid., p. 51.

11. Winifred Aydelotte, "The Miseries of Nudism," *Photoplay* (September 1934), p. 119.

12. Max Horkheimer and Theodor W. Adorno, "The Culture Industry: Enlightenment as Mass Deception," in *Dialectic of Enlightenment* (New York: Herder and Herder, 1972). The Horkheimer/Adorno essay on mass culture is historically specific in nature. Liberally sprinkled with allusions to the way the Nazi influence over the media degraded individuality and expression, it was written during the Holocaust as a cri de coeur against Hitler's Big Lie propaganda machine and as a warning to the "free" world, particularly the United States, against tendencies in its own mass media. As Horkheimer and Adorno later

admitted, their perspective on mass culture at the time had been skewed toward the catastrophic by their horror at the Third Reich. The brilliance of insight in this essay about the potential trivialization of human expression through mass production stands most productively as a description of the excesses of the commercial media and its potential for repression, but the essay should not limit our view of Hollywood to only one aspect of its existence. For example, one of the passages in the essay most pertinent to the present study accurately describes the Hollywood image at its most thoroughly processed, but is utterly blind to Hollywood's potential for spontaneous, raw, originality: "Love is downgraded to romance. And, after the descent, much is permitted; even license as a marketable speciality has its quota bearing the trade description 'daring.' The mass production of the sexual automatically achieves its repression. Because of his ubiquity, the film star with whom one is meant to fall in love is from outset a copy of himself" (p. 140). This may go a long way toward describing the problematic fascination of the Iconic Couple, but it cannot be applied to the liberating, expressively wild energies of the Synergistic Couple.

13. Rudy Behlmer, "Tarzan at MGM," in *The Cinema of Adventure, Romance and Terror*, edited by George E. Turner (Hollywood: ASC Press, 1989). One of the more paradoxical elements of the MGM Tarzan movies is that the Mutia Escarpment, the sacred domain of Tarzan, which does not appear in the Burroughs novels, was named for a black African actor, Mutia Omoolu, who played Trader Horn's faithful "native" gunbearer Rencharo in the relentlessly racist ancestor of the Tarzan films, *Trader Horn* (p. 117).

14. Nielson, "Interview," p. C-12. In response to a question about whether W. S. Van Dyke directed *Tarzan, the Ape Man*, O'Sullivan replied, "He did the first one [*Tarzan, the Ape Man*]. I think he probably picked up a shot or two. Then Jimmy McKay, who was the second unit director, he really did most of the film."

15. Wexman, *Creating the Couple*, emphasizes Hollywood's propaganda for the Nordic Ideal in beauty and its relationship to domination/submission gender relations. Of particular interest to these themes are pp. 47–49, 52–53, 93–96, 140–142.

16. The mechanics of creating African elephants out of Indian elephants and the Tarzan/animal fight scenes are described in detail in Behlmer, "Tarzan at MGM," pp. 119, 121–122, 123, 124, 134–135.

17. Wexman's fascinating analysis of the racism contextualizing the image and narrative function of the land in Hollywood's classical western genre films articulates a situation almost in complete opposition to the representation of land in the MGM Tarzan series. The emptiness of the land, the chaos and mismanagement of the land by Nordic characters tells a convincing story about the racial underpinnings of the western movie (pp. 75–98). In the MGM Tarzan series, the land is emphatically full, and it is the Europeans, with their greedy eyes on profits, who upset its balances and cultures. Particularly interesting is the contrast between Wexman's analysis of how western films depict the difference between the Anglo heroes who want to own land and the cultural "others" (Indians, Latinos) who are already on the land they want to own by creating an "association of the prehistoric with the absence of differentiation"

(p. 78). Thus, Wexman adds immeasurably to our ability to understand the western genre by showing how Hollywood westerns typically validated the seizure of land by the Anglos as they portray the "others" as failing to possess really organized cultures that know how to work the land. Whatever else we may say about the African and animal cultures in the Tarzan films, they are presented as distinct and organized cultures, but beyond that there is also a strong sense that Tarzan models the correct respect for the land and its integrity, quite apart from any work that may be put into it, which ought to be demonstrated by European, African, and animal cultures alike. Wexman refers to the "master of all I survey" shot in western movies, where "the landscape is rendered as an object of discovery by the seer, who is placed in a position of dominance over what is displayed" (p. 78). By contrast, in the Tarzan films, the landscape is not an "object of discovery" but a layered and complex enigma that can never be fully discovered, while Tarzan is never its conqueror. For example, consider the scene in *Tarzan Escapes* where Tarzan arrives to detect the invasion of the Escarpment by trappers. As he stands on a tree limb looking on, he bears witness to invaders that must be repelled. Tellingly, after freeing all the caged animals, Tarzan returns home and tenderly snuggles up to Jane. This is quite unlike the Nordic patriarch, who subdues the woman as he subdues the land.

18. In his on-line correspondence with me over a period of three months, the question that elicited the sharpest response from Johnny Sheffield, who played Boy in the MGM Tarzan series, was about racism in the films. Sheffield categorically and heatedly denied that there was any racism either in the movies or on the set, insisting both that there was no segregation between the white and black actors on the set and that Tarzan *could not* be the kind of person who would judge by skin color. He also maintained that he and Cordell Hickman, who played a black African child unofficially adopted by Tarzan and Jane in *Tarzan's Secret Treasure*, were friends. "Don't be looking for any 'racism' on our set; there wasn't any! We were friends with all our extras and actors. We ate together and worked together. We had some great black extras. Blue Washington, father of Kenny Washington [sic] and Woody Strode come immediately to mind. 'Umagawa Rules and shall apply at all times!' and DID apply on our SET. Can you imagine TARZAN being prejudice [sic] against the natives? Perhaps the Zambizi." (*Umagawa* is a word from MGM Tarzan lore that means anything from "let's go" to the quality of the integrity of all living things.) Sheffield, now a construction contractor in his mid-sixties, was a child of about eight when he became a part of the series in *Tarzan Finds a Son!* and was about eleven when he worked in *Secret Treasure*. He also idealized Johnny Weissmuller, of whom he speaks even today as a second father and with whom he often conflates the character of Tarzan when he speaks about the old days in Hollywood. Thus his testimony may be clouded by youth and romanticism. Nevertheless, it also speaks to the ideals communicated to him when he was a child actor and thus to the best intentions of those around him on the set. Why else would he not have said, as so many others have said about an array of conditions in Old Hollywood, that racism was common at that time?

As for whether the films themselves are racist, the question is far more complex, although there is at least one truly indefensible scene. In *Tarzan's New*

York Adventure, the black janitor of a New York nightclub finds himself in a telephone conversation with someone he cannot understand—it's Cheetah—and assumes he is talking to a fellow African American, screaming finally, "You ain't gettin' fresh with me is you colored boy?"

19. Weissmuller's initial appeal for MGM was his fame as an Olympic swimming champion. The first film, in particular, took every opportunity to display his swimming prowess. Even in 1942, when MGM was publicizing the last O'Sullivan/Weissmuller Tarzan movie, they still depended on his fame as a swimming champion for their public relations campaigns, quoting him in the *Lion's Roar* (no. 10, June 1942) as saying, "First of all, I'm not primarily an actor . . . I am an athlete, and Tarzan is the greatest athlete in fiction." Certainly some publicity person put these words in Weissmuller's mouth to play the Olympic card with the audience. Many of the promotion packets circulated to theaters showing the film depended on his athletic body, touting him as the most perfectly built man in films and recommending that contests be held among male patrons for the man closest to Weissmuller's perfect measurements. This is of interest in terms of gender issues in film. Weissmuller's accomplishments in portraying Tarzan were overlooked in favor of a cynical exploitation of his body in ways predominantly associated with women stars. Interestingly, the *Roar* injects a "fact" amidst its fictions, for some reason admitting that Weissmuller did not really jump from the Brooklyn Bridge as portrayed in *Tarzan's New York Adventure,* adding that no one could survive the jump because of the currents of the East River below.

20. There is a good deal of evidence about the argument over a studio decision to kill Jane at the end of *Tarzan Finds a Son!* In "*Tarzan* at MGM," Rudy Behlmer gives a good account of who held what opinion about Jane's screen demise (pp. 130–132). There is even a picture of Jane's death scene, which was filmed and then removed from the completed movie (p. 134). But there is no evidence about who finally had the authority to make the decision that extended O'Sullivan's screen life as Jane.

21. Ibid., p. 132.

22. Ibid., pp. 132–133.

23. In both *Tarzan, the Ape Man* and *Tarzan and His Mate,* Tarzan takes a stand against the greed and exploitation of Jane's European friends and family, but on the basis of an innate commitment to organic life rather than on any rational understanding of how European-based cultures work. In *Tarzan Escapes,* third film in the series, he only begins to come to grips with the word *money,* and not very successfully, though his congenital defense of the jungle remains effective. Later in the series, when he does understand, Tarzan becomes capable of formulating arguments for his worldview. At first the arguments are indecipherable in English. In *Tarzan Finds a Son!* Tarzan holds a very funny whispered conversation with Boy and Cheetah in mockery of the Europeans when they think they can exploit him for their own venial purposes. At about the same time, he reveals his knowledge of an unidentified African language which he continues to speak in the series. By *Tarzan's Secret Treasure,* Tarzan is ready to theorize the inferiority of money to a direct relationship with organic life. "Gold no good. Tarzan want dinner!" He also articulates his anti-gun policy

for the first time. Most interesting, Tarzan hones his intellectual muscles in a lovely interchange with a German sociologist who proudly speaks of trains that go one hundred miles an hour and that transport people to their destinations faster in order to save time. To all of these, Tarzan asks an iconoclastic "Why?" And finally, "What do with time?" Tarzan wins a point, even if his momentarily speechless enemies continue to implement their devious plans. Finally, in *Tarzan's New York Adventure,* Tarzan finds his voice. He again ponders the use of a big city, a stone jungle, as he calls it, and its frenzy to "save time." He further satirizes conspicuous consumption when he walks into a New York nightclub and says, "Smells like Swahili swamp. Why people stay?" During a court proceeding, when a lawyer tries to demean Tarzan's testimony by asking him if he's read Shakespeare's *Hamlet,* Tarzan makes a fool of the lawyer by demonstrating that the lawyer cannot read the signs of the jungle. He adds, "White man's law lots of words. Jungle law more easy. Man live own life. . . . In jungle, men only kill bad animals. In civilization, men kill good men." Unfortunately, with words come the obligatory PCA platitudes at the end of the movie, as according to the stipulations of the code, Tarzan ends up dutifully conforming to the PCA mandate that "law good."

24. The PCA objections to the Tarzan series are varied and interesting. Among the other objections the Hays office raised, the Tarzan series presented at least one more clear-cut issue for the PCA than any of the other films considered here. Nudity in movies was quite simply prohibited by the code, and there was a nude scene in *Tarzan and His Mate.* There are no documents on file for *Tarzan, the Ape Man,* the previous film, possibly because they have been lost or possibly because the PCA was not as organized in 1932 as in 1934, when it compiled a substantial dossier on the second Tarzan movie. Interestingly a memo on file dated August 3, 1933, detailing a PCA response to a reading of the script for *Tarzan and His Mate* registers no doubts about the film as a potential project. This is significant as another indication of the inconsistency and capriciousness of the Hays office, because even though the script makes clear that Tarzan and Jane are cohabiting without a license, the PCA sounded no serious alarm bells. In another burst of inconsistency, the PCA also warned against the exposure of one of the Englishmen taking a bath, but said nothing about the exposure of Tarzan's body in his loincloth. Women's underwear pushed some buttons, however. Memo author James Wingate, one of the employees who worked for Will Hays and Joe Breen, objects to a scene in which a character holds up a bra and says, "I don't know what you call this—you won't need it anyhow." Wingate also objects to an image of Jane dressing inside a tent seen in silhouette from the outside and to Jane's contented laughter at the end of what is indicated to be a nude swim. The finished film contained some variant of the nude swim in some versions, and in all versions contained the image of Jane in silhouette dressing in her tent, a very contented morning-after smile on her face—never commented on by the PCA—and a contented laugh by Jane during and after the swim, but no line about the bra.

The finished film was condemned by the PCA in a memo of April 12, 1934. The memo also expressed concern about violence against animals. The lions killed in the film were actually being shot to death in front of the camera. They were old and their owners wanted them destroyed in any case, and MGM arranged to have them shot by an SPCA marksman [sic], ostensibly so that the studio could claim that the animals had died quickly and without suffering. The PCA counseled MGM to be even more cautious and get a statement in writing from the local SPCA to forestall any bad publicity. The film opened in late April 1934, but a PCA memo dated August 26, 1935, demands that the shot of Jane dressing in the tent be edited out and states that only a print that does not show the nude underwater scenes will be exhibited.

Rudy Behlmer clears up the mystery of the timing of this memo in "Tarzan at MGM." Behlmer, who had access to the MGM files when they were still stored in a Los Angeles warehouse, relates that in response to the condemnation of *Tarzan and His Mate*, Louis B. Mayer demanded a jury trial, which meant a hearing by executives at his studio and others, and the full membership of the production code office. It took place on April 9, 1934, bringing together representatives from Universal Pictures (Carl Laemmle) and RKO (B. B. Kahane), as well as the upper administration of MGM, including Irving Thalberg and Mayer, the editor of the film, and four members of the PCA. "After a rather animated discussion between the jurors, the representatives of Metro and Mr. Breen, the verdict of this office was sustained by the jury. Thereupon, Mr. Mannix for Metro, suggested some changes in the present sequence: (a) To definitely plan at the start of the sequence that the girl wear some clothes. (b) That several of the shots . . . be deleted either by cutting, or by darkening the print to cloud and confuse the eye [as in *Bird of Paradise*] [sic] . . . the jury agreed that, in the event these changes were made, to again look at the picture and to pass further judgment upon it" (p. 124).

According to Behlmer's best evidence, pursuant to this meeting, three versions of the film were released by MGM, one the original nude print, one with Jane swimming in her Jane costume, and one with Jane swimming topless. The PCA was shown only the print of Jane wearing her full costume and approved it on that basis. However, MGM sent the nude print to some areas of the country, in violation of the code. Eventually, however, MGM was forced to comply and the original eleven-reel film was edited down to nine reels, which suggests that the PCA demanded further deletions as a punitive measure once the violation of the code had been discovered. Only in 1987 was the original made available once more to the public. "A protection master positive (fine grain) of the eleven reel version and a nitrate optical negative of the track were discovered in . . . the MGM archives—but apparently no negative or other prints of the long version are in any of the MGM vaults. The two-minute underwater sequence included in the master positive is the version in which Jane is completely nude rather than a variant. A second print containing the topless version, reportedly from Canada, has been exhibited recently in Los Angeles theaters" (pp. 124, 126).

The consequences of the PCA's unmitigated victory on this issue are hard to evaluate, although there was indisputable immediate aesthetic damage done to the film by the deletions, as the underwater scene is quite lovely visually and was deemed such by the contemporary press. Certainly, the decision had a somewhat chilling effect on future Tarzan films, which never again reached a similarly powerful representation of the innocent eroticism that characterized the Tarzan and Jane relationship. Of course, since the woman in the underwater sequence was not O'Sullivan but a body double named Josephine McKim—like Weissmuller, an Olympic swimmer—if the excision of the scene affected the picture aesthetically, it did not affect the couple chemistry. The censorship was also an inadvertent spur for the series to explore other ways that more directly used the chemistry between Weissmuller and O'Sullivan.

CHAPTER THREE. MYRNA LOY AND WILLIAM POWELL

1. Myrna Loy and James Kotsilibas-Davis, *Myrna Loy: Being and Becoming* (New York: Knopf, 1987), p. 89.

2. Notes for Myrna Loy and James Kotsilibas-Davis, *Myrna Loy*, p. 242. The notes are housed in the Boston University library, Myrna Loy Collection.

3. In *Dialectic of Enlightenment,* their attack on the contemporary mass culture industry, Horkheimer and Adorno address the question of confusion between movies and life, scathingly castigating the movies for blurring the boundaries.

> Real life is becoming indistinguishable from the movies. The sound film, far surpassing the theater of illusion, leaves no room for the imagination or reflection on the part of the audience, who is unable to respond within the structure of the film, yet deviate from its precise detail without losing the thread of the story; hence the film forces its victims to equate it directly with reality. The stunting of the mass-media consumer's powers of imagination and spontaneity does not have to be traced back to any psychological mechanisms; he must ascribe the loss of those attributes to the objective nature of the products themselves, especially to the most characteristic of them, the sound film. (p. 126)

Insofar as the typical mass media film does repress in a significant way imagination and spontaneity, the room left by Loy and Powell in the Thin Man series for their resurgence without the loss of the story is an important fact of Hollywood history.

4. Notes for *Myrna Loy,* p. 209.
5. Loy and Kotsilibas, *Myrna Loy,* p. 88.
6. Ibid.
7. Notes for *Myrna Loy,* p. 234.
8. Loy and Kotsilibas, *Myrna Loy,* p. 214.
9. Ibid., p. 92.
10. Ibid., pp. 91–92.
11. Ibid., p. 89.
12. Notes for *Myrna Loy,* p. 2127.
13. Summary of the plot of *Another Thin Man* may be helpful for the reader in understanding this point. Nick and Nora are called out to the Long Island estate of Colonel McFay because he is receiving death threats seemingly from Phil Church, a known criminal who has recently been released from jail. The threats involve Church's apparent ability to foretell a death in his dreams. While

the police and the Charleses investigate the seeming web of criminal conspiracies, however, the actual perpetrator turns out to be McFay's adopted daughter Lois, who craves immediate possession of her inheritance. She has collaborated with Church because she is in love with him, or perhaps more accurately with the excitement of life on the wrong side of the tracks. Bored with the propriety of the upper class, she nevertheless wants its money to finance her thrills.

14. Wexman, *Creating the Couple*, p. 142.

15. Given the political perspective described in Loy's biography and in the notes for the book, it is ironic that she participated in a film with this kind of isolationist subtext, which at least indirectly supported the unconstitutional harassment of United States citizens by numerous congressional committees from the early 1940s to the early 1950s that were seeking to identify purported Communists in the United States. *Myrna Loy: Being and Becoming* shows that Loy was a persistent adversary of the illegal means used by congressional investigations of Communism in the United States, one example of which was her expression of exasperation about the accusations leveled by Representative Martin Dies and his committee against "people like James Cagney, Fredric March, and Humphrey Bogart.... all good, liberal-minded citizens..." (p. 164). She was a tireless worker for the United Nations during its formative period and was appointed to a three-year term on the National Committee for UNESCO after it was fully established (p. 247).

However, for all her political acumen, Loy did not see the political implications of *The Thin Man Goes Home,* which she described in her autobiography as a very funny movie (pp. 185–186). Loy's blindness to the subtext of her own work, despite her demonstrated courage in facing the reactionary forces in the country and in her industry, suggests how differently Old Hollywood regarded the movies from the way the industry now understands the social ramifications of entertainment.

16. Conversations with a range of screen actors (interviews with prominent soap opera actors Charles Shaughnessy, Terry Lester, and Nancy Lee Grahn; an interview with David Duchovny, a prominent film actor and the star of *The X-Files*; and private conversations with my friend Cynthia King, an aspiring actress just entering the field) all suggest this spectrum. Actors like Shaughnessy and Lester talk of moving into a mode divorced from one's own experience, snapping into a separate psychic space that promotes assumed characteristics of a precise sort. Actors like Grahn, Duchovny, and King speak of going more deeply into one's gut, opening up a psychic space inside oneself from which spontaneous gestures and motivations evolve: in Duchovny's words, "I just try to find the physical and psychic center of the character and radiate out." Julianne Lee, "X Symbol," *Starlog: The X-Files and Other Eerie TV* 1 (December 1995), pp. 35–38.

17. Loy and Powell did not differentiate between their work in the Thin Man series and their collaborations in other films. For them, there was always a sense of a special professional relationship. As quoted in *Myrna Loy,* Powell said generally of his work with Loy that "when we did a scene together, we forgot about technique, camera angles, and microphones. We weren't acting. We were just two people in perfect harmony. Many times I've played with an actress who seemed to be separated from me by a plate-glass window. But Myrna... has the

happy faculty of being able to listen while the other fellow says his lines. She has the give and take of acting that brings out the best" (p. 92). Loy too generalizes a special professional connection, but retains a particular appreciation for their work together in *The Thin Man*: "From that very first scene [in *Manhattan Melodrama*], a curious thing passed between us, a feeling of rhythm, complete understanding, an instinct for how one could bring out the best in the other. In all our work together you can see this strange—I don't know what . . . a kind of rapport. It wasn't conscious. . . . Whatever caused it, though, it was magical, and Woody Van Dyke brought it to fruition in our next picture [*The Thin Man*]— perhaps the best remembered of my hundred and twenty-four features" (*Myrna Loy*, p. 88). This is an excellent characterization of synergy, the opening up of a psychic and physical space between two actors. What I find particularly significant is that once this space is opened, it is experienced by the actors as a continuous rapport whenever they work together regardless of the kind of distinctions in quality and cultural importance made by critics. It is also the case that such a synergy can occur even for actors for whose typical and preferred acting mode is to snap into an external form characterization (see note 16 above). For actors whose typical mode is to open up an inner psychic space (see note 16 above), synergy with a partner is exultation. For more externally motivated actors, like Charles Shaughnessy, a synergistic partner causes a feeling of oppression. When Shaughnessy worked on the soap opera *Days of Our Lives* as part of couple with Patsy (Shane and Kimberly), the power of their professional connection made him restless and uncomfortable. At a certain point, when on public appearance tours excited and enthusiastic fans asked where Kimberly was, an exasperated Shaughnessy would respond, "Kimberly who?" Something of this sort may explain the restiveness of Fred Astaire with Ginger Rogers, despite their extreme success together.

In contrast, when such actors have a professional acting success with a partner with whom they form an Iconic Couple, they don't experience any difference between their work with that partner and other partners despite their knowledge that the public sees a difference. Terry Lester, the original and most seminal Jack Abbott on the perennially popular soap opera *The Young and the Restless*, for example, has described this experience.

CHAPTER FOUR. FRED ASTAIRE AND GINGER ROGERS

1. John Mueller exemplifies the school of criticism that is generally negative in its estimate of the plots of the Astaire/Rogers movies. Of *Swing Time*, Mueller writes that although it "suffers from a rambling, lurching, ill-balanced script, this defect is mitigated by the film's positive qualities: the affecting acting by the leads, the rich and memorable musical score, the splendid Art Deco sets, and, especially, the brilliance of the choreography and the dancing." *Astaire Dancing* (New York: Wing Books, 1985), p. 101. Arlene Croce, another major commentator on Astaire and Rogers, is aware of the plot difficulties in some of the Astaire/Rogers films, but she perceives the organic unity of plot and music in *Swing Time*: "The songs are more tightly interwoven with the script—and with each other—than in any of the other Astaire-Rogers films. . . . Dramatically,

too, the songs establish the scheme from the very first number." *The Fred Astaire and Ginger Rogers Book* (New York: E. P. Dutton, 1972), p. 104. No critic has previously suggested the kind of interconnection between plot and music that I outline in this chapter.

2. Croce takes a narrower view, attributing the omnipresence of inner contradiction and masquerade in the Astaire/Rogers series at least in significant part to Rogers's strengths as an actress: "Almost any Ginger Rogers role is successful to the degree that it reflects the dualism in her personality (tough-vulnerable, ingenuous-calculating) or plays on her curious aptitude for mimicry or fantasy or imposture . . ." *The Fred Astaire and Ginger Rogers Book*, p. 142.

3. David O. Selznik, who took credit for a large number of innovations in Hollywood pictures, wrote a memo on August 30, 1937 expressing anger at Max Steiner, one of the great composers of movie music during the studio system, for his resistance to Selznik's directions about sound track music. Insisting that he had the expertise as well as the authority to guide Steiner, Selznik wrote, "I don't think there is another producer in Hollywood that devotes ten per cent as much time to the score as I do—and it may interest you to know that I was the first producer to use dramatic scores [under dialogue in sound films]." *Memo from David O. Selznik*, selected and edited by Rudy Behlmer (Hollywood: Samuel French), p. 119. Worthy of note, as a brief digression, is that the conventional absence of non-diegetic music at that time was a factor that was helpful to the synergistic Tarzan and Thin Man series. This absence of emotionally manipulated non-diegetic music is most intriguing with respect to the Tarzan series, which is, of all the works under discussion here, most suspect of being shamelessly contrived and manipulative. Surprisingly, though, the emotionally manipulative musical sound track is almost completely absent from MGM's synergistic Tarzan films; even in the later films, when film scoring was the norm, the films are impressively clean of heavy-handed emotional cues in offscreen music. By contrast, the reverse is true of the non-synergistic Tarzan films, including the 1998 Disney cartoon version, which lavishly and reductively employ conventional movie music to heighten the impact of the already oppressively formulaic treatment of the story. However, with the exception of the main title, all the films in the synergistic Tarzan series, including the lesser final two films, tend to use music only within the frame, or diegesis, and most often as it emerges from the African peoples who live in the jungle and the towns abutting it. The sound design of the MGM series tends to be a sophisticated layering of noises in the jungle setting, the many unadorned voices of the live animals forming an especially wild element as a complement to the synergistic chemistry of Weissmuller and O'Sullivan. Tarzan's legendary yell was technically augmented to produce its resonant quality, but, even before Weissmuller had worked with it long enough to do away with the need for electronic amplification, its strangeness, the lack of a verbal or logical translation for what it is and how it affects both the other characters and the audience, renders it a filmic element that complicates as well as serving storyline objectives.

In the MGM synergistic Thin Man series, there is a great deal of music, but again generally from within the context of the social setting Nick and Nora inhabit. The series benefits substantially from the absence of fabricated mood music to artificially stimulate eeriness during suspenseful moments or to sugarcoat the film frame with false cheer, charm, or amorousness during the scenes between Nick and Nora. Such musical sound track prompts are not even employed in the saccharine *The Thin Man Goes Home,* all the more surprising since the defining of emotion by non-diegetic music had already become standard practice by the 1940s. In the last movie of the series, the one exception, the music is usually diegetic; some non-diegetic music wafts in from outside the scene, but this is generally used wittily, in a way that subverts its usually manipulative purposes. One striking example occurs when, in *Song of the Thin Man,* Nick is wandering around a supposedly empty boat at night. There is some non-diegetic music to foster "that creepy feeling," and then a lonesome "three in the morning" jazz melody when Nick is skulking alone in the boat's inner corridor. It turns out, however, that the jazz sounds are really there. A bunch of jazz musicians are jamming in mock elegy for the death of their much-hated band leader.

4. Mueller is representative of those critics who see "Isn't It a Lovely Day to Be Caught in the Rain?" as a mirror dance leading to Rogers's acceptance of Astaire's affection. However, neither Mueller nor his compatriots deal with the question of how and why a mirroring process might result in romantic accord (pp. 80–81). Croce sees this as a challenge dance. She doesn't discuss how and why a challenge evolves into romantic accord, but she does suggest that the excitement of the challenge generates energy for their "ecstatic embrace"—that is, their exuberant pirouette together around the gazebo (pp. 61–62).

5. Croce discusses a fascinating memo that *Top Hat* director Mark Sandrich dictated, but never sent, to producer Pandro Berman concerning the sets for the Lido in the movie: "As the latter part of our picture plays in and around the Lido in Italy, it has occurred to me that we may be able to get some tremendous values if we could have some authentic character scenes and backgrounds photographed in that locale" (p. 75). Croce speculates that Sandrich never sent the memo because he realized that the last thing he wanted to do was remind the audience of Fascist Italy. But many other scenarios are possible and more likely since Hollywood was not exercised about Fascism in 1935. Berman may have walked into Sandrich's office before the memo was sent, and they discussed the issue then and there. (Only David Selznik and the PCA were determined to document all decisions on paper.) What is most significant here is that Sandrich did not seem to understand the importance of artificiality and fantasy to the tone of his film, and that things worked out as they did because of the collaborative nature of the studio system, which prevented any one person from running the show completely.

6. Astaire offered the edict, "Either the camera will dance or I will." He insisted on a minimum of editorial cuts in the filming of his dances to ensure continuity and integrity. Fred Astaire and Bob Thomas, *Astaire the Man the Dancer: The Life of Fred Astaire* (New York: St. Martin's, 1984), p. 112. Mueller also quotes Astaire on this issue, elaborating on the precise rules Astaire applied to editing, including the banning of inserted "foot shots" and reaction shots from the audience watching the dance. *Astaire Dancing,* pp. 27–30.

7. The 180 degree rule: "Typically after a scene is established, an imaginary

line is drawn between the camera and the participants and all subsequent action is shot from only one side of that line." Peter Lehman and William Luhr, *Thinking about Movies: Watching, Questioning, Enjoying* (Fort Worth: Harcourt Brace, 1999), p. 45.

8. Croce has her own version of the inner contradiction of *Swing Time*, which she describes as "a movie about a myth, the myth of Fred and Ginger and the imaginary world of romance they live in. . . . but it is also a middle-class workaday, American world. It is top hats and empty pockets; Fred as a Depression Dandy hopping a freight car . . . The antithetical strain runs through the picture . . . it seems to me the true miracle of the series . . ." *The Fred Astaire and Ginger Rogers Book*, p. 101.

9. Croce calls *Swing Time* an intellectual comedy, "a concept alien to America movies." Ibid., p. 102. I would suggest she senses the same tensions I do but does not use academic vocabulary to enunciate it, nor does she see the intellectual comedy in the majority of the Astaire/Rogers series.

10. Although Lucky emerges from behind the door with lipstick prints on his beaming face, Astaire and Rogers did not kiss off camera. Ginger Rogers, *Ginger: My Story* (New York: HarperCollins, 1991), p. 203. Rogers and Astaire did not kiss onscreen until a dream sequence in *Carefree*, when Sandrich shot Astaire and Rogers lip to lip, in what was barely a kiss, in slow motion to create the effect of the full-fledged kiss that the audience was clamoring for. Rogers recalls that Astaire hated the scene, during which he had no idea what was happening, not knowing what Sandrich had planned; she also notes that Phyllis Astaire was not present, suggesting, as she does all through the book, Mrs. Astaire's jealous nature. In his autobiography, Astaire contradicts the notion that he and Ginger never kissed because his wife didn't approve. "It was my idea to refrain from mushy love scenes, partly because I hated doing them and also because it was somewhat novel not to have sticky clinches in a movie." Fred Astaire, *Steps in Time* (New York: Harper, 1959), p. 233. According to Astaire, both the kiss in *Carefree* and shooting it in slow motion were his idea, and he asked Rogers if she minded "so that we might end this international crisis."

11. Mueller notes that the "Bojangles" number is the only time Astaire ever appeared in blackface "and the number makes some people uncomfortable today." *Astaire Dancing*, p. 108. But though Mueller adds that this number could be considered an homage to Bill Robinson, he claims that Astaire had little regard for the other dancer's work. This conflicts with what I was told by Astaire's widow, Robyn Astaire, who said that Astaire highly esteemed Robinson.

12. The differences between the production number "Goin' to Heaven on a Mule" featuring Al Jolson in *Wonder Bar* (Dir. Lloyd Bacon, 1934) and "Bojangles of Harlem" in *Swing Time* are monumental. Jolson's song is a blatantly patronizing image of the rural black community, rendering the people portrayed as little different from the mule. "Bojangles of Harlem" distinguishes between entertainment and life, portraying the fantasy about Robinson in terms of his role as an entertainer. The theatrical use of blackface is not, by its nature, racist. Portraying it as an artificial mode of representation, as in *Swing Time*, rather than as a naturalized illusion, as in *Wonder Bar*, suggests the theatrical nature of the image, and even the inappropriateness of regarding human nature in terms of skin color.

13. *Roberta* was intended by producer Pandro Berman as a vehicle for Irene Dunne, as Mueller notes in *Astaire Dancing*, p. 65.

14. Rogers, *Ginger*, p. 130. Critics have not missed the particularly spontaneous nature of this number. Croce enthuses over three minutes of "what looks like sheerest improvisation" (p. 47). Mueller endorses Croce's opinion, adding that "part of the illusion [of spontaneity] is created by having the sound recorded live on the set (the usual practice was to dub in the taps later). Though this causes some of the tap sounds to be a bit muffled, it also allows Rogers's little squeals of breathless delight as Astaire swirls her around the dance floor to emerge with exceptional naturalness." *Astaire Dancing*, p. 69. I would suggest that there are documentary elements here that go beyond an *illusion* of spontaneity.

15. Irene Dunne was supposed to play Connie in *Fleet*, as Mueller notes. He thinks Hilliard and Scott an even greater mismatch than Dunne and Scott, though it's hard to believe that he would have preferred Dunne as the forlorn, drab teacher. Ibid., p. 89.

16. When it was supposed that Irene Dunne would take the role of Connie, it was also planned that she would sing "Let's Face the Music and Dance." Mueller, *Astaire Dancing*, pp. 96–97. This shows the importance of the role of inadvertence in Hollywood. If it made sense to use Dunne's voice once they had Dunne, it would have made no sense to use it in this particular musical number.

17. Mueller, who tends to be very literal about plot matters, finds it ludicrous in the extreme that the Astaire character falls in love with the Rogers character in *Shall We Dance* after only seeing her picture: "a script device that elevates to absurdity the love-at-first-glance formula of the two previous Astaire-Rogers films." Ibid., p. 117.

18. The problematic relationship between music and plot is obvious to most critics. Croce is eloquent on the subject, noting that the musical numbers "aren't planted there as firmly as the songs in *Top Hat* or *Swing Time*—they don't well up out of a dramatic situation . . ." *The Fred Astaire and Ginger Rogers Book*, p. 119. She also notes, "These elements—the ballet vs. musical comedy themes and the real vs. false Ginger theme—are merely stated in the course of the plot; they aren't dramatized . . ." Ibid., p. 120.

19. The "Change Partners" dance is evaluated differently by both Mueller and Croce. Mueller sees it as an absurdly comic exaggeration of previous Astaire/Rogers dances in which "Astaire had sought to mesmerize the reluctant Rogers into a dance." *Astaire Dancing*, p. 146. Croce sees it as being on the edge of absurd but notes that it was in fact "dancing at its driest and shapeliest." She further discusses the dancing in *Carefree* as indicative of Astaire and Rogers's "new understanding of each other, a new intimacy and confidence in their dancing" (pp. 147–150). They have both come to conclusions based too narrowly on the relationship of the dance number to previous dance numbers and not on the relationship of the music to the plot as it has evolved or devolved, as the case may be.

20. Svengali and Trilby are the legendary hypnotist and the creature he controls through mind power. Indeed, Croce perceptively speaks of Astaire

making Rogers a goddess. *The Fred Astaire and Ginger Rogers Book*, p. 17. Oddly, Betty Comden and Adolf Green used the image of Svengali and Trilby comically in *The Barkleys of Broadway* in creating the fraught relationship between the Barkleys, even though, as Comden told me in a telephone interview on October 4, 1999, they had originally written the script for Judy Garland and Fred Astaire and knew nothing of the likening of Astaire/Rogers to Svengali and Trilby. Rogers rightly insisted that they created each other: "Over the years, myths were built up about my relationship with Fred Astaire. The general public thought he was a Svengali who snapped his fingers for his little Trilby to obey. . . . What nonsense! . . . Fred and I were colleagues . . ." Rogers, *Ginger*, p. 147.

21. Mueller comments that *Carefree* doesn't "'feel' much like a musical, but that Astaire is experimenting with new dance steps, particularly lifts, which he uses more freely in this film than previously." *Astaire Dancing*, p. 139.

22. Irene Castle was hired as a consultant on *The Story of Vernon and Irene Castle* and used her position to chill the production. She spoke to Berman in Rogers's presence as if Rogers wasn't present, demanding that Rogers's hair be dyed brown and bobbed to reflect the real-life character Rogers played. She complained about the verisimilitude of the costumes. She and Rogers fought over the color of the ribbons on Rogers's dancing shoes. Rogers admits to being intimidated but not defeated. "I felt that Irene Castle looked down her nose at me; I was certain she didn't want me in the film. Since signing the contract with RKO in 1937, she had hounded the studio about one thing or another. Among other requests, she wanted RKO to conduct a nationwide search for just the right actress to portray her, like the Scarlett O'Hara business . . . I'm sure this was an annoyance to the front office, for RKO had bought the rights to this film as a project for Fred and me; they already had their Irene." *Ginger*, pp. 204–206.

23. This was almost verbatim the premise of the film that Arthur Freed asked Betty Comden and Adolph Green to write.

24. According to Betty Comden, the film was indeed written with Judy Garland in mind as Astaire's partner. Garland was a favorite of Comden's and she and Green were disappointed at the cast change. In addition, all the studio records in the script files at UCLA confirm that Garland was taken off the project and replaced by Rogers because she repeatedly failed to show up for work on the set.

25. Astaire's films frequently called for mimicry. He feigned a Russian accent in *Shall We Dance* and French accents in *Roberta* and *The Barkleys of Broadway*. He feigned a lower-class accent in *Follow the Fleet*. According to his widow, Robyn Astaire, he had a perfect ear for voice inflection.

26. The lack of integrity in the relationship between the music and the plot of *The Barkleys of Broadway* is revealed in the several musical numbers given to Oscar Levant. Comden and Green had no say in the choice of the music, but Comden told me that the musical numbers given to Levant were a kind of studio economy, the desire to use whatever talents he had, as he was on the set in any case. Arguably, the original Astaire/Rogers creative team would not have permitted this to happen.

27. Betty Comden told me that had she known in time that Rogers would play Dinah, she and Adolph Green would have written out the Sarah Bernhardt

scene and replaced it with a scene more directed to Rogers's talents. Comden believes the scene would have worked for Garland.

28. Croce too intuits, in language somewhat different from my own, that the forties musical film had lost the balance between music and plot that released the power of music. Referring to the films made by Gene Kelly, who had replaced Astaire in the public mind as the favorite dancing star, Croce says,

> ... the Kelly film is no longer a dance film. It's a story film with dances, as distinguished from a dance film with a story. When Fred and Ginger go into their dance, you see it as a distinct formal entity, even if it's been elaborately built up to in the script. In a Kelly film, the plot action and the musical set pieces preserve a smooth continuity of high spirits, so that the pressure in a dance number will often seem too low, the dance itself plebeian or folksy in order to "match up" with the rest of the picture. Wonderful as *Singin' in the Rain* is, the fun of it hasn't much to do with dancing.
> (*The Fred Astaire and Ginger Rogers Book*, p. 7)

CHAPTER FIVE. KATHARINE HEPBURN AND SPENCER TRACY

1. Speaking of the political messages in *Keeper of the Flame* (1943), screenwriter and outspoken Communist Donald Ogden Stewart noted that the film probably couldn't have been made later. As it was, Louis B. Mayer had been furious at the picture, and the PCA had done its best to straitjacket it, but the picture had been made and Stewart was proud of its anti-Fascism. "Certainly such a picture could never have been produced later, after the Congressional committees had begun to instruct Hollywood in the 'true' brand of Americanism, and the producers had abjectly gone down on their knees to the McCarthy definition of patriotism." Quoted in Christopher Andersen, *An Affair to Remember* (New York: Avon Books, 1997), pp. 290–291. In 1947, J. Edgar Hoover claimed to have files on Hepburn and Tracy that would be "interesting" to HUAC.

> One of the committee members, a freshman congressman from California who was to use the committee as a stepping-stone to higher office, believed Hepburn and Tracy were so admired by the American public that any attempt to drag them through the mud would trigger a backlash. The congressman's name was Richard Nixon. Hoover shelved the files and neither Kate nor Spencer was called before the committee. Aside from a few passing references during the hearings, they escaped the firestorm that consumed so many of their friends and colleagues.   (Andersen, *Affair*, p. xx)

(Andersen took his information from Curt Gentry, *J. Edgar Hoover: The Man and the Secrets* [New York: W. W. Norton, 1991].) This is even more interesting in light of Hepburn's refusal to hide her political opinions from the public. On May 12, 1947, she made a speech against censorship at a rally against HUAC in Gilmore stadium, wearing a red dress. See *An Affair to Remember*, p. 287, and Katharine Hepburn, *Me: Stories of My Life* (New York: Ballantine Books, 1991), pp. 213–214, for her declarations of her belief in free speech and defense of her behavior to Louis B. Mayer. As might be expected, then, the PCA was more involved with the ideas in the films made by Tracy/Hepburn than it was with those of any of the other Synergistic Couples discussed here. By and large, the PCA disgraced itself because of the Fascist, sexist, and racist pressures it brought to bear on the Tracy/Hepburn films, but by and large, unaided by HUAC pressure, it was not often effective in its efforts.

As Hepburn and Tracy were emerging at MGM as a couple, in the early years of World War II, PCA documents clearly indicate concern about a loss of profits resulting from alienating the rich markets of Germany and Italy. With all its emphasis on the sanctity of social institutions, the PCA at no time hints of any concern about the threat to these institutions should Hitler and Mussolini win the war. Whether they were simply Fascist sympathizers or simply too myopic to realize the implications of their alliances is not clear. However, the Hays office outrageously sought to suppress the anti-Fascist ideas of Hepburn and Tracy's *Keeper of the Flame*, even though that film was made after America had entered the war against Germany and Italy.

Hepburn and Tracy were able to make *Keeper of the Flame* by hiding its real nature from Louis B. Mayer. When he saw it completed, he is reported to have fumed with rage, but did not refuse to distribute it, and did not insist on having it recut.

Aside from their attempts to police anti-Fascism in *Keeper of the Flame*, the PCA also sought to protect the family from *Without Love*, which the PCA sternly warned was making light of the institution of marriage, and from *The Sea of Grass*, which includes a child born out of wedlock. All three films retained the "offensive" elements. The PCA also failed to sterilize *Adam's Rib* when it reminded MGM that the code specifically stipulates that adultery may not be presented as funny, nor may the legal system be made light of. Indeed, the PCA could effect none of the smaller changes it demanded in this film, either: the implication of Kip's (David Wayne) homosexuality, the representation of Amanda as naked under her towel when Adam is massaging her, the slap on the buttocks that provokes one of Adam and Amanda's bitterest quarrels—all of which the PCA ordered out of the film—remained in the distributed print. The PCA also failed to affect *Pat and Mike*. The PCA complained that it was in bad taste for Collier (William Ching) to break his engagement with Pat (Hepburn) when he wrongly suspected that "the marital privilege" had been granted between Pat and Mike (Tracy), and that it was in equally bad taste that Pat's love for Mike prompts her to break the law—all of which went with impunity into the distributed films.

PCA objections to *State of the Union* were more effective in terms of the letter of the demand; yet here we find that the deletions that the code won made Lansbury oddly more, rather than less, insidious, and made the adultery as well as the suicide more of a potent factor in the film.

2. Pedestrian scientific explanations for truly mysterious behavior of characters in movies began as early as 1945, when Alfred Hitchcock prefaced *Spellbound* with title cards explaining the scientific basis of psychoanalysis, apparently something he felt he had to do to placate the studio and the audience

demand for "realism." In *Glen or Glenda* (1953), Ed Wood sincerely plays the science card in his inadvertently hilarious attempt to deal honestly and directly with transvestism. Hitchcock wittily used the hollowness of these reductive recipes again in *Psycho* (1960) in juxtaposition to the layers of complication underlying Norman Bates's (Anthony Perkins) behavior. In its time, recipe psychology was impressive to members of the mass audience, though they now sound as shallow as Hitchcock understood them to be.

3. Andersen, *An Affair to Remember*, p. 236.

4. For discussions of Hepburn's already successful recovery of her popularity through her campaign to star in the film version of *The Philadelphia Story* (1940, Dir. George Cukor), please see Andersen, *An Affair to Remember*, pp. 203–208; Hepburn, *Me*, pp. 211, 213; and Charles Higham, *Merchant of Dreams: Louis B. Mayer, M.G.M., and the Secret Hollywood* (New York: Donald I. Fine, 1993), pp. 303–304.

5. *Lion's Roar*, vol. 1, no. 6.

6. See Andersen, *An Affair to Remember*, for extensive discussion of Tracy's alcoholism and womanizing, especially pp. 122, 128, 136–137, 258.

7. *Lion's Roar*, vol. 1, no. 6.

8. The uniqueness of Hepburn and Tracy becomes obvious in contrast with other onscreen/offscreen couples of their time. Robert Taylor and Barbara Stanwyck may have been in love, but they were an Iconic Couple onscreen, and in only two films—*His Brother's Wife* (1936, Dir. W. S. Van Dyke) and *This Is My Affair* (1937, Dir. William Seiter). They never worked together again after they married in 1939. Lauren Bacall and Humphrey Bogart had an onscreen synergy in four films: *To Have and Have Not* (1944, Dir. Howard Hawks), *The Big Sleep* (1946, Dir. Howard Hawks), *Dark Passage* (1947, Dir. Delmer Daves), *Key Largo* (1948, Dir. John Huston). However, unlike the case of Tracy and Hepburn, their publicity tended to emphasize how different they were offscreen than the characters they portrayed, even though it did focus on their real-life love affair and marriage. In the 1960s and 1970s, Elizabeth Taylor and Richard Burton became, in some ways, heirs to the traditions of the Tracy/Hepburn partnership. However, unlike Tracy and Hepburn, who walked a very fine line between realism in movies and offscreen reality, and who were highly political in a very direct way, Taylor and Burton generally played out indulgent, con-fessional, often low-quality commentaries on their private lives. Among their eleven films together, *Cleopatra* (1963, Dir. Joseph Mankiewicz) operated in the public mind as an opulent diary entry about the way they met on the set of the picture, as *Divorce His—Divorce Hers* (1973, Dir. Waris Hussein) operated as a confessional about their divorce. *The Taming of the Shrew* (1967, Dir. Franco Zeffirelli) and *Who's Afraid of Virginia Woolf?* (1966, Dir. Mike Nichols)—arguably their best together and most clearly in the Hepburn/Tracy tradition—both operated as much transformed mirrors of what the public supposed to be the dynamic between the uncontrollable Taylor and her lover, as Burton and Taylor appeared to play out the tension between the two of them. The other seven films approached pure psychodrama: *The VIPs* (1963, Dir. Anthony Asquith), *The Sandpiper* (1965, Dir. Vincente Minnelli), *The Comedians* (1967, Dir. Peter Glenville), *Boom!* (1968, Dir. Joseph Losey)—arguably their worst together and

proof that synergy is no guarantee of quality in films—*Dr. Faustus* (1968, Dir. Richard Burton), *Hammersmith Is Out* (1972, Dir. Peter Ustinov), *Under Milk Wood* (1973, Dir. Andrew Sinclair).

9. Katharine Hepburn's typical embrace of all people on the basis of who they were as individuals and her particularly warm and close friendship with George Cukor, whom she protected against the deeply homophobic Louis B. Mayer, is basis enough for surprise that she would permit what Joe Breen referred to as "pansy humor" in *Woman of the Year*. But the irony is compounded in consideration of the possibility, entertained by many, that she and Tracy were both bisexual or that Hepburn was gay (despite her disclaimers in her autobiography), and that she had a close but completely platonic relationship with Tracy. For a brief discussion of Mayer's homophobia, see Higham, *Merchant of Dreams*, p. 303. For an exploration of the sexuality of both Hepburn and Tracy see Andersen, *An Affair to Remember*, pp. 161–169, 174–175, 237–238.

Beyond the gossip interest of these issues, what is profoundly interesting about Andersen's researched yet hide-and-seek presentation of Tracy and Hepburn's sexuality is the questions it provokes about the relevance of private sexual orientation to screen chemistry. It is certain that in each of the four couples from the studio era, offscreen sexuality was an issue, though it is equally certain, as we shall see in the final chapter, that enormous chemistry can emerge in images of screen partners where one is gay and the other heterosexual and there can be no question of "real" life sexual relationships.

10. See Higham, *Merchant of Dreams*, p. 304; Andersen, *An Affair to Remember*, p. 229. Hepburn dominated the production of this film in all ways. She had the final say in choice of writers for *Woman of the Year*. She would not reveal the potential writers' names to Mayer because the Kanins and Ring Lardner Jr. were not on the approved MGM list. Thus Hepburn precluded the creative wars on this issue by stonewalling Mayer—successfully. The first Hepburn/Tracy film was not made from preexisting source material. It was based on an original story, Garson Kanin's idea, and developed by his brother Michael Kanin and Ring Lardner Jr.—and very much tailored to Hepburn. Garson Kanin had imagined the character eventually played by Hepburn as a variant of Dorothy Thompson, Sinclair Lewis's wife and the only female columnist of her day. The hybrid nature of the project is certain; many heads went into the script, but these were not the same cast of studio characters that usually collaborated on MGM projects. A greater inadvertence had been introduced by Hepburn's refusal to stay inside the studio loop. Moreover, there was always a particular tension on the set of a Hepburn project because she was unusually willing to plunge forcefully into dialogue with her co-workers, who were rarely prepared for her powerful interventions.

She even had some control over the perspective on Tess, who seems at first blush inimical to everything Hepburn believed. We now know that, surprisingly, she was in sympathy with the need for Tess to recognize the problem that she constitutes. While Hepburn was appalled at the relentless and crude humiliation of Tess in the final version of the film's ending, she clearly was and is in sympathy with the need of men to have wives who are concerned first, last, and always with the man's interests—and if she had been born a man, arguably, she wouldn't have married a career woman. Thus Hepburn's concern with Tess's submission was one of tact, not of ideology. For the record, Spencer Tracy has left no documentation of his response to the proliferation of endings for this picture, but Lardner hazards a guess that he probably didn't have one, since he "was pretty used to doing what he was told at the studio."

There was always a fight for control of a Tracy/Hepburn picture. Their first collaboration set the pattern of things to come, making everyone nervous with their strange and very powerful attraction/repulsion dynamic, as if they were immediately locked into an intimate struggle that was both productive and unnerving. On the set of *Woman of the Year*, George Stevens and Tracy would retreat to Tracy's dressing room to discuss acting issues, only to be interrupted by Hepburn. A typical interchange among the three of them would, apparently, go something like this. She would knock, open the door, and ask what the men were conspiring about. Tracy might say that he wanted "guidance" from their director. "What about my guidance?" Hepburn would say. To this, Tracy would reply along the following lines: "How could I be such a damn fool as to get into a picture with a woman producer and *her* director? . . . How could I be such a dumb bastard as that?"

Hepburn wanted to rehearse constantly; Tracy found it a bore and said so. She did research on her roles—for *Adam's Rib* she walked into a courtroom to observe trial conduct—while he relied on instinct, saying that was really all he had as an actor. But with each other, on the set, they probed and explored in the same way. Unlike some screen partners, whose work never really showed up as remarkable until it was on the screen, Hepburn and Tracy provoked awe in the studio. In the words of producer Joe Mankiewicz, "It was rather like an intricately choreographed ballet at first. . . . Very self-conscious as they tried to figure each other out. Early on in the filming I noticed that Spencer was sounding sort of high-brow and Kate's very distinctive, metallic-sounding voice was much lower, her delivery slower. Then it hit me. My God, they were unconsciously imitating each other!" (quoted in Andersen, *An Affair to Remember*, p. 216).

11. Hepburn's submissiveness to Tracy, sitting literally and figuratively at his feet, is discussed in Andersen, *An Affair to Remember,* pp. 281, 305, 389.

12. Mankiewicz's cynical intention to pander to an audience determined to see Hepburn taken down a peg before forgiving her is documented in *An Affair to Remember,* p. 234. Said Mankiewicz, "The average housewife was going to look up at this beautiful, brilliant, accomplished goddess up there on the screen . . . and, well, hate her guts." But with the new ending, "women could turn to their schmuck husbands and say, 'She may know the president, but she can't even make a cup of coffee, you silly bastard.'"

13. Rosalind Russell was the queen of films about successful women in narratives that revolve around "getting her to readopt her abandoned femininity by falling love. . . . Rosalind Russell described this pattern retrospectively, saying: 'I could order the clothes for my pictures in my sleep. I'd say . . . 'Make me a plaid suit, a striped suit, a grey flannel, and a negligee for the scene in the bedroom when I cry.'" Sarah Berry, *Screen Style: Fashion and Femininity in 1930s Hollywood* (Minneapolis: University of Minnesota Press, 2000), p. 179.

14. Max Horkheimer and Theodor W. Adorno's characterization of word use in propaganda captures the quality of the empty, reductive language so prevalent in the Hollywood of the 1940s and 1950s: "The more completely language is lost in the announcement, the more words are debased as substantial vehicles of meaning and become signs devoid of quality; the more purely and transparently words communicate what is intended, the more impenetrable they become." "The Culture Industry," p. 164.

15. Higham, *Merchant of Dreams*, p. 313.

16. I. A. R. Wylie, *Keeper of the Flame* (New York: Grosset and Dunlap, 1942).

17. Higham, *Merchant of Dreams*, p. 312.

18. Phillip Barry, *Without Love: A Comedy in Three Acts* (New York: Coward-McCann, 1943).

19. Conrad Richter, *The Sea of Grass* (Ohio University Press, 1992).

20. In *Mildred Pierce* (1945, Dir. Michael Curtiz), as Linda Williams has pointed out, no direct reference is made to the war, or to Mildred's ability to rise in the business world because the men are away, but the narrative carries an "oblique suggestion of highly selected aspects of wartime reality—in particular the absence of paternal authority..." "Feminist Film Theory: *Mildred Pierce* and the Second World War," in *Female Spectators: Looking at Film and Television*, edited by E. Dierdre Pribram (London: Verso, 1988), p. 23. Thus, when Mildred leaves the business world as her husband returns, reasons Williams, there is an oblique reference to the sudden pressure on women to return to working strictly at home when the armed forces returned. I suggest that a similar but more extreme oblique dynamic is at work in *State of the Union*. The death of Kay Thorndyke's father propels her into power, but the return of Grant Matthews to his right mind undercuts her bid to stay there and raise the stakes. In *Pierce*, where Mildred (Joan Crawford) is falsely accused of murder, she is wrongly suspected of being a demon. In *Union*, Kay is depicted as genuinely all that and more.

21. The PCA file on *State of the Union* is very revealing regarding the kind of influence the Hays office had on Hollywood, even as de facto government censorship was becoming an everyday reality. The point of view of Joe Breen, the head of the office at the time, was that certain things should not be seen by the audience. Absolutely unaware, it would seem, that what is not seen is often more powerful than what is seen in the movies, Breen pressured Capra to erase any visual evidence of a sexual affair between Kay and Grant. This actually intensified the aura of illegitimate sexuality, considering how chastely onscreen kisses were depicted at the time. It supercharged the invisible scene between Kay and Grant in Detroit. The exact words Breen used in his memo of September 25, 1947, reveal his obtuseness about visual storytelling and the onscreen couple: "You have quite effectively pointed up the fact that Kay and Grant have not been engaged in an illicit relationship. We feel, nevertheless, that although it may be shown that Kay and Grant have some attraction for each other, it is going too far to show them actually kissing. This, since Grant is a married man with a wife and child." Actually they had more than one child, but that may have been too racy for Breen to contemplate.

The PCA effectively forced removal of any overt indication about an affair between Grant and Kay, but the deletion of overt representation is a happy one; because there is no screen chemistry between Lansbury and Tracy, only invisibility could have made the audience believe in her power over him.

22. At the end of her autobiography, *Me*, after a deluge of affirmation of her love for Tracy, Hepburn makes the following startling declaration: "I have no idea how Spence felt about me. I can only say I think that if he hadn't liked me he wouldn't have hung around. He wouldn't talk about it and I didn't talk about it. We just passed twenty-seven years together in what was to me absolute bliss" (p. 403). Although Hepburn does not call Matt Drayton's declaration of love Tracy's way of finally making his own declaration, Stanley Kramer is quoted in *An Affair to Remember* as saying of the speech, "Spence was talking about Kate, about their love for each other.... He was paying tribute to her before millions of people and saying good-bye" (pp. 452–453).

CHAPTER SIX. THE POST-STUDIO SYNERGISTIC COUPLE

1. I am indebted to David Sterritt, film critic for the *Christian Science Monitor*, for sharing his considerable knowledge of the film business in New Hollywood. Readers interested in further exploration of the structure of the Hollywood deal will find ample assistance from *Variety: The International Entertainment Weekly*. For example, in the June 26–July 9, 2000, issue alone, in addition to the mass of material about current films in production, there were two articles and one full-page chart outlining the network of allegiances in the production scene: "F/X Alert: Houses on Overload," by Marc Graser, pp. 1, 70; "Passion for Slashin': Studios Ax Producer Pacts, Strip Frills from Deals," by Charles Lyons, pp. 1, 69; "Variety Facts on Pacts," compiled by Claude Brodesser, Paul Duke, Dana Harris, Dade Hayes, Charles Lyons, and Dave McNarry, p. 68. Surprisingly, there is a dearth of book-length studies on this important subject. One, Jonathan Rosenbaum's passionate diatribe about the effect of Hollywood business practices on the pleasures of Hollywood movies, *Movie Wars: How Hollywood and the Media Conspire to Limit What Films We See* (Chicago: A Cappella Books, 2000) is highly informative.

2. For example, the contract guarantee can be the financial foundation of teaming two soap opera stars together. Each soap opera contract actor is guaranteed payment for a certain number of shows per week, regardless of whether he or she is actually used on the show or not; the salary per week naturally varies with the celebrity of the actor. A guarantee of one show per week is fairly standard. Some actors may be guaranteed more. But in any case, a writer may be told to put a scene into a script for no other reason than to use the guarantee. More often, story action is geared to those actors with high guarantees, which basically replicates the effect of the contract player system in Old Hollywood. While the actor is being paid, he or she might as well be used.

3. I am indebted for this formulation to Cynthia King, a young aspiring actress. It has the merit of economically summing up the experience so many co-stars, forced into a strange kind of professional intimacy, have faced in the form of seemingly inexplicable tantrums on the set, and even the refusal to work, as

in the case of Cybill Shepherd and Bruce Willis, to be discussed in Chapter Seven.

4. Penelope Ann Miller, who now works predominantly in made-for-television features, in the early 1990s lent her colorless presence to onscreen romances with a number of great stars: in *The Freshman* (Dir. Andrew Bergman, 1990), Miller was the co-star of Matthew Broderick and Marlon Brando; in *Kindergarten Cop* (1990, Dir. Ivan Reitman) she co-starred with Arnold Schwarzenegger; in *Other People's Money* (1991, Dir. Norman Jewison) she was the principal ingenue in a film featuring Gregory Peck, Danny De Vito, and Piper Laurie; in *Carlito's Way* (1993, Dir. Brian De Palma) she co-starred with Al Pacino and Sean Penn; in *The Shadow* (1994, Dir. Russell Mulcahey) she co-starred with Alec Baldwin.

5. *Eyes Wide Shut* (1999, Dir. Stanley Kubrick) was a controversial movie. Critics who admire it generally concede that Cruise and Kidman were brilliantly used by Kubrick in surprising and riveting scenes in which the two actors frequently do not appear together. Each is considered to be individually beautiful, but there is arguably no onscreen chemistry between them.

6. Beatty and Christie co-starred in *McCabe and Mrs. Miller* (1971, Dir. Robert Altman), *Shampoo* (1975, Dir. Hal Ashby), and *Heaven Can Wait* (1978, Dir. Warren Beatty). Nicholson and Huston co-starred in *Prizzi's Honor* (1985, Dir. John Huston) and *The Crossing Guard* (1995, Dir. Sean Penn). Peters and Martin co-starred in *The Jerk* (1979, Dir. Carl Reiner) and *Pennies from Heaven* (1981, Dir. Herbert Ross).

7. Mia Farrow and Woody Allen have worked together in thirteen films, but have co-starred—in some fashion—in only seven of them (all directed by Allen): *A Midsummer Night's Sex Comedy* (1982), *Zelig* (1983), *Broadway Danny Rose* (1984), *Hannah and Her Sisters* (1986), *New York Stories* (1989), *Crimes and Misdemeanors* (1989), *Husbands and Wives* (1992).

8. Gena Rowlands and John Cassavetes worked together on eleven movies, but co-starred in only two: *Opening Night* (1977, Dir. Cassavetes) and *Tempest* (1982, Dir. Paul Mazursky).

9. There are dozens of internet sites at which anyone who cares to may discuss *The X-Files* or *General Hospital*. Both internet communities share a lively interest in the progression of narrative and in character. Both contain sites that have search engines, although the *X-Files* community has more sophisticated search engines, with a particularly impressive one to be found at http://www.fandom.com/x-files.com. The best soap opera search engine I have found is at http://memberstripod.com/GHTranscripts. Both fan communities are critical of inconsistencies and cliches and excited about performers they consider to be sexy or excitingly villainous. However, the *X-Files* community contains fans with a scholarly inclination. For example, Daniel Wood, who bills himself as the head fanatic on Fandom, posted on April 2, 2000, a systematic attempt to bring together all the details of the seven seasons of the series. By June 27, 2000, he was again churning up the fields with a host of questions that seemed to destabilize the *X-Files* narrative.

10. The centrality to the show of the intimacy between Scully and Mulder shows up subtly in the subtext of the series, but blatantly in the text of the

magazine illustrations for articles about the show, which are unaccountably sexual and unaccountably mocking in tone. The pictures accompanying an article about *The X-Files,* and especially the cover of *Rolling Stone,* no. 734 (May 16, 1996), are the most sensational example of explicit and smirking eroticizing of Scully and Mulder. The cover depicts Duchovny and Anderson naked and in bed together, draped by a sheet and angled so that there is no full exposure. The article, "X-Files under Cover," by David Wild, is even more extravagant. It is a full two-page spread, depicting Anderson in a black lace nightgown, smoking a post-coital cigarette and nestled between the sleeping bodies of Duchovny and creator Chris Carter, both of whom appear to be naked (pp. 38–39). Among other images, other covers depict them kissing, snuggling, and kneeling while Duchovny encircles Anderson, hugging her from behind; one shows Anderson licking Duchovny's face. The importance of this media obsession becomes more impressive when we consider that it differs radically from publicity pictures of any other television series, including the overtly erotic nighttime shows *Twin Peaks, Buffy,* and *Xena.* There are, of course, many romantic publicity pictures for the daytime serials, but nothing as extreme as the illustrations accompanying *X-Files* print media coverage, which verge on soft pornography.

The tone of the print media fantasies about *X-Files* sex that is never shown onscreen is also noteworthy, suggesting a distinct discomfort with the tenderness between them and a cultural need to convert the warmth of intimacy into a kind of raunchy joke. The contrast between publicity images and actual Synergistic Couple dynamics onscreen is in itself a fascinating topic that deserves more scrutiny. In the case of the soaps, the publicity stills are often formatted through the cliches of popular romance novels, and generally those images are reductive references to the complexity of the Synergistic Couples on the daytime serials, where the images only fall into stereotype when the creative community is asleep at the switch or desperate. There are certainly numerous tonal discrepancies of a similar nature between print advertising campaigns and the films of the Synergistic Couples in Old Hollywood.

Equally indicative of the urgency of the intimacy of Scully and Mulder to the series is the battle between two categories of *X-Files* fans on-line, those called "shippers," who are interested in seeing an overt development of Scully and Mulder's relationship, and those called "noromos," who insist, against all evidence to the contrary, that Scully and Mulder are "just good friends." Perhaps the most amusing manifestation of the conflict is a parody of a "pop quiz" in which the episode "all things" [sic] is described in detail, and questions are asked calling for a, b, and c possible interpretations of the increasingly erotic behavior of the pair. The (a) answer is practical, the (b) answer is "noromo," and the (c) answer is "shipper." The following is an example:

> We see Scully changing into her clothes . . . hey, was she undressed for a reason? She quietly leaves the bathroom and walks into a bedroom, walking past a leg barely covered by a bedsheet . . . hey, wait a second. She keeps walking past the sleeping form of a guy lying NAKED IN BED?!?! You scream:
> A) "Condoms! Did you remember the condoms?!?!"

B) "Uh-oh. If that's Mulder, we'll never hear the end of it from those naive 'Shippers who keep answering C) on these surveys!"
C) "That had better be Fox!!! <camera keeps panning up to reveal it is, indeed, Dana's One-In-Five-Billion> YES! YES! THEY DID IT! THEY FINALLY DID IT!" <faint in orgasmic bliss>

11. As immoderate as the visual depiction of Scully and Mulder has been in the print media, it has been met with equal and opposing strength by Chris Carter's persistent vocal denial, until the end of the seventh season, that there was a sexual subtext to *The X-Files*. For a typical statement, please see Ted Edwards, *X-Files Confidential: The Unauthorized X-Philes Compendium* (Boston: Little, Brown, 1996), pp. 12–13.

12. The *X-Files* narratives normalize the clinical symptoms of paranoia, as defined by J. Laplanche and J.-B. Pontalis, *The Language of Psychoanalysis* (New York: W. W. Norton, 1973): "Chronic psychosis characterised by more or less systematised delusion, with a predominance of ideas of reference but with no weakening of the intellect, and generally speaking, no tendency towards deterioration... erotomania, delusional jealousy and delusions of grandeur" (p. 296). "The systematized delusion is frequently of persecution often characterized by a lack of affect" (p. 296). All of this correlates with the tonalities of amusing, yet oddly affectless, theoretical dialogue between Scully and Mulder, clearly floating on top of intense feeling, and the narrative construction of Mulder and Scully's persecution by the FBI, the conspiracy, and most of the aliens.

13. The taping rhythms of the *X-Files* production team is highly conducive to the generation of synergy. It is a hectic affair with the actors often learning their lines on the way to the set and with few if any retakes. Much as "one-shot Woody" generated enormous spontaneous energy, opening the door to couple synergy, with his rapid-fire filming schedule, the *X-Files* method also leaves no room for stilted, over-rehearsed performances characteristic of American nighttime television. (The soaps also generate an impressive percentage of vital performances for the same reasons.) Numerous sources confirm this manner of working, including my e-mail conversations with Autumn Tysko, Julianne Lee's interview with David Duchovny ("X Symbol"), and the many interviews with the *X-Files* creative team in Edwards, *X-Files Confidential*.

Another production incentive to spontaneity and mutual acting energy transfer is the provocatively contrasting work styles of Anderson and Duchovny. While Anderson approaches her work seriously and rarely if ever deviates from the script, Duchovny plays with his lines, changing them from take to take, specifically in search of a joke line, and thus generating more takes than would be necessary were Anderson alone involved. My source here is Autumn Tysko, who has watched the pair work on the set and who has copies of twenty sets of dailies in her personal collection. This kind of contrast usually generates heat between acting partners, and, though it is usually negative in character, provokes the kind of energy that translates onscreen as a powerful connection between the characters.

14. There are practical ways of reading this oddly sexualized scene in the

pilot. J. J. Pierce, a writer who specializes in studying science fiction and especially *The X-Files,* believes that the scene was put in the pilot to reassure the producers and the network that Carter's choice of Gillian Anderson, rather than a Pamela Anderson Lee look-alike, didn't mean an absence of erotic titillation. That may have been on Carter's mind, but it isn't what makes the scene important and significant.

15. The details of Samantha's existence in the series follow: Mulder's motive for joining the FBI is based on a youthful experience, when his little sister Samantha was abducted on November 27, 1973. Mulder went through hypnotic regression therapy to try to recover memories of the trauma. He believes that he saw her taken by aliens who pulled her to them on a light beam. Other times he is not sure of what he saw. His need to find his sister sparked his interest in the X-Files at the FBI. Ultimately Mulder has found that she was part of the alien conspiracy to take over Earth, as part of a plan to clone human/hybrid slaves. In the seventh season, a show called "Closure" depicted Mulder finding that Samantha was rescued from the aliens by mysterious figures called "walk-ins" who turned her into pure light. In worldly terms, she died at the age of fourteen, but is in a better place. At an on-line fan conference on July 25, 2000, Carter gave some hints, greeted by howls of protest on the internet, that this is only what Mulder believes and that further revelations are in store. This is a specific instance of the ambiguities of the elliptical storytelling on the series. Some consider it sloppiness at best. I believe that this is part of the fun of television serial storytelling, and also part of the dreamlike structure of the *X-Files* universe.

16. The Bounty Hunter is another instance of elliptical storytelling in the series. In the early episodes, the Bounty Hunter (Brian Thompson), who abducted selected human beings by changing his body and face to make him resemble trusted friends and family, seemed to be unequivocally part of the alien invasion. More recently, as the aliens have distinguished themselves as belonging to pro- and anti-invasion forces, it has become impossible to say which group the Bounty Hunter belongs to. Possibly he is a renegade from all factions, working for himself, and part of a universe much more complicated than it first appeared. Perhaps the situation is hopelessly confused and out of Carter's control, as some think. Daniel Wood pointed out many inconsistencies about alien life at the Fandom website on April 3, 2000. He notes that the plot point about the search for human/alien hybrids is illogical. They are intended to be slaves, but they would, according to *X-Files* alien lore, also be immune to infection by the black oil, the alien's greatest weapon. If that is so, then why would the aliens agree to create hybrids? That would mean "the creation of a being who is not a slave!" I would say, in response, that the alien/human dichotomy works only as a metaphor for talking about elements of the human condition we don't want to recognize as our own. Whether or not Carter intends this, and he actually may, the inadvertence of his high-energy collaboration with his actors, writers, and so forth was most likely the first cause of the strangely menacing Bounty Hunter.

17. In the Season Three finale called "Talitha Cumi," (Arise Maiden, taken from the Grand Inquisitor chapter of *The Brothers Karamazov,* by Fyodor

Dostoevsky), an odd person named Jeremiah Smith, one of the more equivocal alien characters, tells the evil human C. G. B. Spender, Cancer Man, "You can't kill their love, which makes them what they are. Makes them better than us, better than you." Here is an important touchstone, suggesting the show is about love, not mystery, or the mystery of love. Smith is referring to the human race, but the indeterminacy of the pronoun frees the statement to resonate about Scully and Mulder, who are indeed better, though many humans are not, and it is their love that accounts for their excellence.

18. Arthur Dales is a resonant character. He has appeared on three episodes of the series: "Travellers" (Season Five); "Agua Mala" (Season Six), and "The Unnatural" (Season Seven). In "Travellers" and "Agua Mala," he is played by Darren McGavin, Carter's avowed inspiration for Mulder, appropriately as the FBI agent who first found the X-Files that Mulder later made his special project. In "The Unnatural," played by M. Emmet Walsh, he claims to be that Arthur Dales's brother, also named Arthur, a little in-joke on Duchovny's part.

19. "I always thought the center of Mulder was a kind of detachment from other people's opinions and views... Physically, I felt his center was in the head. He tends to get top heavy from time to time and to get surprised when his center moves to other parts of his body. It's move to the heart and, in one episode, to the groin." This is Duchovny's comment on his character in Julianne Lee, "X Symbol," p. 37. It's a very interesting statement in light of Duchovny's authorship of "The Unnatural," which asks Mulder to look into "the mystery of the heart."

20. The Season Seven finale that discovers Scully pregnant is also illustrative of another feature of *The X-Files*—its extraordinary synergy between creative community and audience. Through the internet, primarily, a collaborative relationship has been established between Chris Carter, the many writers for *The X-Files*, the principal actors, and an international community of fans that is interested in playing with the elliptical, indeterminate universe depicted in the show and the clues about its composition left by the creators. They dialogue at conferences, and over the internet about narrative developments on an extremely high level of sophisticated reading. The show is shot on an open set to which numerous fans flock regularly to see the making of the show, with no loss to the fictional impact. The shooting schedules are posted by the film office of the Entertainment Industry Development Corporation (EIDC) and are easily available on the internet.

With new development, even images, the fan community will search systematically through former episodes to find emerging narrative and image patterns with the dexterity of university scholars (which some are), which is unprecedented for a truly mass audience. The season finale pregnancy sent the fan community back through previous episodes searching for all images and plot arcs connected with birth and children, with Scully's relationship to birth and children, and with Scully and Mulder's relationship to birth and children. In addition, it has generated much discussion about a small gold cross that Scully wears around her throat, which has figured as an icon of connection between Scully and Mulder in previous episodes. In an elliptical moment in "Requiem," the final episode, Scully tells Mulder she will not let him go alone to the site of a paranormal event where Mulder eventually is abducted by aliens. However, when we next see him, he is alone; that is, he is without her as he walks into what turns out to be a trap. Yet the fan community spotted Scully's cross around his neck, or what might have been her cross glinting in the moonlight, since in the last scene she was clearly not wearing it. The passionate speculation about the transfer of the cross, the subtlety of its evocation has a poetry to it, and also all the hallmarks of the inadvertence of synergy, since Anderson herself has been unable to remember whether she was told to take the cross off for the final scene or whether she did so herself. She expressed further ignorance about whether Duchovny was wearing it in the final scene. (I am indebted to Autumn Tysko, one of the above-mentioned mass media *X-Files* scholars, for sharing information in an e-mail conversation, September 1–2, 2000, about the fan community and about Anderson's remarks about Scully's cross.)

Unlike the inadvertence during the studio system, the image of Scully's cross is not merely a live coal suddenly flaring up in the project; by virtue of the interplay between fans and creators it becomes a ball set in motion that the creators can now play with, if they choose, because the fan community has answered the spontaneous energy of the image with its own energy, a potential source of fuel for Scully and Mulder.

21. Allen neither liked the substantial height discrepancy between himself and Keaton when she auditioned for the part of his co-star in *Play It Again, Sam* in 1969 nor thought it funny. He feared that it would be an unwelcome joke, but ultimately the hesitation took a backseat to his interest in working with her. Eric Lax, *Woody Allen, A Biography* (New York: Vintage, 1992), p. 242. The inversion of male-female height in their films, and the benefits it brings, is an inadvertent gain for the Allen/Keaton films.

22. Allen has said that he is influenced by the school of well-made plays from the 1930s: Clifford Odets, Maxwell Anderson, Eugene O'Neill (Lax, *Woody Allen*, p. 241). This is probably true, but Allen identifies equally with his alien side in his imaginative works.

23. Allen's general lack of interest in rehearsing and interest in spontaneity is explored in Lax, *Woody Allen*, pp. 291–299. His rapid style of casting is extensively discussed in an excerpt from a taped conversation between Allen and Juliet Taylor, his casting director of choice in "A Team of Two Who by Now Think as One," Arts and Leisure Section, *New York Times* (May 14, 2000), pp. 17, 24.

24. *Manhattan Murder Mystery* uses the discarded ideas that were supposed to go into *Annie Hall*. The tonal contrasts between the two films are striking; the earlier film is freewheeling and experimental and unable to confirm longevity in love; the second is a more conventionally structured song of praise to enduring affection. Time will tell whether Allen is moving ahead toward a mature use of convention, or regressing back toward a safer place.

25. Eyeline match is a feature of continuity editing, the purpose of which is to create the illusion that we always know where the characters are looking. If the protagonist's eyes shift toward screen right, the next edited image creates the sense that it is on the character's right, giving the impression of an ordered world. If the sequences are not edited that way, the spectator keeps receiving the impression that he or she is not sure where anything is.

26. As far-fetched as the comparison between Scully and Mulder and Keaton and Allen may seem, it has much to recommend it. Scully and Mulder exist in a haunted universe that is no longer trustworthy and often indeterminate; she insists on rational explanations while he inclines toward the intuitive stance. Allen and Keaton exist in a comic universe that is no longer trustworthy and often indeterminate. She insists on rational explanations while he inclines toward the intuitive stance. The scene in the planetarium, locating them in outer space by a trick of the eye, is particularly resonant of Scully and Mulder, separated primarily by genre. This is not to propose in any way that Carter was influenced by Allen, but more to suggest a current, fin de siècle cultural pull toward a certain kind of depiction of the couple.

27. The advent of Luke and Laura encouraged the creation of many other Synergistic Couples on the daytime serials; a few of the best and most provocative onscreen couples of the eighties were Julia (Nancy Lee Grahn) and Mason (Lane Davies) on *Santa Barbara*, Gina (Robin Mattson) and Buzz (Justin Deas) on *Santa Barbara*, Eden (Marcy Walker) and Cruz (A. Martinez) on *Santa Barbara*, Shane (Charles Shaughnessy) and Kimberly (Patsy Pease) on *Days of Our Lives*, Patch (Stephen Nichols) and Kayla (Mary Beth Evans) on *Days of Our Lives*, Bo (Peter Reckell) and Hope (Kristian Alfonso) on *Days of Our Lives*, Trevor (James Kiberd) and Natalie (Kate Collins) on *All My Children*, Angie (Debbi Morgan) and Jesse (Darnell Williams) on *All My Children*, Noah (Keith Hamilton Cobb) and Julia (Sidney Penny) on *All My Children*. Angie and Jesse and Noah and Julia are among very few synergistic pairs involving people of color in soap opera. They distinguish soap opera as being the one venue in popular culture to produce synergistic pairs involving people of color, recognized as such by a mass audience. Because of its radically modernist character as a storytelling form, and because it has been the groundbreaker for so many developments later seen on nighttime television and in the movies—for example, the multi-plot serial form—the chances are quite good that the first gay synergistic pair for a mass audience will also emerge on soap opera.

28. In a paper entitled "Betty Grable Finally Dances with Baron Sacher-Masoch," given at the annual Society for Cinema Studies Conference (March 2000), I explored *That Lady in Ermine* (1948, Dir. Ernst Lubitsch) as a reflexive comment on the split in Betty Grable's star discourse between the feral powerhouse and the cherubic ingenue. The film's interest lies in its unmasking through fantasy, in a manner clearly unsuspected by Grable, of a situation long prevalent in her movies. The transcript is available at http://www.sensesofcinema.com. The pertinence of Grable's situation to the present study is that under current conditions, in an entertainment industry that tolerates complexity in female actors, Genie Francis did not have to mask the double nature of her screen persona. As a result, at least as I see it, her energy was free for the kind of synergy with a partner that Grable never achieved.

29. The plot details of this arc of the Luke and Laura story are as follows. Luke's sister Bobbie (Jacklyn Zeman) was interested in Scot and jealous of Laura. She persuaded Luke to try to sabotage the relationship, and it worked better than either the characters or the writers had planned. Luke fell passionately in love with Laura. And the audience fell passionately in love with that

pairing. Luke had been intended only as a minor character in the Scotty-Laura romance. When Luke and Laura generated excitement, the writers decided to give them a flashy tragic story, with Luke dying in Laura's arms before she returned to Scotty. But the tide of audience interest was too great to adhere to that story, either. Thus the story of Luke and Laura's continuing and enduring passion for each other was initiated. My sources are the writers who worked on these initial segments of the Luke and Laura story: Douglas Marland (in-person interview, April 19, May 10, 1989, February 5, 1990; Sheri Anderson (telephone interview, December 1, 8, 1989); and Pat Falken Smith (in-person interview, November 20, 1984).

30. I am here retracting one element of my discussion of the Luke and Laura story published in my book-length study of the genre, *No End to Her: Soap Opera and the Female Subject* (Berkeley: University of California Press, 1993), pp. 81–82, in which I denied that their first sexual contact was actually a rape. I was wrong. *Luke did rape Laura.* My error was due to a flawed memory of the episode, which I watched when it was first aired; my inability to find a tape of the full episode; and disingenuous statements made by Sheri Anderson, who was a writer on the show at the time. The tapes available to me showed only part of the dance between Luke and Laura that culminated in the rape, which, in combination with my faulty memory, led to a false conclusion. Anderson denied that the writers had intended it as a rape. A fuller viewing of the rape segment of the episode belies her statement. Laura said, "No," emphatically, but with no effect. Moreover, in the 1999/2000 arc of the show, the incident was revisited, the rape being clearly identified as a rape when, in a daring narrative move equal to the courage of the initial story, Lucky (Jonathan Jackson), the couple's son, discovers that part of family history and struggles to come to terms with it. However, that being said, I stand by my interpretation of the couple's relationship as one in which conceptions of male entitlement and female deference are honestly and imaginatively explored. This problem in my earlier work stands as testimony to the need for an archive—of some substance—of soap opera tapes to be made available to scholars, students, and critics, so that those with a serious interest in the genre can pursue serious explorations of their ideas.

31. The widespread critical myopia about this incident would seem to be based in part on an inability or unwillingness to separate the exploitative publicity given Luke and Laura by the media from the complex storytelling. However, another possibility is that a number of critics confused the intensity of the Francis/Geary synergy with approval for the act. The two actors were absolutely riveting together during the unfolding of the rape narrative and afterward. However, the onscreen images told the tale of rape as violence, not raucous pleasure. This was no Rhett/Scarlett rape fantasy in which Scarlett wakes the next day with a smile on her face. The termination of the rape found Laura hysterically stumbling from the scene, her clothes torn and her mascara running down her face and Luke almost catatonic with horror at his behavior.

32. The endurance of the Luke and Laura phenomenon is impressive. If the polls taken casually by the official *General Hospital* website is any indication, the audience by at least three to one was not pleased when Luke and Laura were separated in the 1999/2000 arc of their story and re-paired with other characters.

In a rare interview with the two of them together in *Soap Opera Digest* (January 4, 2000), Francis and Geary themselves registered a typical ambivalence about the power of their work together on their professional lives. Both express the unique pleasure and pain of the intensity of working together: they knew that there was something special about their partnership from the beginning—a special spontaneity and excitement—but also that neither would do it again (pp. 48–51). Yet in the final analysis the two agree that, as characters, they are never really apart: "That bond will not be broken" (p. 51). Should there be skepticism about material appearing in what is primarily a fanzine, there is abundant corroboration of the authenticity of this interview from castmates and writers. My in-person interviews with both Nancy Lee Grahn (May 14, 1998) and writer Patrick Mulcahey (many conversations, 1998–2000) also include mention of the special if fraught bond between Francis and Geary.

33. I am indebted to Tony Geary and Genie Francis for giving me their rarely granted permission to watch the taping of the scene, and to Nancy Lee Grahn for inviting me to the studio as her guest. Their generosity gave me the chance to watch couple synergy in action, and it is breathtaking. I have been on many television and film sets and have never witnessed the intensity of the rapport demonstrated by Geary and Francis. The studio had the atmosphere of a cathedral during their work together; the silence, which of course is standard during taping, resonated with a highly unstandard awe. The reluctance of the two, primarily Francis, according to Geary, to permit observers on the set is understandable in light of the naked intimacy in their work.

34. Luke's scheme to kill Helena Cassadine (Constance Towers) resulted in the near-death injury of Catherine Bell (Mary Beth Evans), the fiancée of Stefan Cassadine (Stephen Nichols). Luke's demonstration of remorseless willingness to kill, unheard of in a soap opera hero, suggests the basis for the radical, complex storytelling provoked by the Luke/Laura pairing. The narrative demands of soap opera required trouble in their marriage, an absolute necessity for the endless drama of soap opera and a necessity that could not be met in any ordinary way. The usual erotic triangle that is the staple of post-marriage soap opera plotting is unthinkable with regard to Luke and Laura, who can only be separated by Luke's tendency to fall into paranoia. Luke's belief—accurate as it turns out—that Helena has returned to Port Charles to avenge herself on Luke and Laura for the death of her husband and oldest son, in connection with their attempt to abuse Laura, and to wreak havoc on the world, left him feeling persecuted enough to trigger his grandiosity and his tendency toward extreme measures. Her survival has left her free to initiate a "Manchurian Candidate plot," whereby she has had Luke and Laura's son kidnapped and hypnotically altered to take dangerous suggestions from her.

35. The sexuality of an actor should only be raised to facilitate discussion of urgent issues regarding his or her work. Geary's sexuality is mentioned here only to demonstrate its irrelevance to the issue of synergy, a distinction that throws light on how powerfully synergy is linked to energy beyond ordinary daily behavior and social codes. Geary's sexual orientation has long been shrugged at by members of the daytime creative community, without prejudice. Patrick Mulcahey, who has written for *General Hospital,* offers a representative

comment: "I've always heard it said that Tony's gay, and I assume it's true. As far as I know, he's never denied it, and the rumor doesn't seem to bother him. Certainly he never produces a female escort merely for appearances' sake in social situations." Mulcahey, a richly accomplished writer who has lifted the level of soap opera discourse since his first major assignment to the innovative daytime serial *Santa Barbara* (1984–1992), is my source about Francis's stipulation that the writers never instruct Laura to kiss Luke. He mentioned her caveat to me in discussing what he needs to consider in drafting their scenes. This limitation has never prevented him from representing the uncanny Luke/Laura relationship, a tribute to the brilliance of Mulcahey, Francis, and Geary.

36. From an internet posting of the interview, http://www.usaweekend.com/00 issues/000326/000326duchovny.html.

37. Lax, *Woody Allen*, pp. 243–244.

CHAPTER SEVEN. THE THEMATIC COUPLE

1. Ronald L. Smith, *Cosby* (New York: St. Martin's, 1986), pp. 123–128, 149. Cosby is an entertainer, but he has a teaching mission, which he demonstrated as early as 1976 in his participation in *The Electric Company*, a PBS production dedicated to the education of children past the *Sesame Street* age. His strong interest in raising expectations and going beyond old stereotypes has led him to success, but also to controversy. Racial representations in the media are lightning rods, regardless of how tactful they may seem to be—and sometimes even because of their tact. Cosby was frequently attacked by what has styled itself as the liberal press, including the *Village Voice*, and by such African American groups as the Black Writers' Caucus (p. 127). He answered complaints against his depiction of the good life of the Huxtables by saying, "All we're trying to show all Americans is that in a lot of ways behavior is the same all over," and "Why do they want to deny me the pleasure of being an American and just enjoying life?" (p. 149). In a sense, Cosby's situation suggests that his stubborn refusal to "make all the black social statements" (p. 149)—that is, statements of raw anger in addition to statements about the basic competency and beauty of African Americans—may turn out to be the most radical project he could have undertaken at the time. That is, ironically, Cosby's determination to fit African Americans into a proto-iconic formula that evokes the elegance and charm of Loy and Powell may be, by its very correspondence to conservative formulas, a very bold move indeed.

The love-hate relationship that the popular culture audience had with Cosby's boldness is demonstrated by the combination of the many years *The Cosby Show* was the top-rated show in the country and the absence of any online discussion groups of his work. I have been able to find many websites at which devoted fans of the top-rated television shows continue to share enthusiasms and questions even more than a decade after some of these shows have ceased taping new episodes. For *The Cosby Show*, I have found websites that fans have created with search engines for basic information about the players and episodes, but not a single site where fans conduct extensive conversations about the show, posting ongoing strings of questions and statements. It appears that the public is hard-pressed to frame about the adventures of the Huxtables the kinds of questions that provoke such "chat," unlike the fans of *Moonlighting*, who still spend days and weeks on the *Moonlighting* Listserv debating whether David Addison (Bruce Willis) is the father of Maddie Hayes's baby, and the wisdom of the show's creators in killing off his possible offspring.

2. Lincoln Theodore Monroe Andrew Perry was an African American actor who achieved stardom during the 1930s portraying highly stereotypical bumbling, cowardly servants who inescapably fulfilled racist ideas about the inferiority of people of color. Ironically, through the magic of movies, he would literally turn white when he was frightened, though the subversive nature of the joke was surely lost on most spectators. However, he was a dexterous physical comedian whose skillful use of his entire body onscreen arguably created an inheritance for all cinematic comedians that eventually served less narrowly abusive comedic portraits of human nature.

3. In creating *The Cosby Show*, Cosby demonstrated very specific goals and aesthetic priorities. He took on as his consultant Harvard University professor of psychology Alvin Poussaint in an effort to discuss human behavior in a serious way—not random zingers about "behinds or breasts or pimples." Smith, *Cosby*, p. 149. My own professional association with Carmen Finestra, one of the show's enduring writer/producers, led to extensive discussions about how difficult it was to structure the show because Cosby insisted that the writers not rely on the usual structure of simple conflict as the through line in the show. As the conventional conflict structure can easily turn into a linguistic machine for producing only those human traits that satisfy its requirements, Cosby's desire to render the Huxtables through a more complex and humane portrait than is common in television shows about African American communities would lead him away from conflict recipes for storytelling.

4. Cosby's stated goal for *The Cosby Show* was to reflect a family of the 1980s with an evolved family dynamic. "If this was 1964, my wife could do the cooking and I could be the guy on the sofa who just says, 'Let your mother handle this.' But today a lot of things have changed and I want the show to reflect those changes. A family where the father cooks, too, and pitches in with the kids, and where everyone has responsibilities." Smith, *Cosby*, p. 148.

5. Bill Cosby maintained a scrupulous commitment to professional discipline on the set. The following anecdote passed on to me by Carmen Finestra illustrates the extremes to which Cosby carried his demand for order. During the preparation to tape an episode in which a dog was to appear, as Cosby walked onto the set he heard the dog, who was intended for the role, bark. On asking whether anyone had told the dog to bark, and learning that no one had, he insisted that the dog be fired, and replaced by another dog who would only act on command. As radical as this behavior is, it certainly demonstrates why Cosby and Rashad belong in the category of Thematic Couple rather than Synergistic Couple. The spontaneity Cosby cultivated was necessarily within bounds that he drew rather than the eruption of energy that he might then welcome into his creation.

6. Cybill Shepherd, with Aimee Lee Ball, *Cybill Disobedience* (New York: HarperCollins, 2000), pp. 211–229. Shepherd is not clear about the chronology

of the rupture between her, Glenn Gordon Caron, and Bruce Willis. However, she appears to have become burned out within the first two years of production, and, from her point of view, tension between her and Willis grew from mutual exhaustion and the pressures of fame and success. However, she is precise about the conflicts that exploded in 1988 that affected her character. Among the problems, she believes, was that Caron took her pregnancy that year as a personal affront and that he punished Shepherd by distorting Maddie. She is particularly resentful about the scripting of Maddie's sudden marriage with a man she met on a train trip, while pregnant. "When I strongly voiced my objection that the character we had created in Maddie would never do such a thing, Glenn said words to the effect of 'Just shut up and do your job, you're not producing this show'" (p. 219). Maddie's sudden marriage certainly does violate the years of dramatizing Maddie as a person who cannot act on spontaneous impulse. And there is no question but that it created a big imbalance in the show's point of view about Maddie and David, making him seem the aggrieved victim of Maddie's selfishness, but also making it unnecessary for Willis to play any love scenes with Shepherd and thus relieving him of the necessity of feigning tenderness for a woman he disliked.

7. Glenn Gordon Caron and Bruce Willis, "Commentary," *Moonlighting, The Pilot*. DVD distributed by Anchor Bay Entertainment, Inc., 2000.

8. In *Cybill Disobedience*, Shepherd notes the particularly patriarchal form that Caron's 1988 vendetta against her took. Specifically, one script called for Maddie to counsel her client to continue a relationship with a man who had been sending her threatening letters. "'No sane person would encourage a woman to engage with a harasser,' I told him. . . . But Glenn was adamant . . ." (p. 223). She also refers to what she believes was Caron's attempt to stack the deck against Maddie as a feminist by revealing her to be an atheist, "My character could go no lower: a feminist atheist" (p. 223). But the low point came for Shepherd in "Atomic Shakespeare," in which Maddie was "made to be an impossibly unsympathetic character so that Petruchio aka David aka Bruce could score" (p. 223). To add insult to injury for Shepherd, the binding and gagging of the character was also played for laughs. "Big Man on Mulberry Street" featured a dream fantasy in which Maddie "looked a lot more like David's fantasy" (p. 225).

9. For all Willis's claims that after the show became a cultural phenomenon, in the second or third year, they did "whatever they wanted to" as far as comedy is concerned, the evidence on the tapes of the show's foray into a moderate form of reflexivity testifies to how narrowly Willis is impelled to define absolute freedom in a medium virtually paralyzed by conservative restrictions, mitigated in a significant way only by miracles, accidents, and acts of God. Caron and Willis, "Commentary."

10. Both Shepherd and Willis sported dark circles under their eyes because of the demanding schedule, as did the crew, "but they don't have the expectations of physical perfection imposed on them as the on-camera people do, and it's worse for women. . . . I was blamed if I looked exhausted, whereas squinty eyes and a two-day stubble only added to David Addison's rakish allure. . . . Gerald Finnerman, the director of photography, very kindly had a special sliding filter made for the lens of the camera, so when it panned from Bruce to

me, the heavier diffusion was slid into place to make me look 'prettier.'" Shepherd, *Cybill Disobedience*, p. 209.

11. Berry, *Screen Style*, p. 179. Rosalind Russell distills the situation of the strong woman in the 1940s movies in the following way: "I could order the clothes for my pictures in my sleep. I'd say . . . 'Make me a plaid suit, a striped suit, a grey flannel, and a negligee for the scene in the bedroom when I cry.'"

12. The full plot of "It's a Wonderful Job" is as follows: Maddie is in the doghouse with David and all her colleagues at the Blue Moon Detective Agency because she wants them to finish a job for a client that would mean working during Christmas week. At the same time, her aunt is in the hospital four blocks from Blue Moon, but Maddie hasn't found the time to visit, and Aunt Ruth dies before Maddie can see her. Maddie is depressed because she put work before Aunt Ruth, and leaves the office, further alienating David and the crew, who think she is taking time off capriciously. Maddie goes to a bar and drinks too much. In an ambiguous moment she slumps on the bar—is she asleep or awake?—and looks up to see a man, ethnic/Semitic in appearance, whom she mistakes for a masher. He is a version of the angel Clarence from the Capra film, and he grants her wish that she had sold the Blue Moon Agency two years before so she would never have had "all this trouble" with ungrateful employees. With the two years demolished, Maddie is taken on a tour of the results of her wish. Lovable Agnes (Allyce Beasley), the rhyming receptionist at the agency, has bought the place and her lust for success at any price has turned her into a terrible virago, worse even than Maddie. David has become successful on his own, and is about to marry model Cheryl Tiegs (as herself) when Maddie catches up with him at the engagement party, held at her apartment, now his. Maddie herself is at the end of her rope, having lost her money, and is about to commit suicide by driving her car into a wall when she wakes up. Returning to the agency, she is met by David, Agnes, and another employee, who have learned of the death of Aunt Ruth and feel bad about the way they treated her when she left. All is forgiven, and Maddie learns the "true meaning of Christmas."

There is a flourishing Listserv for *Moonlighting* which reflects an enduring interest in the show. The conversation tends toward a fairly light dialogue about wanting to kiss Bruce, and arguments over who was the father of Maddie's baby. The conversation does not usually reflect an audience concern with the kinds of gender bending that the series was originally intended to reflect. However, I joined the group temporarily and posed questions about my reservations about "It's a Wonderful Job." The responses revealed a division between the thoughtful and the defensive members of the group. The latter thought that my questions about the way that the episode positioned Maddie were an attack on her, and defended her as a wonderful, even perfect role model for girls. The more thoughtful responses are reflected in the following: "i've always had my criticism of this episode. seemed like they were being hard on her. it's true that she didn't have to have them work on christmas, but as far as mean bosses go, she's not one of them. she only wants them to do a little work. most of them are unemployable anyway. agnes seems the only one who appreciates her in a lot of episodes. and at this point in maddie and david's relationship, he should have defended her. and i think agnes' evil self was a lot harsher than maddie!"

In general, the members of the *Moonlighting* Listserv were neither intellectual nor critical in the best sense of those words. They wanted to find ways to praise the series as a perfect show, despite the flaws Shepherd recounted in her autobiography, with which many of the group were familiar. Unlike the on-line conversations about *The X-Files*, this Listserv tended, in the usual manner of fans, to justify most decisions made by the creative community that produced the show, rather than to keep the creators on their toes. The most convoluted of the defensive statements embraced all the fantasy shows indiscriminately as part of a larger arc that showed that Maddie and David are Old Souls. An excerpt from the very extensive exegesis follows:

> Because M&D are "old souls", and have lived, circling each other, many times before (as Jerome confirmed), it can be safely said that because this is so, we, who all agree (I think all) we equally ache in disappointment over ML's end, can be comforted in knowing that what we experienced to be "MOONLIGHTING" was ONLY ONE of the many life-times shared by M&D. We see examples of their other life-times together in "ATOMIC SHAKESPEARE" and "THE DREAM SEQUENCE ALWAYS RINGS TWICE" (granted these are both ML-inspired stories, but each are independent of M&D's real-life "BLUE MOON"-life). When "BABY HAYES" is scared and put-off by the seeming fighting between M&D, Jerome consoles him by telling him that while they do ". . . this little tango", it is the very wonderfulness that IS M&D, as they are not "fighting", but rather "dancing" around each other in their own funny way of communicating and connecting with one another.

The *X-Files* on-line community demonstrates the more innovative possibilities for the relationship between fans and show; the relationship between *Moonlighting*'s on-line fans and the *Moonlighting* creators is more conventional, though it is impossible to say what might have happened had there been such a flourishing on-line Listserv while the series was being produced.

13. Caron and Willis, "Commentary."

14. For those readers unfamiliar with *The Shop around the Corner*, it is a romantic comedy about the rivalry between two salespeople in a shop in old Vienna, played by James Stewart and Margaret Sullavan, who, as they bicker with each other, are simultaneously carrying on a romantic correspondence as anonymous pen pals. When the man discovers the identity of his unknown lady of the letters, the daily relationship between the two begins to change, mystifying the woman, until he reveals to her his identity, and they embark on an in-the-flesh romance.

15. Lawrence J. Quirk, *Paul Newman* (Dallas: Taylor, 1996), pp. 314–317. *Mr. and Mrs. Bridge* began as an idea Joanne Woodward had for television, a mini-series based on the two novels by Evan S. Connell, *Mr. Bridge* and *Mrs. Bridge*. At a dinner party, a discussion with James Ivory led to the idea to combine the two novels into one movie. Ivory was attracted to the project because "The world of Mr. and Mrs. Bridge is the world I grew up in" (p. 313). Woodward liked the project because it looked at a marriage from competing

viewpoints (husband's and wife's) that had "absolutely no relationship one to the other" (p. 313). And Newman found the project attractive because "on the surface the story seemed to be about nothing. 'But it really is about absolutely everything, life and love and the family'" (p. 313).

16. In *Movie Wars*, Rosenbaum passionately argues against claims that the low caliber of films is a result of a low caliber of spectator. He argues that media market research, which often reaches preordained conclusions, is a smoke screen for self-serving decisions by media executives who claim they are giving a coarse and unsubtle public what it wants but who are actually cynically manipulating the audience. His argument is certainly supported by the *X-Files* phenomenon, which demonstrates the ability of huge numbers of fans to work with intricate subtleties of plot, character, and image structure.

17. Jacques Attali, *Noise: The Political Economy of Music* (Minneapolis: University of Minnesota Press, 1996), p. 5.

APPENDIX ONE. FRED, GINGER, AND RKO

1. Two important sources of biographical information on Rogers and Astaire are their autobiographies: Fred Astaire, *Steps in Time* (New York: Harper, 1959); Ginger Rogers, *Ginger: My Story* (New York: HarperCollins, 1991). The Fred Astaire Collection at the Boston University Library reveals information suppressed in Astaire's official autobiography.
2. Fred Astaire Collection.
3. Fred Astaire Collection.
4. Rogers, *Ginger*, p. 91.
5. Mueller, *Astaire Dancing*, p. 8.
6. Ibid.
7. Richard Brownell Jewell, "A History of RKO Radio Pictures, Incorporated 1928–1942" (Ph.D. diss., University of Southern California, 1978), p. 219.
8. Ibid., p. 220.
9. Astaire, *Steps in Time*, p. 195.
10. Jewell, "A History of RKO Radio Pictures," p. 220.
11. Rogers, *Ginger*, p. 150.
12. Mueller, *Astaire Dancing*, p. 16.
13. Ibid.
14. Ibid., p. 15.
15. Rogers, *Ginger*, p. 136.
16. Croce, *The Fred Astaire and Ginger Rogers Book*, p. 89.
17. Ibid., p. 112.
18. The Columbia University Oral History Project.
19. Croce, *The Fred Astaire and Ginger Rogers Book*, p. 127.
20. Ginger Rogers, Oral History Project, Columbia University.
21. Ibid., p. 284.
22. Rogers, *Ginger*, pp. 151, 162, 177, 201–202, 284.
23. Astaire, *Steps in Time*, p. 210.
24. Rogers, *Ginger*, p. 143.
25. Ibid.

APPENDIX TWO. THEORIZING CHEMISTRY IN ENTERTAINMENT VIA NEUROSCIENCE

1. Damasio, *Descartes' Error*. "My view then is that having a mind means that an organism forms neural representations which can become images, be manipulated in a process called thought, and eventually influence behavior by helping predict the future, plan accordingly, and choose the next action" (p. 90).

2. Antonio Damasio, *The Feeling of What Happens: Body and Emotion in the Making of Consciousness* (New York: Harcourt Brace, 1999) p. 11.

3. Damasio, *Descartes' Error*, p. 4.

4. Damasio presents an extensive, highly accessible, and fascinating account of the Phineas Gage case. Ibid., pp. 3–19.

5. Ibid., p. 172.

6. Ibid., p. 173.

7. Ibid., p. 172.

8. Ibid., p. 228.

9. Ibid., p. 229.

BIBLIOGRAPHY

SECONDARY SOURCES—BOOKS AND ARTICLES

The American Film Industry. Ed. Tino Balio. Madison: University of Wisconsin Press, 1985.
The American Movie Industry: The Business of Motion Pictures. Ed. Gorham Kindem. Carbondale: University of Illinois Press, 1982.
Affron, Charles, and Mirella Jona Affron. *Sets in Motion: Art Direction and Film Narrative.* New Brunswick, N.J.: Rutgers University Press, 1995.
Andersen, Christopher. *An Affair to Remember.* New York: Avon, 1997.
Anderson, Gillian. "The Truth about David Duchovny." http://www.usaweekend.com.
Astaire, Fred. *Steps in Time.* New York: Harper, 1959.
Astaire, Fred, and Bob Thomas. *Astaire the Man the Dancer: The Life of Fred Astaire.* New York: St. Martin's, 1984.
Attali, Jacques. *Noise: The Political Economy of Music.* Minneapolis: University of Minneapolis Press, 1985.
Aydelotte, Winifred. "The Miseries of Nudism." *Photoplay* (September 1934): 26–27, 119.
Baars, Bernard. *In the Theatre of Consciousness: The Workspace of the Mind.* Oxford: Oxford University Press, 1997.
Babbington, Bruce. *Affairs to Remember: The Hollywood Comedy of the Sexes.* Manchester, England: Manchester University Press, 1989.
Balazs, Bela. *Theory of the Film: Character and Growth of a New Art.* New York: Dover, 1970.
Barry, Philip. *Without Love: A Comedy in Three Acts.* New York: Coward-McCann, 1943.
Becker, Paul. "Star of Midnight." *The Friends of Ginger Rogers Society Quarterly* 2.3 (May–July 1998) [unnumbered pages].
Behlmer, Rudy. "Johnny Weissmuller: Olympics to Tarzan." *Films in Review* (July–August 1996): 20–33.

———. "Tarzan at MGM." In *The Cinema of Adventure, Romance and Terror.* Ed. George E. Turner. Hollywood: ASC Press, 1989. 115–137.
Benjamin, Walter. *Illuminations.* Trans. Harry Zohn. New York: Schocken, 1969.
Berry, Sarah. *Screen Style: Fashion and Femininity in 1930s Hollywood.* Minneapolis: University of Minnesota Press, 2000.
Black, Gregory D. *Hollywood Censored.* Cambridge: Cambridge University Press, 1994.
Bordwell, David, Janet Staiger, and Kristin Thompson. *The Classical Hollywood Cinema.* New York: Columbia University Press.
Bringing Up Baby. Ed. Gerald Mast. New Brunswick, N.J.: Rutgers University Press, 1988.
Britton, Andrew. *Katharine Hepburn.* London: Studio Vista, 1995.
Caron, Glenn Gordon. "Glenn Gordon Caron and Tom Fontana." *On Writing* 11 (April 2000): 1–16.
Cavell, Stanley. *Pursuits of Marriage: The Hollywood Comedy of Remarriage.* Cambridge: Harvard University Press, 1981.
Crick, Francis. *The Astonishing Hypothesis: The Scientific Search for the Soul.* New York: Touchstone Books, 1995.
Croce, Arlene. *The Fred Astaire and Ginger Rogers Book.* New York: E. P. Dutton, 1972.
Crowther, Bosley. *Hollywood Rajah: The Life and Times of Louis B. Mayer.* New York: Holt, Rinehart and Winston, 1960.
———. *The Lion's Share: The Story of an Entertainment Empire.* New York: E. P. Dutton, 1957.
Damasio, Antonio R. *Descartes' Error: Emotion, Reason, and the Human Brain.* New York: G. P. Putnam's Sons, 1994.
———. *The Feeling of What Happens: Body and Emotion in the Making of Consciousness.* New York: Harcourt Brace, 1999.
Deny all Knowledge: Reading the X-Files. Ed. David Lavery, Angela Hague, and Marla Cartwright. Detroit: Wayne State University Press.
Durgnat, Raymond. *The Crazy Mirror: Hollywood Comedy and the American Image.* New York: Horizon, 1970.
Dyer, Richard. "Charisma." In *Stardom: Industry of Desire,* ed. Christine Gledhill. London: Routledge, 1991. 57–60.
Edelman, Gerald M. *Bright Air, Brilliant Fire: On the Matter of Mind.* New York: Basic Books, 1993.
Edwards, Ted. *X-Files Confidential: The Unauthorized X-Philes Compendium.* Boston: Little, Brown, 1996.
Eisenstein, Sergei. *Film Form.* Edited and translated by Jay Leyda. San Diego: Harcourt Brace, 1949.
Fury, David. *Kings of the Jungle: An Illustrated Reference to Tarzan on Screen and Television.* Jefferson, N.C.: McFarland, 1994.
Gallagher, Kristin. "Living Legends." *Soap Opera Digest* (January 4, 2000): 48–51.
Gehring, Wes D. *Screwball Comedy: A Genre of Madcap Romance.* Westport, Conn.: Greenwood, 1986.

Gomery, Douglas. *The Hollywood Studio System*. New York: St. Martin's, 1986.
Graser, Marc. "F/x Alert: Houses on Overload." *Variety* (June 26–July 9, 2000): 1, 70.
Hepburn, Katharine. *Me: Stories of My Life*. New York: Ballantine, 1991.
Higham, Charles. *Merchant of Dreams: Louis B. Mayer, M.G.M., and the Secret Hollywood*. New York: Donald I. Fine, 1993.
Hirsch, Foster. *Love, Sex, Death, and the Meaning of Life: The Films of Woody Allen*. New York: Limelight Editions, 1990.
Horkheimer, Max, and Theodor W. Adorno. "The Culture Industry: Enlightenment as Mass Deception." In *Dialectic of Enlightenment*. New York: Herder and Herder, 1972. 120–167.
Jacobs, Lea. *The Wages of Sin: Censorship and the Fallen Woman Film, 1928–1942*. Berkeley: University of California Press, 1995.
Jewell, Richard Brownell. "A History of RKO Radio Pictures, Incorporated 1928–1942." Unpublished Ph.D. diss., University of Southern California, 1978.
Jewell, Richard, and Vernon Harbin. *The RKO Story*. New York: Arlington House, 1982.
Kazan, Elia. *A Life*. New York: Doubleday, 1989.
Kendall, Elizabeth. *The Runaway Bride: Hollywood Romantic Comedy of the 1930s*. New York: Doubleday, n.d. Originally published by Knopf in 1990.
Koenig, Oliver, and Stephen Michael Kosslyn. *Wet Mind: The New Cognitive Neuroscience*. New York: Free Press, 1995.
Lardner, Ring, Jr. "On Writing, A Publication of the Writer's Guild of America, East, Inc." No. 7 (September 1997): 1–60.
Lasky, Betty. *RKO: The Biggest Little Major of Them All*. Englewood Cliffs, N.J.: Prentice-Hall, 1984.
Lax, Eric. *Woody Allen, A Biography*. New York: Vintage, 1992.
LeDoux, Joseph. *The Emotional Brain: The Mysterious Underpinnings of Emotional Life*. New York: Simon and Schuster, 1996.
Lee, Julianne. "X Symbol." *Starlog: The X-Files and Other Eerie TV* 1 (December 1995): 35–38, 67.
Lehman, Peter, and William Luhr. *Thinking about Movies: Watching, Questioning, Enjoying*. Fort Worth: Harcourt Brace, 1999.
Loy, Myrna, and James Kotsilibas-Davis. *Myrna Loy: Being and Becoming*. New York: Knopf, 1987.
Lyons, Charles. "Passion for Slashin': Studios Ax Producer Pact, Strip Frills from Deals." *Variety* (June 26–July 9 2000): 1, 69.
Marx, Samuel. *Mayer and Thalberg: The Make-Believe Saints*. New York: Random House, 1975.
Memo from David O. Selznik. Selected and edited by Rudy Behlmer. Hollywood: Samuel French, 1989.
Moore, Rachel O. *Savage Theory*. Durham, N.C.: Duke University Press, 2000.
Mordden, Ethan. *The Hollywood Studios*. New York: Knopf, 1987.
Mueller, John. *Astaire Dancing*. New York: Wing Books, 1985.

Nielson, Ray. "A Final Interview with Maureen O'Sullivan (1911–1998)." *Classic Images*, no. 278 (August 1998): C-10–C-13.

Nochimson, Martha. *No End to Her: Soap Opera and the Female Subject.* Berkeley: University of California Press, 1993.

Perez, Gilberto. *The Material Ghost.* Baltimore: Johns Hopkins University Press, 1998.

Pickard, Roy. *The Hollywood Studios.* London: Frederick Muller, 1978.

Pierce, John J. "In Dangerous Purpose: The Quest of Mulder and Scully." *Spectrum* 16 (November 1998): 8–9.

———. "The Spiritual Journey of Fox Mulder." *Spectrum* 8 (January 1997): 2–9.

Quirk, Lawrence J. *The Complete Films of William Powell.* Secaucus, N.J.: Citadel Press, 1986.

———. *Paul Newman.* Dallas: Taylor, 1996.

Ray, Robert B. *The Avant-Garde Finds Andy Hardy.* Cambridge: Harvard University Press, 1995.

Richter, Conrad. *The Sea of Grass.* Athens: Ohio University Press, 1992.

Rogers, Ginger. *Ginger: My Story.* New York: HarperCollins, 1991.

Rosenbaum, Jonathan. *Movie Wars: How Hollywood and the Media Conspire to Limit What Films We Can See.* Chicago: A Cappella Books, 2000.

Schachter, Daniel L. *Searching for Memory: The Brain, the Mind, and the Past.* New York: HarperCollins, 1997.

Schatz, Thomas. *The Genius of the System.* New York: Holt, 1988.

———. *Hollywood Genres: Formulas, Filmmaking, and the Studio System.* New York: Random House, 1981.

Sennett, Ted. *Lunatics and Lovers.* New York: Limelight Editions, 1981. Originally published 1973.

Shepherd, Cybill. *Cybill Disobedience.* New York: HarperCollins, 2000.

Sheridan, Morley. *Shall We Dance: The Life of Ginger Rogers.* New York: St. Martin's, 1995.

Sikov, Ed. *Screwball: Hollywood's Madcap Romantic Comedies.* New York: Crown, 1989.

Smith, Ronald. *Cosby.* New York: St. Martin's, 1986.

Sterritt, David. *The Films of Jean-Luc Godard: Seeing the Invisible.* Cambridge: Cambridge University Press, 1999.

Stewart, Donald Ogden. *By a Stroke of Luck.* New York: Paddington Press, 1975.

"A Team of Two Who by Now Think as One." Arts and Leisure Section, *New York Times* (May 14, 2000): 17, 24.

Thomas, Bob. *Thalberg.* New York: Doubleday, 1969.

Thompson, Kristin. *Storytelling in the New Hollywood: Understanding Classical Narrative Technique.* Cambridge: Harvard University Press, 1999.

"Variety Facts on Pacts." *Variety* (June 26–July 9, 2000): 68.

Weales, Gerald. *Canned Goods as Caviar: American Film Comedy of the 1930s.* Berkeley: University of Chicago Press, 1985.

Wexman, Virginia Wright. *Creating the Couple: Love, Marriage, and Hollywood Performance.* Princeton: Princeton University Press, 1995.

Wild, David. "X Files under Cover." *Rolling Stone*, no. 734 (May 16, 1996): 38–41, 74.

Williams, Esther. *The Million Dollar Mermaid.* New York: Simon and Schuster, 1999.
Williams, Linda. "Feminist Film Theory: *Mildred Pierce* and the Second World War." In *Female Spectators: Looking at Film and Television.* Ed. E. Dierdre Pribram. London: Verso, 1988. 12–30.
W. S. Van Dyke's Journal. Edited and annotated by Rudy Behlmer. Filmmakers, no. 46. Lanham, Md.: Scarecrow Press, 1996.
Wylie, I. A. R. *Keeper of the Flame.* New York: Grosset and Dunlap, 1942.

PRIMARY AND SECONDARY SOURCES—ARCHIVAL MATERIALS

Boston University Department of Special Collections: The Fred Astaire Collection, the Myrna Loy Collection.
Louis B. Mayer Library of the American Film Institute: The *Radio Flash* Collection.
The Margaret Herrick Library of the Academy of Motion Picture Arts and Sciences:
The George Cukor Collection
The Production Code Administration Files
Adam's Rib
After the Thin Man
The Barkleys of Broadway
Carefree
Desk Set
Double Wedding
Evelyn Prentiss
Flying down to Rio
The Gay Divorcee
Guess Who's Coming to Dinner
I Love You Again
Keeper of the Flame
Libeled Lady
Love Crazy
Manhattan Melodrama
Pat and Mike
Roberta
The Sea of Grass
Shadow of the Thin Man
Shall We Dance
Song of the Thin Man
State of the Union
The Story of Irene and Vernon Castle
Tarzan the Ape Man
Tarzan and His Mate
Tarzan Finds a Son
The Thin Man
Top Hat

Without Love
Woman of the Year
Woman of the Year Script Collection.
The Oral History Project at Columbia University:
　Fred Astaire
　Ginger Rogers
　Pandro S. Berman
UCLA Arts Special Collections (Script Collection):
　Carefree
　Flying down to Rio
　Follow the Fleet
　The Gay Divorcee
　Shall We Dance
　Swing Time
　The Story of Irene and Vernon Castle
　Top Hat
USC Special Collections.
The *Lion's Roar* Collection.
Script Collections:
　The Barkleys of Broadway
　Song of the Thin Man plus conference notes
　Tarzan the Ape Man plus conference notes
　Tarzan and His Mate plus conference notes
　Without Love plus conference notes

PRIMARY SOURCES—INTERVIEWS

Anderson, Sheri, telephone interview, December 1, 8, 1989.
Astaire, Robyn, in-person, May 14, 1998.
Backstein, Karen, in person, telephone, e-mail, 1998–2000.
Becker, Paul, in-person, May 16, 1998.
Behlmer, Rudy, telephone interview, June 12, 1998.
Comden, Betty, telephone, October 4, 1999.
Grahn, Nancy Lee, in-person, May 14, 1998.
Jewell, Richard Brownell, in-person, May 13, 1998.
Kiberd, James, in-person, April 11, 1998.
Lester, Terry, in-person, e-mail, and telephone, 1998–2000.
Marland, Douglas, in-person, April 19, May 10, 1989, February 5, 1990.
Mulcahey, Patrick, e-mail, telephone, in-person, 1998–2000.
Olden, Roberta J., telephone, July 10, 1998.
Nichols, Stephen, in-person, May 15, 1998.
Pierce, John J., in-person, e-mail, 1999–2000.
Sheffield, Johnny, numerous e-mails, 1998.
Smith, Pat Falken, in-person, November 20, 1984.
Sterritt, David J., telephone, July 20, 2000.
Tysko, Autumn, e-mail, September 1, 2000.

INDEX

Italicized page numbers refer to photographs.

acting modes, 95–96, 125, 130, 290, 340–341nn.16–17
Adam's Rib, 31, 188, 201, 217–224, *220,* 228, 230, 348n.1, 351n.10
Adorno, Theodor W., 43, 333–334n.12, 339n.3, 352n.14
adultery, 189, 215–216, 348n.1, 352–353n.21
Affron, Charles and Mirella Jona, 330n.6
African American performers, 230–232, 260, 286, 288–294, 360n.27, 363–364nn.1–2
African cultures, 44, 67, 68, 69–70, 73, 79–80, 83, 335n.17, 342n.3
After the Thin Man, 99, 110, 111–112
alcohol consumption, 91, 102, 104, *105,* 106, 123
alienness. *See* Otherness/alienness
Allen, Woody: casting by, 269, 359n.23; films of, with Farrow, 241, 354n.7; influences on, 268, 269, 359n.22; offscreen relationship with Farrow, 241; offscreen relationship with Keaton, 233, 240–241, 283; rapid work mode of, 269, 356n.13, 359n.23. *See also* Allen/Keaton couple

Allen/Keaton couple: alienness in films of, 264–265, 268; in *Annie Hall,* 264, 269–271, 359n.24; comedy due to slippages and shifts in films of, 266–271; contradictions of fullness and emptiness in films of, 271–272; freedom from concept in films of, 269–270; as Functional Couple, 263; gender shifts in films of, 267, 273, 302; intimacy in films of, 263–274, 312; length of time working together, 263; in *Love and Death,* 264, 265–269, 270; in *Manhattan,* 264, 270, 271–273; in *Manhattan Murder Mystery,* 264, 273–274, 359n.24; and narrative discontinuities, 245; nonverbal quality in films of, 268–269; offscreen relationship of, 233, 240–241, 283; and paranoia, 264, 274; physical appearance of, and height discrepancy between, 268, 273, *275,* 359n.21; in *Sleeper,* 264, 265, *266,* 267, 268, 270; as Synergistic Couple generally, 233, 240–241, 243, 310; *X-Files* compared with, 264–265, *266,* 268, 271, 360n.26
All in the Family, 287, 294

All My Children, 360n.27
Andersen, Christopher, 347n.1, 350n.9
Anderson, Gillian. *See* Duchovny/Anderson couple
Anderson, Maxwell, 359n.22
Anderson, Pamela, 248
Anderson, Sheri, 361nn.29–30
androgyny. *See* gender issues
animals: in Astaire/Rogers film, 153; on *Cosby Show*, 364n.5; in Tarzan films, 41, 42, 51, 52, 56, 67, 69, 71, 72–73, 82, 83, 335n.17; in Thin Man films, 90, 101–102, 103, *105*, 106, 107, 124; in Tracy/Hepburn films, 201, 208–209
Annie Hall, 264, 269–271, 359n.24
Another Thin Man, 97–98, 99, 109, 112–118, 339–340n.13
Arnaz, Desi, 287
Arnold, Tom, 233
Arthur, Jean, 100
Astaire, Adele, 313–315, 317–318
Astaire, Fred: in "blackface," 156–157, 344n.11; and casting approval for leading ladies, 318; in *Damsel in Distress*, 318; early life of, 313–315; insecurities of, 317–318; marriage of, 314–316, 344n.10; as mimic, 181, 346n.25; mother of, 313–315; sister as dancing partner of, 317–318. *See also* Astaire/Rogers couple
Astaire, Phyllis Potter, 314–315, 344n.10
Astaire, Robyn, 344n.11, 346n.25
Astaire Dolly, 319
Astaire/Rogers couple: and acting skills of Rogers, 342n.2; and artificiality of Hollywood technologies, 19; Astaire's accents in films of, 346n.25; in *Barkleys of Broadway*, 136, 178, 179–184, 320, 346n.20, 346–347nn.24–27; and body, 136, 140–144, 147–150; in *Carefree*, 136, 171–177, 320, 344n.10, 345n.19, 346n.21; collegial relationship between, 320, 345–346n.20; costumes for, 16, 140, 146–147, 166, 321; dancing by, 135–137, 141, 143–149, 152–160, 164–167, 169–170, 172, 174, 176–177, 179–184, 311, 318–320, 343n.6, 345n.14, 345n.19, 346n.21; disputes between, 138, 316–321; early offscreen romance of, 315–316; entropy of last films of, 137, 177–184; financial arrangements with, 317; in *Flying Down to Rio*, 1, 2, 136, 162, 176, 316; in *Follow the Fleet*, 136, 167–171, 320, 345nn.15–16, 346n.25; Functional Couple in minor films of, 161, 163–166, 169; in *Gay Divorcee*, 136, 137–138, 176, 177, 316–317, 321–323; gender and raw energy in films of, 14, 16–18, 31, 36, 140–141, 144–147, 174–177; glamour of, 16–18, *17*, 139–140, 146–147, 166; Hepburn on, 139; images of, 16–18, *17*, *145*, *151*, *175*; interdependence between plot and dancing in, 135–139, 183–184; length of time working together, 4, 135; list of films by, 136; love scenes between, 156, 344n.10; major films of, 137–161; minor films of, 137, 161–171; misrecognition and misperceptions in films of, 141–144, 146, 148–150, 181, 182, 183; and musical score, 319; narrative patterns in films of, 9–10; and perfectionism of Astaire, 319–320; photography and editing of films of, 147, 159, 319, 343n.6; plots of films by, 136, 137, 138, 139, 161, 341n.1, 345nn.17–18; and Production Code Administration (PCA), 321–323; resistance of Astaire to pairing with Rogers, 316–317; restiveness of, 341n.17; and RKO, 2, 313, 316–323; in *Roberta*, 136, 162–167, 345n.14,

346n.25; in *Shall We Dance*, 136, 171–172, 180, 320, 345n.18, 346n.25; social limitations in films of, 149–161, 183; in *Story of Vernon and Irene Castle*, 136, 178–179, 346n.22; in *Swing Time*, 136, 137–138, 140, 149–161, 177, 179, 319, 320, 341–342n.1, 344nn.8–12; in *Top Hat*, 17, 31, 136, 137–138, 140–149, 145, 176, 183–184, 321, 343nn.5–6; transitional films of, 137, 171–177; treatment of, on movie set, 317, 346n.22

Attali, Jacques, 312

audience: and Allen/Keaton films, 270–271; and couple chemistry generally, 3, 4–5, 37, 309–310, 332–333n.13, 368n.16; and escapism, 3, 8, 23, 30, 78, 133, 187, 232, 333n.13; and Hepburn and Tracy, 195, 206, 207; and internet fan communities, 354n.9, 355–356n.10, 357nn.15–16, 358–359n.20, 363–364n.1, 366–367n.12; and *Woman of the Year*, 195; of *X-Files*, 256–258, 368n.16

Austerlitz, Ann, 313–315

Bacall, Lauren, 349n.8
Baldwin, Alec, 354n.4
Ball, Lucille, 287
Bananas, 269
Barkleys of Broadway, 136, 178, 179–184, 320, 346n.20, 346–347nn.24–27
Barr, Roseanne, 233, 287
Beatty, Warren, 240, 354n.6
beauty and glamour: and Allen/Keaton couple, 268, 273, 275, 359n.21; of Astaire/Rogers couple, 16–18, 17, 139–140, 146–147, 166; and domination/submission gender relations, 54–55, 334n.15; and Geary/Francis couple on *General Hospital*, 275, 276; and *Moonlighting*, 296, 302, 365–366n.10; Nordic Ideal in, 54, 119, 268, 334n.15; in Tarzan films, 43, 49–50, 55–57, 58, 71–73, 82, 336n.19; in Thin Man films, 101–102, 107–108, 110–112, 119–120; Wexman on glamour, 110; in *Without Love*, 210–211

Behlmer, Rudy, 336n.20, 338n.24
Bendix, William, 200
Bergman, Ingmar, 267, 269
Bergman, Ingrid, 24
Berkeley, Busby, 157
Berman, Pandro, 316–317, 319, 322, 323, 345n.13, 346n.22
Bishop, Julie, 54, 55
"Blackface," 156–157, 344nn.11–12
blacks. *See* African American performers; African cultures
body: in Astaire/Rogers films, 136, 140–144, 147–150; and *Cosby Show*, 293–294; mind-body connection, 328; in *Mr. and Mrs. Bridge*, 306–307; physicality between Geary and Francis, 281–282; in Tarzan films, 50–53, 55–59, 74, 80; in Thin Man films, 91–92, 101–102, 107; and touch in Tarzan films (MGM), 51–52, 72–82, 83; in Tracy/Hepburn films, 208–211, 219–221; Weissmuller's body used in film promotions, 336n.19; in *X-Files*, 247, 251, 252–254, 256, 257–261
Bogart, Humphrey, 11, 24, 263, 301, 340n.15, 349n.8
"Bojangles," 156–158, 344nn.11–12
Bonanza, 204
Bordwell, David, 7
Boreanaz, David, 287
"Bouncin' the Blues," 181
brain functions, 21, 36, 325–328
Brando, Marlon, 267, 354n.4
Breen, Joe, 104, 322, 338n.24, 350n.9, 352n.21
Bringing Up Baby, 24–25
Broadway Danny Rose, 354n.7
Broderick, Helen, 33, 150–151, 332n.12

Broderick, Matthew, 354n.4
Buffy the Vampire Slayer, 287, 355n.10
Burroughs, Edgar Rice, 43, 45–46, 62–63, 68, 76, 80, 334n.13
Burton, Richard, 233, 349–350n.8
business practices. *See* economics and business practices

Cagney, James, 340n.15
camp couples, 33, 331–332nn.10–11
Capra, Frank, 73, 100, 132, 215, 216, 297, 352n.21
Captain Blood, 27–30, *29*
Carefree, 136, 171–177, *175,* 320, 344n.10, 345n.19, 346n.21
"Carioca," 149, 176
carnivalization, 199–200
Caron, Glenn Gordon, 295–296, 365n.6, 365n.8
Carter, Chris, 245, 247–249, 262, 283, 356n.11, 357nn.14–16, 358n.18, 358n.20
Casablanca, 24
Cassavetes, John, 241, 354n.8
Castellaneta, Dan, 287
Castle, Irene, 178, 346n.22
Castle, Vernon, 178
censorship. *See* Production Code Administration (PCA)
"Change Partners," 176–177, 345n.19
Chaplin, Charlie, 90, 268
charisma, 329n.2. *See also* couple chemistry
"Cheek to Cheek," 146–148, 321
Cheers, 287
chemistry onscreen. *See* couple chemistry; and specific couples and movies
Chevalier, Maurice, 11, 33, 304, 331n.10
Ching, William, 224, 225, 348n.1
Christie, Julie, 240, 354n.6
class issues, 87–89, 99, 108–109, 112–113, 224–227, 275, 276
Colbert, Claudette, 329n.3

"Color Blind," 174
Comden, Betty, 179, 346n.20, 346n.23–24, 346–347nn.26–27
Communism/anti-Communism, 34–35, 132, 185–187, 214, 232, 340n.15
"Continental," 149, 176, 180
Cooper, Gary, 11, 100, 129
Cooper, Merrian C., 322
Cosby Show, 12, 243, 286, 287, 288–294, *289,* 311, 363–364n.1, 364nn.3–5
couple chemistry: artificiality of Hollywood technologies versus, 19–20, 21; and audience, 3, 4–5, 37, 309–310, 332–333n.13, 368n.16; and camp couples, 33, 331n.10; contemporary actors' disinterest in couple work, 238–239; energy versus craft in, 3, 13, 16–18; and ideology, 20–21, 23, 34–37, 57–59, 132, 188–189, 193, 235; neuroscience on, 21, 325–328; and new industrial economics, 236–243, 309; pressure of couple work on individual identity, 238; and star chemistry, 7–8, 18–19, 34, 202–207; and storytelling practice, 7–8; studies on, 12–13, 34; and studio system, 5–6, 18–21, 85–86, 236, 237, 238, 313, 316; on television series, 237–238; in today's mass media couples generally, 235–236. *See also* Functional Couples; Iconic Couples; and specific screen couples and movies; Synergistic Couples; Thematic Couples
Crabbe, Buster, 54, 55
Crawford, Joan, 11, 15–16, 25–26, 330n.3, 352n.20
Crimes and Misdemeanors, 274, 354n.7
Croce, Arlene, 341–342nn.1–2, 343nn.4–5, 344nn.8–9, 345n.14, 345–346nn.18–20, 347n.28
Crouse, Russel, 214

Cruise, Tom, 239–240, 354n.5
Cukor, George, 200, 204, 217, 225, 226, 350n.9

Damascio, Antonio R., 326–328, 369n.1
Damsel in Distress, 318
dance. *See* Astaire/Rogers couple
Dance, Fools, Dance, 11, 330n.3
Dancing Lady, 11, 25–26, 330n.3
Daniels, Jeff, 274
Danson, Ted, 287
Day, Doris, 33, 187, 331n.10
Days of Our Lives, 341n.17, 360n.27
De Havilland, Olivia, 26, 27–30, 29, 46
Del Rio, Dolores, 162
Desk Set, 188–189, 230
De Vito, Danny, 354n.4
Dies, Martin, 340n.15
Dietrich, Marlene, 35, 129
Dirty Harry series, 245
Disney's Tarzan film, 54, 342n.3
domination/submission gender relations: in Astaire/Rogers films, 140; in Iconic Couples, 25–26, 52, 54–55; and Nordic ideal of beauty, 54, 334n.15; as stereotypical male fantasy, 61; and Taming-of-the-Shrew reflex, 109; and Tarzan films, 50–52, 54, 65–66, 74; in Tarzan novels, 63; and Thin Man films, 112; in Tracy/Hepburn films, 193–199, 210–211; in *Trader Horn*, 54. *See also* gender issues; intimacy
Double Indemnity, 301
Double Wedding, 86, 125, 128–130
Douglas, Melvyn, 11, 213
Dovzhenko, Alexander, 34–35
Driving Miss Daisy, 332n.12
Duchovny/Anderson couple: in "all things" episode, 262; and body, 247; and casting decisions on, for *X-Files*, 248–249; in "Closure" episode, 357n.15; creative contributions of, to episodes of *X-Files*, 259, 261–262, 358nn.18–19; debates between Scully and Mulder, 250–252; denial of sex between, 356n.11; Duchovny's explanation of chemistry between, 283; gaze between Scully and Mulder, 251, 252; images of, 251, 354–355n.10; intimacy and synergy between, 246–253, 255–259, 261–263, 283–284, 312, 354–356nn.10–11, 356–357n.14, 358n.17; last episode of, on *X-Files*, 262–263; in "Milagros" episode, 255–259, 286; and Mulder's abduction, 262, 359n.20; original concept of Mulder and Scully, 245–246; in pilot episode of *X-Files*, 249–253, 356–357n.14; and plots of *X-Files*, 246; in "Requiem" episode, 358–359n.20; and Scully's abduction, 247, 253; and Scully's cross, 358–359n.20; and Scully's disrobing in first episode, 252–253; and Scully's pregnancy, 262, 358–359n.20; in "Talitha Cumi" episode, 357–358n.17; and taping rhythms of *X-Files*, 356n.13; in "Unnatural" episode, 255, 259–262, 358n.19; work styles of, 340n.16, 356n.13
Dumont, Margaret, 33, 331–332n.11
Dunne, Irene, 162–164, 345n.13, 345nn.15–16
Dyer, Richard, 329n.2

Earth, 35
Eastwood, Clint, 245
economics and business practices: of contemporary entertainment industry, 236–243, 261–262, 309; link between identity and economics, 312; of studio system, 5–6, 18–21, 85–86, 136, 185, 236, 237, 238, 313, 316, 343n.5, 350n.10
Eddy, Nelson, 26, 331n.9
editing, 147, 159, 272, 319, 343n.6, 359n.25
Edward VII, Prince of Wales, 314
Edwards, Ted, 356n.11, 356n.13

EIDC. *See* Entertainment Industry Development Corporation (EIDC)
Eliot, T. S., 138
Entertainment Industry Development Corporation (EIDC), 358n.20
entropy: of Astaire/Rogers last films, 137, 177–184; Tracy/Hepburn last films, 230–232
escapism, 3, 8, 23, 30, 78, 133, 187, 232, 333n.13
ethnicity: and African American performers, 230–232, 260, 286, 288–294, 360n.27, 363–364nn.1–2; African cultures in Tarzan films, 44, 67, 68, 69–70, 73, 79–80, 83, 335n.17, 342n.3; and *Cosby Show*, 288–294; in *Gay Divorcee*, 322; in *Roberta*, 162–164; in *Sleeper*, 267, 268; in Thin Man films, 106, 119; in *Trader Horn*, 44, 53; and whites in "blackface," 156–157, 344nn.11–12. *See also* racism
Evans, Mary Beth, 360n.27, 362n.34
Evelyn Prentice, 86, 125–127
Ex-Mrs. Bradford, 131
experimental and independent films, 33, 240–241
eyeline match editing, 272, 359n.25
Eyes Wide Shut, 239–240, 354n.5

Fargo, 233
Farrow, Mia, 241, 274, 354n.7
Fascism/anti-Fascism, 188, 201–207, 343n.5, 347–348n.1
Feist, Felix, 40
Fellini, Federico, 269
Fenn, Sherilyn, 287
Fields, W. C., 33, 101, 331n.10
Fiennes, Joseph, 287
film noir, 100–101, 122, 123, 299, 301, 302
"Fine Romance," 155, 161
Finestra, Carmen, 364n.3, 364n.5
Finnerman, Gerald, 365–366n.10
First Amendment rights, 185–187
Flying Down to Rio, 1, 2, 136, 149, 162, 167, 176, 316
Flynn, Errol, 26, 27–30, *29*, 46
Follow the Fleet, 136, 167–171, 320, 345nn.15–16, 346n.25
Fontaine, Joan, 318
Francis, Genie. *See* Geary/Francis couple
Freed, Arthur, 346n.23
free speech, 185–187, 347–348n.1
From the Terrace, 303
Functional Couples: Allen/Keaton couple as, 263; in Astaire/Rogers minor films, 161, 163–166, 169; in contemporary films, 239, 310; definition and description of, 7, 8–9, 10, 11, 35, 132, 235, 248, 311, 328; parodies of, 187; on soap operas, 274; in Thin Man films, 118–119; in wartime and postwar movies, 187
Fury, 201

Gable, Clark: in *Dancing Lady*, 25–26; and domination/submission gender relations, 11, 13, 25–26; in *Gone with the Wind*, 11, 24, 26; as Iconic Couple male, 11, 12, 13, 14–15, 18, 24, 25–26, 46, 329–330n.3; image of, 14–15, *15*; list of films and costars of, 11, 329–330n.3; Loy as costar of, 11, *15*, 26, 32, 95, 330n.3; in *Test Pilot*, 26, 32
Gage, Phineas, 327, 328
Garland, Judy, 33, 179, 298, 331–332nn.10–11, 346n.20, 346n.24, 347n.27
Gay Divorcee, 136, 137–138, 149, 176, 177, 316–317, 321–323
gaze: of Duchovny/Anderson couple, 251, 252, 258; invasive gaze of Padgett in *X-Files*, 256, 258; in *Moonlighting*, 296, 302; of Tracy/Hepburn couple, 195–198, *196*, 206, 208–211, 219–221, 229
Geary/Francis couple: and alienness of Luke and Laura, 276–281; and

Geary's sexual preference, 282, 362–363n.35; image of, 278, 279, 284; and intensity of their work together, 281–282, 312, 362nn.32–33; and Laura's double nature, 275–276, 360n.28; length of time working together, 242–243; and Luke's rape of Laura, 277–278, 279, 361nn.30–31; and Luke's willingness to kill, 279–280, 362n.34; and narrative discontinuities, 244, 245; physical appearance of, 275, 276; physicality between, 281–282; and plots of *General Hospital*, 275–281, 360–361n.29, 362n.34; rehearsal and taping process of, for *General Hospital* scene, 278–283, 362n.33; and separation of Luke and Laura, 361n.32; as Synergistic Couple generally, 242–243, 274–275, 310
Gellar, Sarah Michelle, 287
gender issues: in Allen/Keaton films, 267, 273, 302; androgyny in *Pat and Mike*, 224, 228, 229; associations between narrative and masculinity and sound and femininity, 31; in *Cosby Show*, 291–294; gender crossing in Astaire/Rogers films, 140–141, 144; in *Guess Who's Coming to Dinner*, 230–232; massage incident in *Adam's Rib*, 219–220, 220; in *Moonlighting*, 286, 295–303, 365n.8; in *New Kind of Love*, 304; offbeat gender definition in Synergistic Couples, 12–14, 16–21; in Tarzan films, 50–52, 54, 65–66, 74; in Thin Man films, 93–94, 101, 102, 103, 109–110, 112, 113–114, 132–133; in Tracy/Hepburn films, 193–199, 205–207, 211, 214–229. *See also* beauty and glamour; domination/submission gender relations; Iconic Couples; intimacy; Synergistic Couples
General Hospital, 242–245, 274–284, 279, 310, 312, 354n.9, 360–362nn.28–34
Gere, Richard, 310
Gilda, 300
Girl Crazy, 315, 332n.11
glamour. *See* beauty and glamour
Gleason, Jackie, 287
Gleason, James, 33, 332n.12
Glorifying the American Girl, 40
Godard, Jean-Luc, 330n.5
"Goin' to Heaven on a Mule," 344n.12
Gone with the Wind, 11, 24, 26, 361n.31
Goodman, John, 287
Gordon, Ruth, 217
Grable, Betty, 275, 323, 360n.28
Grahn, Nancy Lee, 340n.16, 360n.27, 362nn.32–33
Grant, Cary, 11, 24–25, 33, 95–96, 331n.10
Green, Adolf, 179, 346n.20, 346nn.23–24, 346–347nn.26–27
Greene, Lorne, 204
Greystoke: The Legend of Tarzan, 71
Guess Who's Coming to Dinner, 189, 201, 230–232, 353n.22

Hall, Jon, 33, 331n.10
Hanks, Tom, 310
Hannah and Her Sisters, 274, 354n.7
Harlow, Jean, 11, 330n.3
Hays, Will, 322, 337n.24. *See also* Production Code Administration (PCA)
Hayward, Leland, 316–317
Hayworth, Rita, 300
Hecht, Ben, 23
Hepburn, Katharine: on Astaire/Rogers couple, 139; as athlete, 225; control over films by, 194, 350–351n.10; films of, without Tracy, 24–25, 287, 349n.4; friendships of, 350n.9; political views of, 186, 347–348n.1; public image and popularity of, 189–190, 194, 195, 214, 216–217, 349n.4; sexual

orientation of, 350n.9. *See also* Tracy/Hepburn couple
Hickman, Cordell, 69, 335n.18
Hildegard Withers series, 33, 332n.12
Hilliard, Harriet, 167, 345n.15
His Girl Friday, 195
historical labeling, 199, 201, 224, 226
Hitchcock, Alfred, 188, 348–349n.2
homosexuality, 193, 219, 282, 350n.9, 360n.27, 362–363n.35
Honeymooners, 287
Honky Tonk, 11, 330n.3
Hoover, J. Edgar, 347n.1
Horkheimer, Max, 43, 333–334n.12, 339n.3, 352n.14
Horton, Edward Everett, 141, 323
House Un-American Activities Committee (HUAC), 185–187, 214, 347–348n.1
Hudson, Rock, 33, 187, 331n.10
Hume, Cyril, 69, 77
Hurston, Zora Neale, 292
Husbands and Wives, 274, 354n.7
Huston, Anjelica, 240, 354n.6
Hyams, Leila, 62
Hyman, Bernard, 41, 62, 70, 77

Iconic Couples: audience reaction to, 332–333n.13, 334n.12; cliched domination/submission patterns in, 25–26, 52, 54–55; compared with Synergistic Couples, 5–12, 22–33, 35–36, 333n.13; compared with Thematic Couples, 286, 287–288; definition of, 9, 235, 310–311; disappearance of, in contemporary media, 238–239; documentary element of, 14–16; and escapism, 23, 30, 333n.13; examples of, 11, 24, 26–27, 329–330n.3; Gable Plus One formula for, 11–15, 18, 24–26, 46, 239, 329–330n.3; neuroscience on, 328; Newman/Woodward couple as, 303; Powell/Loy couple as, 86, 125–130; predictability and familiarity of, 26–30; in soap operas, 341n.17; and star chemistry, 8, 9; and stereotypical representations of intimacy, 10–12, 13, 25–30; synergistic moments by, 32; Taylor/Stanwyck couple as, 349n.8; Tracy/Hepburn couple as, 217
Ideology, 20–21, 23, 34–37, 57–59, 132, 188–189, 193, 235
"I'd Rather Lead a Band," 169
"I'll Be Hard to Handle," 164–165, 166
illegitimacy, 213, 348n.1
I Love Lucy, 287
"I'm Putting All My Eggs in One Basket," 169, 320
independent films. *See* experimental and independent films
internet fan communities, 354n.9, 355–356n.10, 357nn.15–16, 358–359n.20, 363–364n.1, 366–367n.12
intertextuality, 200–201
intimacy: in Allen/Keaton films, 263–274, 283–284, 311; in Astaire/Rogers's dancing, 143–144, 147–148, 156–157, 158–160, 164–167, 169–170, 174, 181, 183–184, 311; audience preferences on, 309–310; on *Cosby Show*, 291–293; of Geary/Francis couple, 281–282, 312, 362nn.32–33; in Hildegarde Withers series, 332n.12; and Iconic Couples, 10–12, 13, 25–30; and interdependence of plot and dancing in Astaire/Rogers films, 135–139, 183–184; older definitions of, 236; oppositionality between Nick and Nora in Thin Man Series, 115–124; of Scully and Mulder in *X-Files*, 246–253, 255–259, 261–263, 283–284, 312, 354–356n.10–11, 356–357n.14, 358n.17; sexuality in *Moonlighting*, 300–302; sexuality in Thin Man films, 97–

98, 104–107; and Synergistic Couples generally, 13–14, 36–37, 311–312; in Tarzan films, 36, 50–53, 55–59, 66–67, 72–83, 83, 125, 311; in Tracy/Hepburn couple, 193–199, 211–212, 229; trivialization of, 334n.12
"Isn't It a Lovely Day to Be Caught in the Rain?," 143–144, 343n.4
It Happened One Night, 11, 329n.3
It's a Wonderful Life, 297

Jackson, Jonathan, 361n.30
Johnson, Van, 214, 215
Jolson, Al, 157, 344n.12
Joy, Jason, 322
Joyce, Brenda, 63
"Just the Way You Look Tonight," 154, 161, 320

Kahane, B. B., 338n.24
Kaiser of Atlantis, 35
Kanin, Garson, 217, 350n.10
Kanin, Michael, 350n.10
Kavner, Julie, 287
Keaton, Buster, 268
Keaton, Diane. *See* Allen/Keaton couple
Keeler, Ruby, 33, 331n.10
Keeper of the Flame, 188, 201–207, 213, 215, 217, 347–348n.1
Kelly, Gene, 33, 331n.10, 347n.28
Kennel Murder Case, 130
Kern, Jerome, 319
Kidman, Nicole, 239–240, 354n.5
King, Cynthia, 340n.16, 353–354n.3
Kolchak: The Night Stalker, 245–246, 248
Kramer, Stanley, 353n.22
Kruger, Stubby, 41
Kubrick, Stanley, 239–240, 354n.3

Laemmle, Carl, 338n.24
Lambert, Christopher, 71
Lansbury, Angela, 214, 348n.1, 353n.21
Laplanche, J., 356n.12

Lardner, Ring, Jr., 350–351n.10
Laurie, Piper, 354n.4
Lax, Eric, 359n.21, 359n.23
Lee, Julianne, 356n.13, 358n.19
Leigh, Vivien, 24, 26
Lerner, Alan Jay, 318
Lester, Terry, 340n.16, 341n.17
"Let's Call the Whole Thing Off," 172, 320
"Let's Face the Music and Dance," 169, 170, 345n.16
"Let's K-knock K-knees," 321–323
"Let Yourself Go," 169
Levant, Oscar, 181, 346n.26
Lewis, Sinclair, 350n.10
Lichtman, Al, 76
Life with Father, 308
Lindsay, Howard, 214
Lion in Winter, 287
listservs. *See* internet fan communities
Long, Shelley, 287
Long Hot Summer, 233, 241, 303
Lost Horizon, 73
love. *See* intimacy
Love and Death, 264, 265–269, 270
"Lovely to Look At," 166
Lover Come Back, 187, 331n.10
Loy, Myrna: costars of, excluding Powell, 11, 15, 26, 32, 95–96, 330n.3; early films of, 88, 102–103; political views of, 340n.15. *See also* Powell/Loy couple; Thin Man films

MacDonald, Jeanette, 26, 33, 331nn.9–10
MacLachlan, Kyle, 287
MacMurray, Fred, 299
Maltese Falcon, 301
Manhattan, 264, 270, 271–273
"Manhattan Downbeat," 181
Manhattan Melodrama, 1, 2, 95, 330n.3, 341n.17
Manhattan Murder Mystery, 264, 273–274, 359n.24
Mankiewicz, Joe, 195, 351n.10, 351n.12
Mannix, Mr., 338n.24

March, Fredric, 340n.15
Martin, Steve, 240, 354n.6
Marx, Groucho, 33, 91, 331–332n.11
Marx, Harpo, 275
Marx Brothers, 129, 332n.11
Mask of Fu Manchu, 103
Mayer, Louis B., 103, 194, 338n.24, 347–348n.1, 350nn.9–10
McCarthy, Joseph, 185, 186, 347n.1
McCrea, Joel, 11
McGavin, Darren, 245, 358n.18
McKay, Jimmy, 40, 44, 334n.14
McKim, Josephine, 339n.24
McLuhan, Marshall, 270–271
Meadows, Audrey, 287
Meadows, Jayne, 107
Me and My Gal, 201
MGM, 2, 40–41, 43, 44, 47, 54, 97, 103, 104, 106, 191, 194, 338–339n.24, 350n.10
Micheaux, Oscar, 288
Midsummer Night's Sex Comedy, 274, 354n.7
Mildred Pierce, 352n.20
Miller, Penelope Ann, 239, 354n.4
Minnelli, Vincente, 318
minstrel show, 156–157, 290, 344nn.11–12
Miracle, 186
Montez, Maria, 33, 331n.10
Montgomery, Robert, 299–300
Moonlighting, 12, 243, 286, 287, 294–303, *300,* 311, 354n.3, 364n.1, 364–365n.6, 365–366nn.8–10, 366–367n.12
Morgan, Dennis, 11
Morocco, 129
Morrow, Rob, 287
Mr. and Mrs. Bridge, 242, 286, 303–309, *306,* 367–368n.15
Mr. Blandings Builds His Dream House, 95–96
Mr. Deeds Goes to Town, 100
Mueller, John, 320, 341n.1, 343n.4, 344n.11, 345nn.14–15, 345n.17, 345n.19, 346n.21

Mulcahey, Patrick, 362n.32, 362–363n.35
Mulvey, Laura, 109, 132
musical films, 138, 157, 347n.28. See also Astaire/Rogers couple
musical scores, 136, 197–198, 201–202, 206, 225, 319, 342–343n.3
My Little Chickadee, 101, 331n.10
"My One and Only Highland Fling," 181
mystery genre, 130–131, 133, 332n.12. *See also* Thin Man films; *X-Files*

narrative: in Allen/Keaton movies, 245; masculinity associated with, 31; of *Mr. and Mrs. Bridge,* 308; and new mass media Synergistic Couples, 244–245; and old Synergistic Couples, 9–10, 244; paranoid narratives, 247, 249, 251, 253–254, 259, 264, 274, 275, 278, 279, 356n.12, 362n.34; and plot emphasis of movies, 7–8, 23; in Tarzan films, 82–83; of television series, 244
Nazism, 186, 199, 333–334n.12, 348n.1
neuroscience, 21, 36, 325–328
"Never Gonna Dance," 158–160
New Kind of Love, 303–304
Newman/Woodward couple, 12, 233, 241–242, 286, 303–309, *306,* 311, 367–368n.15
New York Stories, 354n.7
Nichols, Stephen, 360n.27, 362n.34
Nicholson, Jack, 240, 354n.6
"Night and Day," 177
Night at the Opera, 129, 332n.11
Nixon, Richard, 347n.1
"No, No They Can't Take That Away from Me," 172, 180, 181–182, 320
Northern Exposure, 287
"No Strings," 141
Novak, Kim, 188
No Way Out, 230
Nudity, 42, 52, 56–58, 337–339n.24

O'Connor, Carroll, 287, 294
Odets, Clifford, 359n.22
Oliver, Edna May, 33, 332n.12
180-degree rule, 148, 343–344n.7
O'Neill, Eugene, 359n.22
O'Sullivan, Maureen: personality of, 41; in *Thin Man*, 92–94; Weissmuller's sexual harassment of, 42. *See also* Tarzan films (MGM); Weissmuller/O'Sullivan couple
Otherness/alienness: in Allen/Keaton films, 264–265, 268; in *General Hospital*, 276–281; in *Moonlighting*, 286; and Synergistic Couples, 30–31, 36–37; and Tarzan films, 46–59, 77, 79; and Thin Man films, 132–133; and western film genre, 334–335n.17; in *X-Files*, 253–255, 259–261, 263, 264–265, 268, 357–358nn.15–17
O'Toole, Peter, 287

Pacino, Al, 239, 354n.4
Paltrow, Gwyneth, 287
Pan, Hermes, 319, 321
paranoia, 251, 253–254, 264, 274, 275, 278, 279, 356n.12, 362n.34
Pat and Mike, 188, 201, 217, 224–229, 348n.1
Patch of Blue, 230
Payne, John, 11
PCA. *See* Production Code Administration (PCA)
Peck, Gregory, 354n.4
Penn, Sean, 354n.4
Perkins, Anthony, 349n.2
Perry, Lincoln Theodore Monroe Andrew, 290, 364n.2
Peters, Bernadette, 240, 354n.6
"Piccolino," 149, 176
"Pick Yourself Up, Dust Yourself Off, Start All Over Again," 153–154
Picnic, 195
Pillow Talk, 187, 331n.10
Pitts, Zazu, 33, 332n.12

Pittsburgh, 35
Play It Again, Sam, 263, 359n.21
Poitier, Sidney, 230, 231
Pontalis, J.-B., 356n.12
Postman Always Rings Twice, 301
Potter, Phyllis, 314–315, 344n.10
Poussaint, Alvin, 364n.3
Powell, Dick, 33, 331n.10
Powell, William: family background of, 91; films of, other than Thin Man series, 92, 102–103, 125–131; physical attributes of, 92. *See also* Powell/Loy couple; Thin Man films
Powell/Loy couple: acting modes and performance styles of, 85, 86, 95–96, 125, 130; and body, 91–92, 101–102, 107; and class structure and materialism in films, 87–89, 99, 108–109, 112–113; and collaborative process of studio system, 85–86; compared with *Cosby Show*, 288–289; compared with Weissmuller/O'Sullivan couple, 85, 90; and cultural norms, 86–88, 98, 104; in *Double Wedding*, 125, 128–130; and dumbing down of Nora in later films, 119–122; and equality between Nick and Nora, 101, 103, 109–110; in *Evelyn Prentice*, 125–128; facial expressions of, 88, 103; glamour and beauty of, 101–102, 107–108, 110–112, 119–120; as Iconic Couple, 86, 125–130; images of, 89–98, *89, 93, 105*; and improvisatory tone on movie set, 90–91, 94–95, 97; intimacy between generally, 36, 311; length of time working together, 4, 85–86; and lighthearted repartee between Nick and Nora, 92–94; in *Manhattan Melodrama*, 1, 2, 95; narrative patterns of films of, 10; Nick and Nora as gender doubles, 14, 93–94, 102, 132–133; and Nick's male authority, 92, 101, 109–110, 121;

in non-synergistic films, 86, 124–131, 133; nonverbal interchanges of, 97–98; and Nora's blend of hauteur and playfulness, 88–89, 90, 103; and Nora's wealth in films, 87–88, 92, 133; offscreen friendship of, 96; and Otherness, 132–133; and parenthood in films, 112, 115, 124; and playful/serious struggle between Nick and Nora, 112, 115–124; and sexual exclusivity, 93–94, 108, 114–116; sexuality and double entendres in films, 97–98, 104–107; synergy of, described, 95–96, 340–341n.17; total number of films of, 86. *See also* Thin Man films
Principal Productions, 54
procreation, in Tarzan films, 80–81
Production Code Administration (PCA): and Astaire/Rogers films, 321–323; and conventional values, 13, 23, 82, 139, 202, 221; and documentation, 343n.5; end of, 230, 240; and *Gay Divorcee*, 321–323; and *Miracle*, 186; and Tarzan films, 52, 57, 70, 73, 81, 337–339nn.23–24; and Thin Man films, 91, 104–107, 124, 132; and Tracy/Hepburn films, 202, 216, 221, 347–348n.1
propaganda, 187, 352n.14
Psycho, 188, 349n.2
Purple Rose of Cairo, 274

racism: and Nordic ideal of beauty, 53, 54–55; in Tarzan films, 58–59, 68–70, 72, 335–336n.18; in Tarzan novels, 63; in Thin Man films, 106, 119; in *Trader Horn*, 44, 53; in western genre films, 334–335n.17; and whites in "blackface," 156–157, 344nn.11–12. *See also* ethnicity
Radio Days, 263
rape, 26, 277–278, 279, 361nn.30–31

Rashad, Phylicia. *See Cosby Show*
Raymond, Gene, 162
Rear Window, 333n.13
Red Dust, 11, 330n.3
rehearsals, 278–283, 319–320, 351n.10, 362n.33, 365–366n.10
Richards, Beah, 231
RKO, 2, 131, 276, 316–323, 338n.24, 346n.22
Roberta, 136, 162–167, 169, 345n.14, 346n.25
Roberts, Julia, 310
Robinson, Bill, 156, 344nn.11–12
Rogers, Ginger: early life and mother of, 313–315; films of, without Astaire, 131, 315; salary of, 317. *See also* Astaire/Rogers couple
Rogers, Lela McMath, 313–314
Rooney, Mickey, 33, 331–332n.11
Roosevelt, Franklin Delano, 199, 265
Roseanne, 287
Rosenbaum, Jonathan, 253n.1, 368n.16
Rossellini, Roberto, 186
Rowlands, Gena, 241, 354n.8
Russell, Rosalind, 36n.11, 126, 195, 351n.13
Ryan, Meg, 310
Ryan, Robert, 300

Sandrich, Mark, 138, 317, 319, 343n.5, 344n.10
Santa Barbara, 360n.27, 363n.36
Schwarzenegger, Arnold, 354n.4
science fiction, 187. *See also X-Files*
Scott, Randolph, 11, 162–163, 167, 345n.15
screen chemistry. *See* couple chemistry; and specific couples and movies
Sea of Grass, 188, 213–214, 348n.1
Selznik, David O., 137, 342n.3, 343n.5
Send Me No Flowers, 187, 331n.10
Sennett, Mack, 90
Serrano, Nestor, 256

Seventh Seal, 267
sexism. *See* domination/submission gender relations; gender issues
sexual harassment, 42
sexuality. *See* adultery; homosexuality; intimacy; rape
Shadow of the Thin Man, 99–100, 106, 112, 118–121, 132
Shakespeare in Love, 287
Shall We Dance, 136, 171–172, 180, 320, 345nn.17–19, 346n.25
Shaughnessy, Charles, 340n.16, 341n.17, 360n.27
Sheffield, Johnny, 41, 48, 335n.18
Shepherd, Cybill. *See* Willis/Shepherd couple
Shills, E. A., 329n.2
"Shoes with Wings On," 181
Shop around the Corner, 304, 367n.14
Simpsons, 287
Singin' in the Rain, 347n.28
Sirk, Douglas, 188
sitcoms. *See Cosby Show*; *Moonlighting*; television series
slavery, 28–30
Sleeper, 264, 265, *266*, 267, 268, 270
"Smoke Gets in Your Eyes," 166–167
Snow White, 90
soap operas, 274, 340–341nn.16–17, 353n.2, 355n.10, 356n.13, 360n.27. *See also General Hospital*
social class. *See* class issues
Song of the Thin Man, 100–101, 106–107, 122–124, 343n.3
sound, 31, 73, 342n.3. *See also* musical scores
Splendor in the Grass, 188
sports, 224–229, 260–261
Staiger, Janet, 7
Stanwyck, Barbara, 299, 349n.8
Stapleton, Jean, 287, 294
star chemistry/star system, 7–8, 18–19, 34, 202–207, 329n.2. *See also* couple chemistry; and specific couples and movies

Star of Midnight, 131, 132
Star Trek, 230–231
State of the Union, 188, 213, 214–217, 348n.1, 352–353nn.20–21
Steiner, Max, 342n.3
Stella Dallas, 112
"Stepin Fetchit," 290, 364n.2
Sterritt, David, 330n.5, 353n.1
Stevens, George, 320, 351n.10
Stewart, Donald Ogden, 204, 206, 347n.1
Stewart, James, 111, 188, 367n.14
Stoessel, Ludwig, 199
Story of Vernon and Irene Castle, 136, 178–179, 346n.22
Streetcar Named Desire (Williams), 267
Stromberg, Hunt, 106
studio system, 5–6, 18–21, 85–86, 136, 185, 236, 237, 238, 313, 316, 343n.5, 350n.10
Sullavan, Margaret, 367n.14
Svengali and Trilby, 177, 345–346n.20
Swing Time, 136, 137–138, 140, 149–161, *151*, 177, 179, 319, 320, 341–342n.1, 344nn.8–9, 344nn.11–12
"Swing Time Waltz," 155, 156–157, 158, 159, 319
"Swing Trot," 179–180
Synergistic Couples: Allen/Keaton couple as, 233, 240–241, 243, 263–274, 310; artificiality of Hollywood technologies versus, 19–20, 21; audience reaction to, 3, 4–5, 37, 332–333n.13; and collaborative process of studio system, 5–6, 18–21, 85–86, 313, 316; comparison between Iconic Couples, 5–12, 22–33, 35–36, 333n.13; comparison between old and new Synergistic Couples and, 243–244, 259; comparison between Thematic Couples and, 294, 306, 310; definition and description of, 2–5, 9–10, 310–311;

INDEX 389

Duchovny/Anderson Couple as, 242, 243, 245–263, 310; enduring appeal of, 24; explanations of synergistic processes by, 95–96, 281–283, 340–341n.17, 362n.32; Geary/Francis couple as, 242–243, 274–282, 310; gender definition and raw synergy of, 3, 12–14, 16–23, 30–31, 35–36, 309, 334n.12; and historical labeling, 199; and ideology, 188–189, 193, 235; intimacy between generally, 13–14, 36–37, 311–312; misunderstanding of, 37; narrative patterns of old and new Synergistic Couples, 9–10, 244–245, 259; neuroscience on, 21, 325–328; and new industrial economics, 236–243, 309; new mass media Synergistic Couples described, 236, 243–245, 259; and Otherness, 30–31, 36–37; people of color as, 360n.27; and secure sense of own masculinity/femininity, 60–61; and star chemistry, 7–8, 18–19; in television series and soap operas, 242–243, 360n.27; transformational energies and disruptions of, 30–31, 35–36; wartime and postwar pressures on, 132, 187, 213. *See also* Astaire/Rogers couple; Powell/Loy couple; Thematic Couples; Tracy/Hepburn couple; Weissmuller/O'Sullivan couple

Take a Letter, Darling, 195
talent agencies, 237, 239
Taming of the Shrew, 109, 349n.8
Tarzan and His Mate, 31, 46–48, 52, 56–59, 65, 66, 73, 76, 336n.23, 337–339n.24
Tarzan Escapes, 48, 75, 76, 335n.17, 336n.23
Tarzan film (Disney), 54, 342n.3
Tarzan films (MGM): action scenes in, 69–70; African cultures in, 44, 67, 68, 69–70, 73, 79–80, 83, 335n.17, 342n.3; beauty of Weissmuller/O'Sullivan couple, 49–50, 55; body, physicality, and gestures in, 50–53, 55–59, 74, 80; bond between Tarzan and Jane in, 46–59; Boy in, 48–49, 66, 71, 75–76, 81–82; Cheetah and other animals in, 41, 42, 51, 52, 56, 67, 69, 71, 72–73, 82, 83, 335n.17, 336n.23, 337–338n.24; compared with other Tarzan films, 54, 55, 60, 62, 68, 71–72; compared with Tarzan novels, 43, 45–46, 62–63, 334n.13; compared with *Trader Horn*, 44, 45, 53, 54, 334n.13; decline of, 63, 71, 80, 82–83; dialogue in, 1, 2, 59, 82, 336–337n.23; directors of, 40, 44, 334n.14; energy and couple chemistry in, 43–44, 70–71; and escapism, 78; and Eurocentric value system, 46–49, 57–59, 65–76, 83, 336–337n.23; European male characters in, 50, 56–57, 64, 65–67, 73, 78, 79, 80, 337n.24; female desire and hero's identity in, 44–46, 61–67; film images of Weissmuller/O'Sullivan couple in, 47, 53–59, 56, 58; Hume's ideas for later script for, 77; and ideology, 57–59; intimacy in, 36, 50–53, 55–59, 66–67, 72–83, 125, 311; Jane's character and changing values in, 40, 53, 57, 61–65, 74–76, 333n.1; Jane's father in, 46, 47, 50, 51, 62, 63, 64, 65; Jane's first encounter with Tarzan in, 50–53, 65, 74; Jane's modeling of European clothes in, 56–57, 58; Jane's rescue of Boy in, 75–76; Jane's seduction and betrayal of Tarzan in, 48, 75, 77–78; Jane's wounding in, 76–77, 78; jungle home of Tarzan and Jane in, 52, 82–83; land in, 44, 59–60, 67, 73, 77, 82–83, 334–335n.17; and legal system, 81–82, 337n.23; Mutia Escarpment in, 44, 59–60, 73, 78, 82–83, 334n.13;

narrative action versus image in, 82–83; nature photography in, 60; noble savage image in, 77; nudity in, 42, 52, 56–58, 337–339n.24; without O'Sullivan as Jane, 63, 71, 80; and Otherness, 46–59, 77, 79; plots of, 46–49; and procreation, 80–81; and Production Code Administration (PCA), 52, 57, 70, 73, 81, 82, 337–339nn.23–24; racism in, 58–59, 68–70, 72, 335–336n.18; sound design and music in, 73, 342n.3; studio decision on Jane's death in, 76–77, 336n.20; swimming scenes in, 56–57, *56*, 74, 83, 336n.19, 337–339n.24; Tarzan's articulation of his values in, 336–337n.23; Tarzan's separation from Jane in, 65, 77–78, 80; Tarzan yell in, 49, 74, 342n.3; touch in, 51–52, 72–82, 83; violence and guns in, 50, 67, 69–70, 72, 77, 79, 80, 336–338nn.23–24. See also Weissmuller/O'Sullivan couple; and specific films

Tarzan Finds a Son! 48, 75–76, 80–81, 335n.17, 335n.18, 336n.20, 336n.23

Tarzan novels, 43, 45–46, 62–63, 68, 80, 334n.13

Tarzan's New York Adventure, 48, 59, 68, 71, 81–82, 83, 335–336n.18, 336n.19, 337n.23

Tarzan's Revenge, 76

Tarzan's Secret Treasure, 48, 69, 70, 77, 335n.18, 336–337n.23

Tarzan the Ape Man, 1, 2, 40, 44–46, 50–53, 55–56, 60, 65–66, 68, 74, 75, 333n.1, 334n.14, 336n.23, 337n.24

Tarzan the Fearless, 54, 55

Taylor, Elizabeth, 233, 349–350n.8

Taylor, Juliet, 359n.23

Taylor, Robert, 349n.8

television series: African Americans on, 286, 288–294, 360n.27, 363n.1; couple chemistry on, 237–238, 242–243, 309; narrative of, 244; sitcoms as, 225, 287; Synergistic Couples on, 242–243; Thematic Couples on, 242–243, 285–288. See also *Cosby Show*; *General Hospital*; *Moonlighting*; soap operas; *X-Files*

Test Pilot, 11, 26, 32, 330n.3

Thalberg, Irving, 103, 338n.24

Thematic Couples: compared with Iconic Couples, 286, 287–288; compared with Synergistic Couples, 294, 306, 310; in contemporary films, 286–287, 303–309; definition of, 9, 12, 240, 310–311; examples of, 12, 287; in television series, 242–243. See also *Cosby Show*; Newman/Woodward couple; Synergistic Couples; Willis/Shepherd couple

"They Can't Take That Away from Me," 181

Thin Man (film), 31, 90–94, 97–102, 108, 110–111, 131

Thin Man (novel), 91–92

Thin Man films: alcohol consumption in, 91, 102, 104, *105,* 106; Asta (pet terrier) in, 90, 101–102, 103, *105,* 106, 107, 124; body in, 91–92, 101–102, 107; class structure and materialism in, 87–89, 99, 108–109, 112–113; compared with novel, 91–92; compared with *The Cosby Show*, 288; costumes in, 107, 119–120; cultural norms in, 86–88, 98, 104; dumbing down of Nora in later films, 119–122; equality between Nick and Nora in, 101, 103, 109–110; ethnicity and racism in, 106, 119; facial expressions of Nick and Nora in, 88, 103; Functional Couple in, 118–119; glamour and beauty in, 101–102, 107–108, 110–112, 119–120; and ideology, 132; images of Nick and Nora from, 89–98, *89, 93, 105;* improvisatory tone on set of, 90–91, 94–95, 97; independent women in *Another Thin Man,* 113–114; intimacy in, 36, 86, 248, 311; lighthearted repartee and double entendres between Nick and Nora in, 92–94, 105–106; music in, 342–343n.3; Nick and Nora as gender doubles in, 93–94, 102, 132–133; Nick's father in, 121; Nick's male authority in, 92, 101, 109–110, 121; Nick's voice in, 92; nonverbal interchanges in, 97–98; Nora's blend of hauteur and playfulness in, 88–89, 90, 103; Nora's fall at beginning of *Thin Man,* 90–91, 92, 101–102; Nora's wealth in, 87–88, 92, 113, 133; and Otherness, 132–133; parenthood in, 112, 115, 124; playful/serious struggle between Nick and Nora in, 112, 115–124; plots of, 90, 98–101, 112–124, 339–340n.13; police force in, 87, 106, 119; and Production Code Administration (PCA), 91, 104–107, 124, 132; and sexual exclusivity, 93–94, 108, 114–116; sexuality and double entendres in, 97–98, 104–107; supporting characters' bipolar gender definitions in, 102; synergy of Powell and Loy in, 95–96, 340–341n.17; unease at end of *Song of the Thin Man,* 122–124; Van Dyke as director of, 90–91, 94–95, 97, 103, 104, 106. See also Powell/Loy couple; and specific films

Thin Man Goes Home, 100, 101, 121–122, 132, 340n.15, 343n.3
Thompson, Brian, 254, 357n.16
Thompson, Dorothy, 199, 350n.10
Thompson, Kristin, 7
Top Hat, 17, 31, 136, 137–138, 140–149, *145,* 176, 183–184, 321, 343nn.4–5
"Top Hat, White Tie, and Tails," 144–145, *145,* 320
touch. *See* body; intimacy
Towers, Constance, 362n.34

Tracy, Spencer: as alcoholic and womanizer, 191, 192, 217; early films of, 191, 200–201; FBI file on, 347n.1; hat as prop in films of, 200–201; marriage and children of, 189; public image of, 190–192; sexual orientation of, 350n.9. *See also* Tracy/Hepburn couple
Tracy/Hepburn couple: in *Adam's Rib,* 31, 188, 201, 217–224, 228, 230, 348n.1, 351n.10; adultery in films of, 189, 215–216, 348n.1, 352–353n.21; animals in films of, 201, 208–209; body and gaze in films of, 195–198, *196,* 206, 208–211, 219–221, 229; and carnivalization, 199–200; class structure in *Pat and Mike,* 224–227; compared with other onscreen/offscreen couples, 349–350n.8; in *Desk Set,* 188–189, 230; domesticity in films of, 197–198, 216–217; entropy of last films of, 230–232; fight for control between, 350–351n.10; and glamour in *Without Love,* 210–211; in *Guess Who's Coming to Dinner,* 189, 201, 230–232, 353n.22; historical labeling in films of, 199, 201, 224, 226, 350n.10; images of, *196, 212, 220;* and intertextuality, 200–201; intimacy between generally, 14, 31, 36, 188; in *Keeper of the Flame,* 188, 201–207, 213, 215, 217, 347–348n.1; length of time working together, 4, 185, 188; list of films by, 188–189; massage incident in *Adam's Rib,* 219–220, *220;* musical scores of films of, 197–198, 201–202, 206, 225; narrative patterns of films of, 10; offscreen relationship of, 189, 194, 207, 214, 231–232, 233, 353n.22; in *Pat and Mike,* 188, 201, 224–229, 348n.1; and Production Code Administration (PCA), 202, 204, 347–348n.1;

public image of, 189–192, 214; rehearsal by, 351n.10; in *Sea of Grass*, 188, 213–214, 348n.1; social relevance of films of, 186, 187, 188–189, 311; star images in films of, 202–207, 217; in *State of the Union*, 188, 213, 214–217, 348n.1, 352–353nn.20–21; in *Without Love*, 188, 201, 207–212, 212, 213, 217, 229, 230, 348n.1; in *Woman of the Year*, 1, 2, 188, 190–201, 211, 213, 215, 222, 228, 350–351nn.9–12

Trader Horn, 44, 45, 53, 54, 62, 334n.13
Turner, Janine, 287
Turner, Lana, 11, 330n.3
Twin Peaks, 248, 287, 355n.10
Tysko, Autumn, 356n.13, 359n.20

Ullman, Viktor, 35
Universal Pictures, 338n.24

Valentino, Rudolph, 52
Van Dyke, W. S., 40, 44, 62, 69–70, 90–91, 94–95, 97, 103, 104, 106, 333n.1, 334n.14
Vertigo, 188

Warner Brothers, 27
Wayne, David, 219, 348n.1
Wayne, John, 11, 35
Weber, Max, 329n.2
"Weekend in the Country," 181
Weissmuller, Johnny: and Esther Williams, 42; personality of, 41–42; sexual harassment by, 42; Sheffield's admiration for, 41, 335n.18; as swimming champion, 40, 41, 42, 74, 336n.19. *See also* Tarzan films (MGM); Weissmuller/O'Sullivan couple
Weissmuller/O'Sullivan couple: and animals, 41, 42; beauty of, 43, 49–50, 55; body, physicality, and gestures of, 50–53, 55–59, 74, 80; bond between Tarzan and Jane in films, 46–59; compared with Powell/Loy couple, 85, 90; dialogue for, 1, 2, 59, 82, 336–337n.23; Eurocentric value system rejected by, 46–49, 57–59, 65–76, 83, 336–337n.23; female desire and hero's identity in films, 44–46, 61–67; film images of, 47, 53–59, 56, 58; image versus narrative action in films, 10, 82–83; intimacy between, 14, 31, 36, 50–53, 55–59, 66–67, 72–83, 125, 311; and Jane's character and changing values, 40, 53, 57, 61–65, 74–76, 333n.1; and Jane's father, 46, 47, 50, 51, 62, 63, 64, 65; and Jane's first encounter with Tarzan, 50–53, 65, 74; and Jane's modeling of European clothes, 56–57, 58; and Jane's relationship with European males, 50, 56–57, 64, 65–66; Jane's seduction and betrayal of Tarzan, 48, 75, 77–78; and Jane's wounding, 76–77, 78; and jungle home of Tarzan and Jane, 82–83; and land in Tarzan films, 44, 59–60, 67, 73, 77, 334–335n.17; and language lesson, 55–56, 74; and legal system, 81–82, 337n.23; length of time working together, 4; limited acting skills of, 39–40, 85; and nudity, 42, 52, 56–58, 337–339n.24; offscreen personalities of, 41–42; and Otherness, 46–59, 77; and procreation, 80–81; reluctance of O'Sullivan to continue with role, 76–77; and sexual harassment by Weissmuller, 42; and swimming scenes, 56–57, 56, 74, 83, 336n.19, 337–339n.24; and Tarzan's separation from Jane, 65, 77–78, 80; and touch, 51–52, 72–82, 83. *See also* Tarzan films
Wellman, William, 40
"We Saw the Sea," 169
West, Mae, 33, 101, 331n.10
western genre films, 27, 334–335n.17

Wexman, Virginia Wright, 34, 54, 110, 132, 332–333n.13, 334n.15
White Cargo, 62
Wife vs. Secretary, 330n.3
Wild, David, 355n.10
Williams, Esther, 42
Williams, Linda, 352n.20
Williams, Tennessee, 267
Willis/Shepherd couple, 12, 243, 286, 287, 294–303, *300,* 311, 354n.3, 364n.1, 364–365n.6, 365–366nn.8–10, 366–367n.12
Wingate, James, 337n.24
Withers, Hildegard, films, 33
Without Love, 188, 201, 207–212, *212,* 213, 217, 229, 230, 348n.1
Woman of the Year, 1, 2, 188, 190–201, *196,* 211, 213, 215, 222, 228, 350–351nn.9–12
Wonder Bar, 157, 344n.12
Wood, Daniel, 354n.9, 357n.16
Wood, Ed, 349n.2
Woodward, Joanne. *See* Newman/Woodward couple
Written on the Wind, 188

Xena, 355n.10
X-Files: "Agua Mala" episode of, 358n.18; aliens on, 253–255, 259–261, 263, 264–265, 268, 357–358nn.15–17; "all things" episode of, 262; birth of Scully and Mulder's baby on, 262–263; body, touch and gaze in, 247, *251,* 252–254, 256, 257–261; Bounty Hunter in, 254, 260, 357n.16; casting decisions for, 248–249; claims of factual basis of, 233; "Closure" episode of, 357n.15; compared with Allen/Keaton films, 264–265, 266, 268, 271, 360n.26; compared with *General Hospital,* 278; debates between Scully and Mulder on, 250–252; Doggett/Reyes couple on, 262; Duchovny's and Anderson's creative contributions to, 259, 261–262, 358nn.18–19; FBI hierarchy in, 246, 247, 249–250; and Internet fan community, 354n.9, 355–356n.10, 357nn.15–16, 358–359n.20, 367n.12; intimacy between Scully and Mulder in, 246–253, 255–259, 261–263, 283–284, 312, 354–356nn.10–11, 356–357n.14, 358n.17; last episode of Scully/Mulder couple on, 262–263; "Milagros" episode of, 255–259, 286; Mulder's abduction in, 262, 359n.20; Mulder's sister in, 253, 357n.15; narrative discontinuities in, 244, 245; original concept of, 245–246, 248; paranoid narrative of, 247, 249, 251, 253–254, 259, 274, 356n.12; pilot episode of, 249–253, 356–357n.14; plots of, 246, 247, 255–262, 357n.15; "Requiem" episode of, 358–359n.20; Scully's abduction in, 247, 253; Scully's cross on, 358–359n.20; Scully's disrobing in first episode of, 252–253; Scully's pregnancy in, 262, 358–359n.20; sexual relationship between Scully and Mulder in, 262, 354–356nn.10–11; "Talitha Cumi" episode of, 357–358n.17; taping rhythms of, 356n.13; "Travellers" episode of, 358n.18; "Unnatural" episode of, 255, 259–262, 358nn.18–19

"Yam," 176, 320
"You'd Be Hard to Replace," 181
Young, Loretta, 329–330n.3
Young and the Restless, 341n.17

Zelig, 354n.7
Zeman, Jacklyn, 360n.29

www.ingramcontent.com/pod-product-compliance
Lightning Source LLC
Chambersburg PA
CBHW031702230426
43668CB00006B/78